Developing Alternative Frameworks for Explaining Tax Compliance

Over the past several decades, there has been a growing interest in theoretical, empirical, and experimental work on all aspects of tax compliance and tax evasion. A common theme in much of this work is that the traditional economics-of-crime approach to compliance, while containing many insights, is simply inadequate as a framework for more fully understanding why people pay taxes. Rather, the basic model of individual choice must be expanded by introducing some aspects of behavior or motivation considered explicitly by other social sciences. Many of these aspects can be discussed under the general rubric of behavioral economics.

The original essays in this volume represent an attempt to provide exactly this new framework on compliance – one that moves beyond the economics-of-crime perspective, one that provides a more complete understanding of individual (and group) decisions, and one that is more consistent with empirical evidence. In their entirety, these essays make a convincing case for broadening the scope of analysis of tax evasion to include factors not traditionally viewed as essential policy tools, especially those suggested by behavioral economics.

There are several specific themes that emerge in these essays: What is the existing state of knowledge of tax compliance decisions? How can theory be expanded to reflect more accurately the many factors that underlie these decisions? What is the empirical evidence on the role of these many factors? Each of these themes represents a section in this volume. This collection will be of interest to postgraduates, researchers, and anyone interested in the analysis of tax compliance from an inter-disciplinary perspective.

James Alm is Professor of Economics at Georgia State University. **Jorge Martinez-Vazquez** is Professor of Economics at Georgia State University. **Benno Torgler** is Professor of Economics at Queensland University of Technology.

Routledge international studies in money and banking

Developing Alternative Frameworks for Explaining Tax Compliance

Edited by James Alm,
Jorge Martinez-Vazquez and
Benno Torgler

Routledge
Taylor & Francis Group

LONDON AND NEW YORK

First published 2010
by Routledge
2 Park Square, Milton Park, Abingdon, Oxon OX14 4RN

Simultaneously published in the USA and Canada
by Routledge
270 Madison Avenue, New York, NY 10016

Routledge is an imprint of the Taylor and Francis Group, an informa business

© 2010 Selection and editorial matter, James Alm, Jorge Martinez-Vazquez, and Benno Torgler; individual chapters, the contributors

Typeset in Times by Wearset Ltd, Boldon, Tyne and Wear
Printed and bound in Great Britain by TJI Digital, Padstow, Cornwall

British Library Cataloguing in Publication Data
A catalogue record for this book is available from the British Library

Library of Congress Cataloging in Publication Data
Developing alternative frameworks for explaining tax compliance/edited by James Alm, Jorge Martinez-Vazquez, and Benno Torgler.
p. cm.
Essays presented at a conference held in Atlanta in Oct. 2007 and sponsored by the International Studies Program of the Andrew Young School of Policy Studies at Georgia State University.
Includes bibliographical references and index.
1. Taxpayer compliance–Congresses. 2. Tax evasion–Congresses. I. Alm, James. II. Martinez-Vazquez, Jorge. III. Torgler, Benno, 1972– IV. Georgia State University. School of Policy Studies.
HJ2319.D48 2010
336.2'91–dc22

2009046099

ISBN10: 0-415-57698-9 (hbk)
ISBN10: 0-203-85161-7 (ebk)

ISBN13: 978-0-415-57698-7 (hbk)
ISBN13: 978-0-203-85161-6 (ebk)

Contents

Figures

Tables

Contributors

James Alm is a Professor of Economics in the Department of Economics, Andrew Young School of Policy Studies, Georgia State University, Atlanta, Georgia, USA.

Julie Ashby is a Postdoctoral Fellow at the Institute of Education, University of London, London, United Kingdom.

Calvin Blackwell is an Assistant Professor in the Department of Economics and Finance, College of Charleston, Charleston, South Carolina, USA.

Valerie Braithwaite is a Professor at the Regulatory Institutions Network (RegNet), RSPAS, College of Asia and the Pacific, The Australian National University, Canberra, Australia.

John Cullis is Professor or Economic, University of Bath, Bath, United Kingdom.

Brian Erard is an Owner of Erard and Associates, Reston, Virginia, USA.

Jonathan S. Feinstein is Professor of Economics and Management at the Yale School of Management, New Heaven, Connecticut, USA.

Lars P. Feld is a Professor of Economics at the Ruprecht-Karls-Universität Heidelberg, Alfred Weber Institute for Economics, Chair of Public Economics, Heidelberg, Germany.

Bruno S. Frey is a Professor of Economics at the University of Zurich and Research Director of CREMA – Centre for Research in Economics, Management and the Arts, Switzerland.

Philip Jones is a Professor of Economics in the Department of Economics and International Development, University of Bath, Bath, United Kingdom.

Barbara Kastlunger is a Professor of Psychology in the Department of Economic Psychology, Educational Psychology and Evaluation, University of Vienna, Vienna, Austria.

Erich Kirchler is Vice Dean and Professor of the Faculty of Psychology in the Department of Economic Psychology, Educational Psychology and Evaluation, University of Vienna, Vienna, Austria.

Alan Lewis is a Professor of Economic Psychology in the Department of Psychology, University of Bath, Bath, United Kingdom.

Alison Macintyre is a PhD Student in Economics at the School of Economics and Finance, Queensland University of Technology, Brisbane, Queensland, Australia.

Jorge Martinez-Vazquez is a Professor of Economics and Director of the International Studies Program, Andrew Young School of Policy Studies, Georgia State University, Atlanta, Georgia, USA.

Stephan Muehlbacher is a Professor of Psychology in the Department of Economic Psychology, Educational Psychology and Evaluation, University of Vienna, Vienna, Austria.

Kristina Murphy is a Professor in the Alfred Deakin Research Institute, Deakin University, Geelong, Victoria, Australia.

Monika Reinhart is a Researcher at the Centre for Tax System Integrity, The Australian National University, Canberra, Australia.

Markus Schaffner is a PhD Student in Economics at the School of Economics and Finance, Queensland University of Technology, Brisbane, Queensland, Australia.

Jan Schnellenbach is a Professor of Economics in the Ruprecht-Karls-Universität Heidelberg, Alfred Weber Institute for Economics, Chair of Public Economics, Heidelberg, Germany.

Michael Smart is a Researcher at the Centre for Tax System Integrity, The Australian National University, Canberra, Australia.

Benno Torgler is a Professor of Economics at the School of Economics and Finance, Queensland University of Technology, Brisbane, Queensland, Australia.

Eric Uslaner is a Professor of Government and Politics, University of Maryland–College Park, College Park, Maryland, USA.

Ingrid Wahl is a Professor of Psychology in the Department of Economic Psychology, Educational Psychology and Evaluation, University of Vienna, Vienna, Austria.

Paul Webley is the Director and Principal of the School of Oriental and African Studies, University of London, and a Professor at the School of Psychology, University of Exeter, United Kingdom.

Part I
Introduction to the volume

1 Developing alternative frameworks for explaining tax compliance

James Alm, Jorge Martinez-Vazquez, and Benno Torgler

Over the past several decades, there has been a growing interest in theoretical, empirical, and experimental work on all aspects of tax compliance and tax evasion. A common theme in much of this work is that the traditional economics-of-crime approach to compliance, while containing many insights, is simply inadequate as a framework for more fully understanding why people pay taxes. Rather, the basic model of individual choice must be expanded by introducing some aspects of behavior or motivation considered explicitly by other social sciences. Many of these aspects can be discussed under the general rubric of *behavioral economics*, broadly defined as an approach that uses methods and evidence from other social sciences (especially psychology) to inform the analysis of individual and group decision-making. The original chapters in this volume represent an attempt to provide exactly this new framework on compliance – one that moves beyond the economics-of-crime perspective, one that provides a more complete understanding of individual (and group) decisions, and one that is more consistent with empirical evidence.

The chapters in this volume summarize the existing state of knowledge of tax compliance and tax evasion, present new thinking about this issue, and analyze the empirical relevance of these new perspectives. They were presented at a conference entitled "Tax Compliance and Tax Evasion", held in Atlanta in October 2007 and sponsored by the International Studies Program of the Andrew Young School of Policy Studies at Georgia State University.

It is useful at the start to identify more fully the basic insight – and the basic problem – with the standard economic approach to compliance. To date, the basic theoretical model used in nearly all research on tax compliance begins with the economics-of-crime model of Becker (1968), first applied to tax compliance by Allingham and Sandmo (1972).[1] Here, a rational individual is viewed as maximizing the expected utility of the tax evasion gamble, weighing the benefits of successful cheating against the risky prospect of detection and punishment, and individuals pay taxes because they are afraid of getting caught and penalized if they do not report all income. This approach gives the plausible and productive result that compliance depends upon audit rates and fine rates. Indeed, the central point of this approach is that an individual pays taxes because – and *only* because – of this fear of detection and punishment. The obvious policy implication here is that enforcement matters because enforcement can affect the financial considerations that motivate – at least in part – an individual's compliance choices. However, it is essential to recognize that this approach also concludes that an individual pays taxes because – and *only* because – of the economic consequences of detection and punishment. Again, this is a plausible and productive insight, with the obvious implication that the government can encourage greater tax compliance by increasing the audit and the penalty rates. The many extensions of this economics-of-crime approach considerably complicate the theoretical analyses, and generally render clear-cut analytical results impossible. Nevertheless, these extensions retain the basic approach and the basic result: individuals focus exclusively on the financial incentives of the evasion gamble, and individuals pay taxes solely because they fear detection and punishment.

However, it is clear to many observers that compliance cannot be explained entirely by such purely financial considerations, especially those generated by the level of enforcement. The percentage of individual income tax returns that are subject to a thorough tax audit is generally quite small in most countries – almost always considerably less than 1 percent of all returns. Similarly, the penalty on even fraudulent evasion seldom exceeds more than the amount of unpaid taxes, and these penalties are infrequently imposed; civil penalties on non-fraudulent evasion are even smaller. Taxpayer audits are a central feature of the voluntary compliance system in all countries, largely because more frequent audits are thought to reduce tax evasion. Even so, a purely economic analysis of the evasion gamble suggests that most rational individuals should either under-report income not subject to source withholding or overclaim deductions not subject to independent verification because it is extremely unlikely that such cheating will be caught and penalized. However, even in the least compliant countries evasion never rises to levels predicted by a purely economic analysis, and in fact there are often substantial numbers of individuals who apparently pay all (or most) of their taxes all (or most) of the time, regardless of the financial incentives they face from the enforcement regime.

The basic model of individual compliance behavior therefore implies that rational individuals (especially those whose incomes are not subject to third-party sources of information) should report virtually no income. Although compliance varies significantly across countries and across taxes, and is often quite low, compliance seldom falls to a level predicted by the standard economic theory of compliance. It seems implausible that government enforcement activities alone can account for these levels of compliance; the basic model is certainly unable to explain this behavior. Indeed, the puzzle of tax compliance behavior may well be why people pay taxes, not why they evade them (Slemrod, 1992; Torgler, 2007). This observation suggests that the compliance decision must be affected in ways not fully captured by the basic economics-of-crime approach.

What other factors may explain why people pay taxes? It is this fundamental question that motivates the chapters in this volume, and it is the insights of behavioral economics that provide many of the bases for these chapters.

There are several specific themes that emerge in these chapters: What is the existing state of knowledge of tax compliance decisions? How can theory be expanded to reflect more accurately the many factors that underlie these decisions? What is the empirical evidence on the role of these many factors? Each of these themes represents a part in this volume.

In Part II, Erich Kirchler, Stephan Muehlbacher, Barbara Kastlunger, and Ingrid Wahl provide a useful summary of much the existing tax compliance literature. Their basic conclusion echoes that of this volume: there is much to be said for the standard economics-of-crime approach to tax compliance, but this approach goes only so far in explaining why people pay taxes. Indeed, they believe that alternative perspectives can help solve the puzzle of compliance. They argue especially for models that examine compliance choice as a *social dilemma*, that incorporate *tax morale* or *social norms*, and that utilize their own *slippery slope* framework.

The *slippery slope* model suggests that authorities' position towards taxpayers is relevant for compliance: in an antagonistic tax climate, when tax authorities communicate a "cops and robbers" attitude, taxpayers will try to maximize their individual expected utility and only comply when forced to do so. On the other hand, in a synergistic climate, when authorities communicate a "service and clients" attitude, taxpayers will act on the basis of the perceived fairness of the system and comply voluntarily. As they conclude, "[t]he problem of tax compliance seems much too complex to be explained by a purely economic approach". Rather, "[i]ncluding alternative approaches could help to understand the irrational behavior of taxpayers, and could expand the toolbox for an efficient tax policy". These themes are repeated throughout the volume.

Part III develops the theoretical bases for these alternative approaches, by incorporating broader sets of individual motivations than simply financial considerations. John Cullis, Philip Jones, and Alan Lewis start with the standard *homo economicus* model, and then introduce *social norms* as an explanatory factor, including the ways in which one's own norms can over time be influenced by others, and can in turn influence the dynamic path of the norms of others. Although difficult to define precisely, a social norm can be distinguished by the feature that it is process oriented, unlike the outcome orientation of individual rationality. A social norm therefore represents a pattern of behavior that is judged in a similar way by others, and which therefore is sustained in part by social approval or disapproval. Consequently, if others behave according to some socially accepted mode of behavior, then the individual will behave appropriately; if others do not so behave, then the individual will respond in kind. In particular, Cullis, Jones, and Lewis distinguish in their theoretical model between the *prevalence* of the social norm (e.g., the proportion of people actually pay their taxes honestly) and the *strength* of the norm (e.g., the proportion of individuals who think that they ought to pay taxes whether they actually do so or not). Clearly, the strength of the social norm can influence its prevalence, and can in turn be affected by the prevalence, and it is through these interactions that Cullis, Jones, and Lewis demonstrate the endogeneity of the norm, and also derive complicated dynamic effects. Some empirical evidence, derived largely from country estimates of the underground economy and also from the World Values Survey (WVS) questions on tax morale, provides some aggregate evidence that is at least somewhat consistent with their endogenous social norms theory.

Jan Schnellenbach also develops an alternative theory of tax compliance that moves well beyond the standard economic approach. In particular, he examines the impact of vertical reciprocity and horizontal reciprocity on individual compliance behavior. *Vertical reciprocity* represents the relationship between the individual and the state, and has sometimes been used in models of tax compliance; that is, do individuals feel that they are getting a fair return from government for their tax payments. *Horizontal reciprocity* is related to the relationship between individuals: individuals may be more likely to pay their taxes if they feel that others are doing so as well. Schnellenbach demonstrates that both types of reciprocity enter the calculus of a rational taxpayer; indeed, he argues that both types help influence the existence of a social norm, or a tax morale, that encourages compliance. He also demonstrates that the notions of reciprocity can be incorporated in a model of compliance, and that the resulting model enriches our understanding of compliance behavior. As Schnellenbach concludes, his model is only "...a first step towards incorporating results from the vast literature on reciprocity into theoretical reasoning about tax compliance". Even so, his model is a useful first step.

Lars Feld and Bruno Frey take a somewhat similar approach, but shift the perspective to a voluntary individual compliance motivated mainly by trust in authorities – what they term a *psychological tax contract* approach. They develop their contractual approach by discussing the role of positive and negative incentives in paying taxes, building upon their previous work on how an *intrinsic motivation* to pay taxes can emerge and also on how this intrinsic motivation can be crowded out by government deterrence. If paying taxes is viewed as a contract, then government must provide appropriate levels of services to citizens when citizens make their tax payments. Failure by government to provide this quid pro quo can destroy the contract between individuals and the state. Deterrence itself can also negatively affect the psychological tax contract, because deterrence may lead taxpayers to believe that they are not being treated with mutual respect and mutual honesty. Feld and Frey identify a number of ways in which this contract can be either encouraged or discouraged by government (including the use of tax amnesties). They conclude by arguing that tax morale is a function of the fiscal exchange between government and taxpayers, political procedures that define the exchange, and the personal relationship between taxpayers and tax administrators. Feld and Frey make a convincing case that it is largely though the positive/reward channels that tax morale – and so tax compliance – can be improved.

The remaining chapters provide various types of empirical support for a broader, interdisciplinary approach to tax compliance. This empirical evidence can be separated into several categories: evidence on financial incentives (including audit systems), evidence on governance, and specific case studies. Each of these three categories is organized as a separate section.

In Part IV, Calvin Blackwell examines the role of financial incentives. He uses data generated from the large number of tax compliance experiments that have been published in the past 30 years, and combines these separate data sets into a single data set using *meta-analysis,* an econometric method that increases the power of the statistical analysis from the increased number of data points and from the increased variation in the dependent variable(s). He focuses his meta-analysis on the compliance impact of the tax rate, the fine rate, the audit rate, and the public good return rate. Blackwell's empirical results largely confirm those of the previous 26 experimental papers that he includes in his data set; that is, compliance increases with increases in the fine rate, the audit rate, and the public good return rate. He finds that the estimated compliance elasticities are comparable to but slightly larger than those of the previous studies. He also finds that compliance declines with an increase in the tax rate, but that this impact is not statistically significant.

Brian Erard and Jonathan Feinstein also focus on the financial incentives, this time looking at audit mechanisms employed by the tax authorities. They are able to make two major improvements over much previous empirical work. First, they incorporate fully the multi-stage aspect of most audit schemes. There are numerous distinct, decisions made by auditors in the course of a typical "audit": which returns should be audited, what type of audit should be conducted, what mandatory classification issues should be examined, what additional unclassified issues should be examined, and the like. These decisions are made at different points in the audit process and by different individuals, and these types of sequential issues require sophisticated econometric modeling methods to be examined correctly. Second, they are able to use data collected from the recent Internal Revenue Service (IRS) National Research Program (NRP), in order to examine the effectiveness of the audit processes. Erard and Feinstein find that there is considerable heterogeneity across auditors (and across income types) in their ability to detect non-compliance. They also find that the NRP classification scheme is largely successful in identifying specific income types that should be examined in an audit, although there are some cases in which the classification process can – and should – be improved. In short, Erard and Feinstein demonstrate that the financial impact of audits matters in individual compliance decisions, but that the specific details of the audit process also matter.

Part V contains three chapters that look at the empirical impact of more broadly defined societal institutions, especially those of government and governance. Benno Torgler, Markus Schaffner, and Alison Macintyre first provide convincing empirical evidence that *tax morale,* defined as one's intrinsic motivation to pay taxes, has a significant impact on tax evasion. They use data from a wide range of sources – survey data, laboratory experimental data, and field data – and they find in each instance that lower tax morale is strongly correlated with greater tax evasion. Importantly, they then go on to explore empirically the determinants of tax morale, focusing specifically on how governance and attitudes toward governance affect tax morale. Torgler, Schaffner, and Macintyre use survey evidence from the European Values Survey (EVS), which has a number of questions that relate to citizen attitudes toward the quality of governance. They use these responses to construct six different measures of governance quality: citizen voice and government accountability; political stability and the absence of violence; government effectiveness; regulatory quality; the rule of law; and control of corruption. There are also variables in the EVS that measure trust in the parliament and trust in the justice system, and these variables are included in the ordered probit estimation. Their results consistently indicate that governance quality, however measured, has a positive and significant impact on tax morale, with the strongest effects associated with voice and accountability and the rule of law. As Torgler, Schaffner, and Macintyre conclude, "our analysis highlights the relevance of extending the standard economic theory of tax evasion" to include elements of political economy as a basis for understanding tax morale.

Eric Uslaner finds a similar result regarding the relevance of governance for compliance, focusing specifically on transition countries. His premise is that people obey the law – and pay their taxes – when they are treated fairly by the legal system; when the law is seen as unfair, arbitrary, and corrupt, then individuals will respond by cheating on their taxes. Survey information from the Business Enterprise and Environment Performance Survey (BEEPS) provides information on how businessmen and -women perceive the level of corruption and the fairness of the legal system for over 6,000 firms in nearly 30 transition countries for 2002 and 2005. Uslaner uses these responses to estimate how various measures of business compliance (e.g., the share of income reported by firms, payments to tax collectors) are correlated with governance quality measures. His estimation results indicate that compliance increases significantly with greater quality of government services and with reduced levels of government corruption. Like Torgler, Schaffner, and Macintyre, he concludes that governance is a crucial element in the compliance decisions of business people.

The role of *procedural justice* (e.g., the fair treatment of individuals by the legal system) in tax compliance is also emphasized by Kristina Murphy, but she also argues that *personal norms* (e.g., the existence of moral values consistent with the law) can affect these outcomes. There is much empirical evidence that indicates that people who feel they have been treated fairly by legal authorities are more likely to trust that authority, and so are more likely to obey the law. However, there may well be other factors that can moderate or enhance these impacts. In particular, Murphy suggests that the effectiveness of procedural justice can be influenced by personal norms; that is, even when individuals perceive the legal system as unfair, the existence of a strong sense of ethical behavior can mitigate the otherwise negative effect on compliance. Murphy provides empirical evidence to support this suggestion from survey evidence of 652 Australian taxpayers who had previously been caught and punished by the Australian Tax Office (ATO) for investing in illegal tax avoidance schemes. The survey contains over 200 questions that measured the respondents' attitudes toward the

ATO, questions that allowed the construction of various measures of *procedural justice*; the survey also contains questions that measured the respondents' *personal norms*, as well as their self-reported compliance behavior. Using hierarchical regression analysis, Tyler finds that compliance increases when individuals feel that they are treated fairly by the ATO. She also finds that, even when individuals feel that they have been treated unfairly by the ATO, they nonetheless increase their compliance when they believe that paying taxes is the "right" thing to do. Put differently and more generally, Tyler's empirical results provide further support for the role of an intrinsic motivation to pay taxes, whether that motivation goes under the label of *personal norms* or *tax morale*.

The final part, Part VI, contains more specific case study evidence. Valerie Braithwaite, Monika Reinhart, and Michael Smart focus on the behavior of younger taxpayers (those under 30 years of age), asking whether the well-documented lower compliance of younger taxpayers is due to a lack of knowledge of their true tax liabilities, a lower moral obligation to pay taxes, or a greater distrust of government. They use survey evidence of a random sample of Australian taxpayers, in which 2,040 individuals were asked about their perceptions of the Australian tax system. The responses indicate that younger taxpayers (those under 30 years of age) are in fact less compliant than older taxpayers. The responses also indicate that the lower compliance is due largely to a significantly lower feeling among the under-30 respondents that paying taxes is the "right" thing to do. Younger taxpayers are somewhat more distrustful of government, although the age differences here are small, and there is little evidence that lower compliance in the under-30s is due to a lack of knowledge. Braithwaite, Reinhart, and Smart conclude that encouraging greater compliance among younger taxpayers "…must rely first and foremost on role models … who exemplify the high standards of a community that openly promotes taxpayer honesty and commitment to the tax system".

Most studies on compliance, including most of the chapters in this volume, examine only compliance with the individual income tax. Paul Webley and Julie Ashby extend the analysis of evasion to one of the most important taxes in many countries around the world: value-added tax (VAT). VAT is a tax whose base is the difference between final sales and purchased inputs, and (under some circumstances) it is equivalent to a general consumption tax. There are numerous ways to evade the VAT tax liability, such as failing to register for VAT, under-reporting sales, overstating sales of good taxed at lower tax rates, and submitting false claims of VAT refunds (e.g., fake invoices), especially on exports. Webley and Ashby argue that understanding VAT evasion requires recognizing the occupational group identity of firm owners – what Webley and Ashby term a *social identity* approach (in contrast to the *individualistic* approach more common used); that is, different types of occupations have different attitudes toward paying VAT taxes, attitudes that are reflected in the mental accounting used in the occupations (e.g., are tips viewed as "my money" versus "their money", taxable by the tax authorities), the sources used for tax advice (e.g., are colleagues and friends asked for advice versus tax specialists like accountants), and the view of paying taxes as a legal obligation (e.g., are the authorities seen as trusted and fair versus corrupt and arbitrary). Webley and Ashby use previously collected survey responses, mainly from small business owners in Britain and in Australia in several different occupations, to demonstrate that there are significant differences across these occupations in their attitudes toward VAT compliance. Specifically, they find that factors affecting VAT compliance are closely tied to occupational group membership. They conclude that the culture of compliance differs across occupations in ways that can affect the resulting compliance decision of individuals in these occupations. As they say, "…attention to occupational group membership … can help improve our understanding of why people hold certain tax attitudes and why they do (or do not) pay VAT".

In the final chapter, James Alm and Jorge Martinez-Vazquez incorporate many of these main compliance factors, both economic and non-economic, in their own empirical work, focusing especially on countries in the Latin American and Caribbean (LAC) region of the world. Using the size of the informal sector as a rough proxy for the amount of tax evasion, they find that tax evasion is common in LAC countries. They also find that evasion is likely due to administrative problems that allow evasion to escape detection/punishment, and to societal attitudes that view evasion as acceptable behavior. Alm and Martinez conclude that the role of societal institutions, broadly defined to include both tax administration and tax morale, is *the* crucial element in explaining and in encouraging compliance. They emphasize that enforcement of the tax laws is a necessary part of any compliance strategy, what they term the *punishment paradigm* of tax compliance, and one that is consistent with the standard economics-of-crime approach. However, they also emphasize that changing the social norm of compliance is an equally essential part of any overall compliance strategy, via a tax administration that is a facilitator and a service provider. They term this approach the *service paradigm*, and it is one that is increasingly utilized around the world.

In summary, the common theme running throughout most of the chapters in this volume is that the basic model of individual choice must be expanded, by introducing some aspects of behavior or motivation considered explicitly by other social sciences. As we noted earlier, many of these aspects can be discussed under the rubric of behavioral economics, and many of the chapters emphasize one specific aspect of behavioral economics whose application to tax compliance is especially obvious and useful: the role of a social norm of compliance, whether this is alternatively called tax morale, or personal norms, or procedural justice, or reciprocity, or a tax contract, or social identity, or any other related term of taxes.

However, and in conclusion, we believe that there are other elements in behavioral economics that are relatively unexplored in these chapters but that nonetheless hold some potential for significant expansion in our understanding of compliance behavior.

One such factor is the way in which individuals perceive probabilities. There is overwhelming evidence from psychology that individuals *overweight* the low probabilities that they face in tax compliance; that is, even when fully informed, individuals will systematically act as if the probability of audit that they face is much higher than its actual probability. Overweighting of probabilities may therefore provide an additional explanation for tax compliance. If taxpayers give more weight to the probability of an audit than they ought to (at least relative to an expected utility model), then compliance will be greater than the level predicted by the standard economics approach.

A related factor is that many individuals apparently adapt to an unchanged environment and perceive stimuli relative to the environment. Many individuals react much differently to gains than to (equal-but-opposite valued) losses. Individuals may therefore act on the basis of a *value function* (rather than the utility function in economic models). The value function is assumed to depend upon changes in income from some reference point, rather than the level of income itself. It is also assumed to be steeper for losses than for gains because a loss in income is disliked much more than an equal gain, and it is concave for gains (e.g., risk aversion) but convex for losses (e.g., risk seeking), so that individuals may exhibit risk-averse behavior when confronted with risky but positive gambles, while the same individuals may become risk-lovers when faced with gambles that involve possible losses. The relevance of these assumptions for tax compliance is subtle yet powerful. Since some individuals frame any payment of taxes as a loss, these individuals will be likely to engage in risk-seeking behavior; that is, these individuals will declare less income than predicted by the basic model of expected utility theory.

Other elements may also be relevant. Individuals are not always purely self-interested. They face limits on their ability to compute (e.g., "bounded rationality"), they systematically misperceive the true cost of actions (e.g., "fiscal illusion"), they face limits on their "self-control", and they are affected by the ways in which choices are "framed" (e.g., reference points, gains versus losses, loss aversion). Eventually, these other elements may be more fully incorporated into the analysis of tax compliance and tax evasion.

In their entirety, then, we believe that these chapters make a convincing case for broadening the scope of analysis of tax evasion to include factors not traditionally viewed as essential policy tools, especially those suggested by behavioral economics. It is our hope that the chapters in this book will deepen our understanding of why people pay taxes, and of what government can do to enhance voluntary compliance with the tax system.

Note

1 See See Cowell (1990), Andreoni, Erard, and Feinstein (1998), Alm (1999), and Slemrod and Yitzhaki (2002) for comprehensive surveys.

Bibliography

Alm, J. (1999) "Tax compliance and administration", in W. Bartley Hildreth and J. A. Richardson (eds.), *Handbook on Taxation*, New York, NY: Marcel Dekker, Inc.

Allingham, M. G. and Sandmo, A. (1972) "Income tax evasion: A theoretical analysis", *Journal of Public Economics*, 1 (3–4): 323–38.

Andreoni, J., Erard, B., and Feinstein, J. (1998) "Tax compliance", *Journal of Economic Literature*, 36 (2): 818–60.

Becker, G. S. (1968) "Crime and punishment – an economic approach", *Journal of Political Economy*, 76 (2): 169–217.

Cowell, F. (1990) *Cheating the Government: The Economics of Evasion*, Cambridge, MA: MIT Press.

Slemrod, J. (ed.) (1992) *Why People Pay Taxes: Tax Compliance and Enforcement*, Ann Arbor, MI: University of Michigan Press.

—— and Yitzhaki, S. (2002) "Tax avoidance, evasion, and administration", in A. J. Auerbach and M. Feldstein (eds.), *Handbook of Public Economics*, New York, NY: Elsevier.

Torgler, B. (2007) *Tax Compliance and Tax Morale: A Theoretical and Empirical Analysis*, Cheltenham, UK: Edward Elgar.

Part II

A review and critique of the existing literature

2 Why pay taxes?

A review of tax compliance decisions

*Erich Kirchler, Stephan Muehlbacher,
Barbara Kastlunger, and Ingrid Wahl*

Introduction

Tax compliance has evolved into a major research topic in economic psychology. The issue has been approached from various viewpoints, shedding light on different aspects of taxpayers' behavior. Attitudes have been measured, prevailing social norms captured, and those lay theories explored which people have in mind when brooding over their annual tax declarations (for an overview, see Kirchler, 2007).

One line of research focuses on judgment and decision processes in tax compliance. In the seminal works of Allingham and Sandmo (1972) and Srinivasan (1973), income tax evasion was modeled as a decision under uncertainty.[1] Since then, parameters specified in the formal model have been empirically studied in various publications. This review summarizes results and conclusions of research on tax compliance decisions within the paradigm of maximizing expected utilities. Similar work has been published in the past (see, for example, Alm, 1999; Slemrod and Yitzhaki, 2002). The present chapter catches up with and incorporates the more recent empirical studies. After illustrating the model, each of its parameters is addressed separately, and empirical evidence for or against their effects on tax compliance is reported. Finally, a summary of results is provided, and the typical problems of tax compliance research and alternative theoretical approaches are discussed from the psychologists' perspective.

Allingham and Sandmo's (1972) and Srinivasan's (1973) analyses are restricted to income tax evasion. Research dealing with value added tax, other taxes or related duties is therefore omitted in the present review. Most of the cited studies focus on self-employed taxpayers, because this group has the greatest opportunities to evade income taxes.

Tax evasion as a decision under uncertainty

Following the neoclassical approach in economics, Allingham and Sandmo (1972) and Srinivasan (1973) assume that taxpayers are rational agents whose choice behavior conforms to the Von Neumann-Morgenstern axioms, and who try to maximize utility of their taxable income. They do so by weighing costs and benefits of compliance with the expected utility of evasion. Choosing the risky strategy of tax evasion on all or part of their actual income will result in a better outcome *if* the respective tax file is not audited. In the case of an audit, however, compliance would have been the better strategy, since paying a fine decreases income even further than honest payment of taxes.

Accordingly, a compliance decision depends on (i) the level of actual income, (ii) tax rates, (iii) audit probabilities, and (iv) the magnitude of fines. Though Allingham and Sandmo (1972) admit that other, less economic variables might also be important in understanding tax compliance (and exemplarily outline a more complex model incorporating changes in a taxpayer's reputation in society due to his or her compliance behavior), their analysis is based on the simpler model with the four parameters described above.

Since their analysis – often (and herein after) referred to as the standard economic model – was published, empirical research has gathered evidence for (and against) the significance of its parameters in tax compliance decisions. The following four sections provide a review of these studies, structured by the respective variable being tested. Each section begins with predictions of the formal model, and concludes with potential explanations for empirical deviations. Implications for tax policy and everyday operations of fiscal authorities are discussed.

Level of actual income

Predictions of the standard economic model regarding income effects are ambiguous. Though wealthier citizens are more likely to evade their taxes, since the level of absolute risk aversion decreases with income, it is not clear if severity of evasion is an increasing or a decreasing function of income. Once taxpayers have decided to evade taxes, the degree of under-reporting depends on their relative risk aversion (i.e., the risk attitude at a specific point of the utility function). The relation of income and relative risk aversion is not unique and, consequently, Allingham and Sandmo (1972: 329) conclude "...that, when actual income varies, the fraction [of income] declared increases, stays constant or decreases according as relative risk aversion is an increasing, constant or decreasing function of income".

The empirical evidence for income effects on compliance is just as ambiguous as the predictions of the standard economic model. If any impact of income level was found, both proposed directions of the effect were supported.

A *negative relation* of income and tax compliance is reported by Slemrod (1985), who analyzed archival data from the United States' Treasury tax file for 1977, and by Ali *et al.* (2001), who analyzed IRS data for the period between 1980 and 1995. Consistently, Weck-Hannemann and Pommerehne (1989; Pommerehne and Weck-Hannemann, 1996) found lower compliance among high-income earners in archival data on Swiss taxpayers. Lang *et al.* (1997) showed, with survey data from 33,000 West German households, that wealthier citizens are particularly prone to evading and avoiding taxes. Further evidence for a negative relation is reported from laboratory experiments. Baldry (1987) manipulated participants' income (among other variables), and found lower compliance at higher income levels. Anderhub *et al.* (2001) report similar results from a multi-period experiment, where participants had to earn their income in small tasks. The importance of how one's economic status is *perceived* was demonstrated by Vogel (1974). Taxpayers who reported improvement of their economic status were less compliant than others who reported deterioration of their financial well-being.

A *positive relation* of income and tax compliance has also found empirical support. Christian (1994) analyzed data from the Taxpayer Compliance Measurement Program (TCMP) of the Internal Revenue Service (IRS) in the United States. On average, taxpayers with an annual income of more than $100,000 reported 96.6 percent of income, but only 85.9 percent if income was below $25,000. Higher compliance at higher income levels is also reported by Dubin *et al.* (1990), who analyzed data from American taxpayers. Fishlow and Friedman (1994) found decreased compliance at low income levels in archival-empirical data from Argentina, Brazil, and Chile – three countries with low economic growth and high inflation rates. A single laboratory experiment also found support for a positive relation of income and compliance. Alm *et al.* (1992a) report that compliance significantly increased with income in their experiment. In a survey by Mason and Calvin (1978), low-income earners were more likely to admit failure to file a return.

Other studies found *no relation* between income level and tax compliance. Feinstein (1991) compared pooled data from the 1982 and 1985 TCMP, and found no significant effects of income on tax compliance. In a laboratory experiment conducted in Korea, Park and Hyun (2003) varied experimental income (among other variables). No effect of income on compliance behavior was found. Self-reported compliance behavior was not related to income among American (Porcano, 1988; Spicer and Lundstedt, 1976) or Swedish taxpayers (Wärneryd and Walerud, 1982).

Definite conclusions cannot be drawn from the empirical studies reported. Evidence for income effects is inconsistent – as Andreoni *et al.* (1998) had already concluded in their earlier review). Though a slight majority of studies report a negative relation of income and compliance, opposite and zero effects have also been found.

The ambiguous evidence could possibly be explained by other variables moderating or mediating the effect of income. Besides the problem of relative risk aversion, several variables can be hypothesized to weaken the income effect or to influence its direction. For instance, Pencavel (1979), Cowell (1985), and Sandmo (1981) added labor supply to the standard economic model, and consequently made income an endogenous variable. Accordingly, taxpayers are able to reduce their tax burden either by evading taxes or by working less. Another confounding variable is the opportunity for tax avoidance, which is likely to vary with income. High-income earners are able to afford professional tax advisors, who know about the loopholes in the tax law (Slemrod *et al.*, 2001; Wärneryd and Walerud, 1982). If tax avoidance is possible, the tax burden can be reduced without breaking the law and taking the risk of paying a fine. Spicer and Lundstedt (1976) point out that the self-employed also have more possibilities to avoid taxes than employed taxpayers. However, self-employed taxpayers also have more opportunities for tax evasion, and opportunities might further increase with the number of different income sources. Hence, in compliance decisions the level of income might interact with the source of that income. A different aspect of the income source – if income was earned by hard work or an effortless job – has been studied in experiments by Kirchler and colleagues (Kirchler *et al.*, 2009; Muehlbacher and Kirchler, 2008). Participants were less compliant when they reported income earned by low effort than when they reported hard-earned income. It seems that taxpayers are reluctant to lose their hard-earned money by "gambling" with tax authorities.

Given the present results on income and compliance, it is too early to consider practical implications for tax policy. The issue, however, is important not only for designing proper audit strategies, but also for tax ethics, since a negative relation of income and compliance would put "[...] into question the intended (or pretended?) distributional effects of progressive income taxation." (Lang *et al.*, 1997: 328)

Tax rate

Would higher tax rates decrease compliance? No clear hypothesis emerges from the standard economic model. Two counteracting effects are proposed. On the one hand, a high tax rate reduces effective income, and therefore makes tax evasion more profitable. On the other hand, by reducing effective income absolute risk aversion increases. Consequently, evasion should be reduced.[2]

Both of the model's predictions regarding the impact of tax rates on compliance found empirical support, though most studies report that compliance is lower at high tax rates.

A *negative relation* of tax rate and compliance was found by Clotfelter (1983), who analyzed American taxpayers' data from the 1969 TCMP; by Slemrod (1985), who studied data from the United States' Treasury tax file of 1977; and by Dubin *et al.* (1990), who also used American data from the period between 1977 and 1986. Consistently lower compliance at high marginal tax rates is reported by Lang *et al.* (1997) for German taxpayers, and by Pommerehne and Weck-Hannemann (1996; Weck-Hannemann and Pommerehne, 1989) for Swiss taxpayers. An analysis of IRS data for the period between 1980 and 1995 revealed that the negative effect of tax rate on compliance is more pronounced among high-income earners (Ali *et al.*, 2001). Experimental evidence for the negative impact of high tax rates is reported by Alm *et al.* (1992a). In 25 periods, participants received an income, paid taxes and were randomly audited and fined. Tax policy changes were introduced during the experiment, including changes in tax rate (10 percent, 30 percent, and 50 percent). When the tax rate increased, participants' compliance decreased. Park and Hyun (2003) found that higher tax rates lead to less compliance. Similar results are reported by Friedland *et al.* (1978), from an experiment where the tax rate varied between subjects (25 percent and 50 percent). Thus, instead of the impact of an increasing or decreasing tax burden, this experiment tested for the effect of absolute differences in tax rates. Actually studying the effect of different audit schemes, Collins and Plumlee (1991) also tested for the effect of different tax rates (30 percent vs 60 percent). Again, lower compliance was observed at the higher tax rate. An experiment by Moser *et al.* (1995) revealed the importance of perceived fairness when studying the impact of different tax rates. A negative effect of a high tax rate was found only if participants felt inequitably treated compared to others.

A *positive relation* of tax rates and compliance, as proposed by Yitzhaki (1974), is less often reported. Feinstein (1991) found higher compliance at higher tax rates in aggregate data on American taxpayers from the TCMP. In an experiment conducted in Spain by Alm *et al.* (1995), participants were more compliant when tax rate increased over time.

No effect of the tax rate was found in an experiment by Baldry (1987) and in a study by Porcano (1988), both dealing with self-reported compliance behavior.

To summarize, most empirical studies on the impact of tax rates support the assumption that high tax burdens have negative impact on compliance. However, the strong connection of income and tax rate makes final conclusions difficult (Andreoni *et al.*, 1998; Slemrod, 1985). In experimental studies it is hard to separate the effects of tax rates and income, if both variables are varied at the same time. In field studies it is possible to make a similar critique to that in the discussion on income effects – i.e., opportunities for tax evasion or avoidance and source of income are likely to interact with tax rate. Regarding the source of income, Boylan and Sprinkle (2001) report that participants in their experiment reacted to a tax rate increase with lower compliance if they were endowed with income by the experimenters, but reacted with higher compliance to a tax rate increase if they had to earn their income by performing in a one-hour multiplication exercise. Findings by Moser *et al.* (1995) seem to suggest that perceived fairness of the tax rate is more important than its absolute level. Judging the fairness of taxation requires comprehensive knowledge and correct interpretation of the tax law; however, complex tax rate structures, such as progressive taxation, are not perfectly understood by taxpayers. Roberts *et al.* (1994) showed that taxpayers' preferences for progressive, flat, and regressive taxation depend on the form in which the respective tax rates are presented – for example, whether tax rates are described as an abstract concept or in concrete terms by giving hypothetical examples. McCaffery and Baron (2004) asked their participants to indicate what they consider a fair tax for different levels of income. Preference for progressive taxation was stronger when the amount of taxes had to be indicated in percentages of income than when it had to be indicated in absolute amounts. Such framing effects suggest that tax policies are hard to understand and can easily be misinterpreted. Knowledge about framing effects could help authorities in promoting changes in tax policy, such as tax rate increases, without undermining taxpayers' compliance.

Audit probability

The economic model assumes that taxpayers try to maximize the outcome of the compliance decision by weighing the gain of successful evasion against the risk of detection and punishment. The expected value of non-compliance depends on the audit probability and the amount of fines. Allingham and Sandmo (1972: 330) therefore conclude that "...an increase in the probability of detection will always lead to a larger income being declared" .

Most empirical studies found support for the effect of audit probability on compliance, though the reported effects are sometimes weak (cf. the specific review on audit rates by Fischer *et al.*, 1992).

A *positive effect* was found in aggregate data on tax compliance behavior of Swiss taxpayers. Pommerehne and Weck-Hannemann (1996; Weck-Hannemann and Pommerehne, 1989) compared 25 Swiss cantons, and report that compliance was slightly higher in cantons where more audits occurred in the observed period. Between 1977 and 1986, individual audit probability in the US dropped from about 2.5 percent to 1 percent. Dubin *et al.* (1990) estimated that maintaining the 1977 audit rate in 1986 would have increased the total reported tax by 15.6 billion dollars. Witte and Woodbury (1985) and Ali *et al.* (2001) report similar results, also using American samples. In the latter study, however, audit probability affected compliance more among high-income earners. An opposite interaction of audit probability and income was found in a field experiment, with a sample of 1,724 American taxpayers, by Slemrod *et al.* (2001). The experimental group in this study received a notification by mail that their next tax files would be audited. While low- and middle-income earners increased tax payments compared to previous years, high-income earners reacted differently and indicated a lower tax liability. The authors assumed that the notification letter induced high-income taxpayers to seek the help of professional tax advisors to minimize their tax liability. The effectiveness of frequent audits also found support in laboratory experiments. Webley *et al.* (1991), for instance, confirmed the effect of audit probabilities, but not the impact of sanctions. Park and Hyun (2003) analyzed (among other variables) the effect of audit and fine rates on tax compliance, and found a positive effect for both variables. However, the impact of fines gave a higher result. Alm *et al.* (1995) compared audit rates of 5, 30, and 60 percent, and found a corresponding increase in compliance. Support, however, for very weak effects of audit probabilities on tax compliance was found in the experiment by Alm *et al.* (1992a). In the experiments by Trivedi *et al.* (2003, 2004), audit rates were either zero or 25 percent. As expected, compliance was higher in the latter condition. Gërxhani and Schram (2006) conducted experiments in Albania and in the Netherlands. Participants in Albania were not affected by audit rates (16.6 percent and 50 percent), but Dutch participants evaded more when audit probability was low. An experiment by Alm *et al.* (1992b) revealed that the relation between audit probability and compliance is non-linear. At audit probabilities of 0, 2, and 10 percent, participants declared 20, 50, and 68 percent of their income, respectively. Spicer and Thomas (1982) varied audit rates and provided their participants with either concrete (1 in 20, 5 in 20, or 3 in 20) or non-concrete (*low*, *high*, and *medium*) information regarding the probability of being audited. Again, with increasing audit rates, evasion declined. Furthermore, precise information had a stronger impact than imprecise information. By contrast, Friedland (1982) reports that at small audit probabilities, imprecise information can enhance compliance.

Dubin and colleagues (1990) emphasize that, in reality, audit rates might respond to compliance levels. Therefore, they consider it fundamental to allow for the possible endogeneity of audit probability when modeling tax compliance. Martinez-Vazquez and Rider (2005) make a similar argument. They suggest that taxpayers may employ different forms of tax evasion to manage the risk of detection. For instance, if they obtain income from different sources and attribute different audit probabilities to the sources, they could misreport some income sources more intensively than others. With audit probability as the endogenous variable, subjective probabilities may become more important than the objective audit rate. Fischer *et al.* (1992) point out that perceived and objective probabilities differ widely. Given the extremely low audit probabilities in most countries, tax evasion should approach 100 percent if no overweighting occurs, as suggested in prospect theory (Kahneman and Tversky, 1979). Subjective rather than objective probabilities should therefore be of greater interest in tax research. Survey research revealed that taxpayers who admit tax evasion perceive the chances of being caught as lower than do honest taxpayers (Mason and Calvin, 1978). However, correlations of perceived risk and compliance are sometimes weak or even not present (Elffers *et al.*, 1987; Spicer and Lundstedt, 1976; Wärneryd and Walerud, 1982). Subjective probability that an audit will occur may partly depend on prior experience. In an experiment by Spicer and Hero (1985), participants paid taxes on a given income and were randomly checked in ten periods overall. Compliance in the tenth period was correlated with the number of audits in previous rounds. Similar results from a business simulation study are reported by Webley (1987). The experience of an audit induces a learning process for evaluating audit probabilities, according to findings from Guala and Mittone (2005; Mittone, 2006). Participants in their experiments paid taxes in a total of 60 periods, and were audited either only in the first or only in the latter 30 periods. If participants were audited early in the experiment, compliance was relatively high and remained at a high level in the latter 30 periods, though no more audits had occurred. By contrast, if participants were not audited in the first half of the experiment, compliance was comparably low and did not increase even when audits started in the latter 30 periods. Learning and understanding the objective probabilities of uncertain events by experiencing (or observing) their occurrence can be understood as applying the availability heuristic (Tversky and Kahneman, 1974). Analogous to Tversky and Kahneman's example that seeing a burning house influences judgments on the occurrence of such accidents, experiencing an audit could increase the subjective probability of being audited. On the other hand, it was frequently observed in tax experiments that compliance decreases sharply after an audit (Guala and Mittone, 2005;

Mittone, 2006). Such a reaction to an audit has been coined the "bomb-crater" effect by Mittone (2006). In a recent study, Kastlunger *et al.* (2009) investigated whether the "bomb-crater" effect is caused by misperception of chance or by the attempt to repair losses from paying a penalty. Results suggest that misperception of chance is the major cause for the strong decrease in compliance immediately after an audit. At least in some cases, however, loss repair tendencies also seem to reduce compliance. The "bomb-crater" effect affects only the earlier periods after an audit, before compliance increases again. After a "bomb-crater" occurred in an experiment by Maciejovsky *et al.* (2007), compliance increased faster to its baseline in a condition with a high audit rate (30 percent) than in a condition with a lower audit rate (15 percent). Thus, the duration of this effect seems to depend on when the next audit is expected.

To summarize, empirical evidence for the impact of high audit probabilities is quite strong. Yet, in practice, tax audits are costly, and research consequently changes its focus towards alternative control mechanisms. Reinganum and Wilde (1985), Collins and Plumlee (1991) and Alm *et al.* (1993) contrasted random audit schemes with several alternatives. Alm *et al.* (1993) tested the effectiveness of a cut-off rule (i.e., when the declaration falls below a certain threshold), a retrospective audit scheme (i.e., when the random detection of non-compliance results in examination of previous tax files), and a prospective audit scheme (i.e., when the detection of non-compliance increases future audit probability). Alternative audit mechanisms led to higher tax compliance even if the audit rules implicated fewer audits than random control systems. Also, the findings by Guala and Mittone (2005; Mittone, 2006) can be used to design an efficient audit scheme. According to their results, it might be advisable to audit particularly young and inexperienced taxpayers. It is possible that they will "learn" to be compliant if their very first tax file is checked by authorities.

Fines

The second parameter determining the expected value of being non-compliant, besides audit probabilities, is the amount of fines. Due to their multiplicative linkage, fines and audit rates may substitute each other, as long as neither of them is set to zero. Higher fines simply make evading taxes more hazardous for taxpayers, and should therefore deter them from evasion.

Empirically, the deterrent effect of fines could not always be supported. The observed effects were weaker than expected, and some studies even suggest that an increase of penalties can have undesirable effects and result in more tax avoidance.

Supporting evidence for the effect of fines is reported by Alm *et al.* (1992a), though its impact on compliance was found to be virtually zero. In the experiment by Park and Hyun (2003), compliance was more strongly affected by the amount of fines than by audit probabilities. Similar results are reported by Friedland *et al.* (1978), though their study does not allow disentangling audit effects from the effects of fines. By contrast, Friedland (1982) reports that audit rates affected compliance more than the amount of fines. Finally, Alm *et al.* (1995) point out that fines are only effective in combination with high audit rates. The interaction of both variables seems to be more important than their separate effects.

Several studies found *no support* for the deterrent effects of fines. Pommerehne and Weck-Hannemann (1996; Weck-Hannemann and Pommerehne, 1989) found no impact of penalty rate in their comparison of tax compliance in different Swiss cantons. Ali and colleagues (2001) analyzed compliance behavior of American taxpayers between 1980 and 1995. In this period, the penalty rate increased from 5 percent to 30 percent of the evaded tax. Overall, increasing the fines had no impact on compliance. However, high- and low-income earners reacted differently. Whereas low-income earners showed no change in compliance, high-income earners reacted as expected and increased their tax payments. In experiments by Collins and Plumlee (1991) and by Webley *et al.* (1991), compliance was unaffected by the amount of fines, though fines should have stronger effects in the laboratory than in the field due to the artificial situation of gambling with the experimenters. Perceived rather than objective severity of fines was studied in a survey by Spicer and Lundstedt (1976). Tax evasion was not related to the perceived severity of fines.

Interestingly, increasing the fines can also have the *opposite effect*, by initiating tax avoidance. In a field experiment by Schwartz and Orleans (1967), a random selection of American taxpayers received a letter emphasizing the severity of sanctions available to the government. Reported adjusted gross income did not increase compared to previous years, but amount of deductions increased substantially. It seems that taxpayers had tried to get back the higher income they were forced to declare due to the threat of a fine. Fjeldstad and Semboja (2001) report comparable results from a survey study they conducted in Tanzania. Oppressive tax enforcement and harassment of taxpayers increased resistance to paying taxes. Accordingly, a survey study by Strümpel (1969) revealed that unfair penalties have a negative impact on attitudes toward the tax office and taxes. Martinez-Vazquez and Rider (2005) point out that taxpayers often have the possibility of evading the authorities' enforcement efforts by switching to a different mode of tax evasion than the targeted one.

The conclusion from the empirical evidence reported above is that deterrent effects of fines are weak, if not negligible (as earlier reviews had already concluded; cf. Andreoni *et al.*, 1998; Fischer *et al.*, 1992; Pommerehne and Weck-Hannemann, 1992). Some of the findings suggest that a policy based on deterrence is effective only in combination with frequent audits. The most extreme penalties will have no effect, if it is common knowledge that audits virtually never occur.

The increasing tax avoidance and tax resistance due to an increase of fines raises the question of how fines should be assessed as being effective. On the one hand, fines should be high enough to decrease the expected value of tax evasion and to assure their deterrent effect on taxpayers. On the other hand, if fines are too high, the tax system would be perceived as unjust und unfair, and taxpayers would use any opportunity to legally avoid their taxes. In most countries, fines are relative to the evaded tax. In Austria, for instance, the maximum (monetary) penalty for tax evasion is 200 percent of the evaded amount, though in practice the typical sentence is a fine of 40 percent. However, depending on the income of the accused, such a system might yield fines too low to have a deterrent effect. An alternative would be to adjust the fine to the income of taxpayers. In an experimental survey study by Muehlbacher *et al.* (2007), income-adjusted fines had more impact on the sentenced taxpayer's intention to commit the same offense again than fines which were solely adjusted to the severity of evasion.

Summary and discussion

The standard economic model frames the tax compliance problem as a decision under uncertainty. Taxpayers are assumed to maximize income by weighing the pros and cons of evading taxes. Though the model provides useful tools for tax policy, and its publication stimulated a variety of tax research, empirical evidence for its validity is rather weak. Most of its parameters have unstable and unclear effects, and it is hard to draw definite conclusions from the studies we have reviewed. Whether high- or low-income earners are more prone to evading their taxes remains unclear. Regarding the effects of tax rate increases, most studies seem to support a negative relation to compliance – i.e., more tax evasion at high tax rates. The impact of audits and fines can hardly be separated, though a combination of both seems to be effective. Since audits are costly, however, tax policy has a wider scope in adjusting fines. Table 2.1 provides an overview of the empirical findings that have been reported in this review.

The weak empirical support of the economic model could be either due to constraints in the methodology applied to gather and analyze data, or because the economic approach is too narrow for a comprehensive explanation of compliance behavior.

Regarding methodology, empirical research on tax compliance faces severe problems – mainly the problem of low external validity. Most tax experiments deal with students as participants, and often are designed as "gambling" experiments rather than providing more realistic tax-paying environments. An experiment without monetary incentives has low external validity, but providing participants with windfall endowments enhances the mentioned gambling situation in the laboratory. Additionally, if participants' profit is based on their behavior in the experiment, the impact of tax morale and the possibility of other, non-financial consequences are ruled out completely. Further methodological constraints were demonstrated in an extensive study done by Elffers *et al.* (1987). The authors compared actual tax files of Dutch taxpayers with self-reported compliance within the same sample. As expected, actual tax-evaders frequently indicated in self-reports that they were fully compliant. More surprisingly, several participants admitted non-compliance, though their tax files proved that income had been honestly reported. Accordingly, experimental data, and especially self-reported data, have to be interpreted very carefully before generalization.

Regarding the theoretical approach to the tax compliance problem, the standard economic model has been extended in various ways. The exogeneity of its variables has been criticized (see, for example, Dubin *et al.*, 1990); additionally, variables have been included (e.g., labor supply; Cowell, 1985) and existing variables have been split up (e.g., tax evasion in multiple modes of tax evasion; Martinez-Vazquez and Rider, 2005). It might be useful, however, to enrich compliance research by considering alternative theories, which are based on a more relaxed rationality assumption and take into account peoples' actual tax behavior. Prospect Theory (Kahneman and Tversky, 1979), for instance, has been successfully applied in the field of tax research (see, for example, Elffers and Hessing, 1997; Kirchler and Maciejovsky, 2001; Yaniv, 1999). Framing effects – that is, presenting outcomes as losses or gains – were studied (Schepanski and Kelsey, 1990), and the withholding phenomenon was explained by introducing the notion of a reference point (Schepanski and Shearer, 1995). However, Prospect Theory is of limited use for predicting behavior. It is not always clear which reference point taxpayers naturally adopt, unless this is given externally by framing (Copeland and Cuccia, 2002).

Another research paradigm that has already been applied in tax research describes compliance decisions as a social dilemma (Dawes, 1980). According to such models, taxpayers try to balance egoistic goals (i.e., maximizing effective income) and collective goals (e.g., establishing health care and welfare systems). The individual is better off by defecting and evading taxes. If too many individuals behave egoistically and evade taxes, collective goals cannot be achieved and everyone would have been better off by cooperating. The standard economic model fully neglects the utility of the collective.

Probably an even stronger constraint of the economic model is that tax morale is neglected. Braithwaite (2003) suggests that taxpayers follow quite diverse motivational postures in paying their taxes. While some may pay their taxes due to their commitment to the community, others are disengaged, or enjoy tax evasion as sort of game playing with the state. According to Braithwaite, only a small proportion of taxpayers are driven by the latter postures and should be pursued with full rigor of the law. Therefore, Ayres and Braithwaite (1992) argue for responsive regulation, where tax authorities treat taxpayers according to their motivational posture. Responsive regulation suggests maintenance and stabilization of compliant taxpayers, and severe punishment for notoriously noncompliant taxpayers. It is likely that the economic model fits best for the group of disengaged and game-playing taxpayers, and loses validity among taxpayers with different motivational postures.

A related idea was proposed in the "slippery slope" framework by Kirchler *et al.* (2008). Their approach is based on the interaction between taxpayers and authorities, and distinguishes enforced and voluntary compliance. Whereas enforced compliance is determined by how taxpayers perceive the power of authorities to prosecute and punish them, voluntary compliance can be achieved

Table 2.1 Overview of empirical findings reported in the text

Publication	Method	Effect on tax compliance of:			
		Level of income	*Tax rate*	*Audit probability*	*Fines*
Ali *et al.* (2001)	Aggregate data	–	–	+	0/+**
Alm *et al.* (1992a)	Experiment	+	–	+	+
Alm *et al.* (1992b)	Experiment			+	
Alm *et al.* (1995)	Experiment		+	+	+**
Anderhub *et al.* (2001)	Experiment	–			
Baldry (1987)	Experiment	–	0		
Christian (1994)	Aggregate data	+			
Clotfelter (1983)	Aggregate data	+	–	+	
Collins and Plumlee (1991)	Experiment		–		0
Dubin *et al.* (1990)	Aggregate data	+	–	+	
Feinstein (1991)	Aggregate data	0	+		
Fishlow and Friedman (1994)	Aggregate data	+			
Friedland (1982)	Experiment			+	+
Friedland *et al.* (1978)	Experiment		–		~**
Gërxhani and Schram (2006)	Experiment				
	Dutch sample			+	
	Albanian sample			0	

Study	Method			
Lang et al. (1997)	Survey*	−	−	
Mason and Calvin (1978)	Survey*	+	+	+
Moser et al. (1995)	Experiment	0	0/−**	
Park and Hyun (2003)	Experiment	−	+	+
Pommerehne and Weck-Hannemann (1996)	Aggregate data	0	−	0
Porcano (1988)	Survey*	0	0	
Schwartz and Orleans (1967)	Experiment	−	−	0**
Slemrod (1985)	Aggregate data	−		
Slemrod et al. (2001)	Experiment		+**	
Spicer and Lundstedt (1976)	Survey*	0	0	0
Spicer and Thomas (1982)	Experiment		+**	
Trivedi et al. (2003, 2004)	Experiment		+	
Vogel (1974)	Survey*	−		
Wärneryd and Walerud (1982)	Survey*	0	0	
Webley et al. (1991)	Experiment		+	0
Weck-Hannemann and Pommerehne (1989)	Aggregate data	−	+	0

Notes

+, Positive effect on tax compliance; −, negative effect on tax compliance; 0, no effect on tax compliance; ~, ambiguous effect on tax compliance.

* In surveys, fines and audit probabilities are sometimes measured by subjectively perceived audit and fine rates.

** Interactions with other variables; for further details, please consult the text.

if the taxpayers perceive authorities as trustworthy and benevolent. Hence, in a climate where trust in authorities is low, a tax policy based on audits and fines is effective. In a climate of trust, however, tax morale, perceived fairness of the tax system, tax knowledge, and social norms are important to foster compliance. Further, a dynamic interaction of power and trust has to be considered. Changes in trust might influence power (e.g., by whistle-blowing of compliant citizens) and vice versa (e.g., if frequent audits are perceived as a signal of distrust). The slippery slope framework emphasizes the interaction of taxpayers and authorities, and suggests that tax authorities move from a "cops-and-robbers" to a "service-and-client" view.

The problem of tax compliance seems much too complex to be explained by a pure economic approach. Including alternative approaches could help in understanding the irrational behavior of taxpayers, and could expand the toolbox for an efficient tax policy.

Notes

1 In fact, Allingham and Sandmo (1972) and Srinivasan (1973) published their analyses of tax evasion at almost the same time without knowing about each other's work.
2 The latter proposition is also supported by Yitzhaki (1974), who suggests that if fines are imposed on the evaded tax instead of undeclared income, compliance will be related positively to tax rates.

Bibliography

Ali, M. M., Cecil, H. W., and Knoblett, J. A. (2001) "The effects of tax rates and enforcement policies on taxpayer compliance: A study of self-employed taxpayers", *Atlantic Economic Journal*, 29: 186–202.

Allingham, M. G. and Sandmo, A. (1972) "Income tax evasion: A theoretical analysis", *Journal of Public Economics*, 1: 323–38.

Alm, J. (1999) "Tax Compliance and Administration", in W. B. Hildreth and J. A. Richardson (eds.), *Handbook of Taxation*, New York, NY: Marcel Dekker, Inc.

Alm, J., Cronshaw, M. B., and McKee, M. (1993) "Tax compliance with endogenous audit selection-rules", *Kyklos*, 46: 27–45.

Alm, J., Jackson, B., and McKee, M. (1992a) "Estimating the determinants of taxpayer compliance with experimental-data", *National Tax Journal*, 45: 107–14.

Alm, J., McClelland, G. H., and Schulze, W. D. (1992b) "Why do people pay taxes?" *Journal of Public Economics*, 48: 21–38.

Alm, J., Sanchez, I., and De Juan, A. (1995) "Economic and noneconomic factors in tax compliance", *Kyklos*, 48: 3–18.

Anderhub, V., Giese, S., Güth, W., Hoffmann, A., and Otto, T. (2001) "Tax evasion with earned income – an experimental study", *Finanz Archiv*, 58: 188–206.

Andreoni, J., Erard, B., and Feinstein, J. S. (1998) "Tax compliance", *Journal of Economic Literature*, 36: 818–60.

Ayres, I. and Braithwaite, J. (1992) *Responsive Regulation: Transcending the Deregulation Debate*, New York, NY: Oxford University Press.

Baldry, J. C. (1987) "Income tax evasion and the tax schedule: some experimental results", *Public Finance*, 42: 347–83.

Boylan, S. J. and Sprinkle, G. B. (2001) "Experimental evidence on the relation between tax rates and compliance: The effect of earned vs. endowed income", *Journal of the American Taxation Association*, 23: 75–90.

Braithwaite, V. (2003) "Dancing with tax authorities: motivational postures and non-compliant actions", in V. Braithwaite (ed.), *Taxing Democracy*, Aldershot, UK: Ashgate.

Christian, C. W. (1994). *Voluntary Compliance with the Individual Income Tax: Results from the 1988 TCMP Study.* Washington, DC.

Clotfelter, C. (1983) "Tax evasion and tax rates: an analysis of individual returns", *The Review of Economics and Statistics*, 65: 363–73.

Collins, J. H. and Plumlee, R. D. (1991) "The taxpayers labor and reporting decision – the effect of audit schemes", *Accounting Review*, 66: 559–76.

Copeland, P. V. and Cuccia, A. D. (2002) "Multiple determinants of framing referents in tax reporting and compliance", *Organizational Behavior and Human Decision Processes*, 88: 499–526.

Cowell, F. A. (1985) "Tax evasion with labour income", *Journal of Public Economics*, 26: 19–34.

Dawes, R. M. (1980) "Social dilemmas", *Annual Review of Psychology*, 31: 169–93.

Dubin, J. A., Graetz, M. J., and Wilde, L. L. (1990) "The effect of audit rates on the federal individual income tax, 1977–1986", *National Tax Journal*, 43: 395–409.

Elffers, H. and Hessing, D. J. (1997) "Influencing the prospects of tax evasion", *Journal of Economic Psychology*, 18: 289–304.

Elffers, H., Weigel, R. H., and Hessing, D. J. (1987) "The consequences of different strategies for measuring tax evasion behaviour", *Journal of Economic Psychology*, 8: 311–37.

Feinstein, J. (1991) "An econommometric analysis of income tax evasion and its detection", *RAND Journal of Economics*, 22: 14–35.

Fischer, C. M., Wartick, M., and Mark, M. M. (1992) "Detection probability and taxpayer compliance: A review of the literature", *Journal of Accounting Literature*, 11: 1–46.

Fishlow, A. and Friedman, J. (1994) "Tax evasion, inflation and stabilization", *Journal of Development Economics*, 43: 105–23.

Fjeldstad, O. H. and Semboja, J. (2001) "Why people pay taxes: The case of the development levy in Tanzania", *World Development*, 29: 2059–74.

Friedland, N. (1982) "A note on tax evasion as a function of the quality of information about the magnitude and credibility of threatened fines: Some preliminary research", *Journal of Applied Social Psychology*, 12: 54–9.

Friedland, N., Maital, S., and Rutenberg, A. (1978) "A simulation study of income tax evasion", *Journal of Public Economics*, 10: 107–16.

Gërxhani, K. and Schram, A. (2006) "Tax evasion and income source: A comparative experimental study", *Journal of Economic Psychology*, 27: 202–22.

Guala, F. and Mittone, L. (2005) "Experiments in economics: External validity and the robustness of phenomena", *Journal of Economic Methodology*, 12: 495–515.

Kahneman, D. and Tversky, A. (1979) "Prospect theory: An analysis of decision under risk", *Econometrica*, 47: 263–91.

Kastlunger, B., Kirchler, E., Mittone, L., and Pitters, J. (2000) "Sequences of audits, tax compliance and taxpaying strategies", *Journal of Economic Psychology*, 30: 405–18.

Kirchler, E. (2007) *The Economic Psychology of Tax Behaviour*, Cambridge, UK: Cambridge University Press.

Kirchler, E. and Maciejovsky, B. (2001) "Tax compliance within the context of gain and loss situations, expected and current asset position, and profession", *Journal of Economic Psychology*, 22: 173–94.

Kirchler, E., Hoelzl, E., and Wahl, I. (2008) "Enforced versus voluntary tax compliance: The "slippery slope" framework", *Journal of Economic Psychology*, 29: 210–25.

Kirchler, E., Muehlbacher, S., Hoelzl, E., and Webley, P. (2009) "Effort and aspirations in tax evasion: Experimental evidence", *Applied Psychology: An International Review*, 58: 488–507

Lang, O., Nöhrbaß, K.-H., and Stahl, K. (1997) "On income tax avoidance: The case of Germany", *Journal of Public Economics*, 66: 327–47.

Maciejovsky, B., Kirchler, E., and Schwarzenberger, H. (2007) "Misperception of chance and loss repair: On the dynamics of tax compliance", *Journal of Economic Psychology*, 28: 678–91.

Mason, R. and Calvin, L. D. (1978) "A study of admitted income tax evasion", *Law and Society Review*, 13: 73–89.

Martinez-Vazquez, J. and Rider, M. (2005) "Multiple modes of tax evasion: Theory and evidence", *National Tax Journal*, 58: 51–76.

McCaffery, E. J. and Baron, J. (2004) "Framing and taxation: evaluation of tax policies involving household composition", *Journal of Economic Psychology*, 25: 679–705.

Mittone, L. (2006) "Dynamic behaviour in tax evasion: An experimental approach", *Journal of Socio-Economics* 35: 813–35.

Moser, D. V., Evans, J. H. III, and Kim, C. K. (1995) "The effects of horizontal and exchange inequity on tax reporting decisions", *Accounting Review*, 70: 619–34.

Muehlbacher, S. and Kirchler, E. (2008) "Arbeitsaufwand, Anspruchsniveau und Steuermoral", *Zeitschrift für Arbeits- und Organisationspsychologie*, 26: 91–6.

Muehlbacher, S., Hölzl, E., and Kirchler, E. (2007) "Steuerhinterziehung und die Berücksichtigung des Einkommens in der Strafbemessung", *Wirtschaftspsychologie*, 24: 116–21.

Park, C. G. and Hyun, J. K. (2003) "Examining the determinants of tax compliance by experimental data: A case of Korea", *Journal of Policy Modeling*, 25: 673–84.

Pencavel, J. H. (1979) "A note on income tax evasion, labor supply and nonlinear tax schedules", *Journal of Public Economics*, 12: 115–24.

Pommerehne, W. and Weck-Hannemann, H. (1992) "Steuerhinterziehung: Einige romantische, realistische und nicht zuletzt empirische Befunde", *Zeitschrift für Wirtschafts- und Sozialwissenschaften*, 112: 433–66.

——. (1996) "Tax rates, tax administration and income tax evasion in Switzerland", *Public Choice*, 88: 161–70.

Porcano, T. M. (1988) "Correlates of tax evasion", *Journal of Economic Psychology*, 9: 47–67.

Reinganum, J. F. and Wilde, L. L. (1985) "Income-tax compliance in a principal agent framework", *Journal of Public Economics*, 26: 1–18.

Roberts, M. L., Hite, P. A., and Bradley, C. F. (1994) "Understanding attitudes toward progressive taxation", *Public Opinion Quarterly*, 58: 165–90.

Sandmo, A. (1981) "Income tax evasion, labor supply, and the equity-evasion tradeoff", *Journal of Public Economics*, 16: 265–88.

Schepanski, A. and Kelsey, D. (1990) "Testing for framing effects in taxpayer compliance decisions", *Journal of the American Taxation Association*, 12: 60–77.

Schepanski, A. and Shearer, T. (1995) "A prospect-theory account of the income-tax withholding phenomenon", *Organizational Behavior and Human Decision Processes*, 63: 174–86.

Schwartz, R. and Orleans, S. (1967) "On legal sanctions", *University of Chicago Law Review*, 34: 274–300.

Slemrod, J. (1985) "An empirical test for tax evasion", *Review of Economics and Statistics*, 67: 232–38.

Slemrod, J., and Yitzhaki, S. (2002) "Tax avoidance, evasion and administration", in A. J. Auerbach and M. Feldstein (eds.), *Handbook of Public Economics*, Vol. 3, Amsterdam: Elsevier.

Slemrod, J., Blumenthal, M., and Christian, C. (2001) "Taxpayer response to an increased probability of audit: evidence from a controlled experiment in Minnesota", *Journal of Public Economics*, 79: 455–83.

Spicer, M. W. and Hero, R. E. (1985) "Tax evasion and heuristics: a research note", *Journal of Public Economics*, 26: 263–7.

Spicer, M. W. and Lundstedt, S. B. (1976) "Understanding tax evasion", *Public Finance*, 21: 295–305.

Spicer, M. W. and Thomas, J. E. (1982) "Audit probabilities and tax evasion decision: an experimental approach", *Journal of Economic Psychology*, 2: 241–5.

Srinivasan, T. N. (1973) "Tax evasion: a model", *Journal of Public Economics*, 2: 339–46.

Strümpel, B. (1969) "The contribution of survey research to public finance", in A. T. Peacock (ed.), *Quantitative Analysis in Public Finance*, New York, NY: Praeger.

Trivedi, V. U., Shehata, M., and Lynn, B. (2003) "Impact of personal and situational factors on taxpayer compliance: An experimental analysis", *Journal of Business Ethics*, 47: 175–97.

Trivedi, V. U., Shehata, M., and Mestelman, S. (2004) "Attitudes, incentives, and tax compliance", unpublished manuscript, Hamilton: McMaster University, Department of Economics.

Tversky, A. and Kahneman, D. (1974) "Judgment under uncertainty: Heuristics and biases", *Science*, 185: 1124–31.

Vogel, J. (1974) "Taxation and public opinion in Sweden: An interpretation of recent survey data", *National Tax Journal*, 27: 499–513.

Wärneryd, K. and Walerud, B. (1982) "Taxes and economic behaviour: some interview data on tax evasion in Sweden", *Journal of Economic Psychology*, 2: 187–211.

Webley, P. (1987) "Audit probabilities and tax evasion in a business simulation", *Economics Letters*, 25: 267–70.

Webley, P., Robben, H. S. J., Elffers, H., and Hessing, D. J. (1991) *Tax evasion: An Experimental Approach*, Cambridge, UK: Cambridge University Press.

Weck-Hannemann, H. and Pommerehne, W. (1989) "Einkommensteuerhinterziehung in der Schweiz: Eine empirische Analyse" *Schweizerische Zeitschrift für Volkswirtschaft und Statistik*, 125: 517–56.

Witte, A. D. and Woodbury, D. F. (1985) "The effect of tax laws and tax administration on tax compliance: The case of the US individual income tax", *National Tax Journal*, 38: 1–13.

Yaniv, G. (1999) "Tax compliance and advance tax payments: a prospect theory analysis", *National Tax Journal*, 52: 753–64.

Yitzhaki, S. (1974) "A note on income tax evasion: a theoretical analysis", *Journal of Public Economics*, 3: 201–2.

Part III

Expanding the standard theory of compliance

3 Tax compliance

Social norms, culture, and endogeneity

John Cullis, Philip Jones, and Alan Lewis[1]

Introduction

Neoclassical welfare economics offers normative prescriptions premised on the preferences and capabilities of *homo economicus*. This actor is described as:

i   "rational";
ii egoistic;
iii with egoism predicated on self-interest narrowly defined in terms of income or wealth.

(Brennan and Lomasky, 1993)

"Rational" behavior is consistent behavior. Predictions are made when *homo economicus* faces new constraints (relative prices, income) but when preferences are assumed exogenous and constant (Stigler and Becker, 1977). This is the essence of the Allingham and Sandmo (1972) tax evasion as a crime model of evasion. In this chapter, the focus is on the extent to which *homo economicus* might be deemed "unrepresentative" and the associated implications when considering the question of tax evasion in the light of a different actor.

An established behavioral empirical literature now describes a *homo-realitus* (see Cullis and Jones, 2007) as:

i   reliant on bounded rationality;
ii concerned with more than pure self-interest;
iii responsive to reference frames (with endogenous preferences).

This suggests three dimensions of concern that form the substantive sections of this chapter.

Homo realitus displays anomalous behavior (individual failure) which might be interpreted as a form of bounded rationality. Defenders of neoclassical theory see conventional predicted behavior as a close enough approximation to sustain the argument that *homo economicus* is representative. They argue that anomalous behavior observed, largely, in laboratory testing arises because participants lack a "correct" understanding and that, in practice, anomalous behavior is far less than implied in experiments. In short, they see neoclassical theory as being applied in "evolved" settings, where similar decisions are repeated. However, study after study reports the ubiquity of anomalies and tax evasion theory and policy should reflect this. Tax framing is a particularly important issue here. Closer analysis of "ego" suggests that narrow self-interest is far from representative.

There seems to be some dissatisfaction with narrow instrumental rationality when modeling tax evasion so that psychic and stigma costs and "norms of convention" have been noted. There are a number of authors who have sought to introduce a variety of related concepts to give greater content to *homo economicus*. Further, neoclassical microeconomics predicts the behavior of *homo economicus* when preferences are assumed constant. However, if it is accepted that preferences are context-laden and to some extent endogenous, then a third dimension needs to be added to the analysis of tax evasion. The tax policy context and statutes employed by government itself informs preferences (Jones *et al.*, 1998), and the question of tax evasion may be better addressed in the light of this.

If neoclassical microeconomics appears to address the question "how much tax evasion will there be?", in practice it is addressing the question "how much tax evasion should be undertaken by *homo economicus*?". However, the argument here is that the question cannot be satisfactorily addressed without recognizing research in behavioral economics and economic psychology (and the questions that are raised concerning the degree to which *homo economicus* is representative). How much tax evasion will be undertaken by *homo realitus*? The general view is that people evade less than is predicted by the Allingham–Sandmo "instrumentally rational economic actor" approach – there appears to be too little evasion!

A growing literature calls into question the proposition that the decision to evade tax is as instrumental as implied by the Allingham–Sandmo model. A "…purely economic analysis of the evasion gamble implies that most individuals would evade if they are rational because it is unlikely that cheaters will be caught and penalised" (Alm *et al.*, 1992: 22), but Andreoni *et al.* (1998) surveyed a plethora of studies to demonstrate that tax compliance exceeds predictions premised on self-interested instrumental behavior.[2] Risk aversion is lower than required to explain such high levels of compliance (Alm *et al.*, 1992; Feld and Frey, 2002; Graetz and Wilde, 1985).

Slemrod (2007) has qualified this criticism. The probability of audit may be low across the population as a whole, but a wage- or salary-earner (whose employer submits the employee's taxable income) realizes that dishonesty will be transparent. Yet even with this qualification, Slemrod (2005) accepts that "…there is more to the story than … amoral … cost benefit calculation…". Allingham and Sandmo's (1972) model points to the tax rate, the probability of detection and the fine for evasion as the determinants of tax compliance. An empirical literature explains the determinants of "tax morale" when "tax morale" is defined as the difference between tax compliance and compliance that would be predicted with reference to instrumental self-interest.

The first objective in this chapter is to present a critique of arguments designed to reconcile differences between reported levels of tax evasion and levels predicted by the Allingham–Sandmo model. When assessing these arguments, there is evidence that social norms are an important determinant of "tax morale". But if social norms are important, how does this inform predictions of the way that tax evasion is likely to change? The second objective in this chapter is to present and test a "social norms model" that has a role to play when analysing the dynamics of tax evasion.

Alternative explanations

A "market" for alternative explanations was already developing as early as 1982, where a review of the literature, based on experimental and social survey evidence, revealed that taxpayer compliance was determined by the "tax mentality" or "tax morale" of taxpayers: whether or not taxpayers were aware of the benefits of paying taxes by making the "fiscal connection" between taxation and public expenditure, whether they felt a sense of civic duty or perceived tax evasion to be morally wrong (Lewis, 1982). In the intervening years a considerable amount of relevant work has been undertaken and the list of explanations has become lengthy; it includes the role of government in increasing or crowding out intrinsic motivation; framing effects; social norms; perceptions of justice and fairness; even the nature of democracy itself (Kirchler, 2007). Since Allingham and Sandmo's floodgates were opened, we have become awash with explanations: how are we to choose between them?

It may be helpful to consider three categories of explanation: "tinkering", "cognitive" and "social". In the first, exemplified by the work of Spicer (1986), the model remains analytic and individualistic. Spicer (1986) amends the Allingham–Sandmo model to embrace analysis of the expected tax gain, the expected punishment for evasion, and the "psychic costs" experienced if individuals prefer to act honestly. Citizens evade if:

$$(1 - p)t\theta Y - pst\theta Y - c > 0 \tag{1}$$

where t = the tax rate
θ = the fraction of taxable income not reported
Y = income
s = the fine rate imposed on evaded tax
p = the probability of detection
c = the psychic costs of tax evasion.

Here the trick is to specify a source of utility, namely concern with your own conscience, that will save the theory. In Frey and Eichenberger's (1989) terms, it represents an attempt to, minimally, rewrite the underlying objective function so that results at odds with the initial theory are now apparently predicted by the revised one. This *ex-post* rewriting appears methodologically unsound.

The second development is driven by a contemporary interest in the findings of cognitive psychology, and in particular the work of Kahneman and Tversky (1979) on heuristic decision-making. The "framing effect" is especially relevant to the study of tax compliance (see Kirchler, 2007, for a helpful review). If, for example, income in one tax system is declared at the end of the fiscal year and tax is then subsequently deducted, this may be "framed" by taxpayers as a loss, encouraging tax evasion. Alternatively, if taxpayers have already had tax deducted and are likely to receive a rebate on completion of a tax return, this will be framed as a gain, encouraging compliance. For the interpretation of this result to be attributed to framing effects, the total liability in both cases must be the same. Using self-reported measures of tax evasion, Kirchler and Maciejovsky (2001) were able to show that, among a sample of 60 self-employed respondents, an unexpected demand for payment led to low tax compliance (risk-seeking for losses) and a surprise refund led to high tax compliance (risk aversion for gains). An analysis of US Internal Revenue Statistics convincingly shows that compliance decreases as a function of supplementary payments due (Cox and Pumley, 1988; Schepanski and Shearer, 1995). Here, the unit of analysis is the brain and the way it works. The implication appears to be that, if the tax system can be set up to exploit "framing", tax evasion will be minimal.

The "social" category seems to be the largest (covering studies which are at the social/cognitive margins, with much broader considerations of the influence of culture on compliance). Some examples include the following:

i   Tax morale might reflect altruism. When Orviska and Hudson (2002) employ the concept of civic duty, they define this (in part) in terms of concern for **others**.[3] The problem with this explanation is that altruistic individuals have no incentive to take altruistic action if they feel that action by one individual would have no impact. If each individual feels that personal tax will have only a miniscule impact on the provision of services there is no incentive to comply beyond the instrumental levels predicted by Allingham and Sandmo, because altruism has the hallmarks of a public good (Collard, 1978). In "large" number situations there is no instrumental motivation to pay tax even if taxpayers are concerned for others, because in a "large" number situation individual action is (by definition) insignificant (Buchanan, 1968).

ii A second approach distinguishes between utility from action and utility derived from outcome contingent on action. Individuals are described as "...intrinsically motivated to perform an activity when one receives no apparent reward except the activity itself..." (Deci, 1971: 105). A growing empirical literature presents evidence that perceptions of the intrinsic value of action depend on moral considerations and low-cost signals that acknowledge action (see, for example, Deci and Ryan, 1980, 1985; Frey 1997a). In this context, taxpayers' response depends on signals that are emitted by tax policy and by the administration of tax policy (Frey 1997b; Feld and Frey 2002). Taxpayers are also more compliant if the action of other taxpayers acknowledges the value of honest response. Frey and Torgler (2007: 23) emphasize that taxation is a "social act": "An individual taxpayer is strongly influenced by what he or she perceives to be the behavior of other taxpayers. If taxpayers believe tax evasion to be common, their tax morale decreases..." (our emphasis).They report that, on average, "...the percentage of persons reporting a high tax morale falls by 7.4 percentage points when the extent of tax evasion rises by one unit (on a scale from 1 to 4)...".

iii   A third approach focuses on reciprocity. Individuals are sensitive to the way they "...are treated by others..." (Bowles and Gintis, 2006: 172). "Reciprocity means that in response to friendly actions, people are frequently much nicer and much more cooperative than predicted by the self interest model: conversely, in response to hostile actions they are frequently much more nasty and even brutal" (Fehr and Gachter, 2000: 159). Once again, behavior by others is a very important consideration.

Individuals repay gifts (or take revenge), incurring cost that generates neither present nor future material rewards. In "public good experiments" Fehr and Gachter have found that where there are punishment opportunities, "reciprocal types" can induce "selfish types" to choose cooperative action as opposed to free-riding. Individuals are more willing to trust one another when there are signals that it is possible to trust one another.[4] In this way, it is also the case that a tax system perceived to be fair will increase willingness to reciprocate. Slemrod (2007: 40) argues that taxpayer behavior depends on government behavior. As Levi (1998: 91) notes (our emphasis),

> ...if citizens believe that the government will act in their interests, that its procedures are fair, and that their trust of the state and **others** is reciprocated, then people are more likely to become "contingent consenters" who cooperate in paying taxes even when their short term material interest would make free-riding the individual's best option.

If there is overlap between different studies of tax morale, this overlap is perhaps most obvious when focusing on analysis that highlights the importance of the behavior of others (hence the bold type). This is in line with one of the general findings from public goods experiments, where the rational egoist will make zero contribution no matter what others do: "Those who believe others will cooperate in social dilemmas are more likely to cooperate themselves..." (Ostrom, 2000: 140).

Hindricks and Myles (2006) illustrate the importance of social context by comparing "payoffs from non-compliance" (determined by the tax to be paid, the probability of detection and the fine for evasion) and "payoffs from compliance" (determined by perceptions of the value of acting honestly). Any shift from equilibrium leads to "corner solutions". Fixing enforcement parameters, the payoff from non-compliance in Figure 3.1 (i.e. NP) increases with the number of non-compliers (because the chance of getting away with evasion increases when tax auditors have more evaders to monitor). Focusing on reciprocity (or response to the intrinsic value of action signaled by others), the more others evade, the lower is the perception of compliance payoff. In Figure 3.1, the compliance payoff (CP) falls the more others evade. "The reasoning behind this social inter-action can be motivated along the following lines: The amount of stigma or guilt I feel if I do not comply may depend on what others do and think" (Hindricks and Myles, 2006: 534).

At a non-compliance rate ε taxpayers are indifferent between compliance and non-compliance, but a small reduction in non-compliance would alter incentives. The payoff from compliance now exceeds the payoff from non-compliance. This change triggers a reaction that leads to increased compliance. Hindricks and Myles (2006: 535) argue that "...a short but intense audit policy backed by a harsh punishment in order to change the decisions of enough taxpayers" means "...that the dynamics switch toward full compliance".

Of course, a small increase in non-compliance triggers a chain reaction in the opposite direction, making non-compliance progressively more and more attrac-tive. The important concern here is that, if tax evasion depends on "how others behave", analysis of the dynamics of tax evasion suggests that the outcome will be at one or two extremities (all comply, or no one complies).[5] While analysis of tax morale highlights the relevance of perceptions of the way that others behave, the observation that there is a positive relationship leads to "corner-equilibria". In the neoclassical world, with all adjustments generally being conceived of as marginal ones, "corner solutions" (although good for exercise sets) fit oddly, and an analysis yielding interior solutions seems attractive.

Some lines of criticism

It is accepted that social norms, taking into account what other people do, is an important ingredient of tax morale, yet both concepts are surely more complex

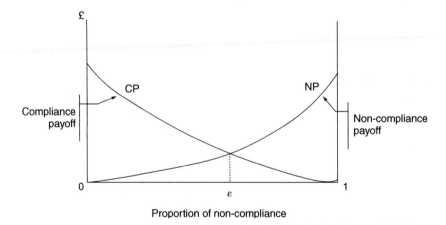

Figure 3.1 The behavior of "others" and the incentive to comply.

than this. "Social norms are shared understandings about actions that are obligatory, permitted or forbidden" (Crawford and Ostrom, 1995, in Ostrom, 2000). Which norms are learned, however, varies from one culture to another, across families, and with exposure to diverse social norms expressed within various types of situations" (Ostrom, 2000: 143–4). In this vein, tax morale is about the attitudes, values and beliefs which represent elements of choice and preference among taxpayers. Social norms, or what constitutes acceptable behavior within a given culture, can vary within cultures – for example, there are differing speech styles and varying manners deemed appropriate to wealthy people compared to poorer people in manual occupations (there are cultures within cultures). Social norms are not about aping the behavior of nebulous others; rather, normative behavior requires that one follows the manners of people in the social group with whom one identifies.

In the case of tax compliance, this may be other self-employed people or other workers in the construction industry. Whether instrumental behavior is acceptable or not is also determined by social norms and cultural understandings. For example, Frank *et al.* (1993) have shown that students who study economics are often less cooperative than other students; Cullis *et al.* (2006) present evidence that economics students are more instrumental and more likely to do the rational calculations in tax evasion scenarios. Rational economic man (an individual who does the relevant tax evasion calculations) is likely to be unevenly distributed across cultures and within them.

This chapter began with a relatively simple analytic model (Allingham and Sandmo), but now considerable complexity has emerged. Parsimonious models and *homo realitus* are not readily compatible bedfellows. The problem is, which of these alternative explanations are the most pertinent, and how is it possible to choose between them? Take framing effects as an example. Studying framing effects is very popular at the moment, and there is extensive evidence that these effects can be reproduced outside laboratory settings and when real money is involved. Studies of this kind are very persuasive, as they are easy to understand, repeatable, and appear to have something to do with how the brain works. Nevertheless, some aspects of the methodology are akin to a party game where participants are tricked by a kind of mental illusion in a very restricted-stimulus environment. It is therefore a simplification of a more complex world, and should not be taken as a comprehensive description of the way people make decisions. When Martinez-Vazquez *et al.* (1992) consider the tendency to be more evasive (because tax is framed as a "loss"), they draw attention to an alternative explanation. If tax payment is "underwitheld" (so that taxpayers must pay the difference), a tendency to be more evasive (than if overpayment of tax was available for refund) can be explained with reference to the liquidity constraint taxpayers face.

When studies identify framing effects, they are more complex than is usually acknowledged. Framing effects may be underpinned by something else – i.e., by tax morale, which includes the attitudes, beliefs and preferences of the actors concerned. The perception of tax liability as a loss is dependent not only on the framing effect, but also on whether the money is ever seen as "mine" as opposed to the revenue's in the first instance; some people would never see the money as their own however it was framed (see endnote 3). The question of property rights emerges. Framing effects are not purely mechanical; they require interpretation from participants, and are constructed differently depending on the value systems of the participants and the social context (similar points have been made by Reckers *et al.*, 1994). Cullis and colleagues (2006) show that framing effects may not always be powerful. Furthermore, Cullis *et al.* argue that there is an interaction between these effects and micro-cultural understandings. Economists and, presumably, other instrumental people are more susceptible to framing effects, so it is not purely a cognitive phenomenon.

With a litany of possible explanations of differences between predicted and observed levels of tax evasion, a critical examination of the relative merits of alternatives warrants a chapter (or perhaps a book) of its own. The emphasis here is more on the question of tax morale /tax mentality and culture. It may be that the cultural (national) level of analysis is something newer (and a refreshing change from micro-analytic perspectives). Furthermore, tax morale /tax mentality are useful generic terms which include a range of variables of relevance to comprehending tax compliance, beyond instrumental assumptions and heuristic biases.

A model with norms and endogeneity

The proposition is that there is a relationship between the *prevalence* of a norm to comply and the *strength* of the norm. The *strength* of the norm is the proportion of individuals who think that they ought to honestly pay taxes whether they actually do or not. The *prevalence* of the norm depends positively on the strength of the norm of honest tax-paying. More individuals actually act honestly the greater the proportion who think they ought to act honestly.

Predictions of the way in which tax evasion will change are possible by comparing the strength of the norm with the prevalence of the norm. The following discussion applies insight drawn from Hargreaves-Heap (1992). When the strength of the norm (S) exceeds the proportion actually conforming to the norm (P), more individuals will be induced to behave in accordance with the norm, and vice versa. Equilibrium occurs when the norm is self-supporting (in that the proportion thinking they ought to conform equals the proportion that conforms).

The following two examples demonstrate some of the different equilibria possible and the dynamics of tax evasion:

i   In the "square box" figure (Figure 3.2), the 45° line is the equilibrium line. In Figure 3.2, the tax compliance equilibrium is EE. Below EE (e.g., at point 1), the strength of the norm (S) exceeds the prevalence of the norm (P) and increased prevalence is induced (i.e., $\Delta P/\Delta S > 0$).[6] Above point EE (say at point 2), the strength of the norm (S) falls short of the prevalence of the norm (P) and prevalence is reduced (i.e., $\Delta P/\Delta S < 0$). Equilibrium EE is stable. Any deviation will be self-correcting, as $\Delta P/\Delta S > 1$ at EE.

ii   In Figure 3.3, the equilibrium EEu is an unstable equilibrium (as any devia-
     tion, or tremble, to points like 1 and 2 from EEu induces feedback effects
     that make EE and 0' the stable equilibria – ΔP/ΔS < 1 at EEu). Figure 3.3
     shows multiple equilibria that have a paradoxical element in that a low or
     complete stable equilibria tax-compliant population would be observed.

Many other patterns are clearly possible. However, in order to proceed it is
necessary to consider the strength of the norm concerning honest compliance.
This norm might depend on culture, political, religious and other factors. In
summary, when the strength of a norm exceeds the proportion actually conforming to the norm, more individuals will be induced to behave in accordance with a
norm, and vice versa. Equilibrium occurs when the norm is self-supporting, in
that the proportion who think they ought to conform to the norm equals the
number who actually conform to the norm (strength = prevalence).

An empirical application

Using available data, it is possible to carry out an exercise that can tabulate a
version of the strength of the norm for honest tax-paying with the prevalence of
honest tax-paying. As regards the strength of the honesty norm, questionnaire
responses have been employed. Torgler and Schneider (2007) use a tax morality

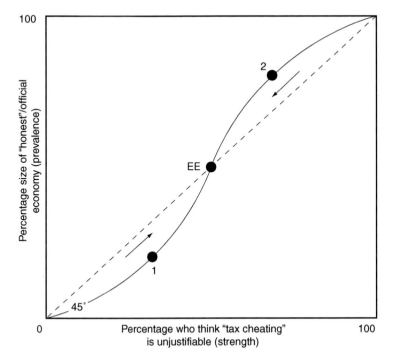

Figure 3.2 Stable intermediate equilibrium.

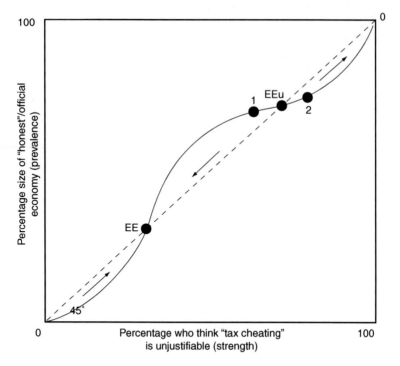

Figure 3.3 Low and complete equilibria.

variable from the World Values Survey, where responses to the general question "Please tell me for each of the following statements whether you think it can always be justified, never be justified, or something in between (…) Cheating on tax if you have the chance" are coded into ranks ranging from 1=Never justifiable to 10=Always justifiable. This is essentially an attitudinal question relating to the morality of tax evasion, as opposed to a behavioral one, and can be construed as data on norm strength of tax honesty. These data are used here. It must be recognized that proxying tax morality in this way is telescoping a fairly rich concept into a very humble measure.

As regards the prevalence of the norm, a major element in measures of the shadow economy is tax evasion, so the estimated size of the shadow economy might be interpreted as the prevalence of the norm of tax honesty in a country. A typical interchange in some areas of the UK economy is: Customer; "Can I write you a check?" Tradesperson; "Why are you swearing at me?". Capturing quantitatively the outcomes of a myriad of such relatively subtle interchanges is clearly a difficult task. Fortunately, however, Schneider (2005) provides estimates of the shadow economy for a number of years for many countries.

In order to abstract from problems associated with considering economies with very different underlying structures, the focus is OECD countries. The years considered are for each country as close to 1989 and 1999 as possible.

Whilst it must be readily recognized that the data must be viewed very cautiously, they must nevertheless be worthy of consideration.

The size of the shadow economies for 19 of 21 OECD[7] countries as reported in Schneider (2005) were converted into percentages that gave the size of the official or honest economy for each of those countries compared to the size of the official plus shadow economy (a measure of the actual economy). These figures are used to proxy the prevalence of the honesty norm in each economy. For the same countries, a measure of the strength of the norm of honesty came from the World Values Survey as noted above. There is an obvious problem in that only code 1 corresponds to complete honesty as regards tax paying, while the remainder are increasing degrees of dishonesty. As a starting point, it was decided to treat all respondents coded 1–5 as "honest" (a sort of democratic 50 percent view of honesty!).

Figure 3.4 plots the outcome of this exercise and shows, via the bunching in the North-East corner, that, visually, the sample is of countries that are fairly honest. A country in apparent equilibrium, in that the strength of the norm equals the prevalence of the norm, would be on the diagonal line. Choosing as a measure of equilibrium a 1 percent or less difference between the strength and prevalence of the norm, only the Netherlands (0.95 percent) was in this position. Taking the numbers at face value, with other things being equal, predictions for 1999 can be formed. Of the 19 countries, 14 are located above the diagonal. As prevalence of the economic honesty norm exceeds the strength of that norm, the prediction would be a future fall in the size of the honest economy.

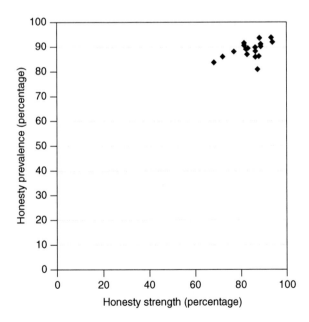

Figure 3.4 Honesty prevalence vs honesty strength, 1989.

The data for 1999 are fairly supportive of this prediction (see Figure 3.5), in that the percentage size of the honest economy fell in all 19 countries (the prediction would have been a rise in Austria, Ireland, Italy, Spain and Sweden). Evidence of "equilibrium" adjustment seems weak, in that only three countries seem to be in equilibrium on the above definition. These were Austria, Finland and the Netherlands.

This analysis seems ideal for the Dutch! As for post-1999, rises in the honest economy are predicted for 11 of the "non-equilibrium" countries and falls for the other five countries.

Evidence is consistent with the proposition that changes in tax evasion can be predicted with reference to difference between the strength and the prevalence of social norms. Of course, there are qualifications to make:

i   In the first instance, tax evasion dynamics can be predicted if individuals act instrumentally. Engle and Hines (1999) argue that tax evasion cycles are possible when a taxpayer's current evasion is a decreasing function of earlier evasion. They show that tax evasion is likely to be lower in a recession because taxpayers fear that there are past (as yet undiscovered) large evasions relative to their new reduced income. A social norms model is not the only model that can be employed to predict tax evasion dynamics. However, it is clear that changes that occurred between 1989 and 1999 (as illustrated above) are largely consistent with predictions premised on a social norms model.

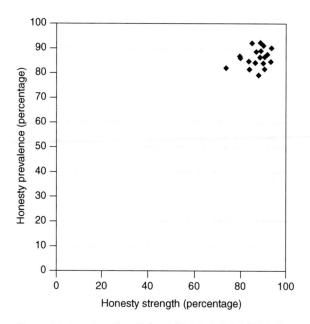

Figure 3.5 Honesty prevalence vs honesty strength, 1999.

ii   A vast number of other charts and predictions based on a more or less strin-
gent view of honesty could be drawn up and doubtless, with a different definition for each country for each year, a "good fit" might be obtained.
However, this would appear to be a somewhat arbitrary process. Correlat-
ing the size of the honest economy with different aggregations of the codes
1 to 10 reveals, helpfully, that the sum of codes 1 to 5 has the highest correlation for 1989 (r=0.53). Using only code 1 results in r=0.43. For 1999
overall the correlations are lower, with, ironically, code 1 in isolation yielding the highest correlation (r=0.29). Using this "correction", Figure 3.6
appears to suggest a massive post-1999 fall in the honest economy. Japan
is closest to a "blue eyed economy", with a 90 percent honest economy and
81 percent reporting "cheating on tax if you have the chance is never justifiable" (but even here more honesty is apparently displayed than is
claimed).

iii   Inevitably, there are always questions concerning the way respondents interpret questionnaires. Responses to questionnaires are sensitive to the way
questions are interpreted. Orviska and Hudson (2002) focused on the British
Social Attitudes Survey (Jowell *et al.*, 1997). The questions were:

- "A householder is having a job done by a builder. He is told that if he
  pays cash, he will not be charged VAT. So he pays cash and saves
  £500. Do you feel he is right or wrong?" The possible responses were:
  Not wrong, A bit wrong, Wrong and Seriously wrong, which the
  authors coded 0 to 3 respectively.

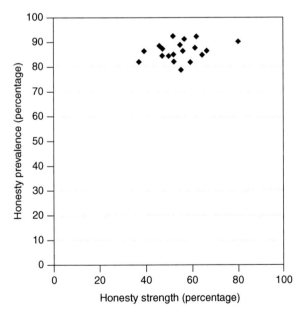

Figure 3.6 Honesty prevalence vs "pure" honesty strength, 1999.

- "And how likely do you think it is that *you* would do this if you found yourself in this situation". The responses were coded 0 (Very likely), 1 (Fairly likely), 2 (Not very likely) and 3 (Not at all likely).
- "An unemployed person on benefit takes a casual job and is paid in cash. He does not report it to the benefit office and is £500 in pocket. Do you feel this is right or wrong?" (Possible responses as above.)
- "A person in paid work takes on an extra weekend job and is paid in cash. He does not declare it for tax and so is £500 in pocket. Do you feel that this is right or wrong?" (Possible responses as above)

In the first instance, it is clear that response was highly sensitive to the way that cheating on tax was framed. Compare the different responses in Table 3.1.

Attitudes are clearly most hostile to the evasion involving benefits and least hostile to the one involving VAT. With respect to the latter question, almost 60 percent of the sample thought it at most only "A bit wrong" whilst almost 70 percent of the sample thought it at least "Fairly likely" that they would do this. Even with respect to benefits, over a quarter of the population thought it at least "Fairly likely" that they would engage in such behavior. Clearly, there is a considerable culture in the UK which condones tax evasion, and this must be of concern to the revenue agencies. Moreover, the problem would appear to be greatest amongst younger people, as the figures in parentheses show. One possible explanation for the differing levels of response between the three types of question is their coding in respondents' minds. How might respondents "see" these scenarios? The VAT question condones evasion by someone else you have met, which you gain from,[8] but does not directly lead you into breaking the law yourself (perhaps coded "I personally am not cheating/stealing"?). The benefits question, however, is not so much evading tax, but the false acquisition of welfare benefits (perhaps coded: "Cheating/stealing from other anonymous taxpayers"?).

Table 3.1 Attitude and behavior responses to tax evasion questions (1997)

Response	VAT (%)	Benefits (%)	Pay (%)
Morally wrong			
Not wrong	29.9 (37.8)	6.9 (12.0)	16.6 (23.2)
A bit wrong	29.6 (34.1)	18.4 (26.5)	30.6 (38.0)
Wrong	32.8 (22.8)	51.2 (43.0)	44.1 (32.9)
Seriously wrong	7.7 (5.3)	18.5 (23.5)	8.8 (5.9)
Would do			
Very likely	36.2 (46.9)	9.8 (13.7)	15.9 (21.3)
Fairly likely	33.0 (35.3)	16.7 (19.4)	25.6 (32.7)
Not very likely	19.3 (14.6)	32.9 (34.5)	28.9 (27.5)
Not at all likely	11.5 (5.2)	42.6 (32.4)	29.6 (18.5)

Note
Figures in parentheses relate to that part of the sample aged under 40.

The public, apparently, see a difference between evading tax on "extra" earned income (perhaps coded: "Cheating/stealing from the anonymous taxmen who have already had their share"?) and the acquisition of transfers which have not been earned.

Data from the 2002 British Social Attitudes Survey provides the most recent comparable data to those in Table 3.2. Unfortunately the question relating to VAT fraud was not asked in this wave, but the key responses to the other two questions are recorded in Table 3.2.

Fuller pictures of the complete set of responses are recorded in Figures 3.7 and 3.8.

With respect to the benefits question, there appears to be a shift towards increasing tax morality between 1997 and 2002. Regarding the "cash in hand" work question there seems to have been a softening of attitudes, with a shift from it being viewed as "Seriously wrong" to "Wrong". The behavioral part of this question suggests increasing tax morality. That said, 18.5 percent of respondents were fairly likely to commit benefit fraud given the opportunity, and 28.7 percent accepted "cash in hand" arrangements. These are not negligible numbers. Overall, there are significant variations in responses to the different questions.

Of course everything depends on interpretation. Referring back to the second section of this chapter, is the variation in responses "cognitive" or "social"? The different responses obtained may be seen as artefacts of "framing" in that the underlying prospect remains the same at least for the benefits and pay questions (an individual dishonestly obtaining his marginal tax rate times £500). Only the wording for different contexts is changed, so are individuals inappropriately choosing different responses across effectively identical questions? That said, the words describe different contexts, and the variation in responses may reflect genuine aspects of British tax mentality – a "social" explanation. Where does framing end and revelation of genuine preferences begin?

Table 3.2 Attitudes and behavior responses to tax evasion questions (2002)

Response	Benefits (%)	Pay (%)
Morally wrong	1.7 (–5.2)	11.6 (–5.0)
Not wrong	9.9 (–8.5)	25.8 (–4.8)
A bit wrong	40.4 (–10.8)	40.8 (–3.3)
Wrong	44.5 (+26.0)	15.9 (+7.1)
Seriously wrong		
Would do		
Very likely	6.4 (–3.4)	10.2 (–5.7)
Fairly likely	12.1 (–4.6)	18.5 (–7.1)
Not very likely	29.1 (–3.8)	30.1 (+1.2)
Not at all likely	46.1 (+3.5)	33.9 (+4.3)

Note
Figures in parentheses relate to changes since 1997.

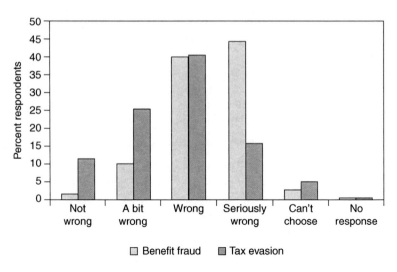

Figure 3.7 Attitudes to benefit fraud and tax evasion in the UK (2002).

There are many considerations when interpreting responses. For example, with respect to the VAT question, a builder who expresses a desire to evade VAT may simply be viewed differently to one who does not. The data are also subject to the criticisms (see, for example, Elffers *et al.*, 1987) that responses are strategic and imply little or nothing about real tax behavior – a common fear in economics. A healthy scepticism needs to be exercised about the value of survey data, and the same applies when using questionnaire responses to estimate the "strength" of social norms. Of course, this qualifica-

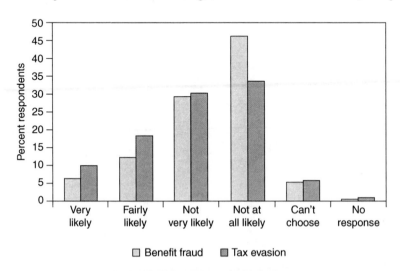

Figure 3.8 Probability of committing benefit fraud and tax evasion in the UK (2002).

tion is even more apposite when comparing responses in different countries. If there is a tendency to interpret questions differently in different countries, difference must be consistent (if relative positions are to be trusted).

iv There are many different methods of estimating the shadow economy (see Schneider, 2005: Appendix A). As Schneider (2005) notes: "There are many obstacles to overcome in measuring the size of the shadow economy ... but progress has been made." While measures of "prevalence" are dependent on received estimates, this approach relies on faith in sufficient progress not to invalidate the exercise above.

With these qualifications, the social norms model offers insight into tax evasion dynamics. Analysis of the strength of social norms (tax morale) is relevant when predicting changes in tax compliance. It is also the case that any assessment of the effectiveness of policy to deter tax evasion is likely to be sensitive to analysis of the role that is played by tax morale. A bold interpretation of the data in Figure 3.6 might reason that the gap between the strength and prevalence of the norm is a crude measure of the effectiveness of the tax regulations and administration in operation in different countries in preventing evasion – an "enforced equilibrium" above the diagonal. Table 3.3 ranks 19 OECD countries on this "prevented evasion", or, to coin a phrase, Tax Value Added (TVA) criterion. This ranking records the difference between the percentage size of the honest economy and the percentage number of purely honest individuals for *c*.1999.

Table 3.3 Tax Value Added (TVA) country rankings circa 1999

Rank	Countries	
1	Germany	46.6
2	Belgium	44.4
3	The Netherlands	42.1
4	France	39.6
5	Switzerland	39.5
6	Norway	36.8
7	Austria	33.8
8	GB	33.5
9	Sweden	33.5
10	Finland	32.5
11	USA	30.0
12	Ireland	29.7
13	Portugal	28.8
14	Australia	25.7
15	Italy	23.0
16	Spain	21.8
17	Denmark	19.5
18	Canada	19.3
19	Japan	9.4

Sources: Calculated from Schneider (2005) and World Values Survey.

Table 3.3 offers a ranking of the extent to which tax authorities in different countries are able to increase compliance beyond levels that would be predicted solely with reference to social norms.

Conclusions

This chapter has highlighted a number of important questions that are relevant when attempting to explain levels of tax compliance. A fundamental observation is that once analysis goes beyond the relative safety of "*homo or femina economicus*", the tax evasion waters get muddier and (perhaps misplaced) clarity is lost. As James (2006: 598) notes, "...factors such as social norms, morals, perception of justice, various attitudes and particular beliefs can influence the way people behave...". There is now a raft of competing labels for "amending/intervening" behavior. The question raised in this chapter is the extent to which different labels are helpful. Analysts now refer to "altruism", "intrinsic action", "civic duty" and "social norms". The objective is to provide a consistent analysis of behavioral response that will explain tax morality/tax mentality.

Questions have also been raised with respect to the relevant unit of analysis. Should the unit of analysis be the workings of the brain, the individual, or an organic view of society? Are individuals victims of their limited brain capacity, instrumentally rational, altruistic, or what? Is it that the mysteries of tax compliance and evasion in any society become no mysteries to those sharing a culture but are, as it were, in the air they breathe and learnt unconsciously as children?[9] Do individuals comprise all or some of these aspects, and do differing societies systematically contain individuals with differing proportions of these attributes?

In this chapter, the individual as the unit of analysis has been retained. Tax morality has been explained with reference to the observation that individuals are responsive to the actions of others around them (an attenuated form of "social" analysis). A crude "social norms numerical exercise" has been employed to explain the dynamics of tax evasion. This analysis has been applied to predict the direction of change in the size of "shadow economies" in different countries.

The same analysis has also been applied to assess policy set to deter tax evasion. Analysis of disequilbrium between estimates of tax compliance (determined by the strength of social norms) and reported tax compliance also proves useful when assessing the contribution that is made by tax authorities. If compliance differs from compliance predicted with reference to social norms, this difference can be attributed to tax legislation and the execution of tax legislation. In this context, the same analysis has been applied to construct a "Tax Value Added" league table. This table compares the success that tax authorities achieve in generating higher levels of compliance than would be predicted solely with reference to "social norms". First estimates of 19 OECD countries indicate that Germany is top and Japan is bottom. While confidence in this ranking depends on the weight that can be attached to estimates of tax morality in different countries (see later chapters), this yardstick comparison analysis offers a more balanced assessment of the success of tax authorities in achieving compliance beyond levels that would be predicted with reference to social norms.

Notes

1 The authors are Reader in Economics, Professor of Economics and Professor of Economic Psychology at the University of Bath respectively.
2 For example, Andreoni *et al.* (1998) comment that, in 1995, the audit rate in the United States for individual tax returns was 1.7 percent, the civil penalty for underpayment of taxes was 20 percent of the underpayment; very large values for risk aversion would be required to predict tax compliance.
3 In addition, they want to recognize the fact that some people are honest and law-abiding (accepting that a legal authority has a right to dictate their behavior).
4 Positive reciprocity has been documented in "trust", or "gift exchange" games. A "proposer" receives an amount of money x from the experimenter, and can send between zero and x to the "responder". The experimenter then triples the amount of money sent, y, so the responder has 3y. The responder is then free to return anything between zero and 3y to the proposer. In experiments, proposers usually send money and responders usually give back some of the money.
5 It is interesting to note that the Allingham and Sandmo (1972) model will never predict a separating equilibrium (where some individuals evade and others do not) because of the rule connecting the probability of detection and surcharge rate.
6 Below EE the curve is strictly convex ($f' > 0$ and $f'' > 0$), whereas beyond EE the curve is strictly concave ($f' > 0$ and $f'' < 0$).
7 Greece and New Zealand were excluded, as necessary data were missing.
8 Smart thinkers will assume the builder will charge the same as if VAT was included, and therefore not going along with him actually financially punishes them.
9 This is a corruption of Marshall's description of pure external economies that take, using more modern terminology, the form of informational spillovers. "The mysteries of the trade become no mysteries; but are as it were in the air, and children learn many of them unconsciously." (Marshall, 1920: 271).

Bibliography

Allingham, M. G. and Sandmo, A. (1972) "Income tax evasion: A theoretical analysis", *Journal of Public Economics*, 1: 323–38.

Alm, J., Jackson, B. R., and McKee, M. (1992) "Estimating the determinants of taxpayer compliance with experimental data", *National Tax Journal*, 45: 107–14.

Andreoni, J., Erard, B., and Feinstein, J. (1998) "Tax compliance", *Journal of Economic Literature*, 36: 818–60.

Bowles, S. and Gintis, H. (2006) "Social preferences, homo economicus and zoon politikon", in R. E. Goodin and C. Tilly (eds.), *The Oxford Handbook of Contextual Political Analysis*, Oxford, UK: Oxford University Press.

Brennan, G. and Lomasky, L. (1993) *Democracy and Decision; the Pure Theory of Electoral Preference*, Cambridge, UK: Cambridge University Press.

Buchanan, J. M. (1968) *The Demand and Supply of Public Goods*, Chicago, IL: Rand McNally.

Collard, D. (1978) *Altruism and Economy; A Study in Non-Selfish Economics*, Oxford, UK: Martin Robertson.

Cox, D. and Plumley, A. ((1988) *Analyses of Voluntary Compliance for Different Income Source Classes*, IRS Research Division, Washington, DC.

Cullis, J. G. and Jones, P. R. (2008) "How big should government be?", in A. Lewis (ed.), *The Cambridge Handbook of Psychology and Economic Behaviour*, Cambridge, UK: Cambridge University Press.

Cullis, J. G., Jones, P. R., and Lewis, A. (2006) "Tax evasion: Artful or artless dodging?", in E. J. McCaffery and J. Slemrod (eds.), *Behavioral Public Finance: Toward a New Agenda*, New York, NY: Russell Sage Foundation.

Deci, E. L. (1971) "Effects of externally mediated rewards on intrinsic motivation", *Journal of Personality and Social Psychology*, 18: 105–15.

Deci, E. L. and Ryan, R. M. (1980) "The empirical exploration of intrinsic motivational processes", *Advances in Experimental Social Psychology*, 10: 39–80.

Deci, E. L. and Ryan, R. M. (1985) *Intrinsic Motivation and Self Determination in Human Behavior*, New York, NY: Plenium Press.

Elffers, H., Weigel, R. H., and Hessing, D. J. (1987) "The consequences of different strategies for measuring tax evasion behaviour", *Journal of Economic Psychology*, 13: 311–37.

Engle, E. M. R. A. and Hines, J. R. Jr (1999) "Understanding tax evasion dynamics", Working Paper 6903, January, National Bureau of Economic Research: Cambridge, MA.

Fehr, E. and Gachter, S. (2000) "Fairness and retaliation: The economics of reciprocity", *Journal of Economic Perspectives*, 14: 158–81.

Feld, L. P. and Frey, B. S. (2002) "Trust breeds trust: how taxpayers are treated", *Economics of Governance*, 3: 87–99.

Frank, R. H., Gilovich, T., and Regan, D. T. (1993) "Does studying economics inhibit cooperation?", *Journal of Economic Perspectives*, 7: 159–71.

Frey B. S. (1997a) "A constitution for knaves crowds out civic virtues", *Economic Journal*, 107: 1043–53.

Frey, B. S. (1997b) *Not Just For the Money: An Economic Theory of Personal Motivation*, Cheltenham, UK: Edward Elgar.

Frey, B. S. and Eichenberger, R. (1989) "Anomalies and institutions", *Journal of Institutional and Theoretical Economics*, 145: 423–37.

Frey, B. S. and Torgler, B. (2004) "Taxation and conditional cooperation", CREMA Working Paper No. 2004–20, August, 1–28.

Graetz, M. J. and Wilde, L. L. (1985) "The economics of tax compliance: Facts and fantasy", *National Tax Journal*, 38: 355–63.

Hargreaves-Heap, S. (1992) "Bandwagon effects in Hargreaves-Heap", in S. Hargreaves-Heap, M. Hollis, B. Lyons, R. Sugden, and A. Weale (eds.), *The Theory of Choice: A Critical Guide*, Oxford, UK: Blackwell.

Hindricks, J. and Myles. G. (2006) *Intermediate Public Economics*, Cambridge, MA: MIT Press. www.data-archive.ac.uk/doc/4838/mrdoc/pdf/4838userguide.pdf.

James, S. (2006) "Taxation and the contribution of behavioral economics", in M. Altman (ed.), *Handbook of Contemporary Behavioral Economics: Foundations and Development.* New York, NY: M. E. Sharpe, pp. 589–601.

Jones, P. R, Cullis, J. G., and Lewis, A. (1998) "Public versus private provision of altruism: Can fiscal policy make individuals "better" people?", *Kyklos*, 5: 3–24.

Jowell, R., Brook, L., and Taylor, B. (1997) *British Social Attitudes: The 14th Report: The End of Conservative Values*, Aldershot, UK: Ashgate.

Kahneman, D. and Tversky, A. (1979) "Prospect theory: An analysis of decision under risk", *Econometrica*, 47: 263–91.

Kirchler, E. (2007) *The Economic Pyschology of Tax Behaviour*. Cambridge, UK: Cambridge University Press.

Kirchler, E. and Maciejovsky, B. (2001) "Tax compliance within the context of gain and loss situations, expected and current asset position, and profession", *Journal of Economic Psychology*, 22: 173–94.

Levi, M. (1998) "A state of trust", in V. Braithwaite and M. Levi (eds.), *Trust and Governance*. New York, NY: Russell Sage Foundation

Lewis, A. (1982) *The Psychology of Taxation*, Oxford, UK: Martin Robertson.

Marshall, A. (1920) *Principles of Economics*, 8th edn, London, UK: Macmillan.

Martinez-Vazquez, Harwood G. B., and Larkins E. R. (1992) "Witholding position and income tax compliance: Some experimental evidence", *Public Finance Quarterly* 20(2): 152–74.

Ostrom, E. (2000) "Collective action and the evolution of social norms", *Journal of Economic Perspectives*, 14: 137–58.

Orviska, M. and Hudson, J. (2002) "Tax evasion, civic duty and the law abiding citizen", *European Journal of Political Economy*, 19: 83–102.

Reckers, P. M. J., Sanders, D. L., and Roark, S. J. (1994) "The influence of ethical attitudes on taxpayer compliance", *National Tax Journal*, 47: 825–36.

Schepanski, A. and Shearer, T. (1995) "A prospect theory account of the income tax withholding phenomenon", *Organizational Behaviour and Human Decision Procesess* 63: 174–86.

Schneider F. G. (2005) "Shadow economies around the world: What do we really know?" *European Journal of Political Economy*, 21: 598–642.

Slemrod, J. (2002) "Tax systems", *NBER Reporter*, Summer: 8–13.

Slemrod, J. (2007) "Cheating ourselves: The economics of tax evasion", *Journal of Economic Perspectives*, 21: 25–48.

Spicer, M. W. (1986) "Civilization at a discount: The problem of tax evasion", *National Tax Journal*, 39: 13–20.

Stigler, G. and Becker, G. (1977) "De gustibus non est disputandum", *American Economic Review* 67: 76–90.

Torgler, B. and Schneider, F. (2007) "What shapes attitudes toward paying taxes? Evidence from multicultural European countries", *Social Science Quarterly*, 88: 443–70.

4   Vertical and horizontal reciprocity in a theory of taxpayer compliance

Jan Schnellenbach

Introduction

Not too long ago, Cullis and Lewis (1997: 309) stated, with regard to the analysis of tax evasion, that the "economic approach has obvious analytic appeal but lacks realism and humanity." A lot has changed since then in theoretical research, while in empirical research contributions as early as that of Spicer and Becker (1980) have argued for the relevance of fairness considerations in explaining actual tax evading behavior. In a similar spirit, Maital (1982) has argued that high levels of tax compliance can be explained by the wish of individuals to support policies that are in concurrence with their preferences. Later, Frey (1997) extended such arguments to the hypothesis that individuals are endowed with civic virtues. These supposedly render cooperation with government, and in collective action in general, the default behavior. If this is indeed the case, then not only are the surprisingly high levels of tax compliance a theoretical puzzle, but it is defection that needs to be explained theoretically. Frey argues that civic virtues can be crowded out if the government violates norms of procedural fairness, or if it conducts policies that are perceived as being fundamentally unfair.

In this way, reciprocity in the form of vertical reciprocity – i.e., in the relationship between the individual and the public sector – enters the theoretical reasoning on tax compliance. Gouldner (1960) has argued that reciprocity is a ubiquitous characteristic of human interaction across cultural boundaries. The basic norm to which, according to Gouldner, individuals tend to adhere is that we ought to cooperate with those who cooperate with us. In the economics literature, which we discuss in detail below, there is widespread belief that there is also a complementary norm at work, which states that those who do not behave cooperatively, and who do so in a harmful way, ought to be punished.

Reciprocal behavior may, however, not only occur in the relationship between taxpayers and their government; it may also play a role as horizontal reciprocity among taxpayers, where one individual's cooperation in paying taxes increases if he or she has reason to believe that the other taxpayers also comply. In this chapter, we attempt to show how both types of reciprocity enter the decision-making calculus of a rational taxpayer. Furthermore, we probe into the interaction of both types of reciprocity, and in particular argue that a taxpayer's ability to retaliate against a non-cooperative government depends crucially on the individual being endowed with a feeling of guilt related to the activity of tax evasion. In the next section, we review the literature on reciprocity and hint at some connections to the tax compliance problem. Both types of reciprocity in tax evasion are then discussed separately in the following section, while the subsequent section discusses the interaction of both. Finally, there are some conclusions.

Reciprocity and tax evasion

How reciprocity is understood in this chapter

Fueled in particular by experimental evidence, economics has in recent years experienced a lively debate regarding whether the assumption of strictly self-interested behavior reflects reality or not. The evidence indicates that, frequently, individuals do appear to deviate from a narrowly defined, short-term, self-interested motivation, and one pattern of behavior that stands out is that of reciprocal decision-making. Fehr and Gächter (2000a) offer a broad overview of the issues, and in particular of the empirical evidence.

Reciprocity can be defined as conditional kindness and conditional retaliation, depending on the observed behavior of other individuals, and, as Fehr and Gächter point out, it is in this sense different from self-interested cooperation or retaliation in repeated interactions, where costly cooperation or retaliation can be seen as an investment to secure benefits in the future. Reciprocity, on the other hand, is only of a responsive nature. It is also important to note that not all individuals exhibit the same propensity to reciprocate; indeed, a substantial minority of individuals in experiments do not do so. The empirical evidence thus suggests that it is reasonable to assume different types of individuals in theoretical discussions. The plausibility of co-existing groups of reciprocally minded and strictly self-interested individuals has also been demonstrated by Gintis (2000) in an evolutionary model incorporating group selection.

We do not elaborate in detail on the controversial discussion regarding the sources of reciprocity here – i.e., the question of whether intentions or results of observed behavior are relevant in determining which reciprocal response is chosen by an individual (see, for example, Dufwenberg and Kirchsteiger, 2004; Falk *et al.*, 2008; Rabin, 1993; Sobel, 2005). As Fehr and Schmidt (1999) point out, this dispute is in any event of limited relevance for many applications of reciprocity in economic theory. If intentions matter – i.e., if only pure kindness evokes a reciprocal reaction, as argued by, for example, Rabin (1993) – then this kindness will lead to the implementation of a distributional result that is considered fair and acceptable. Normally, a fair result that follows from the cooperative action of one individual will be attributed to a fairness-oriented mindset of this individual. Discriminating between different motivations for cooperative behavior may become relevant if short-term cooperation can be attributed to some overarching strict self-interest, but this is unlikely to be the case for individuals who decide to pay taxes honestly. Thus, we restrict ourselves here to an outcome-based notion of reciprocity: reciprocally minded individuals have a propensity to positively (negatively) reciprocate if the observed actions of other indviduals yield a result that is considered fair (unfair).

Reciprocity and contributions to public goods

The literature on reciprocity in public good games is of some interest here. The reason is that evading fewer taxes than predicted by Allingham and Sandmo (1972) is to some degree akin to voluntarily contributing to the financing of a public good under the condition of individual insignificance for the overall quantity supplied. Fehr and Gächter (2000b) conducted an experiment allowing them to compare behavior in a public good game both with and without punishment opportunities. They show that a substantial fraction of individuals bears the costs of punishing free-riders, and that the threat of punishment secures on average a relatively high, positive contribution by the subjects in the experiments. The mechanism of punishment in experiments of this class is a direct reduction of payoffs: individuals may invest into "punishing points", which they can assign to another individual in order to have her payoff reduced. The magnitude of payoff-reduction increases with the number of points assigned.

Fischbacher *et al.* (2001) make another interesting observation regarding a public good experiment that did not allow for punishment. Using the strategy method to extract information on individual preferences, they also found that a large fraction of individuals is conditionally cooperative: if the average contributions of the other individuals rise, then half of the subjects react to this by raising their own contribution to the public good. However, even a conditional cooperator will contribute less than the average contribution of the rest of the population. Thus, Fischbacher and colleagues predict that, in a repeated game, conditional cooperation will eventually diminish – a downward spiral of conditional cooperation is to be expected. It appears to be the case that the availability of a mechanism for reciprocal punishment is indeed crucial to ensure positive cooperation levels that are stable over time.

At this point, we can hint at an important difference between public good games and tax evasion. Fehr and Schmidt (1999) assume a very precise mechanism of punishing uncooperative individuals: The actions of every subject can be observed, and any subject can be singled out for punishment by another individual. Fehr and Schmidt show that a full-cooperation equilibrium can be reached if a sufficiently large group of reciprocal punishers is present in the population. However, this result can obviously not simply be carried over to a model of tax compliance. Here, it is hardly possible to single out uncooperative individuals for reciprocal punishment, since, at best, aggregate estimates of overall evasion activity become common knowledge, while information on the compliance levels of single individuals is not publicly disclosed. Reciprocal punishment is then directed at an uncooperative collective of individuals: if a taxpayer observes a large magnitude of overall evasion activity, he or she may feel inclined to punish the population of (on average) disingenuous other taxpayers by evading tax him- or herself.

There is another point to be made regarding the suggestion of Fehr and Schmidt to model reciprocity as inequality aversion. Cox and Sadiraj (2007) confront the model with experimental data, and show that inequality aversion is ill-suited to account for several stylized facts of public good experiments. An alternative model with an egocentric but mildly altruistic utility function that meets the standard criteria of strict convexity and strict monotonicity in payoffs is shown to perform much better in predicting these stylized facts. And on the empirical side, Charness and Rabin (2002) report evidence which indicates that individuals aim much more at increasing social welfare rather than being motivated by inequality aversion. However, Charness and Rabin also note that reciprocity matters; their results strongly indicate that reciprocity and a concern for equality are to be treated separately. They also report from their experiments that negative reciprocity in the form of disregard for the welfare of other individuals appears to play a greater role than positive reciprocity.

Given these general considerations, some skepticism regarding the identification of a propensity to reciprocate with inequality aversion is in order. It is very premature to assume an egalitarian distribution of net incomes as the reference point by which individuals judge the fairness of an actual distribution. This may be warranted for laboratory experiments, where the payoffs do not depend (or depend only to a small extent) on effort and labor, but is by no means a natural starting point for models of real-world economic activity. Thus, it is difficult to see how the now canonical models of fairness and reciprocity by Bolton and Ockenfels (2000), as well as Fehr and Schmidt (1999), with their focus on equity as distributional equality could be directly applied to the issue of tax compliance.

Reciprocity and tax compliance

On a very general level, reciprocity in tax morale implies that an individual's own evasion activity depends on the fiscal policy conducted, and on the evasion decisions of other individuals. As we have seen above, if this interdependence is indeed reciprocity related, then some notion of fairness will be needed as a benchmark, with deviations from the benchmark evoking negative reciprocity. There are already some contributions to the literature that suggest an interdependence of decisions, without explicitly referring to reciprocity. For example, Alm and McKee (2004) investigated taxpayers' reactions to endogenous audit probabilities in an experiment where the likelihood of being audited increased for a taxpayer if his or her reported income differed from that of other taxpayers in the same cohort. They found that taxpayers have difficulties in coordinating on a zero-compliance equilibrium, and that endogenous audit probabilities depending on individual peculiarities in reporting can indeed induce high compliance levels.

Other papers have aimed directly at the relationship between the taxpayer and the government. Cowell (1992) presents some very counterintuitive results. If consumption c and a fairness measure φ both enter a standard utility function, $U = u(c, \varphi)$, that is strictly concave in both arguments, and if this is used in a standard Allingham–Sandmo model of tax evasion, then individuals will actually adjust to a decline of the fairness measure by evading less. The reason is that the decline of utility that results from a ceteris paribus reduction of fairness leads to a reduced willingness to take the risk involved in tax evasion. A more intuitive result can, in this framework, only be obtained if increasing evaded income e made the individually perceived situation more equitable for the taxpayer – i.e., if $\varphi = \varphi(e)$ with $\partial\varphi/\partial e > 0$, and if the fairness effect was sufficiently large to overcompensate the risk aversion effect. In this case, evasion increases with inequity. Falkinger (1995) extends this approach by incorporating public goods whose utility in consumption rises with income, and shows that, for this type of public goods, evasion increases with a declining quantity of goods provided, and vice versa. However, this again is a special case, and it is not obvious at all that this condition should hold for all or even most publicly provided goods.

Here, an important distinction between mere individual equity concerns and reciprocity has to be made. The condition $\partial\varphi/\partial e > 0$ can plausibly be fulfilled in very small groups, where the individual evasion activity matters directly and to a quantitatively relevant degree for the collective outcome. It is, however, also fulfilled in large societies if the individually perceived inequity is corrected by only increasing the individual evader's welfare, without reducing perceived inequity for society as a whole. This distinction is important: both a purely self-interested individual in the Cowell (1992) model and a reciprocally minded individual increase their evasion activity as a response to increased inequity if one the two above conditions is fulfilled so that $\partial\varphi/\partial e > 0$. If, however, a large society exists with $\partial\varphi/\partial e = 0$, then Cowell (1992) cannot explain increasing tax evasion (tax morale) as a response to decreasing equity (inequity) – although a model based on reciprocity could.

A very important question, therefore, regards what the true relationship between φ and e is, because this relationship indicates what kind of fairness benchmark individuals use in their decision-making. Individuals who are only concerned about being treated fairly themselves can, starting from a perceived unfair situation, increase fairness in their own relationship with the public sector and with other taxpayers by improving their own welfare, and only their own welfare, and even at the expense of other individuals. In contrast, those who care about a societal measure of fairness and who decide behind a veil of insignificance in a large society cannot expect to improve the fairness measure by evading taxes. How self-centered is the fairness concept that is usually employed, then? Not too surprisingly, the empirical evidence suggests that both fairness measures matter, with the work cited above by Charness and Rabin (2002) being one contribution that emphasizes the relevance of motivations concerned with social welfare.

The intuition that taxpayers use tax evasion to restore equity if they perceive themselves as personally being treated unfairly is corroborated by, for example, experimental evidence reported by Fortin *et al.* (2004). They found that individuals who are themselves taxed at a higher rate than the mean tax rate for their reference group tend to increase evasion if the gap between their rate and the mean tax rate increases. On the other hand, Crane and Nourzad (1986) found, using US data, that inflation has a positive impact on tax evasion. Suppose that this reflects not only an attempt to counterveil the increase in the tax burden triggered by inflation, but also that there is an equity effect at work here – i.e., that taxpayers are disgruntled with a state that cannot supply stable money. Certainly, tax evasion can do nothing directly to put an end to this unfair state of affairs (i.e., $\partial\varphi/\partial e=0$ in this case). In contrast, a reciprocal motive, the wish to punish the government that is perceived to be responsible for inflation, may still be at work. In a similar vein, a very interesting finding by Weck-Hannemann and Pommerehne (1989) for Swiss cantonal data suggests that political participation rights of citizens (for example, in the form of direct democracy) have a negative impact on tax evasion (see also Alm *et al.*, 1993, as well as Feld and Tyran, 2002, for experimental evidence, and Kucher and Götte, 1998, for field evidence in this regard). Related to this, Torgler (2003) reports evidence that tax morale increases with trust of individuals in the procedures of political decision-making in their polity.

Generally, it may therefore be reasonable not only to distinguish between reciprocally minded and purely self-interested individuals in theoretical reasoning, but also to distinguish between those reciprocally minded individuals who have a self-centered and those who have a society-centered fairness benchmark guiding their judgments on equity. In order to keep matters simple, however, in the following discussion we employ a modeling approach to tax evasion where only $\partial\varphi/\partial e=0$ matters. In contrast to models and experiments concerned with reciprocity in small groups of sometimes only two members, it should be warranted to make this simplifying assumption for an issue like tax compliance. If we observe a situation where few people honestly pay their taxes while many taxpayers cheat, then this unfair situation will not change substantially in the direction of fairness due to our decision to negatively reciprocate by cheating also. On the contrary, if we expected that some taxpayers still remain honest in the next round, we might even expect to increase the overall unfairness of the situation.

Modeling tax evasion with vertical or horizontal reciprocity

Vertical reciprocity

By the term "vertical reciprocity" we denote the tendency of individuals to make evasion decisions conditional on the fiscal policy parameters set by the government. This, however, is not trivial, since standard modeling techniques yield results that are not in line with empirical evidence. For example, it is a well-known result of the Allingham–Sandmo model that with declining absolute risk aversion, the effect of an increase in the tax rate on evasion is ambiguous, due to counterveiling income and substitution effects. Yitzhaki (1974) has even shown that an increased tax rate leads to unambiguously less tax evasion if the penalty tax of detected evaders depends on evaded taxes (and not on income concealed) – in this case, the substitution effect vanishes. Cowell and Gordon (1988) investigated whether incorportating public good supply in a standard model of tax evasion leads to more intuitive, and more empirically reasonable, results. However, they show that raising the tax rate to increase the quantity of supplied public goods still leads to lower evasion if public goods are oversupplied in the status quo ante, and to higher evasion if they are initially undersupplied. In other words, moving towards the preferred level of public goods increases tax evasion, and moving away from it decreases it. The rationale is again that individuals become more willing to take the risk of evasion if fiscal policy provides them with a higher utility.

In an extension of the Cowell–Gordon framework, Bordignon (1993) even argues that taxpayers never evade if the supply of public goods is below the pareto-efficient level. In spite of all their theoretical coherence and elegance, these propositions are still at odds with the vast number of empirical and experimental studies that indicate rising evasion with rising tax rates and declining public good levels (Andreoni *et al.*, 1998). Furthermore, experimental evidence suggests that it is not a pure feeling of guilt, stemming from the perception that evasion is wrong, that deters honest individuals from evading taxes; rather, it appears that indeed the connection of paying taxes with receiving public goods in return is relevant in inducing compliance (Alm *et al.*, 1992).

The basic approach

Following the fairness model of Falkinger (1995), let the utility of a taxpayer be represented by a function

$$U = u\left(c - v(\varphi)\right) \tag{1}$$

with $u' > 0$ and $u'' < 0$. Here, c is the disposable income, which is determined through a tax evasion lottery with

$$c_1 = y(1 - \tau) + e\tau$$

$$c_2 = y(1 - \tau) - e\tau s$$

where y is the taxpayer's gross pecuniary income, p is the probability of detection, τ is the uniform rate of a flat income tax, s is a penalty tax to be paid by detected evaders and e denotes, as above, some amount $0 \leq e \leq y$ of income concealed from the tax administration. With the function $v(\varphi)$ for which $dv/d\varphi > 0$ always holds, the willingness to cooperate enters the taxpayer's calculus. In accordance with the empirical evidence on reciprocity discussed above, we can interpret $v(\varphi)$ as an individual guilt function: with increasing perceived fairness, tax evasion becomes less attractive to a reciprocally minded individual; evading would be at odds with that individual's general motivation to honor his or her obligations as long as these obligations are perceived as legitimate. The taxpayer thus chooses an $0 \leq e \leq y$ to solve

$$\max (1-p)u(c_1 - v(\varphi)) + pu(c_2 - v(\varphi)) \qquad (2)$$

for an optimal level of tax evasion $e^* = e^*(y, p, \tau, s, \varphi)$. As Falkinger (1995) shows, for such a model specification we always have $\partial e^*/\partial \varphi < 0$. Note that φ matters only to the taxpayer if he evades – in this case, his utility is diminished by $v(\varphi)$, and his decision-making shifts into an area of his utility function with higher absolute risk aversion. Straightforwardly, he evades less. The simple, but important, difference to the Cowell framework is thus the assumption that here, equity enters the utility function not as a good but as a "bad", because equity in combination with cheating evokes guilt.

Of course, it could be argued that guilt as a result of non-cooperation does not accurately capture reciprocity, or that a correct notion of reciprocity should rest on a taste for fairness. Such a dispute would, in essence, be about the correct reference point for reciprocal decision-making. In the case depicted above, cooperation evoked by guilt in case of defection is the default choice, and the non-cooperation of others reduces guilt. In a different approach, pure self-interest could be the default option, and, due to a preference for fairness, positive reciprocity would lead away from self-interest. From a behavioral perspective, both approaches ought to be more or less equivalent. From a modeling point of view, the former approach can more easily be integrated into a tax compliance model.

Two stylized facts: perfect compliance and the impact of the tax rate

So how does this approach fare with regard to the other stylized facts of the empirical literature on tax compliance? Given that guilt matters only for cheaters, not only the marginal calculus is relevant, but also a comparison of different states of the world. Let c_i^* with $i = 1, 2$ denote the disposable incomes in case of optimal evasion e^* according to (2). Then the taxpayer also has to make the choice whether to evade or not, and if

$$u(y(1-\tau)) > (1-p)u(c_1^* - v(\varphi)) + pu(c_2^* - v(\varphi)) \qquad (3)$$

holds, he or she has an unambiguous preference not to evade. Since the value of the right-hand side of the inequality decreases unambiguously with $v(\varphi)$, there must exist some threshold level of guilt v^T where complete non-evasion is the strictly preferred action for any $v(\varphi) > v^T$. In other words, the empirical observation that some individuals never evade is consistent with the approach, if individuals in a population are heterogeneous in their propensity to feel guilt in case of tax evasion. One class of v-functions consistent with the evidence is of the form

$$v(\varphi) = \alpha v(\varphi) \tag{4}$$

where $v(\varphi)$ is an arbitrary, strictly increasing function with $v(0)=0$ that is identical for all taxpayers, and α is an individual multiplier distributed over an interval $[\alpha_L,\alpha_H]$ with $\alpha_L>0$. Using α as a multiplier ensures that for sufficiently low values of φ, even the most honest taxpayer with a very high value of α will begin evading taxes. Furthermore, the individual levels of α in this initial distribution ought to be understood as "natural" propensities to feel guilty that may, for example, result from an individual's upbringing. As we will see in the next section of this chapter, these individual propensities can change if the individual observes decisions of other taxpayers. In other words, the initial value of α should be interpreted as the propensity to feel guilt if all other taxpayers are honest. If the taxpayer discovers dishonesty among other taxpayers, he adjusts his own tendency to feel guilt accordingly.

With regard to the empirical observation that usually $\partial e^*/\partial \tau>0$, the model has prima facie the same problems as the Allingham–Sandmo–Yitzhaki model – the effect of a change of τ appears to be ambiguous due to an interaction of an income and a substitution effect. However, it is very unlikely that φ is independent of the tax rate. Since φ characterizes the perceived fairness of the relationship between taxpayer and government, it must depend on the policy parameters chosen by the government, with the quantities of public goods and the tax rate being the most prominent political choices to be made. Whenever $\partial \varphi/\partial \tau<0$, the income effect that is responsible for the counterintuitive results of the Allingham–Sandmo–Yitzhaki-model is directly countered by a fairness effect. If the reduction of a taxpayer's guilt as a response to an increase of the tax rate is sufficiently strong, it can (possibly together with the substitution effect) over-compensate the income effect.

How plausible is a negative reaction of fairness to increasing tax rates? It is hardly possible to answer this question in general, without also taking the expenditure side of the budget into consideration, as well as the perceived fairness of the overall tax system. If an increase in the tax rate is associated with an increase in public spending that is in line with a taxpayer's preferences, such a negative effect is not to be expected. On the other hand, an individual may feel, for example due to an extremely progressive tax schedule, that he or she is forced to finance a too large portion of additional spending, relative to households with lower taxable incomes. In this case, a negative fairness effect of increased tax rates can be observed. Experimental evidence gathered by Alm *et al.* (1993) does indeed suggest that the willingness to pay taxes depends on both procedural fairness and the perceived fairness of the result: Taxpayers evade less if they can vote on public goods, and compliance is significantly reduced if an unpopular expenditure program is imposed. This evidence does not, however, allow direct inferences regarding the fairness effects of marginal changes in the tax rate.

Given these considerations, a view of the whole picture in a particular scenario appears to be necessary to estimate what to expect from increased tax rates. However, if our analytical starting point is an equilibrium where taxing and spending is in line with the taxpayer's preferences, and if taxes are increased from there, then a negative effect prevails. Once again, the value of the parameter α of a single taxpayer is also important: if α assumes a relatively high value, the condition for an intuitive response to increased tax rates is likely to be met.

The interpretation of this result may be somewhat surprising, because it implies that a reasonably strong feeling of guilt entering the taxpayer's utility function is necessary to explain unequivocally a result that a reader not familiar with the issues would probably associate with simple self-interested behavior. It also implies that if for some reason the tendency of taxpayers to associate guilt with tax evasion has been diminished, we would converge towards the counter-intuitive results of the Allingham–Sandmo–Yitzhaki model. We return to this issue in greater detail below, in the fourth section of this chapter.

Fairness

A likely criticism regarding this approach to modeling vertical reciprocity is that a model involving reciprocity should involve an explicit taste for fairness in the taxpayer's utility function. Let (1) be modified such that

$$U = u(c - v(\varphi), \varphi) \tag{5}$$

with the assumption that $u(\cdot, \cdot)$ is strictly concave in both arguments. Furthermore, let the utility function be defined such that the direct effect of an increase in φ (without accounting for its effect on guilt) would, ceteris paribus, increase the willingness to take risks in the tax evasion gamble. In determining the net effect of a fairness increase on tax compliance, the value of α would again be crucial, since it determines the magnitude of the guilt effect vis-à-vis the effect on risk aversion. Taxpayers with a high value of α overcompensate the decreased risk aversion with increased guilt and evade less; for taxpayers with a low value of α the opposite is true. With α being sufficiently large, the qualitative statements regarding the stylized facts do still hold, while individuals with a small enough propensity to feel guilt make decisions that are qualitatively akin to those predicted by the Allingham–Sandmo–Yitzhaki model. Incorporating an explicit positive utility from fairness is thus not at odds, in principle, with the approach pursued here.

Finally, some comments on the concept of fairness used here are also in order. For analytical reasons, it is convenient to restrict heterogeneity in the population of taxpayers to the guilt parameter α. We therefore assume a Rawlsian concept of fairness – i.e., we propose that in thinking about policy, individuals are able to evaluate the policy parameters set by their government from an impartial point of view. In such a process of evaluation, not only policy outcomes but also procedural criteria may matter. For example, I may consider a tax rate that I do not prefer personally nevertheless as fair if it is the result of transparent democratic decision-making, while I would not consider it fair if it was imposed through a dictatorial process. This leads to the assumption that there is some compact set of different policy parameters that are all considered as acceptable (as fair) under given, formal political institutions (see Schnellenbach, 2006). The further the government deviates from this set, the more φ deteriorates.

Horizontal reciprocity

Gordon (1989) assumes a psychological disutility stemming from being dishonest as a taxpayer, which is added to an Allingham–Sandmo model. In contrast to the "flat" guilt disutility used in our approach, Gordon's disutility is assumed to rise proportionally with the concealed income. Gordon shows that his model can explain some of the stylized facts found in the empirical literature – in particular, the fact that some people do not evade at all. Also, for individuals who are initially small evaders, a positive relation between the tax rate and evasion is shown to exist – but only for small evaders. In a further step towards incorporating horizontal reciprocity too, Gordon adds a social custom component as an additional disutility from evading taxes; this component is assumed to rise with the fraction of other taxpayers who are known to be honest. For plausible parameter values, an interior equilibrium in which evaders and non-evaders co-exist is shown to exist.

A different model, by Bordignon (1993), assumes that taxpayers have an ethical disposition and determine a fair tax payment by asking themselves the question: what contribution would I wish all the others to make? This so-called Kantian tax burden is then corrected in reciprocal terms: the more the other taxpayers evade, the lower becomes the fair tax burden that a taxpayer assigns to him- or herself, which generates an upper bound in that individual's evasion decision. However, it is the Kantian rule that guarantees unambiguous results. In a pure reciprocity variant of the model, there are either multiple equilibria, or the unique equilibrium guaranteed by restrictions on the parameters has empirically doubtful implications: the rich never evade taxes, while the poor behave according to the Allingham–Sandmo model.

Myles and Naylor (1996) analyzed a model that has social customs and a taste for conformity at its center. Individuals either evade not at all, if they enjoy sufficient utility from adhering to the social custom of being honest taxpayers, or they behave like the ruthless evaders of the Allingham–Sandmo world. Myles and Naylor show that, for each individual, there exists a threshold fraction of evaders in the population where they begin to evade themselves, as the utility from being a conformist decreases with this fraction. They then went on to analyze the social dynamics of tax evasion, showing that, depending on parameter values, there may be equilibria with full evasion, no evasion at all, or some interior fraction of individuals who behave as unscrupulous tax evaders.

These contributions illustrate some of the difficulties that are associated with modeling horizontal reciprocity in tax evasion; in particular, the difficulty of finding empirically relevant conditions for the different equilibria to be reached. If we define horizontal reciprocity in a very narrow sense, it predicts only that the evasion decision of one taxpayer will be conditional on those of all other taxpayers. It then becomes immediately clear that employing the solution concept of a Nash equilibrium, as Bordignon (1993) does, is somewhat problematic. Suppose that for any individual taxpayer i in a population of N taxpayers with (to simplify) identical pre-tax incomes we have $\partial e_i * / \partial e^M \geq 0$ where $e^M = \sum_{j \neq i} e_j * / (N-1)$. Obviously, any symmetric state of affairs with $e_i^* = e^*(e^M) \forall i$ would be an equilibrium – but it is doubtful that N taxpayers could coordinate on any common e_i^*, especially since tax evasion is usually a rather clandestine activity. While it is quite likely that a taxpayer can receive some information ex post – for example, on the approximated overall evasion activity in his or her jurisdiction in the past fiscal year – coordination on one of multiple Nash equilibria ex ante is an entirely different issue.

Instead of imposing an equilibrium concept with empirically doubtful preconditions, we follow a different path and keep matters very simple: suppose that an individual experiences guilt from evading taxes, in the Falkinger (1995) sense discussed above, and that, ceteris paribus, guilt is reduced if the individual finds out that tax evasion is a common activity. In this case, and only on the individual level, the comparative statics necessarily yield that individual tax evasion increases with the observed frequency of tax evasion in the rest of the population. Suppose, then, that instead of coordinating on some Nash equilibrium ex ante, individuals adapt at any time t to the information on e_{t-1}^M that they by assumption receive at no cost, such that $e_{it}^* = e^*(e_{t-1}^M)$. Clearly, the system is potentially unstable. The necessary condition for an equilibrium for each single individual is that $e_{it}^*(e_{t-1}^M) = e_{it-1}^*(e_{t-2}^M)$. In other words, as long as the functional relationship $e_i^*(\cdot)$ is constant in time, only a stable evasion activity of all other individuals would secure an equilibrium for a single taxpayer, and of course for the model economy as a whole: there is no stable individual equilibrium level of tax evasion without a stable societal level of tax evasion. But what could the functional relationship between an individual's own evasion activity and that of the rest of the population reasonably look like? There are three economic conditions that are straightforward:

i $e^*(0) \geq 0$. A single taxpayer who has a reasonably low guilt parameter α would decide to evade some arbitrarily small amount, even if all others would not evade at all. In other words, the horizontal fairness considerations for that individual do not dominate the entire decision-making on tax compliance. This assumption is consistent with the empirical and experimental evidence discussed above in the second section, which indicates that reciprocal cooperation is not perfect cooperation, but that self-interested and reciprocal motives interact. However, individuals with very high levels of guilt are known not to evade at all. For these individuals, we have $e_{it}^*(0) = 0$.

For them, a positive number of other taxpayers have to evade in order to reduce their value of α, and to induce them to evade taxes themselves.

ii $e_{ii}^*(e^{max}) < e^{max}$. A single taxpayer who observes that all other taxpayers evade the maximum amount (where e^{max} is reasonably determined as the evasion activity in a completely amoral Allingham–Sandmo–Yitzhaki model) conceals strictly less than this maximum amount. There is some autonomous (and maybe very small), degree of morality that does not depend on the behavior of fellow taxpayers.

iii $e_{ii}^*(e_{t-1}^M)$ is strictly increasing in the average amount of income concealed by all other taxpayers if the first condition holds with strict inequality. If it holds with equality, there is some positive interval of evasion levels of other taxpayers where i does not yet evade and $\partial e^*/\partial e_{t-1}^M = 0$. But some reciprocal punishment of a cheating population of other taxpayers is always taking place.

These simple conditions suffice to broadly characterize horizontal reciprocity in the relationship between taxpayers. In the next section of this chapter, we discuss how both types of reciprocity interact.

The interaction of vertical and horizontal reciprocity

The possible interaction of horizontal and vertical reciprocity in taxpayers' decision-making on tax evasion has already been discussed within the framework of a simulation model developed by Pommerehne et al. (1994). They analyzed a rather complex structural model in order to compare evasion behavior under direct and under representative democracy. They assumed a heterogeneous population with individuals who are motivated by civic duty and are therefore (at first) honest taxpayers, while a minority of purely self-interested individuals always evades. Individuals who are initially honest can react to observed evasion of the minority and to a resulting divergence from optimal public good supplies by refusing to cooperate themselves. A downward spiral of tax compliance can be prevented by choosing appropriate deterrence and enforcement policies, and it is assumed that this process is more reliable under direct than under representative democracy. Accordingly, Pommerehne and colleagues predict that direct democracies are characterized by relatively lower levels of tax evasion compared to representative systems.

Since Pommerehne et al. analyzed a very special case, with a focus on the choice of tax enforcement policies under different institutions of collective decision-making, the somewhat higher degree of generality of the present chapter hopefully offers some added value. The three conditions for the existence of a stable, interior equilibrium with horizontal reciprocity are a good starting point for bringing the two types of reciprocity in tax compliance together. The third condition states that a taxpayer wants to evade more, once the other taxpayers reduce their tax compliance. Psychologists who research the origins of feelings of guilt find it obvious that guilt is typically caused by "infliction of harm, loss, or distress on a relationship partner" (Baumeister et al., 1994: 245).

In our case, the relationship partners are the other taxpayers, who, if they were honest, we would cheat if we decided to evade taxes. In this sense, it appears to be natural to assume that the guilt function $v(\varphi)$ not only depends on the perceived fairness of the government's fiscal policy, but also on the evasion activity of fellow taxpayers. We can therefore modify (4) to

$$v(\varphi, e^M) = \alpha(e^M)v(\varphi) \tag{6}$$

with $\partial\alpha/\partial e^M < 0$ and $\alpha > 0 \forall e^M$. The solution of the maximization problem (2) now becomes

$$e^* = e^*(y, p, \tau, s, \varphi, e^M) \tag{7}$$

and what we have simply postulated above is now shown to be consistent with individual utility maximization. An increased intensity of tax evasion in the population reduces the impact of the vertical reciprocal relationship (i.e., the impact of the fairness measure). With a lower fixed cost of tax evasion in terms of guilt, the resulting income effect renders a taxpayer less risk averse and increases that taxpayer's propensity to evade taxes. For those individuals whose "natural" initial value of α was already low enough for inequality (3) not to hold, we accordingly have $\partial e_{it}^*/\partial e_{t-1}^M > 0$ over the entire range of feasible values of e_{t-1}^M. By definition, the first condition of the model with only horizontal reciprocity is also fulfilled by these individuals – after all, they have already evaded taxes even before their feeling of guilt was reduced through receiving information on the evasion behavior of other taxpayers. Finally, the second condition is met by the (relatively innocent) assumption that $\alpha > 0$ always holds. This implies that the individual susceptability for guilt may become arbitrarily close to zero, but never vanishes completely.

Matters are a bit more complicated for those individuals whose "natural" level of α is so high that inequality (3) holds for them, implying that they do not evade taxes initially. For them, the first condition does not necessarily hold, because there might exist a range of tax evasion activities in the population where, for these individuals, $\partial e_{it}^*/\partial e_{t-1}^M = 0$ simply because the costs imposed by guilt are still sufficiently high to deter them from tax evasion altogether. For these individuals, we might find a situation where, even when they start to evade, they evade consistently less than the average evasion activity of the rest of the population.

In Figure 4.1, two examples are shown to illustrate the discussion of different types of tax evaders. The left-hand figure illustrates the reaction function to levels of e_{t-1}^M for a typical tax evader, who always evades some income. The right-hand figure shows a possible reaction function of a taxpayer with a very high "natural" level of α. With increasing evading activities in the population as a whole, the guilt factor α is diminished for both individuals and they increase their evasion activities, but the taxpayer on the right starts evading only when α is lower than a threshold value. It may be the case that, as we see here, the resulting reaction function of such an individual never intersects with the 45° line, which illustrates how this taxpayer always wants to evade less than the average taxpayer.

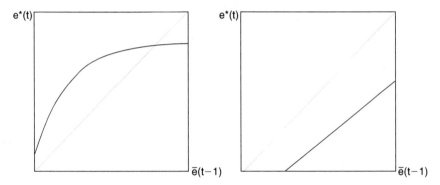

Figure 4.1 Examples of horizontal reciprocity for taxpayers with normal (left) and extremely high (right) initial levels of α.

At this point, a cautionary remark regarding the equilibrium of the economy appears to be in order. Note again that the 45° lines in the two diagrams in Figure 4.1 do not represent an equilibrium condition; they are only there to illustrate whether an individual taxpayer reciprocates by evading more or less than the average of other taxpayers. The existence of a stable equilibrium for society as a whole that is actually reached by the adaptive process described here can, unfortunately, not be guaranteed. To illustrate this point, suppose that at $t=1$, all individual decisions on tax evasion determine a value for e_1^M. In a population that is heterogenous with regard to α, the responses to e_1^M may differ between individuals – for example, their respective local attractors might induce individuals 1 and 2 to choose $e_{12}^*(e_1^M)>e_1^M$ and $e_{22}^*(e_1^M)<e_1^M$. The relative magnitude of the adjustments of 1 and 2 might, however, be reversed in the next period – and the result would be an oscillating overall intensity of tax evasion for society as whole.

Even without having secured the existence of a societal equilibrium, we can make some unambiguous, but also some ambiguous, predictions regarding the effect of government policies on tax compliance:

i   An increase of the probability of the deterrence parameters p and s always leads to a decrease of aggregate tax evasion, since those who do evade taxes always react by shifting their reaction function to e_{t-1}^M downward: they want to evade less themselves for any intensity of tax evasion in the rest of the population.

ii An increase of taxpayers' incomes y always increases tax evasion on aggregate. Taxpayers become more willing to take risks, so that those who already evade now prefer higher levels of evasion and some of those individuals who have been perfectly compliant before may now find it worthwhile to take part in the evasion lottery.

iii If $\partial\varphi/\partial\tau=0$, the effect of a change of the tax rate is ambiguous or even counterintuitive, as in the Allingham–Sandmo–Yitzhaki model. Only if individually felt guilt deteriorates with an increasing tax rate, and if this effect is sufficiently large, do individual taxpayers react with an increase of tax evasion to a heavier de jure tax burden. Another important relationship in this regard is that between α and $v(\varphi)$. Obviously, the higher the individual guilt factor, the larger is the impact of a change of perceived vertical fairness. In fact, the more the deterioration of horizontal fairness has already diminished the individual levels of α, the more likely it is that we will observe counterintuitive effects of tax rate changes. This leads to a more general point (iv).

iv The taxpayers' ability (or willingness) to negatively reciprocate against the government if it imposes unfair policies rises with the value of their guilt factor, i.e. with horizontal fairness.

The fourth statement might appear as very counterintuitive at first sight. It stems from the fact that individuals never employ an irrational reciprocal reaction. There is an upper bound to the evasion activity of individuals, and it is given by the rational magnitude of evasion in the Allingham–Sandmo–Yitzhaki model. The feeling of guilt induces what is commonly called "tax morale"; it leads individuals to evade less than they would evade in the morale-free world of the standard model, and this can be used as a reserve from which a taxpayer can reciprocate against other taxpayers, or against the public sector. This rules out costly punishment, as it is often reported in the experimental evidence – for example, from ultimatum games, as discussed above. And the reason is that costly retaliation against the public sector beyond the amount evaded in the standard model is not possible. If taxpayers evade more than the morale-free rational amount, they decrease their own expected income and increase the expected income of the public sector, in particular from expected penalty taxes. In other words, evading more would not evoke punishment, but gratification. Only a taxpayer influenced by guilt and morality, who initially evades less than an Allingham–Sandmo–Yitzhaki taxpayer, can retaliate against the public sector at all.

This leads to another interesting implication of the model. Suppose that the initial, "natural" distribution of α shifts to the left due to some exogenous shock, which would depict a sudden reduction of the propensity to feel guilty in the entire population of taxpayers. This would lead to both an increase of tax evasion for the population as a whole, and a decrease in the ability of taxpayers to reciprocate against the public sector in the future. If something crowds out the initial goodwill of the taxpayers, this has not only straightforward fiscal implications, but also implications for the relationship between the taxpayers and the government – it reduces the possibility of disciplining the government in the future. Several possible influences on this initial goodwill come to mind, such as social capital and trust, which are both magnitudes that become increasingly researched by economists. Having a detailed look at such possible relationships will, however, be a matter for future research.

Conclusions

In this chapter, we have sketched the interaction of two types of reciprocity in decision-making regarding tax evasion. Having criticized the application of a

Nash equilibrium to a multiple equilibrium setting with massive coordination problems such as tax evasion, we have instead proposed a simple, adaptive rule according to which individual taxpayers reciprocate vis-à-vis an evading population of fellow taxpayers. We have argued that, even without having a formal equilibrium, the signs of the impacts of political measures on the magnitude of tax evasion can be identified.

Furthermore, we have argued that the feeling of guilt by taxpayers is crucial as a precondition for vertical reciprocity. Taxpayers who do not behave morally when they are treated fairly (which could also be catagorized as positive reciprocity) have no means of retaliation against the public sector when they become treated unfairly. Obviously, the present chapter can only be seen as a first step towards incorporating results from the vast literature on reciprocity into theoretical reasoning about tax compliance. Further steps could, for example, be the modeling of endogenous decision-making in the public sector under conditions of reciprocal tax evasion, or further research into the sources and determinants of the individual propensity to feel guilt when evading taxes.

Bibliography

Allingham, M. G. and Sandmo, A. (1972) "Income tax evasion: a theoretical analysis", *Journal of Public Economics*, 1: 323–38.

Alm, J. and McKee, M. (2004) "Tax compliance as a coordination game", *Journal of Economic Behavior and Organization*; 54: 297–312.

Alm, J., Jackson, B. R., and McKee, M. (1993) "Fiscal exchange, collective decision institutions, and tax compliance", *Journal of Economic Behavior and Organization*, 22: 285–303.

Alm, J., McClelland, G. H., and Schulze, G. H. (1992) "Why do people pay taxes?", *Journal of Public Economics*, 48: 21–38.

Andreoni, J., Erard, B., and Feinstein, J. (1998) "Tax compliance", *Journal of Economic Literature*, 36: 818–60.

Baumeister, R., Stillwell, A., and Heatherton, T. (1994) "Guilt: An interpersonal approach", *Psychological Bulletin*, 115: 243–67.

Bolton, G. E. and Ockenfels, A. (2000) "ERC: A theory of equity, reciprocity and competition", *American Economic Review*, 90: 166–93.

Bordignon, M. (1993) "A fairness approach to income tax evasion", *Journal of Public Economics*, 52: 345–62.

Charness, G. and Rabin, M. (2002) "Understanding social preferences with simple tests", *Quarterly Journal of Economics*, 117: 817–69.

Cowell, F. A. (1992) "Tax evasion and inequity", *Journal of Economic Psychology*, 13: 521–43.

Cowell, F. A. and Gordon, J. P. F. (1988) "Unwillingness to pay: Tax evasion and public good provision", *Journal of Public Economics*, 36: 305–21.

Cox, J. C. and Sadiraj, V. (2007) "On modeling voluntary contributions to public goods", *Public Finance Review*, 35: 311–32.

Crane, S. E. and Nourzad, F. (1986) "Inflation and tax evasion: An empirical analysis", *Review of Economics and Statistics*, 68: 217–23.

Cullis, J. G. and Lewis, A. (1997) "Why people pay taxes: From a conventional economic model to a model of social convention", *Journal of Economic Psychology*, 18: 305–21.

Dufwenberg, M. and Kirchsteiger, G. (2004) "A theory of sequential reciprocity", *Games and Economic Behavior*, 47: 268–98.

Falk, A., Fehr, E., and Fischbacher, U. (2008) "Testing theories of fairness: intentions matter", *Games and Economic Behavior*, 62, 287–303.

Falkinger, J. (1995) "Tax evasion, consumption of public goods and fairness", *Journal of Economic Psychology*, 16: 63–72.

Fehr, E. and Gächter, S. (2000a) "Fairness and retaliation: The economics of reciprocity", *Journal of Economic Perspectives*, 14: 159–81.

Fehr, E. and Gächter, S. (2000b) "Cooperation and punishment in public goods experiments", *American Economic Review*, 90: 980–94.

Fehr, E. and Schmidt, K. M. (1999) "A theory of fairness, competition, and cooperation", *Quarterly Journal of Economics*, 114: 817–68.

Feld, L. P. and Tyran, J.-R. (2002) "Tax evasion and voting: An experimental analysis", *Kyklos*, 55: 197–222.

Fischbacher, U., Gächter, S., and Fehr, E. (2001) "Are people conditionally cooperative? Evidence from a public goods experiment", *Economics Letters*, 71: 497–504.

Fortin, B., Lacroix, G., and Villeval, M.-C. (2004) "Tax evasion and social interactions", IZA Discussion Paper 1359, Bonn: Institute for the Study of Labor.

Frey, B. S. (1997) "A constitution for knaves crowds out civic virtues", *Economic Journal*, 107: 1043–53.

Gintis, H. (2000) "Strong reciprocity and human sociality", *Journal of Theoretical Biology*, 206: 169–79.

Gordon, J. P. F. (1989) "Individual morality and reputation costs as deterrents to tax evasion", *European Economic Review*, 33: 797–805.

Gouldner, A. W. (1960) "The norm of reciprocity: A preliminary statement", *American Sociological Review*, 25: 161–78.

Kucher, M. and Götte, L. (1998) "Trust me: An empirical analysis of taxpayer honesty", *Finanzarchiv*, 54: 429–44.

Maital, S. (1982) *Mind, Markets and Money*, New York, NY: Basic Books.

Myles, G. D. and Naylor, R. A. (1996) "A model of tax evasion with group conformity and social customs", *European Journal of Political Economy*, 12: 49–66.

Pommerehne, W. W., Hart, A., and Frey, B. S. (1994) "Tax morale, tax evasion and the choice of policy instruments in different political systems", *Public Finance/Finance Publiques*, 49 (Supplement): 52–69.

Rabin, M. (1993) "Incorporating fairness into game theory and economics", *American Economic Review*, 83: 1281–302.

Schnellenbach, J. (2006) "Tax morale and the taming of Leviathan", *Constitutional Political Economy*, 17: 117–32.

Sobel, J. (2005) "Interdependent preferences and reciprocity", *Journal of Economic Literature*, 43: 392–436.

Spicer, M. W. and Becker, L. A. (1980) "Fiscal inequity and tax evasion: An experimental approach", *National Tax Journal*, 33: 171–5.

Torgler, B. (2003) "Tax morale, rule-governed behaviour and trust", *Constitutional Political Economy*, 14: 119–40.

Weck-Hannemann, H. and Pommerehne, W. W. (1989) "Einkommensteuerhinterzie-hung in der Schweiz: Eine empirische Analyse", *Swiss Review of Economics and Statistics*, 125: 515–56.

Yitzhaki, S. (1974) "Income tax evasion: a note", *Journal of Public Economics*, 3: 201–2.

5 Tax evasion and the psychological tax contract

Lars P. Feld and Bruno S. Frey

Introduction

Tax compliance has many facets. Tax evasion by wealthy people not declaring their capital incomes received in foreign tax heavens may nurture particular prejudices regarding what is involved, but is far from providing a comprehensive picture. Tax non-compliance also comprises the taxes evaded when individuals are working in the shadow economy; or tax avoidance by multinational firms becoming illegal when a (financial) court reaches a final verdict on particular tax saving schemes; or the sophisticated trading schemes which allow evasion of commodity taxes; or donations by family members to their supposed heirs to evade inheritance taxes; and so on. Tax compliance is, moreover, related to the broader concept of tax morale, which also includes the attitudes of honest taxpayers, who have never under-reported their true incomes, towards potential tax non-compliance by their dishonest fellow citizens. Is cheating on the tax code partly accepted as a minor disobedience, and which part of it is? Is tax non-compliance seen as undermining the functioning of a state in general? Or is it even accepted as a kind of popular gaming activity in which the state sometimes loses, sometimes wins? All these issues matter for tax compliance.

In spite of the implied need to cope with tax non-compliance in a differentiated way, economic policy reactions to this complex phenomenon not infrequently appear to be uni-dimensionally focused on deterrence measures or incentives in general. For example, in Germany, just to give a flavor, the recent efforts comprise:

- increases in deterrence – for example, the so called "Black Activities' Act" or, more exactly, the "Law to intensify the fight against black activities and accompanying tax evasion" (SchwarzArbG, Bundesrats-Drucksache 155/04a) in 2004, aiming at both raising fines and the intensity of control;
- measures to coordinate capital and corporate income taxation in the EU – for example, the European Savings Directive in 2005, which implements a (partial) system of information exchange, or the still ongoing negotiations regarding a Common Consolidated Corporate Income Tax Base;

- several measures to intensify auditing by increasing the transparency of monetary transactions between individual bank accounts that in sum almost abolish the German bank secrecy laws;
- tax rate reductions in the case of personal and corporate income taxation in 2000 and, in particular, as of 2008 onwards, including a new source tax on capital income and capital gains to be implemented in 2009;
- a tax amnesty in 2003.

Overall, this will have amounted to a decade of tax policy changes targeted at increasing tax compliance, or, as a former German finance minister put it, fighting tax evasion from cleansing services in households to the international capital markets.

Such policy efforts are in line with the traditional economic approach, which has relied heavily on deterrence as the most important determinant of tax compliance (Allingham and Sandmo, 1972; Sandmo, 2006). However, modern research from different fields, including economics and psychology, raises doubts as to the validity of this approach (see, extensively, Torgler, 2007, with many references to the literature).

Feld and Frey (2007) therefore analyze tax compliance following the approach of a psychological tax contract. They start from the Wicksellian perspective of voluntary exchange between citizens that implies a contractual justification of the state (Wicksell, 1896). Individuals subject themselves to the coercion inherent in collective action because the underlying constitutional exchange is in their well-understood long-term interest (Buchanan, 1987). With respect to fiscal issues, the psychological tax contract pushes the idea of taxation as fiscal exchange (Buchanan, 1976)[1] beyond narrow direct incentives, such as deterrence, but also beyond narrow monetary benefits as they could be provided by public goods and services following the benefit principle of taxation. For such a contract to be upheld, loyalties and emotional ties must also be considered. These bonds between taxpayers and the state shape individual tax morale and thus positively affect tax compliance. Incentives are an important ingredient of the psychological tax contract, but their role is assessed in a much more differentiated fashion than in the traditional economic approach. More importantly, the psychological tax contract is influenced by government policy, tax authorities' behavior, and state institutions.

In a related interdisciplinary analysis, Kirchler (2007) supports this approach by concluding that tax morale, and subsequently tax compliance, depends on tax knowledge, attitudes, norms, perceived opportunity, fairness considerations, and motivational postures.[2] Tax morale thus implies an intrinsic motivation to comply with the tax laws. Deterrence contributes to some of these factors, but does not always do so in the same qualitative fashion. It may on the one hand have the standard effect expected by the traditional economic approach, that the anticipated fine serves as a price on tax non-compliance and thus negatively affects it (Gneezy and Rusticchini, 2000). On the other hand, the intrinsic motivation to pay taxes may be crowded out by the state's intrusion into individuals' privacy (Frey, 1997a, 1997b).

Following this broader research strategy, Kirchler's (2007: 188) suggestion for tax compliance research is the shift from a perspective of compliance enforced by authorities' power (the "cops and robbers approach") to voluntary compliance driven by trust in authorities (the "service and client approach"). He shapes this suggestion by a slippery slope model according to which deterrence and trust as two equally valid ways of achieving compliance could dynamically interact with each other. This interaction would finally evolve into a system of responsive regulation. These conclusions and suggestions are rather cautious, and leave much room for continuous reinterpretations.

Alm and Martinez-Vazquez (2003) similarly argue that two paradigms emerge from tax compliance research. The first paradigm considers taxpayers as potential criminals putting exclusive emphasis on deterrence. The second paradigm acknowledges the importance of social norms to shape tax compliance, and of tax administrations to provide services to citizens. Governments could therefore affect tax compliance by also influencing social norms. In the same vein, Kristina Murphy (see Chapter 10 of this volume) argues (and provides evidence) that a process-based model of regulation as one which emphasizes fair treatment is particularly promising in the regulation of taxpayers. According to her view, procedural justice is the most crucial motivational force to shape taxpayer behavior.

In this chapter, we push the analytics of a psychological tax contract developed in our earlier work a bit further. Our analysis results in similar conclusions to those mentioned before, but we are more radical in leaving aside those approaches which are not captured by this contractual thinking and, moreover, we continuously ask what deterrence does at the different stages of state–taxpayer interaction. In the following section, the theoretical basis of the psychological tax contract is provided by discussing the interactions between incentives and the intrinsic motivation to pay taxes. Positive (rewards) or negative incentives (deterrence) play a role, but it cannot be taken for granted that they induce tax compliance, because they may also crowd out tax morale. Thoughts on the impact of deterrence and rewards on tax compliance highlight the importance of a differentiated approach.

A contractual relationship implies duties and rights for each contract partner. This is looked at from an exchange perspective, according to which the government should provide public services to citizens in exchange for their tax payments. If the benefit principle of taxation that implies a fiscal equivalence between public goods and tax prices is violated by setting those prices too high, citizens think they have a justification for evading taxes. However, citizens may perceive their tax payments as contributions to the "*bonum commune*" such that they are willing to honestly declare their income even if they do not receive a full public good equivalent to their tax payments. Income redistribution is more accepted by affluent citizens the more the political process is perceived to be fair and the more policy outcomes are legitimate: the psychological tax contract has elements of gain (or distributive justice) and participation (or procedural justice).

The contractual relationship has additional implications at the procedural level: the way the tax office treats taxpayers in auditing processes plays a role. As Frey and Feld (2002) argue, the psychological tax contract presupposes that taxpayers and the tax authority treat each other like partners – i.e. with mutual respect and honesty. If tax administrations instead treat taxpayers as inferiors in a hierarchical relationship, the psychological tax contract is violated and citizens have good reason not to stick to their part of the contract, and to evade taxes. The psychological tax contract also has elements of respect (or interactional justice). The notion of a psychological tax contract also helps to highlight the difficulties of upholding tax compliance when tax amnesties are offered.

In the final section, we draw some conclusions regarding the policy implications of such a contractual view of tax compliance. It implies that simple policy proposals are inadequate to shape the psychological tax contract successfully. The right mixture of incentives and of respectful treatment of taxpayers by tax officials needs to be found.

The psychological tax contract

Nobody likes paying taxes, not least because it involves a public good and there are incentives to free-ride. Therefore, incentives are needed to enforce taxation. This is the central insight of Allingham and Sandmo's (1972) deterrence approach to tax evasion. However, several scholars have empirically shown that for selfish individuals it would be rational not to pay taxes, because the probability of being detected is so low and the size of the fines so small in many countries that it is advantageous to evade.[3] Tax payment is taken to be a "quasi-voluntary" act (see Levi, 1988), and the tax authority must acknowledge that external interventions in the form of rewards or sanctions may crowd out that intrinsic motivation to pay taxes. The idea of intrinsic motivation is largely attached to psychology. A group of cognitive social psychologists has identified that, under particular conditions, monetary (external) rewards undermine intrinsic motivation.[4] Giving of rewards for undertaking an activity has indirect negative consequences, as rewards lead to the expectation of future rewards such that desired behavior is undertaken only if rewards are provided. Frey (1997a) generalizes this basic idea in three ways:

1   All types of external interventions may negatively affect intrinsic motivation – i.e., not only offering rewardsm but also issuing commands, imposing rules and regulations as well as punishments. Thus, *deterrence* imposed by the tax authority may undermine individuals' intrinsic willingness to conform to tax laws.
2   The intrinsic motivation affected by external intervention is broadly conceived. It comprises actions undertaken for their own sake – i.e., without expectation of external reward – as well as *internalized norm guided behavior*. The latter is the relevant concept as far as tax paying is concerned.

3   External interventions undermine intrinsic motivation when they are perceived to be intrusive by the individuals concerned (the "crowding-out"), and they maintain or raise intrinsic motivation when they are perceived to be supportive. The underlying psychological processes depend on how self-determination and self-esteem are affected (Deci and Ryan, 1985; Deci and Flaste, 1995). Tax audits as intrusion by tax authorities can undermine tax morale more strongly if the taxpayers' sense of self-determination is high.

Tax officials are assumed to be aware of the effects on taxpayers' behavior suggested by crowding theory. They know that disrespectful treatment of taxpayers undermines their tax morale and thereby increases the cost of raising taxes. Tax authorities will only behave in a respectful way towards taxpayers when they are aware that there exists a substantial extent of tax morale to begin with. Tax officials know at the same time that tax payments do not solely depend on tax morale, but that extrinsic incentives also play a major role. In particular, incentives are used to prevent taxpayers with low (or lacking in) tax morale from exploiting the more honest taxpayers and escaping paying their due share. A combination of respectful treatment and incentives is possible and widely practiced. The sole reliance on extrinsic incentives, as suggested by a large part of the tax compliance literature based on subjective expected utility maximization, represents a special case which only applies under restrictive conditions. Such a special case occurs when the tax officials are convinced that individuals' tax morale is low or does not exist at all. In general, however, it is optimal to simultaneously use both respectful treatment as well as incentives. The higher the initial level of tax morale, and the stronger the crowding effect, the less weight is put on negative incentives, and the more respectfully taxpayers are treated.

This relationship between taxpayers and tax authorities can be modeled as an implicit or relational contract (Akerlof, 1982) which involves strong emotional ties and loyalties. Social psychologists (Rousseau and McLean Parks, 1993; Schein, 1965) have been using this concept for a long time, calling it a "psychological" contract to set it clearly apart from formal contracts, which are obeyed because the parties respond to the explicit and material sanctions previously agreed upon. Osterloh and Frey (2000), for example, use psychological contracts to successfully analyze the organization of firms. Psychological contracts could also be used in tax compliance analysis, suggesting that incentives and respectful treatment are important determinants of tax compliance. This contract can be thought of as a contractual relationship between the taxpayer and the state, while the latter comprises the other fellow taxpayers on the one hand and the official authorities on the other hand. The official authorities are considered to be the government and the legislature, which decide about tax laws and the public services provided, but also the bureaucracy and the tax authority which execute or enforce these decisions. The psychological tax contract must therefore be interpreted as an inclusive relation between state and citizens.

In a psychological tax contract, punishment still plays a role in order to restrict possible exploitation by others; however, the satisfaction of taxpayers with what they get from the other contract party (i.e., the government) mainly influences their tax morale. Taxpayers' reward from that contract must be understood in a broad sense, going beyond pure exchanges of goods and services for the payment of a tax price. In addition to such direct exchange components, the fairness of the procedures leading to particular political outcomes as well as the way the government and the taxpayers treat each other are part of the contractual relationship. A genuine reward is therefore obtained only if taxpayers as citizens have an inclusive, respectful relationship with the community. Both sides of the contract perceive the other as a contract partner and treat each other with mutual respect. As deterrence and tax morale interact, it would be counterproductive to rely solely on punishment or monetary rewards because tax morale may be undermined. A dynamic relationship results in which deterrence, monetary rewards and fiscal exchange, but also decision-making procedures and treatment of taxpayers, play a role.

The contractual metaphor has many advantages over traditional theoretical approaches. First, it underlines that paying taxes is a quasi-voluntary act. Each party has to agree to the contents of the contract. In practice, it is seldom the case that each public good is individually contracted with each taxpayer for a certain tax price. However, a steady reduction in tax compliance needs to be not only interpreted as a violation of the law, but also as taxpayers' discontent with what they receive for their taxes. Second, the contractual approach emphasizes the role of fair procedures decided upon at a constitutional stage. Tyler (1990) argues that people comply with the law in general if they perceive the process that leads to this law as being fair. Most obviously, it will be difficult to think of a psychological tax contract in autocratic regimes. The inclusiveness of political decision-making could, however, also be very different in democratic regimes, depending on the extent of citizens' involvement in political decision-making. This second advantage of the contractual metaphor stems from its potential to include notions of procedural fairness almost by construction. Third, the way people are treated by the tax authorities affects cooperation levels.

At this procedural level, respectful treatment can be split into two different components. The procedures used by auditors in their contact with taxpayers are to be transparent and clear. In the case of arbitrary procedures, taxpayers feel helpless and get the impression that they are not taken seriously. Such behavior reduces their perception of being obliged to pay taxes. In addition, respectful treatment has a direct personal component in the sense of how the personality of taxpayers is respected by tax officials. If they treat taxpayers as partners in a psychological tax contract, instead of inferiors in a hierarchical relationship, taxpayers have incentives to pay taxes honestly. In addition, respectful treatment of taxpayers enforces the effects of emotions on compliance behavior. Grasmick and Bursik (1990) show, for example, that shame affects tax compliance. Makkai and Braithwaite (1994) report similar evidence regarding the impact of avoidance of humiliation on compliance with nursing home regulation.

Two opposing methods of treating taxpayers can be distinguished: (i) a respectful treatment supporting, and possibly raising, tax morale; and (ii) an authoritarian treatment undermining tax morale. The tax officials can choose between these extremes in different ways. For instance, when they detect an error in the tax declaration, they can suspect an intention to cheat, and impose legal sanctions. Alternatively, the tax officials may give taxpayers the benefit of the doubt and seriously inquire about the reason for the error. If the taxpayer in question indeed did not intend to cheat but simply made a mistake, he or she will most likely be offended by the disrespectful treatment by the tax authority. The feeling of being controlled in a negative way, and being suspected of tax cheating, tends to crowd out the intrinsic motivation to act as an honorable taxpayer and, as a consequence, tax morale will fall. In contrast, if the tax official makes an effort to find out the reason for the error by contacting the taxpayer in a friendly way, the taxpayer will appreciate this respectful treatment and tax morale will be upheld.

The impact of deterrence on tax compliance

Given the requirements of a psychological tax contract, it is necessary to identify what role deterrence plays. According to surveys by Andreoni et al. (1998), Alm (1999), and Slemrod and Yitzhaki (2002), an overwhelming majority of theoretical studies predict a positive impact of deterrence on tax evasion. The higher the fines, the lower the tax evasion – ceteris paribus; the higher the intensity of control, the lower the tax evasion – ceteris paribus. However, the empirical evidence looks less convincing. This already holds for experimental studies, although the meta-study of tax compliance experiments conducted by Blackwell (see Chapter 6 of this volume) indicates that higher deterrence raises tax compliance. More recent experiments, which deviate from the simple public good games used in earlier studies of tax compliance, carefully identify the crowding-outs emphasized by the psychological tax contract approach. For example, Falk and Kosfeld (2006) highlight the crowding out of intrinsic motivation as the hidden costs of control in a principal–agent experiment in which the agent is controlled by the principal. In a crime and punishment experiment, Hörisch and Strassmair (2008) even found that, for some subjects in their experiments, higher punishment *increases* criminal behavior in the lab if the incentives do not become overwhelmingly large.

In field studies, many scholars[5] find a negative impact of a higher probability of detection on tax compliance. Some authors[6] report a positive impact of fines on tax complianc, while others[7] present ambiguous evidence. For example, Slemrod et al. (2001) report a significant positive impact of the probability of detection on tax evasion for high-income groups. Scholz and Lubell (2001) find a crowding out of tax compliance when penalties are introduced. The results by Feld and Frey (2002a) support the ambiguous impact of deterrence on tax compliance. According to their evidence from Swiss cantons, a higher intensity of control increases tax evasion, while fines and penalties reduce tax evasion. Martinez-Vazquez and Rider (2005) report evidence for the US that enforcement efforts affect the mode of tax evasion targeted by these efforts negatively, but the untargeted mode positively. While an overall positive effect of enforcement on tax compliance is reported, it remains generally open whether the unintended side effect on the untargeted mode overcompensates the intended effect.

This mixed evidence can occur for many different reasons, ranging from measurement errors in the empirical analysis to a social sanctions approach of deterrence (Ekland-Olson *et al.*, 1984) and the impact of personal and social norms as moderators of deterrence (Wenzel, 2004). It may, however, also be convincingly explained by crowding theory. Higher control intensities increase deterrence and thus tax compliance on the one hand, but may be perceived as intrusive by taxpayers and thus reduce tax compliance on the other hand (Kirchler, 1999; Scholz and Pinney, 1995). Feld and Frey (2002a) provide evidence that fines and penalties are part of a non-linear punishment schedule that allows for low levels of fines in the case of minor offenses against the tax code – even a standing tax amnesty in the case of self-denunciation – in order to reduce taxpayers perception of intrusiveness, but requires high penalties in cases of tax fraud or major convictions in order to make it clear that the psychological tax contract is at stake. Put differently, nobody is perfect, and to cheat a little bit on taxes is a common and minor human weakness, and should be considered as such, while basic violations of the tax code undermine the basic contractual relationship between citizens and the state and must therefore be punished more heavily. Minor and major offenses could thereby be distinguished with respect to the amount evaded, but also to procedural categories – for example, by differentiating between active tax fraud by manipulation of the balance sheet and passive tax evasion when taxpayers forget to report particular income components.

Deterrence thus has two different aspects. On the one hand, in order to keep up a psychological tax contract between the tax office and the taxpayers, honest taxpayers must be confident that they are not being exploited by dishonest tax cheaters. Thus, deterrence for major violations of the tax code reduces tax evasion. On the other hand, each taxpayer may make a mistake, and thus minor offenses can be penalized less without undermining the psychological tax contract. A non-linear punishment schedule, with low fines for minor tax evasion and high penalties for tax fraud, will serve the purpose of shaping tax morale. All in all, the evidence suggests that an exclusive reliance on deterrence is not a reasonable strategy to increase tax compliance.

Rewarding taxpayers

In contrast to the standard model of tax evasion which raises the relative cost of *not paying* taxes, rewards raise the benefits of *paying* taxes. A reward, which is given to taxpayers for correctly fulfilling their duties, changes the relative prices in favor of paying taxes, and against evading them (Falkinger and Walther, 1991). For this result to obtain, two conditions must be met:

1   The income effect induced by the higher wealth position must not work in the opposite direction. However, this is unlikely if the reward is small

compared to the tax liability so that the income effect also tends to be small. Moreover, there is little reason to expect that higher wealth should induce more, rather than less, tax evasion.

2   The reward may induce strategic behavior by the taxpayers if it depends on the reduction of evasive behavior. In that case, it may be rational first to increase tax evasion and thereafter to reduce it in order to benefit from the rewards offered. As the rewards considered here depend on *being* a "good" taxpayer, strategic behavior is not a rational option.

It is crucial to consider effects of rewards on behavior going beyond those ana- lyzed by standard theory. From the perspective of crowding theory, receiving certain types of rewards may undermine the intrinsic motivation to pay taxes. The more rewards are perceived as an acknowledgment for being a good tax- payer, the more they are perceived as supporting, and tend to bolster and raise tax morale quite in contrast to deterrence. This motivational effect then works in the same direction as the relative price effect, and strengthens the attractiveness of giving rewards to "good" taxpayers. In the case of the normally applied pun- ishment for failing to pay the taxes due, the relative price effect and the motiva- tional crowding-out work in opposite directions. The *way* in which rewards are handed out to "good" taxpayers is thus significant for its effects on taxpayer behavior.

The reward may take the form of a *direct monetary* payment. It may be pro- portional to the size of the tax payment (i.e., a percentage rebate) or, at the other extreme, may be the same size for all "good" taxpayers. The relative price effect is larger in the first case, but this beneficial effect may easily be overcompen- sated by a crowding-out effect. A reward received in the same monetary dimen- sion as the tax payments is likely to be discounted by the taxpayers as a "right", and therefore does not positively influence tax morale. In contrast, a reward clearly distinguished from the taxes due tends to be perceived as a sign of acknowledgment. If this is indeed the case, it is even better to give the reward in a *non-monetary* form. Providing "good" taxpayers with better and less costly access to public services is likely to raise tax morale more strongly than money will. Such a "gift" also emphasizes the exchange relationship between the tax- payer and the state based on reciprocity (Fehr *et al.*, 1997). There are many pos- sible ways to reward "good" taxpayers in these terms – for instance, they may be offered free entry to museums, exhibitions and other cultural activities under- taken by the state, or they may be given a reduction (say, 50 percent) on all public transport. Most taxpayers receiving a reward in these terms take it as a sign of appreciation rather than simply a reduction in taxes (which would quickly be taken as a matter of course).

It is well known from psychological research that punishment and rewards lead to different behavioral outcomes. Indeed, it appears to be common know- ledge among psychologists that rewards lead to better outcomes than punish- ment. As early as 1948, Skinner (1948, 1953) was emphasizing the importance of positive incentives. In the literature on social loafing (see Diehl and Stroebe,

1987; Witte, 1989), the impact of reward and punishment is emphasized, and it is shown that rewards particularly help to solve the problem of "hiding in the crowd" (Davis, 1969).

Tax compliance and social exchange

From the perspective of standard economic theory, a much more direct incentive for tax compliance than deterrence or rewards consists in the goods and services that the state provides to citizens in exchange for their tax payments (Mackscheidt, 1984; Smith and Stalans, 1991). If the analogy to private contracts is considered, the goods or services purchased provide the foremost incentives to pay the price for these goods and services. The incentives from private law to stick to the duties fixed by the contract mainly serve as insurance if the individuals' desire to get a product is insufficient, or the terms of trade are unfavorable. Similarly, rewards in the form of gifts for loyal customers serve as a positive means to bind them. Because the state supposedly provides public goods, services, and infrastructure, which are not necessarily traded in private markets, or redistributes income and wealth, the fiscal exchange relationship poses additional difficulties.

From the perspective of a psychological tax contract, respectful treatment occurs at two different levels of action: the fiscal exchange, and the procedural level. The fiscal exchange between the state and its citizens requires that citizens' tax payments are met by a corresponding supply of public services provided by the government. According to the benefit principle of taxation, taxes are prices for particular public goods (Buchanan, 1976). However, the benefit principle does not necessarily imply that income redistribution becomes impossible and only infrastructural goods as well as public consumption goods are provided by the state. Citizens may perceive their tax payments as contributions to the "*bonum commune*" such that they are willing to honestly declare their income even if they do not individually receive a full public good equivalent to their tax payments. Income redistribution is more accepted by affluent citizens the more the political process is perceived to be fair, and the more policy outcomes are legitimate.

Establishing social exchange between citizens and the government

Empirically, the more governments follow the benefit principle of taxation and provide public services according to the preferences of taxpayers in exchange for a reasonable tax price, the more taxpayers comply with the tax laws. Many scholars[8] present experimental evidence that governments which stick to the principle of fiscal exchange achieve more tax compliance. Pommerehne *et al.* (1994) used a simulation study design to analyze the impact of fiscal exchange on tax compliance. They show that the more the citizens' optimal choice of a public good and the actual provision level and quality deviate from each other, the higher is tax evasion. Tax compliance also increases with reductions in government waste. In experimental papers, the proposed fiscal exchange relationship is based on the provision of a public good financed by taxes. Several authors use this analogy to public good games in order to analyze additional variables that influence tax evasion (Feld and Tyran, 2002). According to the benefit principle of taxation, such a restricted view of government action could be rationalized.

However, in real-world settings the state undertakes many activities that cannot be subsumed under the heading of public consumption or public infrastructure. In particular, pure redistribution is not covered by such a design. Whenever redistribution of income is at stake, problems of tax evasion become pertinent. There are only a few studies that consider the relationship between tax evasion and redistribution in a fiscal exchange setting. In an experiment, Güth and Mackscheidt (1985) chose a simple tax-transfer scheme to approximate the principle of vertical equity – i.e., taking from the rich and giving to the poor – as closely as possible. They found that subjects had a compliance rate of 93 percent. Becker *et al.* (1987) report, however, that evasion rises if taxpayers fear to lose from redistribution.

Obviously, the satisfaction with what the government provides in exchange for tax payments strongly depends on the experimental setting or, in the real world, on the environmental conditions. In particular, notions of fairness or justice shape the extent to which the fiscal exchange paradigm increases tax compliance. Kinsey and Grasmick (1993)[9] report evidence that horizontal equity plays a role. If an individual's tax burden is of similar magnitude as that of comparable others, tax compliance increases. According to Kinsey and Grasmick (1993) as well as Roberts and Hite (1994), vertical unfairness of the tax schedule (the progressivity of the income tax) increases tax evasion. This is in line with the results by Scott and Grasmick (1981), who report evidence that deterrence is more effective for taxpayers who perceive the tax system to be unfair. Moreover, Scholz and Lubell (1998) emphasize the importance of trust in government for tax compliance. In contrast to their definition (1998: 411), trust in government is more than a "rough measure of the net benefits from governing institutions". It also involves the effectiveness of the government in conducting the policies and programs promised to citizens. In particular, trust in government can be eroded if government waste is high (Ahmed and Braithwaite, 2004; Braithwaite, 1998, 2003).

Establishing fiscal exchange by political decision-making procedures

The fiscal exchange relationship between taxpayers and the state therefore depends on the politico-economic framework within which the government acts. According to Alm *et al.* (1999: 149), rational egoists should vote for the lowest control intensities and fines that are necessary to ensure compliance. However, the possibility for voters to vote directly on matters of content increases the legitimacy of policies and serves as an insurance against exaggerated government waste. Direct political participation particularly activates the public-spiritedness of taxpayers (Feld and Kirchgässner, 2000).

In an experimental study, Feld and Tyran (2002) found that tax compliance is higher on average in an endogenous fine treatment in which subjects are allowed to approve or reject the proposal of a fine as compared to an exogenous fine treatment where the fine is imposed by the experimenter (see also Alm *et al.*, 1999). People exhibit higher tax morale when they are allowed to vote on a fine because they find it more legitimate. Not only do subjects who approve the fine in the endogenous fine treatment have considerably higher tax compliance than subjects in the exogenous fine treatment compliance rates are also higher if the fine is accepted than if the fine is rejected. Subjects who reject the proposal of the fine show a higher compliance rate than subjects in the exogenous fine treatment even if they know that the dominant strategy under the existence of the low fine is non-compliance. Finally, individuals who vote against the fine contribute effectively more if the fine is adopted than do individuals who vote for the fine if the symbolic fine is rejected.

Field studies provide additional support for the experimental findings. Focusing on tax evasion in the Swiss cantons between 1965 and 1978, Pommerehne and Weck-Hannemann (1996), Pommerehne and Frey (1992) and Frey (1997b) found that the more direct democratic the political decision-making procedures of a canton are, the lower the tax evasion is. These results were replicated by Feld and Frey (2002a) and Frey and Feld (2002) by extending the sample to the period 1985–1995. Torgler (2005) used an alternative approach to study tax morale in the Swiss cantons by investigating two micro-data sets (the World Value Survey and the International Survey Program) that contain questions about the tax morale of respondents. His results provide evidence that direct democracy shapes tax morale. According to his estimates, tax morale is significantly higher in direct democratic cantons. Distinguishing between different instruments of direct democracy, the fiscal referendum has the highest positive influence on tax morale. Moreover, the tax morale of respondents is higher if they have a higher trust in government, or in the courts and the legal system. Since studies for the US (Gerber, 1999) and Switzerland (Pommerehne, 1978) show that policies in direct democratic jurisdictions are more strongly in line with citizens' preferences, institutions of direct democracy can be seen as a means to establish a relationship of fiscal exchange between taxpayers and the government.

Torgler (2005, 2007) also reports evidence that local autonomy as an indicator of fiscal federalism has a marginally significant positive impact on tax morale. Güth *et al.* (2005) report a stronger effect of fiscal decentralization on tax compliance in an experimental setting. Subjects show higher tax morale if public goods are provided and financed regionally or locally, because their taxes are spent on their own regional or local public goods. The fiscal equivalence of the theory of fiscal federalism then holds more strongly.

The treatment of taxpayers

The psychological tax contract is also supported by interactional justice – in particular, a respectful treatment of taxpayers by tax authorities. In order to investigate the relationship between taxpayers and tax authorities, Feld and Frey (2002a) sent a survey to the tax authorities of the 26 Swiss cantons asking detailed questions about the legal background of tax evasion, and including questions on the treatment of taxpayers by tax authorities in day-to-day audits – in particular, when a taxpayer is suspected of not declaring his or her true taxable income. According to this survey, the extent of *respectful treatment* of the taxpayers is captured by:

i   fully observing procedures based on formal and informal rules – i.e., what typically happens if a taxpayer does not declare taxable income at all (procedures, fines), if a tax declaration is mistakenly filled out or, in a second stage, if taxpayers do not react?

ii   acknowledgment of individual citizens' rights and personality – i.e., what does the tax administration do if taxpayers make a mistake by declaring a too high taxable income? Are there attempts to find out whether taxpayers intentionally or mistakenly declare too low a taxable income? Are mistakes in the tax declaration to the advantage or to the disadvantage of *taxpayers*?

The way taxpayers are treated by tax authorities reveals interesting differences between the Swiss cantons. Only 58 percent of Swiss cantonal tax authorities believe that mistakes in reported incomes are, on average, in favor of taxpayers; 31 percent believe that mistakes are neither to the advantage nor to the disadvantage of taxpayers, and 12 percent believe that mistakes are to the disadvantage of taxpayers. These answers indicate that distrust towards taxpayers is not universal. If the tax authorities presume that a taxpayer does not report his or her true taxable income, they contact that taxpayer in several different ways: 54 percent of the cantons phone the person concerned and ask how the mistake(s) occurred in the tax declaration and how it can be explained; all of the cantons send a letter to the taxpayer, half of them with a standard formulation; and nearly 85 percent ask the taxpayer to come to the tax office. Only half of the cantons mention the possibility of punishment. Thus, while one-half of the tax authorities rarely adopt the strategy of explicit deterrence, the other half seek to gain additional information. Of the cantonal tax authorities, 96 percent correct reported incomes that are too high (i.e., reduce taxable incomes when taxpayers commit mistakes that are to their disadvantage), and 27 percent correct reported taxable income even if taxpayers fail to apply legal tax savings.

The impact of the treatment of taxpayers on tax evasion was studied more thoroughly in a regression analysis by Frey and Feld (2002) and Feld and Frey (2002a). With a sample of 26 Swiss cantons in the years 1970–1995, they showed that the tax authorities in Switzerland do indeed behave *as if* they were aware of the reaction of taxpayers to being treated with respect. Tax evasion turns out to be lower, the more fully the tax office observes formal and informal procedural rules. The observation on procedural rules is indicated by a distinction between friendly treatments (for example, implementing a respectful procedure) and unfriendly treatments (such as using an authoritarian procedure or having the tax authorities' direct imposing an arbitrarily determined fine). The friendly treatment has a stronger dampening effect on tax evasion, particularly in cantons using referendums and initiatives in political decision-making, while the authoritarian procedure, the threat of deterrence, reduces tax evasion particularly in representative democracies, but is counter-productive in direct democracies. Moreover, Swiss citizens are more respectfully treated by the tax authority the more strongly developed the citizens' participation rights are (Feld and Frey, 2002b). In addition, tax authorities in more direct democratic cantons appear more frequently to give taxpayers the benefit of the doubt. Feld and Frey (2002b) report evidence that tax authorities in more direct democratic cantons believe to a significantly lesser extent that mistakes in tax declaration are in favor of taxpayers.

The role of tax amnesties

How tax amnesties affect tax compliance is intensively debated in the literature. Two main arguments oppose each other. On the one hand, when offering a tax amnesty, taxpayers are given the opportunity to return to normal and honest compliance behavior. This is the well-known bridge to tax honesty often stressed by governments. On the other hand, previously honest taxpayers may be negatively affected by tax amnesties. They could have the impression that it pays to behave dishonestly and get away with only small penalties. Moreover, when they have illusions about the true extent of tax evasion of their fellow taxpayers, they may realize that tax evasion is much more widespread and may fear that they are the last to pay their taxes honestly. This will induce them to comply with tax law to a lesser extent.

Including tax amnesties in the standard economic theory of tax evasion, the negative effects must be emphasized. Tax amnesties reduce the credibility of governments to commit to a deterrence policy, and thus lead to a decline in actual deterrence. The analytics of the psychological tax contract allow for inclusion of the positive argument for tax amnesties, however. The representatives of the state are reaching out to renew that contract with taxpayers who had become non-compliant in the past. They are confident that the components of fiscal exchange now fit those taxpayers' needs and wishes better than before. When tax amnesties occur infrequently – for example, only every two generations - the negative side effects on honest taxpayers are moderate. From governments' perspective, the additional fiscal revenue is often crucial for tax amnesty proposals. This desire stands in stark contrast to the requirement that tax amnesties should take place infrequently.

In general, tax amnesties do not generate much additional revenue for governments.[10] Alm *et al.* (2001), drawing lessons from Russian tax amnesties, support this conclusion. In addition, they found that tax amnesties generate higher revenue when accompanied by bigger changes in the tax system, often reductions of the tax burden, and that taxpayers must perceive a tax amnesty as a one-time opportunity. The revenue impact becomes smaller when tax amnesties occur repeatedly (Luitel and Sobel, 2007). Interestingly, the introduction of a tax amnesty in US states depends on political economic factors (Le Borgne, 2006). States are more likely to introduce tax amnesties when their tax levels are high (Dubin *et al.*, 1992), but also when state indebtedness is growing (Le Borgne, 2006). Amnesties are thus perceived by governments as raising revenues. Moreover, governors are half as likely to declare a tax amnesty during an election year, because law-abiding taxpayers consider a tax amnesty as unfair and thus would punish governors at the polls. This evidence supports the argument regarding negative side effects of amnesties.

Torgler and Schaltegger (2005) conducted a tax amnesty experiment in which a referendum on the introduction of a tax amnesty was incorporated. They found that taxpayers usually refuse a tax amnesty. However, tax compliance rose significantly after the vote had occurred. When a tax amnesty is accompanied by higher enforcement mechanisms, higher tax compliance results. It is interesting to note that the latest federal tax amnesty in Switzerland, in 1968, became a success because it had to pass a referendum and was accompanied by *less* auditing efforts than a previous proposal (Pommerehne and Zweifel, 1991). In this case, the return of taxpayers to honest behavior dominated the crowding out of honest taxpayers.

Conclusions

Tax compliance is the result of a complicated interaction of deterrence measures and responsive regulation. Citizens and the state develop their fiscal relationships according to a psychological tax contract that establishes fiscal exchange between taxpayers and tax authorities. It reaches beyond pure exchanges, and involves loyalties and ties between the contract partners. Tax morale is therefore a function of (i) the fiscal exchange where taxpayers get public services for the tax prices they pay, (ii) the political procedures that lead to this exchange, and (iii) the personal relationship between the taxpayers and the tax administrators.

Empirical evidence on Switzerland summarized in this chapter underlines these arguments by showing a family of tax jurisdictions where a psychological tax contract appears to be in place. Tax authorities take into account that the way they treat the taxpayers systematically affects the latter's tax morale, and therefore their willingness to pay taxes, which in turn affects the costs of raising taxes. In addition, tax compliance in Switzerland is shaped by direct democracy establishing a fiscal exchange relationship between taxpayers and the state. This also holds for the latest successful tax amnesty in Switzerland, although even more complicated issues are at stake when tax amnesties are introduced.

Finally, it should be noted that the approach of a psychological tax contract shifts the emphasis in tax compliance research from deterrence and its effects towards the ways in which tax morale can be raised and social norms are shaped. As in pure market exchange, reciprocity norms, trust, and pro-social behavior are important pre-conditions for a fiscal system, and thus the state in general, to work smoothly. Without knowledge of these fundamental normative concerns, pure deterrence might easily backfire.

Notes

1 See also the comment by Frey (1976) on Buchanan's paper. In contrast, Musgrave (1939) argues that fiscal exchange theory is highly unrealistic given the compulsory nature of the actual revenue–expenditure process.
2 See also the Special Issue on Responsive Regulation and Taxation, *Law and Policy*, 29 (1) (Braithwaite, 2007).
3 Alm *et al.* (1992a), Graetz and Wilde (1985), Skinner and Slemrod (1985) and Pommerehne and Frey (1992) conclude that the risk aversion that is needed in order to raise compatibility with actual compliance rates is not supported by evidence. In a more recent paper, Slemrod (2007) questioned such an interpretation of the evidence by arguing that the way tax authorities collect information on taxpayer compliance matters such that the probability of detection increases considerably for large parts of the taxpaying population. In a recent work on the effectiveness of the IRS, Erard and Feinstein (see Chapter 7 of this volume) reported detection rates of 88 percent for wage earners (excluding tip income), 47 percent for recipients of rents and royalties, and 32 percent for self-employed individuals. The detection rate of capital income (including capital gains) was not reported. Even for wage earners, these figures do not amount to 100 percent, as claimed by Slemrod (2007).
4 Headed by Deci (1971). Extensive surveys are given in, for example, Pittman and Heller (1987), and Lane (1991). The effect is also known as "The Hidden Cost of Reward" (see Lepper and Greene, 1978). For meta-analyses, see Deci *et al.* (1999), and Cameron *et al.* (2001). That external interventions may crowd out intrinsic motivation is introduced into economics as "crowding theory" (Frey, 1997; Le Grand, 2003), and is supported by much empirical evidence (Frey and Jegen, 2001).
5 For example, Dubin *et al.* (1987), Dubin and Wilde (1988), Beron *et al.* (1992), Slemrod *et al.* (2001), Alm and McKee (2006), and Bergman and Nevarez (2006).
6 Schwartz and Orleans (1967), Friedland *et al.* (1978), Klepper and Nagin (1989), De Juan *et al.* (1994), Alm *et al.* (1995).
7 Spicer and Lundstedt (1976), Friedland (1982), Elffers *et al.* (1987), and Varma and Doob (1998).
8 Spicer and Lundstedt (1976), Porcano (1988), Alm *et al.* (1992a), and Alm *et al.* (1992b, 1992c, 1993).
9 See also Spicer and Becker (1980), De Juan *et al.* (1994).
10 Alm and Beck (1990), Hasseldine (1998), Feld (2003).

References

Ahmed, E. and Braithwaite, V. (2004) "When tax collectors become collectors for child support and student loans: Jeopardizing the revenue base", *Kyklos*, 57: 303–26.

Akerlof, G. A. (1982) "Labor contracts as partial gift exchange", *Quarterly Journal of Economics*, 84: 488–500.

Allingham, M. G. and Sandmo, A. (1972) "Income tax evasion: A theoretical analysis", *Journal of Public Economics*, 1: 323–38.

Alm, J. (1999) "Tax compliance and administration", in W. B. Hildreth and J. A. Richardson (eds.), *Handbook of Taxation*, New York, NY: Marcel Dekker.

Alm, J. and Beck, W. (1990) "Tax amnesties and tax revenues", *Public Finance Quarterly*, 18: 433–53.

Alm, J. and Martinez-Vazquez, J. (2003) "Institutions, paradigms, and tax evasion in developing and transition countries", in J. Alm and J. Martinez-Vazquez (eds.), *Public Finance in Developing and Transition Countries: Essays in Honor of Richard Bird*, Cheltenham, UK: Edward Elgar.

Alm, J. and McKee, M. (2006) "Audit certainty, audit productivity, and taxpayer compliance", *National Tax Journal*, 59: 801–16.

Alm, J., Jackson, B. R., and McKee, M. (1992b) "Estimating the determinants of taxpayer compliance with experimental data", *National Tax Journal*, 45: 107–14.

Alm, J., Jackson, B. R., and McKee, M. (1992c) "Institutional uncertainty and taxpayer compliance", *American Economic Review*, 82: 1018–26.

Alm, J., Jackson, B. R., and McKee, M. (1993) "Fiscal exchange, collective decision institutions and tax compliance", *Journal of Economic Behavior and Organization*, 22: 285–303.

Alm, J., McClelland, G. H. and Schulze, W. D. (1992a) "Why do people pay taxes?", *Journal of Public Economics*, 48: 21–38.

Alm, J., McClelland, G. H., and Schulze, W. D. (1999) "Changing the social norm of tax compliance by voting", *Kyklos*, 52: 141–71.

Alm, J., Martinez-Vazquez, J., and Wallace, S. (2001) "Tax amnesties and tax collections in the Russian Federation", in: National Tax Association (ed.), *Proceedings of the 93rd Annual Conference 2000*, Washington, DC, pp. 239–47.

Alm, J., Sanchez, I., and De Juan, A. (1995) "Economic and non-economic factors in tax compliance", *Kyklos*, 48: 3–18.

Andreoni, J., Erard, B., and Feinstein, J. (1998) "Tax compliance", *Journal of Economic Literature*, 36: 818–60.

Becker, W., Büchner, H. J., and Sleeking, S. (1987) "The impact of public transfer expenditures on tax evasion: An experimental approach", *Journal of Public Economics*, 34: 243–52.

Bergman, M. and Nevarez, A. (2006) "Do audits enhance compliance? An empirical assessment of VAT enforcement", *National Tax* Journal, 59: 817–32.

Beron, K. J., Tauchen, H. V., and Witte, A. D. (1992) "The effect of audits and socio-economic variables on compliance", in J. Slemrod (ed.), *Why People Pay Taxes*. Ann Arbor, MI: University of Michigan Press.

Braithwaite, V. (1998) "Communal and exchange trust norms: Their value base and relevance to institutional trust", in V. Braithwaite and M. Levi (eds.), *Trust and Governance*. New York, NY: Russel Sage Foundation.

Braithwaite, V. (ed.) (2003) *Taxing Democracy*, Aldershot, UK: Ashgate.

Braithwaite, V. (ed.) (2007) Special Issue on Responsive Regulation and Taxation, *Law and Policy*, 29 (1).

Buchanan, J. M. (1976) "Taxation in fiscal exchange", *Journal of Public Economics*, 6: 17–29.

Buchanan, J. M. (1987) "The constitution of economic policy", *American Economic Review*, 77: 243–50.

Cameron, J. A., Banko, K. M., and Pierce, W. D. (2001) "Pervasive negative effects of rewards on intrinsic motivation: The myth continues", *Behavioral Analyst*, 24: 1–44.

Davis, J. H. (1969) *Group Performance*. Reading, MA.: Addison-Wesley.

Deci, E. L. (1971) "Effects of externally mediated rewards on intrinsic motivation", *Journal of Personality and Social Psychology*, 18: 105–15.

Deci, E. L. and Flaste, R. (1995) *Why We Do What We Do. The Dynamics of Personal Autonomy*. New York, NY: Putnam.

Deci, E. and Ryan, R. M. (1985) *Intrinsic Motivation and Self-Determination in Human Behavior*. New York, NY: Plenum Press.

Deci, E. L., Koestner, R., and Ryan, R. M. (1999) "A meta-analytic review of experiments examining the effects of extrinsic rewards on intrinsic motivation", *Psychological Bulletin*, 125: 627–68.

De Juan, A., Lasheras, M. A., and Mayo, R. (1994) "Voluntary tax compliant behavior of Spanish income taxpayers", *Public Finance*, 49: 90–105.

Diehl, M. and Stroebe, W. (1987) "Productivity loss in brainstorming groups: Towards the solution of a riddle", *Journal of Personality and Social Psychology*, 53: 497–509.

Dubin, J. A. and Wilde, L. L. (1988) "An empirical analysis of federal income tax auditing and compliance", *National Tax Journal*, 41: 61–74.

Dubin, J. A., Graetz, M. J., and Wilde, L. L. (1987) "Are we a nation of tax cheaters? New econometric evidence on tax compliance", *American Economic Review*, 77: 240–5.

Dubin, J. A., Graetz, M. J., and Wilde, L. L. (1992) "State income tax amnesties: Causes", *Quarterly Journal of Economics*, 107: 1057–70.

Ekland-Olson, S., Lieb, J., and Zurcher, L. (1984) "The paradoxical impact of criminal sanctions: Some microstructural findings", *Law and Society* Review, 18: 159–78.

Elffers, H., Weigel, R. H., and Hessing, D. J. (1987) "The consequences of different strategies for measuring tax evasion behavior", *Journal of Economic Psychology*, 8: 311–37.

Falk, A. and Kosfeld, M. (2006) "The hidden costs of control", *American Economic Review*, 96: 1611–30.

Falkinger, J. and Walther, H. (1991) "Rewards versus penalties: On a new policy against tax evasion", *Public Finance Quarterly*, 19: 67–79.

Fehr, E., Gächter, S., and Kirchsteiger, G. (1997) "Reciprocity as a contract enforcement device", *Econometrica*, 65: 833–60.

Feld, L. P. (2003) "Rückführung von fluchtkapital als voraussetzung für den fiskalischen erfolg einer abgeltungssteuer?", in G. Schick (ed.), *Veranlagung – Abgeltung – Steuerfreiheit: Besteuerung von Kapitalerträgen im Rechtsstaat*, Berlin: Stiftung Marktwirtschaft/Frankfurter Institut.

Feld, L. P. and Frey, B. S. (2002a) "The tax authority and the taxpayer: An exploratory analysis", unpublished manuscript, University of Zurich.

Feld, L. P. and Frey, B. S. (2002b) "Trust breeds trust: How taxpayers are treated", *Economics of Governance*, 3: 87–99.

Feld, L. P. and Frey, B. S. (2007) "Tax compliance as the result of a psychological tax contract: The role of incentives and responsive regulation", *Law and Policy*, 29: 102–20.

Feld, L. P. and Kirchgässner, G. (2000) "Direct democracy, political culture and the outcome of economic policy: A report on the Swiss experience", *European Journal of Political Economy*, 16: 287–306.

Feld, L. P. and Tyran, J. R. (2002) "Tax evasion and voting: An experimental analysis", *Kyklos*, 55: 197–22.

Frey, B. S. (1976) "Taxation in fiscal exchange – A comment", *Journal of Public Economics*, 6: 31–5.

Frey, B. S. (1997a) *Not Just for The Money. An Economic Theory of Personal Motivation*. Cheltenham. UK: Edward Elgar.

Frey, B. S. (1997b) "A constitution for knaves crowds out civic virtues", *Economic Journal*, 107: 1043–53.

Frey, B. S. and Feld, L. P. (2002) "Deterrence and morale in taxation: An empirical analysis", CESifo Working Paper No. 760, August 2002.

Frey, B. S. and Jegen, R. (2001) "Motivation crowding theory: A survey of empirical evidence", *Journal of Economic Surveys*, 15: 589–611.

Friedland, N. (1982) "A note on tax evasion as a function of the quality of information about the magnitude and credibility of threatened fines: Some preliminary research", *Journal of Applied Social Psychology*, 12: 54–9.

Friedland, N., Maital, S., and Rutenberg, A. (1978) "A simulation study of income tax evasion", *Journal of Public Economics* 10: 107–16.

Gerber, E. R. (1999) *The Populist Paradox: Interest Group Influence and the Promise of Direct Legislation*, Princeton, NJ: Princeton University Press.

Gneezy, U. and Rustichini, A. (2000) "A fine is a price", *Journal of Legal Studies*, 29: 1–17.

Graetz, M. J. and Wilde, L. L. (1985) "The economics of tax compliance: Facts and fantasy", *National Tax Journal*, 38: 355–63.

Grasmick, H. G. and Bursick, R. J. (1990) "Conscience, significant others, and rational choice: Extending the deterrence model", *Law and Society Review*, 24: 837–61.

Güth, W. and Mackscheidt, K. (1985) "Die erforschung der steuermoral", Working Paper, University of Cologne.

Güth, W., Levati, V., and Sausgruber, R. (2005) "Tax morale and (de-)centralization: An experimental study", *Public Choice*, 125: 171–88.

Hasseldine, J. (1998) "Tax amnesties: An international review", *Bulletin for International Fiscal Documentation*, 52: 303–10.

Hörisch, H. and Strassmair, C. (2008) "An experimental test of the deterrence hypothesis", unpublished manuscript, University of Munich.

Kinsey, K. A. and Grasmick, H. G. (1993) "Did the tax reform act of 1986 improve compliance? Three studies of pre- and post-TRA compliance attitudes", *Law and Policy*, 15: 239–325.

Kirchler, E. (1999) "Reactance to taxation: Employers' attitudes towards taxes", *Journal of Socio-Economics*, 28: 131–8.

Kirchler, E. (2007) *The Economic Psychology of Tax Behaviour*. Cambridge, UK: Cambridge University Press.

Klepper, S. and Nagin, D. (1989) "Tax compliance and perceptions of the risks of detection and criminal prosecution", *Law and Society Review*, 23: 209–40.

Lane, R. E. (1991) *The Market Experience*. Cambridge, UK: Cambridge University Press.

Le Borgne, E. (2006) "Economic and political determinants of tax amnesties in the US States", in National Tax Association (ed.), *Proceedings of the 98rd Annual Conference 2005*, Washington, DC.

Le Grand, J. (2003) *Motivation, Agency, and Public Policy. Of Knights and Knaves, Pawns and Queens*. Oxford, UK: Oxford University Press.

Lepper, M. R. and Greene, D. (eds.) (1978) *The Hidden Costs of Reward: New Perspectives on Psychology of Human Motivation*. Hillsdale, NY: Erlbaum.

Levi, M. (1988) *Of Rule and Revenue*. Berkeley, CA: University of California Press.

Luitel, H. S. and Sobel, R. S. (2007) "The revenue impact of repeated tax amnesties", *Public Budgeting and Finance*, 27: 19–38.

Mackscheidt, K. (1984) "Konsolidierung durch erhöhung von steuern und abgaben?", in H. Herbert von Arnim and K. Littmann (eds.), *Finanzpolitik im Umbruch: Zur Konsolidierung öffentlicher Haushalte*, Berlin: Duncker and Humblot.

Makkai, T. and Braithwaite, J. (1994) "Reintegrative shaming and regulatory compliance", *Criminology*, 32: 361–85.

Martinez-Vazquez, J. and Rider, M. (2005) "Multiple modes of tax evasion: Theory and evidence", *National Tax Journal*, 58: 51–76.

Musgrave, R. A. (1939) "The voluntary exchange theory of public economy", *Quarterly Journal of Economics*, 53: 213–37.

Osterloh, M. and Frey, B. S. (2000) "Motivation, knowledge transfer and organizational forms", *Organization Science*, 11: 538–50.

Pittman, T. S. and Heller, J. F. (1987) "Social motivation", *Annual Review of Psychology*, 38: 461–89.

Pommerehne, W. W. (1978) "Institutional approaches to public expenditure: Empirical evidence from Swiss municipalities", *Journal of Public Economics*, 9: 255–80.

Pommerehne, W. W. and Frey, B. S. (1992) "The effects of tax administration on tax morale", unpublished manuscript, University of Zurich.

Pommerehne, W. W. and Weck-Hannemann, H. (1996) "Tax rates, tax administration and income tax evasion in Switzerland", *Public Choice*, 88: 161–70.

Pommerehne, W. W. and Zweifel, P. (1991) "Success of a tax amnesty: At the poll, for the fisc?", *Public Choice*, 72: 131–65.

Pommerehne, W. W., Hart, A., and Frey, B. S. (1994) "Tax morale, tax evasion and the choice of policy instruments in different political systems", *Public Finance*, 49 (Supplement: *Public Finance and Irregular Activities*): 52–69.

Porcano, T. M. (1988) "Correlates of tax evasion", *Journal of Economic Psychology*, 9: 47–67.

Roberts, M. L. and Hite, P. A. (1994) "Progressive taxation, fairness and compliance", *Law and Policy*, 16: 27–47.

Rousseau, D. M. and McLean Parks, J. (1993) "The contracts of individuals and organizations", *Research in Organizational Behavior*, 15: 1–43.

Sandmo, A. (2006) "The theory of tax evasion: A retrospective view", *National Tax Journal*, 58: 643–63.

Schein, E. H. (1965) *Organization Psychology*. Englewood Cliffs, NJ: Prentice-Hall.

Scholz, J. T. and Lubell, M. (1998) "Trust and taxpayers: Testing the heuristic approach to collective action", *American Journal of Political Science*, 42: 398–17.

Scholz, J. T. and Lubell, M. (2001) "Cooperation, reciprocity and the collective action heuristic", *American Journal of Political Science*, 45: 160–78.

Scholz, J. T. and Pinney, N. (1995) "Duty, fear, and tax compliance: The heuristic basis of citizenship behavior", *American Journal of Political Science*, 39: 490–512.

Schwartz, R. D. and Orleans, S. (1967) "On legal sanctions", *University of Chicago Law Review*, 34: 282–300.

Scott, W. J. and Grasmick, H. G. (1981) "Deterrence and income tax cheating: Testing interaction hypotheses in utilitarian theories", *Journal of Applied Behavioral Science*, 17: 395–408.

Skinner, B. F. (1948) *Walden Two*. New York, NY: MacMillan.

Skinner, B. F. (1953) *Science and Human Behavior*. New York, NY: MacMillan.

Skinner, J. S. and Slemrod, J. (1985) "An economic perspective on tax evasion", *National Tax Journal*, 38: 345–53.

Slemrod, J. (2007) "Cheating ourselves: The economics of tax evasion", *Journal of Economic Perspectives*, 21(1): 25–48.

Slemrod, J. and Yitzhaki, S. (2002) "Tax avoidance, evasion and administration", in A. J. Auerbach and M. Feldstein (eds.), *Handbook of Public Economics*, Vol. 3, Amsterdam: North-Holland.

Slemrod, J., Blumenthal, M., and Christian, C. W. (2001) "Taxpayer response to an increased probability of audit: Evidence from a controlled experiment in Minnesota", *Journal of Public Economics*, 79: 455–83.

Smith, K. W. and Stalans, L. J. (1991) "Encouraging tax compliance with positive incentives: A conceptual framework and research directions", *Law and Policy*, 13: 35–53.

Spicer, M. W. and Becker, L. A. (1980) "Fiscal inequity and tax evasion: An experimental approach", *National Tax Journal*, 33: 171–5.

Spicer, M. W. and Lundstedt, S. B. (1976) "Understanding tax evasion", *Public Finance*, 31: 295–305.

Torgler, B. (2005) "Tax morale and direct democracy", *European Journal of Political Economy*, 21: 525–31.

Torgler, B. (2007) *Tax Compliance and Morale. A Theoretical and Empirical Analysis.* Cheltenham, UK: Edward Elgar.

Torgler, B. and Schaltegger, C. (2005) "Tax amnesties and political participation", *Public Finance Review*, 33: 403–1.

Tyler, T. R. (1990) *Why People Obey the Law*. New Haven, CT: Yale University Press.

Varma, K. N. and Doob, A. N. (1998) "Deterring economic crimes: The case of tax evasion", *Canadian Journal of Criminology*, 40: 165–84.

Wenzel, M. (2004) "The social side of sanctions: Personal and social norms as moderators of deterrence", *Law and Human Behavior*, 28: 547–67.

Wicksell, K. (1896) *Finanztheoretische Untersuchungen nebst Darstellung und Kritik des Steuerwesens Schwedens*, Jena: Gustav Fischer.

Witte, E. H. (1989) "Köhler rediscovered: The anti-Ringelmann effect", *European Journal of Social Psychology*, 19: 147–54.

Part IV

Empirical evidence on financial incentives

6 A meta-analysis of incentive effects in tax compliance experiments

Calvin Blackwell[1]

Introduction

Since 1978, economists, psychologists, sociologists, and accountants have used experiments to investigate the determinants of tax compliance. Numerous experimental treatments have been tested, including economic incentive effects (such as changing the probability of audit, the severity of the fine for non-compliance, or the tax rate) and more psychological effects (for example, the use of "neutral" terminology instead of tax terminology, or appeals to morality). This chapter adds to the existing survey literature on tax compliance (see Andreoni *et al.*, 1998, and Slemrod, 2007) by using a meta-analysis to test some of the traditional incentive-effect hypotheses regarding tax compliance.

A compelling argument for a need to combine data from multiple studies is made by Goldfarb (1995). He argues that economists need a "methodology of Plausible Inference (MPI)", and suggests that economists should use meta-analysis as that MPI. The advantages of meta-analysis are evident in the increasing number of such studies appearing in the economics literature.[2] Meta-analysis allows for a large increase in power – an important consideration in experimental research. This increase in power comes from two sources: increased number of data points, and an increased variability in the dependent variables. Because data are relatively expensive to collect, experimentalists collect as little as possible, which means the power of any particular study will be small. By combining studies, meta-analysis increases the power of statistical tests to detect significant results. If reviewers use significance as a criterion, then many low-power studies showing little or no significance will cause the reviewer to conclude no effect of the particular treatment. However, a properly done meta-analysis will be able to combine the results of these small samples into one large sample, and take advantage of the increase in power to test for the hypothesized effect. An additional advantage of a meta-analysis on experiments is that multiple treatment effects can be examined. For example, a typical experimental paper might examine the impact of having a fine rate of two or four, while a second paper might look at fine rates of three and five. Combining the data from these two studies increases the variability in the independent variables, and allows for more powerful statistical tests.

In this chapter I will examine the impacts of the tax rate, the fine rate, the probability of audit, and the marginal-per-capita return to the public good upon tax compliance. The data set used for this analysis consists of all the research papers written in the economics and accounting literature that address this issue with an experiment. I show that the theoretical predictions made regarding the impact of the fine rate, the probability of audit and the marginal-per-capita return to the public good are confirmed. I also show that although most experimental papers examining the effect of the tax rate upon compliance find a negative relationship, this relationship is not statistically significant. This indeterminate relationship is consistent with the theoretical prediction.

Data

The two primary criteria for inclusion in this meta-analysis were as follows:

1   The study must have used an experimental design – i.e., a controlled environment with multiple treatments.
2   The study must report an average level of tax compliance by treatment effect. Tax compliance must be observable directly – i.e., no reports of compliance behavior, but measurable compliance behavior.

The data for this study consist of 26 experimental studies. The papers used are listed in Table 6.1. The search process for these studies was as follows. I first performed a keyword search of ECONLit on the terms "tax compliance" and "tax evasion", and found abstracts that seemed to describe experimental papers. I procured all these papers, and kept the ones that fit my criteria. I also searched the five most recent issues of the *Journal of Economic Literature* for recent papers on these topics, and kept those that fit my criteria. I then searched the reference sections/bibliographies of all the papers deemed acceptable for inclusion in the meta-analysis for other experimental papers, and procured those papers. This searching of bibliographies was recursive – all bibliographies were searched until all possible papers had been discovered.

A typical tax compliance experiment

The general design of the compliance experiments has several common elements.

Subjects: Generally student subjects were used, although occasionally tax professionals or adults were used. Subjects came from the United States, Central America, Europe and Israel.

Incentives: Subjects may have been unpaid, or paid only a show-up fee, or paid a show-up fee and paid for their performance in the experiment.

Setting: Experiments were run using simply a pencil and paper, or in a computer environment. The instructions used either a tax frame (similar to a standard tax form) or a neutral frame that does not use tax-related terminology. Sometimes tax compliance was mis-directed, so as not to be a focus of the experiment.

Dependent variables: The amount/percentage of income was reported, the amount/percentage evaded was reported, or a dichotomous variable – did the subject evade or not? – was reported.

Independent variables: The effects of numerous independent variables have been examined, including the tax rate; the penalty rate; the audit probability; the subject's income; the existence and return to a public good; the effect of neutral or contextual instructions; the type of audit "scheme" (exogenous or endogenous, back audits or not, etc.); the existence of amnesty; the effect of framing the decision problem as a loss or gain; uncertainty regarding the subject's true income, tax rate, penalty rate and audit probability; collective decision making about any of the above; and equity.

Co-variates: Measured covariates have included the subject's age, income, sex, and risk-preference

Researchers: Economists, psychologists, accountants and lawyers have all run experiments investigating tax compliance.

The basic framework of the type of experiment considered is as follows. Subjects are asked to make a decision regarding their own tax compliance given a set of circumstances. Only experiments in which subjects decide their own level of compliance are considered – many experiments ask for other types of choices to be made, and those experiments are not part of this analysis.[3] In a typical experiment, subjects are presented with a set of circumstances and asked to make a decision. This decision is typically to report some amount of income to the tax agency, or to fully comply or evade in a particular scenario. Most experiments use the model presented in Allingham and Sandmo (1972) and the Yitzhaki (1974) model as the basis for the experimental setting.

Allingham and Sandmo/Yitzhaki tax compliance model

In the Allingham and Sandmo (1972) model, and as slightly modified by Yitzhaki (1974),[4] the taxpayer's choice variable is declared income. Taxpayers are assumed to maximize expected utility.[5] There are two possible states of the world – the taxpayer is audited, or the taxpayer is not audited. Using the following variables:

x = declared income
y = true income
t = tax rate owed on declared income, $0 \le t \le 1$
p = probability of audit, $0 \le p \le 1$
f = fine rate applied to unpaid taxes, $f \ge 1$
U = utility function over wealth position[6]

if the taxpayer is not audited, his or her wealth is:

W_{NA} = Wealth if not audited
$W_{NA} = y - tx$

if the taxpayer is audited, his or her wealth is:

W_A = Wealth if audited
$W_A = y - tx - ft(y - x)$

The taxpayer expected utility:

$$\max_x EU = (1 - p)U(W_{NA}) + pU(W_A)$$

This maximization yields the following first-order condition:

$$U'(W_A)/U'(W_{NA}) = (1 - p)/p(f - 1)$$

This model indicates that any risk averse taxpayer should evade some positive amount if:

$$pf < 1 \tag{1}$$

Given equation (1) is true, an increase in p will cause compliance to rise, as will an increase in f. Yitzhaki (1974) shows that an increase in the tax rate will cause a decrease in tax evasion.

This basic model can be (and has been) altered. In particular, Allingham and Sandmo (1972) examined the impact of allowing the probability of detection to be a function of declared income. A more general model might allow for some (or all) of the following possibilities:

$$p = p(y, x) \tag{2}$$

$$t = t(x) \tag{3}$$

$$f = f(y, x) \tag{4}$$

These possibilities make the probability of audit a function of "true" income and declared income, make the taxes owed a more complex function of declared income (e.g., a progressive income tax), and make the penalty rate a more complex function of undeclared income.

Later work has further added to the model's complexity. Some, like Cowell (1981), have included labor supply in the tax compliance decision, or added public goods to the model. Generally, as the models become more complex, it becomes more difficult to make predictions about the effects of the tax rate, the probability of audit, or the fine rate upon compliance.

Hypotheses

The experiments analyzed in this chapter all create an environment broadly consistent with the basic Allingham and Sandmo model (1972). When models incorporating equations (2), (3), and (4) are used, some of the comparative statics change. This change is most evident with regards to the effect of increasing the tax rate on compliance. The basic Allingham and Sandmo (1972) model makes an ambiguous prediction, while Yitzhaki's (1974) model makes the counter-intuitive prediction that higher taxes lead to higher compliance. Other versions of the model also make ambiguous predictions (see, for example, Cowell, 1981). Given that most of the experiments here follow the Yitzhaki penalty structure (hereafter, the "basic" model), this suggests the following hypothesis (H1):

H1: Increasing the tax rate has a positive effect upon compliance.

Empirical studies provide some counter-evidence against this hypothesis. The earliest study by Clotfelter (1983) found a negative relationship. Andreoni and colleagues (1998) wrote, "A number of other studies have investigated the effects of income and marginal tax rates on evasion. Some of these corroborate the finding of Clotfelter, while others contradict it." Andreoni *et al.* concluded, "In general, therefore, the effect of tax rates on evasion remains unclear. Given the importance of this topic, it surely deserves further investigation."

No matter what modifications are made to the basic model, the probability of audit is always predicted to have a positive relationship with compliance. The basic model makes the following hypothesis (H2):

H2: Increasing the probability of audit has a positive effect upon compliance.

In their summary of the literature, Andreoni and colleagues concluded the empirical evidence supports the claim that increases in the probability of audit increase tax compliance.

The basic model makes a clear prediction regarding fine rate. As the fine-rate rises, compliance should rise. The basic model suggests a test of the following hypothesis (H3):

H3: Increasing the fine rate has a positive effect upon compliance.

Some papers incorporate fiscal exchange into the model via the introduction of a public good. In these experiments tax revenues are used to fund a public good, and the benefits of the public good are returned to the participants. The marginal-per-capita return is typically between 0 and 1, so that a dollar put into the public good returns less than a dollar to the participant, while the social return is typically greater than 1, reflecting the fact that contributing to the public good is Pareto superior to not contributing. Although the Nash equilibrium is typically not to contribute (pay taxes), research on public goods (see Ledyard, 1995, for a survey) suggests a significant portion of subjects will contribute, and that their contributions will vary positively with the marginal-per-capita return. This analysis leads to the following hypothesis (H4):

H4: Increasing the marginal-per-capita return on the public good has a positive effect upon compliance.

Meta-regression analysis

First developed by Glass (1976), a meta-analysis is a statistical analysis of empirical results of prior research. Where it was first developed in psychology and education research, the statistical analysis was applied to estimate the effect size of a particular treatment. Meta-regression analysis, as introduced by Stanley and Jarrell (1989), is used to statistically analyze a common parameter estimate (γ), such as the gender wage gap (Stanley and Jarrell, 2005), the size of the inefficiency "gap" created by oligopoly (Engel, 2007), the income turning point for an environmental Kuznets' curve (Li *et al.*, 2007), or an exchange rate (Egert and Halpern, 2006). A meta-regression analysis then uses the various estimates made by different research studies as its inputs to estimate:

$$g_j = \gamma + \sum_{k=1}^{K} \alpha_k Z_{jk} + e_j \quad (j = 1, 2, ...L) \tag{5}$$

where g_j is the reported estimate of γ of the jth study in a literature comprised of L studies, γ is the "true" value of the parameter of interest, Z_{jk} is the meta-independent variables that measure relevant characteristics of a study and explain its variation from other studies, α_k is the meta-regression coefficients, and e_j is the meta-regression error term (Stanley and Jarrell, 1989). Stanley, Doucouliagos, and Jarrell (2008) suggest numerous variables that should be considered in Z_{jk}, including measures of each study's accuracy, model specification characteristics, or characteristics of the author or data.

In the studies examined here, the most commonly reported statistic (and hence the most useful statistic for conducting a meta-analysis) is the average compliance rate (x, the mean level of declared income, measured as a proportion of true income) for each treatment in the study. For example, Alm *et al.* (1992a) used a 2×4 experimental design, with one variable being the presence of a public good, and the second variable being uncertainty regarding the tax rate, the fine rate or the probability of audit. Their design produced eight treatment means (i.e., eight average compliance rates). Given the data set consists of these treatment means, the natural analog of equation (5) is:

$$x_{j\tau} = \beta_0 + \beta_1 t_{j\tau} + \beta_2 f_{j\tau} + \beta_3 p_{j\tau} + \beta_4 p_{j\tau} f_{j\tau} + \beta_5 \alpha_{j\tau} + \beta_6 pos_{j\tau} + \beta_7 neg_{j\tau} + \delta_i + \varepsilon_{j\tau} \tag{6}$$

where

$x_{j\tau}$ = mean level of declared income (measured as a proportion of true income) for treatment τ in paper j

$t_{j\tau}$ = tax rate on declared income for treatment τ in paper j

$p_{j\tau}$ = probability of audit for treatment τ in paper j

$f_{j\tau}$ = penalty rate on undeclared income for treatment τ in paper j

$p_{j\tau} f_j$ = interaction term between the probability of audit and the penalty rate

$\alpha_{j\tau}$ = marginal-per-capita return to the public good for treatment τ in paper j

$pos_{j\tau}$ = a dummy variable taking the value of 1 if there is a factor that should increase compliance relative to the basic model and 0 otherwise for treatment τ in paper j

neg$_{j\tau}$ = a dummy variable taking the value of 1 if there is a factor that should decrease compliance relative to the basic model and 0 otherwise for treatment τ in paper *j*

δ = an unobservable component unique to paper *j*, which will be modeled as a random or fixed effect.

$\varepsilon_{j\tau}$ = a normally distributed error term with mean zero and standard deviation σ associated with each treatment τ in paper *j*.

This model is analogous to equation (5) in that there are variables to control for treatment effects (*t*, *p*, etc.) and also to control for researcher effects (δ). As noted above, Stanley *et al.* (2008) suggest that a control for quality be included. Ideally, I would use the standard error of the treatment mean to control for quality (and for heteroscedasticity), but I do not have access to this information for many of the studies. Instead I estimate equation (6) with weights (the inverse of the square root of the sample size) to control for study quality and heteroscedasticity.

Note that I include the interaction term *pf* in equation (6) because the basic model indicates that for risk averse taxpayers, this interaction term creates a threshold effect. Equation (1) illustrates this relationship.

The variables *pos* and *neg* are used in an attempt to capture additional treatment effects in a parsimonious way. Instead of creating a dummy variable for each possible treatment used in these experiments, I made the decision to "fold" the less frequent treatment effects into these two variables. For example, the existence of an endogenous audits scheme is used as a treatment in several papers.[7] Rather than creating a dummy variable for this treatment effect, I instead chose to note that, compared to the basic model, a model with endogenous audits should increase compliance, and used the *pos* variable to capture this effect. The *neg* variable was used in a similar way for treatment effects that should reduce compliance relative to the basic model.

Results

Twenty-six papers contain usable data for regression analysis; information on these papers is shown in Table 6.1. These papers report values for the following experimental parameters: the proportion of income declared, the tax rate, the probability of audit, the penalty rate, and the marginal per capita return on the public good.

Summary statistics are presented in Table 6.2, and are given using weighted and unweighted observations. The weights used are the inverse of the number of observations in each treatment. Equation (6) is estimated in a variety of ways, the results of which are shown in Tables 6.3–6.5. I estimate equation (6) using OLS, random effects, and fixed effects. I also estimate these models using unweighted and weighted observations. Note that individual intercept terms (δ_i) from the random effects estimation are suppressed in Table 6.5. Table 6.6 presents elasticity estimates of the average compliance rate with respect to the tax rate, the fine rate, and the probability of audit for each of the respective models.

Table 6.1 Number of observations in each paper

Authors	Date	# Treatments	# Rounds	# Subject-rounds
Friedland, Shlomo, Rutenberg	1978	4	4	240
Spicer, Becker	1980	3	10	570
Friedland	1982	16	1	240
Webley, Halstead	1986	15	8	256
Webley	1987	4	2	184
Beck, Davis, Jung	1991	16	30	13,440
Alm, Jackson, McKee	1992a	8	25	9,000
Alm, Jackson, McKee	1992b	8	15	3,000
Alm, Jackson, McKee	1992c	3	20	1,125
Alm, McClelland, Schulze	1992d	9	25	3,240
Alm, Cronshaw, McKee	1993a	8	6	1,600
Alm, Jackson, McKee	1993b	5	18	1,875
Alm, Sanchez, De Juan	1995	14	18*	4,446
Callihan, Spindle	1997	1	1	39
Alm, McClelland, Schulze	1999	42	10	4,260
Wartick, Madeo, Vines	1999	4	14	1,260
Feld, Tyran	2002	6	1	264
Kim	2002	4	8	368
Torgler	2003	4	2	74
Alm, Mckee	2004	2	25	500
Clark, Friesen, Muller	2004	18	10	6,920
Güth, Strauss, Sutter	2005	1	12	576
Cadsby, Maynes, Trivedi	2006	10	1	305
Cullis, Jones, Lewis	2006	6	1	1,617
Cummings, Martinez-Vazquez, McKee	2006	16	24	8,352
Mittone	2006	8	15	1,845
Sum		235		65,596

Note
*18 is the average number of rounds for this paper. Some subjects participated in 6 rounds, some in 18 rounds and some in 36 rounds.

Table 6.2 Summary statistics

Variable	Unweighted mean	Unweighted standard deviation	Weighted* mean	Weighted* standard deviation	Minimum	Maximum
x	0.559	0.288	0.591	0.301	0.01	1.275
t	0.341	0.136	0.345	0.090	0.1	1
f	4.092	4.275	3.142	3.741	0	25
p	0.229	0.226	0.231	0.224	0	1
α	0.069	0.130	0.065	0.136	0	0.75
pf	0.662	0.754	0.452	0.537	0	3.766
pos	0.328	0.471	0.302	0.459	0	1
neg	0.098	0.298	0.054	0.226	0	1

Note
*The weights are the inverse of the number of observations associated with that particular treatment.

Table 6.3 Regression estimates: OLS

Variable	Model 1 estimate (Unweighted)	Model 2 estimate (Unweighted)	Model 3 estimate (Unweighted)	Model 4 estimate (Weighted)	Model 5 estimate (Weighted)	Model 6 estimate (Weighted)
Constant	0.470ᶜ (0.049)	0.446ᶜ (0.050)	0.451ᶜ (0.051)	0.313ᶜ (0.060)	0.314ᶜ (0.061)	0.320ᶜ (0.063)
t	-0.271 (0.139)	-0.144 (0.151)	-0.250 (0.155)	0.169 (0.169)	0.166 (0.175)	0.175 (0.178)
f	0.012ᵇ (0.004)	0.006 (0.005)	0.008 (0.005)	0.006 (0.004)	0.006 (0.005)	0.006 (0.005)
p	0.762ᶜ (0.082)	0.571ᶜ (0.123)	0.609ᶜ (0.123)	0.907ᶜ (0.072)	0.912ᶜ (0.100)	0.908ᶜ (0.101)
α	-0.645ᶜ (0.132)	-0.579ᶜ (0.135)	-0.484ᶜ (0139)	-0.125 (0.113)	-0.126 (0.040)	-0.144 (0.118)
pf		0.068ᵃ (0.033)	0.055 (0.033)		-0.003 (0.040)	-0.002 (0.040)
pos			0.080ᵃ (0.035)			-0.021 (0.033)
neg			-0.068 (0.053)			-0.009 (0.066)
R^2	0.318	0.331	0.350	0.467	0.467	0.468
$Adj. R^2$	0.306	0.316	0.330	0.458	0.456	0.452
F	26.84ᶜ	22.65ᶜ	17.49ᶜ	50.43ᶜ	40.17ᶜ	28.56ᶜ

Notes
*Standard errors are in parentheses.
a indicates significance at the 5% level.
b indicates significance at the 1% level.
c indicates significance at the 0.1% level.

Table 6.4 Regression estimates: random effects MLE

Variable	Model 1 estimate (Unweighted)	Model 2 estimate (Unweighted)	Model 3 estimate (Unweighted)	Model 4 estimate (Weighted)	Model 5 estimate (Weighted)	Model 6 estimate (Weighted)
Constant	0.414c (0.073)	0.440c (0.068)	0.446c (0.067)	0.334c (0.061)	0.368c (0.061)	0.384c (0.062)
t	-0.236 (0.142)	-0.166 (0.134)	-0.282a (0.128)	0.054 (0.137)	0.088 (0.131)	0.044 (0.131)
f	0.013c (0.003)	0.004 (0.004)	0.004 (0.004)	0.012b (0.004)	0.001 (0.005)	0.001 (0.005)
p	0.800c (0.071)	0.420c (0.108)	0.476c (0.102)	0.846c (0.066)	0.508c (0.106)	0.512c (0.105)
α	0.138 (0.131)	0.165 (0.124)	0.219 (0.117)	0.189a (0.086)	0.205a (0.083)	0.230b (0.083)
pf		0.113c (0.025)	0.100c (0.025)		0.123c (0.030)	0.121c (0.030)
pos			0.104c (0.033)			0.037 (0.023)
neg			-0.112c (0.067)			-0.081 (0.044)
Wald				460.43c	484.44c	485.64c
lnL	84.867	94.586	107.992	-553.492	-545.674	-542.589
LR	110.30c	129.74c	156.55c			

Notes
*Standard errors are in parentheses.
a indicates significance at the 5% level.
b indicates significance at the 1% level.
c indicates significance at the 0.1% level.

Table 6.5 Regression estimates: fixed effects

Variable	Model 1 estimate (Unweighted)	Model 2 estimate (Unweighted)	Model 3 estimate (Unweighted)	Model 4 estimate (Weighted)	Model 5 estimate (Weighed)	Model 6 estimate (Weighted)
t	−0.054 (0.151)	−0.046 (0.146)	−0.189 (0.141)	0.541 (0.140)	0.057 (0.134)	−0.010 (0.132)
f	0.013[c] (0.003)	0.005 (0.004)	0.004 (0.04)	0.016[c] (0.005)	0.003 (0.005)	0.001 (0.005)
p	0.854[c] (0.073)	0.497[c] (0.118)	0.539[c] (0.111)	0.848[c] (0.068)	0.452[c] (0.110)	0.466[c] (0.107)
α	0.279[a] (0.133)	0.277[a] (0.129)	0.309[a] (0.122)	0.250[b] (0.086)	0.255[b] (0.083)	0.286[c] (0.082)
pf		0.101[c] (0.027)	0.090[c] (0.025)		0.137[c] (0.031)	0.134[c] (0.030)
pos			0.107[c] (0.026)			0.047[a] (0.023)
neg			−0.113[b] (0.034)			−0.140[b] (0.046)
F	38.35[c]	35.63[c]	32.72[c]	35.75[c]	38.44[c]	38.73[c]

Notes
* Standard errors are in parentheses.
a indicates significance at the 5% level.
b indicates significance at the 1% level.
c indicates significance at the 0.1% level.

Table 6.6 Elasticity estimates for all models

Model type	Model #	Elasticity estimate for t	Elasticity estimate for f	Elasticity estimate for p
OLS regression	1	−0.165	0.088	0.312
	2	−0.088	0.044	0.234
	3	−0.153	0.059	0.249
	4	0.099	0.032	0.355
	5	0.097	0.032	0.356
	6	0.102	0.032	0.355
Random effects MLE	1	−0.144	0.095	0.328
	2	−0.101	0.029	0.172
	3	−0.172	0.029	0.195
	4	0.032	0.064	0.331
	5	0.051	0.005	0.199
	6	0.026	0.005	0.200
Fixed effects	1	−0.033	0.095	0.350
	2	−0.028	0.037	0.204
	3	−0.115	0.029	0.221
	4	0.316	0.085	0.331
	5	0.033	0.016	0.177
	6	−0.006	0.005	0.182

Although I present the OLS results here, all tests for either random or fixed effects indicate either of these two models are preferred. The OLS estimates are generally less significant, suggesting that controlling for across-paper variability is important. Tests to determine the appropriateness of random effects versus fixed effects could not be run due to the nature of the data (specifically, the fact that the data are a highly unbalanced panel). However, the estimated coefficients from the fixed effects and random effects models are not qualitatively different.

From the regression results, hypotheses two, three, and four can be tested. The first hypothesis is not supported by my results. It does not appear that raising the tax rate consistently increases or decreases compliance. Depending upon the model, the estimated coefficient on tax rate is either positive or negative (generally the unweighted models estimate a positive tax rate effect, while the weighted models estimate a negative tax rate effect), but it is significantly different from zero in only model 3 with random effects. There appears to be little support for hypothesis one.

Hypothesis two receives strong support. In every model, the estimated coefficient on p is positive and highly statistically significant. Hypothesis three also receives support, but in a qualified manner. The coefficient on f is positive and statistically significant in models that omit the interaction term pf. When the interaction term is introduced, the coefficient on f becomes insignificant. This result could occur because of collinearity between f and pf, but we do not observe such an impact of p, which should also be somewhat collinear with pf. The positive coefficient on the pf parameter indicates that raising the fine rate will increase compliance, but it does not appear to have as dramatic an effect as raising the probability of detection. One interpretation of this result is that the fine rate is important in effecting compliance when the probability of audit is sufficiently high that taxpayers are concerned about being caught, but if the probability of being caught is low, then the penalty rate has little effect because taxpayers do not expect to be caught.

Hypothesis four receives support; the coefficient on α is generally positive and statistically significant when estimated by either fixed or random effects. This result is consistent with the vast literature on public goods.

The results regarding these four hypotheses hold whether I include the *pos* and *neg* variables or not. These variables were included to capture other aspects of the experiments that have an impact on compliance but do not directly change $t, p, f,$ or α. The estimated coefficients on *pos* and *neg* are generally of the correct sign and significant. Goodness of fit tests and also likelihood ratio tests indicate that these variables ought to be included in the statistical model.

Conclusion

The experimental tax compliance literature unambiguously shows that raising either the fine rate or the probability of audit will increase tax compliance. The theory of fiscal exchange receives support; increasing the return received from contributing to the public good increases tax compliance. This data set does not return clear results as to the impact of raising the tax rate on tax compliance.

Clearly, more research is needed regarding the effect of tax rates upon compliance. This issue has important implications for tax policy, and, as the state of the literature is confused (results conflict both in experiments and from field data), more research must be done. Raising the stakes in an experiment (so that monetary incentives more closely approximate those found in the real world) would seem to be a next step, so as to more accurately measure the tax rate elasticity of compliance.

Other variables play a role in tax compliance, and these variables have been examined in multiple papers, making them excellent candidates for future meta-analyses. In this chapter these factors were controlled by using the *pos* and *neg* variables, but direct measurement and control of factors like the audit scheme (endogenous or exogenous audit selection), uncertainty regarding some or all of the parameters, equity, sex, income, the type of incentives used in the experiment, and the framing of the experiment (neutral or with tax terminology) will become possible as the experimental literature on tax compliance grows.

Notes

1 I would like to thank Spencer Banzhaf, Gary Charness and Paul Ferraro, as well as participants at the 2002 Public Choice Conference, the 2002 Southern Economic Association Conference and the 2007 Tax Compliance Conference at Georgia State University for their many helpful comments. All mistakes are the author's alone.
2 An ECONLit search in December 2007 on meta-analysis yielded 316 papers.

3 For example, Pei *et al.* (1992) examined experimentally the impact of client's preferences upon tax professionals' advice to that client. Although this paper describes an
experiment, the experimental subjects were not asked about their own compliance
behavior; therefore, this paper is not included in my analysis.

4 Allingham and Sandmo's (1972) model assumes only that the fine rate is a function of
undeclared income. Yitzhaki (1974) makes the penalty paid by a tax evader a multiple
of the unpaid taxes.

5 Although in the model taxpayers are assumed to maximize utility, given the small
stakes gambles involved in the experiments, a useful simplification is to assume subjects maximize earnings. See Starmer (2000) for a good review of issues involving
expected utility.

6 Assume the individual is risk averse, or $U' > 0$, $U'' < 0$.

7 An example of this type of paper is Clark *et al.* (2004). The authors investigate a conditional audit scheme that places taxpayers in different "pools." These pools have different fine rates and probabilities of audits. Because the regulatory authority moves
taxpayers from one pool to another on the basis of their compliance behavior (the
more a taxpayer complies, the more likely that taxpayer is to move into a low-fine,
low-probability pool), taxpayers have a stronger incentive to comply than under the
basic model.

Bibliography

Allingham, M. and Sandmo, A. (1972) "Income tax evasion: A theoretical analysis",
Journal of Public Economics, 1: 323–38.

Alm, J. and McKee, M. (2004) "Tax compliance as a coordination game", *Journal of
Economic Behavior and Organization*, 54: 297–312.

Alm, J., Cronshaw, M. B., and McKee, M. (1993a) "Tax compliance with endogenous
audit selection rules", *Kyklos*, 46: 27–45.

Alm, J., Jackson, B., and McKee, M. (1992a) "Institutional uncertainty and taxpayer compliance", *American Economic Review*, 82: 1018–26.

——. (1992b) "Estimating the determinants of taxpayer compliance with experimental
data", *National Tax Journal*, 45: 107–14.

——. (1992c) "Deterrence and beyond: Toward a kinder, gentler IRS", in J. Slemrod
(ed.), *Why People Pay taxes: Tax Compliance and Enforcement*, Ann Arbor, MI: University of Michigan Press.

——. (1993b) "Fiscal exchange, collective decision institutions and tax compliance",
Journal of Economic Behavior and Organization, 22: 285–303.

Alm, J., McClelland, G. H., and Schulze, W. D. (1992d) "Why do people pay taxes?",
Journal of Public Economics, 48: 21–38.

Alm, J., McClelland, G. H., and Schulze, W. D. (1999) "Changing the social norm of tax
compliance by voting", *Kyklos*, 52: 141–71.

Alm, J., Sanchez, I., and De Juan, A. (1995) "Economic and non-economic factors in tax
compliance", *Kyklos*, 48: 3–18.

Andreoni, J., Erard, B., and Feinstein, J. (1998) "Tax compliance", *Journal of Economic
Literature*, 36: 818–60.

Beck, P. J., Davis, J. S., and Jung, W. (1991) "Experimental evidence on taxpayer reporting under uncertainty", *Accounting Review*, 66: 535–58.

Cadbsy, C. B., Maynes, E., and Trivedi, V. U. (2006) "Tax compliance and obedience to
authority at home and in the lab: A new experimental approach", *Experimental Economics*, 9: 343–59.

Callihan, D. S. and Spindle, R. M. (1997) "An examination of contingent and noncontingent rewards in a tax compliance experiment", *Advances in Taxation*, 9: 1–23.

Clark, J., Friesen, L., and Muller, A. (2004) "The good, the bad, and the regulator: An experimental test of two conditional audit schemes", *Economic Inquiry*, 42: 69–87.

Clotfelter, C. T. (1983) "Tax evasion and tax rates: An analysis of individual returns", *Review of Economics and Statistics*, 65: 363–73.

Cowell, F. A. (1981) "Taxation and labour supply with risky activities", *Economica*, 48: 365–79.

Cullis, J., Jones, P., and Lewis, A. (2006) "Tax framing, instrumentality and individual differences: Are there two different cultures?", *Journal of Economic Psychology*, 27: 304–20.

Cummings, R. G., Martinez-Vazquez, J., and McKee, M. (2006) "Experimental evidence on mixing modes in income tax evasion", *Public Finance Review*, 34: 663–86.

Egert, B. and Halpern, L. (2006) "Equilibrium exchange rates in central and eastern Europe: a meta-regression analysis", *Journal of Banking and Finance*, 30: 1359–74.

Engel, C. (2007) "How much collusion? A meta-analysis of oligopoly experiments", *Journal of Competition Law and Economics*, 3: 491–549.

Feld, L. P. and Tyran, R. (2002) "Tax evasion and voting: An experimental analysis", *Kyklos*, 55: 197–222.

Friedland, N. (1982) "A note on tax evasion as a function of the quality of information about the magnitude and credibility of threatened fines: Some preliminary research", *Journal of Applied Social Psychology*, 12: 54–9.

Friedland, N., Shlomo, M., and Rutenberg, A. (1978) "A simulation study of income tax evasion", *Journal of Public Economics*, 10: 107–16.

Glass, G. V. (1976). "Primary, Secondary, and Meta Analysis of Research", *Educational Researcher*, 5: 3–8.

Goldfarb, R. S. (1995) "The economist-as-audience needs a methodology of plausible inference", *Journal of Economic Methodology*, 2: 201–22.

Güth, W., Strauss, S., and Sutter, M. (2005) "Tax evasion and state productivity – An experimental study", *Metroeconomica*, 56: 85–100.

Kim, C. K. (2002) "Does fairness matter in tax reporting behavior?", *Journal of Economic Psychology*, 23: 771–85.

Ledyard, J. O. (1995) "Public goods: A survey of experimental research", in J. H. Kagel and A. E. Roth (eds.), *Handbook of Experimental Economics*, Princeton, NJ: Princeton University Press.

Li, H., Grijalva, T., and Berrens, R. (2007) "Economic growth and environmental quality: a meta-analysis of environmental Kuznets curve studies", *Economics Bulletin* 17: 1–11.

Mittone, L. (2006) "Dynamic behaviour in tax evasion? An experimental approach", *Journal of Socio-Economics*, 35: 813–35.

Pei, K. W. B., Reckers, P. M. J., and Wyndelts, R. W. (1992) "Tax professionals belief revision: The effects of information presentation sequence, client preference and domain experience", *Decision Sciences*, 23: 175–99.

Slemrod, J. (2007) "Cheating ourselves: The economics of tax evasion", *Journal of Economic Perspectives*, 21: 25–48.

Spicer, M. W. and Becker, L. A. (1980) "Fiscal inequity and tax evasion: An experimental approach", *National Tax Journal*, 33: 171–5.

Stanley, T. D. and Jarrell, S. B. (1989). "Meta-regression analysis: a quantitative method of literature surveys", *Journal of Economic Surveys*, 3(2): 161–70.

Stanley, T. D. and Jarrell, S. B. (2005). "Meta-regression analysis: a quantitative method of literature surveys", *Journal of Economic Surveys*, 19(3): 299–308.

Stanley, T. D., Doucouliagos, C., and Jarrell, S. B. (2008). "Meta-regression analysis as the socio-economics of economics research", *Journal of Socio-Economics*, 37(1): 276–92.

Starmer, C. (2000) "Developments in non-expected utility theory: The hunt for a descriptive theory of choice under risk", *Journal of Economic Literature*, 38: 332–82.

Torgler, B. (2003) "Beyond punishment: A tax compliance experiment with taxpayers in Costa Rica", *Revista de Analisis Economico*, 18: 27–56.

Wartick, M. L., Madeo, S. A., and Vines, C. V. (1999) "Reward dominance in tax reporting experiments: The role of context", *Journal of the American Taxation Association*, 21: 20–31.

Webley, P. (1987) "Audit probabilities and tax evasion in a business simulation", *Economics Letters*, 25: 267–70.

Webley, P. and Halstead, S. (1986) "Tax evasion on the micro: Significant simulations of expedient experiments?", *Journal of Interdisciplinary Economics*, 1: 87–100.

Yitzhaki, S. (1974) "A note on income tax evasion: A theoretical analysis", *Journal of Public Economics*, 3: 201–2.

7 Econometric models for multi-stage audit processes

An application to the IRS National Research Program

Brian Erard and Jonathan S. Feinstein[1]

Introduction

Auditing is a standard and essential tool for assessing the validity and reliability of information and processes. Three of the most common forms of audit are financial, operational, and compliance. Financial audits are used to verify the accuracy of financial statements of governments and businesses. Operational audits are employed to assess managerial performance through an analysis of the effectiveness and efficiency of the operational structure, internal control procedures, and processes. Compliance audits are used to evaluate whether, and to what extent, policies, procedures, and other requirements for individuals, businesses, or organizations are being met. Compliance audits are frequently conducted by governments. Examples include examinations of tax returns; audits to assess compliance with regulatory policies, such as environmental regulations; and audits to evaluate whether reporting, spending, and other requirements are being met with respect to government-funded programs.

A common feature of these various forms of audit is that they normally seek only to provide reasonable assurance. Due to practical constraints, it is often infeasible to exhaustively examine every detail or aspect of an operation, system, or report.

Hence, audits normally rely on sampling and testing, either at random, or in areas deemed to be of greatest risk for substantial non-compliance with reporting, procedural, or other requirements. Moreover, even when an issue or process is evaluated, there is often potential for imperfect detection of non-compliance. For example, in tax audits, examiners are not always successful in uncovering certain forms of income that have been understated. Thus, audit findings are frequently subject not only to sampling errors, but also to errors in detection. In this chapter, we introduce some econometric methods for controlling for such errors when analyzing the results of audits, and we apply these methods to a sample of individual income tax audit results to develop estimates of detected and undetected tax non-compliance. Our approach is based on the detection controlled methodology introduced by Feinstein (1990, 1991), which we have adapted to account for the multi-stage nature of the tax return examination process.

Typically, audit processes involve several stages, and it is important to account for impact of the decisions made during these stages on the outcome of the audit. In our tax audit application, some of the key decisions made during the audit include: which returns to audit; the type of audit to be conducted; the classification of mandatory issues to be examined; and whether additional unclassified issues should be examined. These decisions are made at different stages of the process, and by different individuals. In particular, selection of returns for audit is conducted early in the process according to a stratified random sampling design. Under this design, returns considered at higher risk of non-compliance are subject to a higher sampling rate. Once selected, a return is assigned to a seasoned examiner known as a "classifier", who assesses what type of audit should be conducted (accept as filed; correspondence audit involving only one or a few issues; or a more intensive face-to-face audit) as well as which issues should be examined on the return. At the examination stage, examiners must audit all issues assigned by the classifier and may, at their discretion, audit additional unclassified issues.

In this chapter, we develop an econometric methodology to control for errors in assessments that result from multi-stage audit processes. We then apply our methodology to data from a random sample of individual income tax audits collected under the Internal Revenue Service's National Research Program (NRP) to assess the extent to which non-compliance is successfully identified on various income line items of the tax return. The majority of returns in our data were subjected to a face-to-face audit, and it is these returns that are the focus of our analysis.

Our work builds on an earlier model that we developed (Erard and Associates, 2005, 2006, 2007) to assist the IRS in estimating the aggregate tax reporting gap associated with federal individual income tax returns. The current framework extends our earlier work down to a more detailed level of analysis at the level of individual income components, focusing on estimating non-compliance associated with these income components. It is hoped that the resulting estimates from this approach will serve as key inputs for a microsimulation model of individual income tax reporting non-compliance under development by the IRS. The IRS has a sophisticated tax calculator that can be used to combine our estimates of under-reporting by income component with separate estimates of non-compliance with respect to deductions, credits, and other offsets for each return, generating detailed estimates of tax non-compliance.

Our preliminary estimates document considerable heterogeneity in detection rates across examiners for some income items, a finding consistent with earlier work, for example by Feinstein (1989, 1991), Alexander and Feinstein (1987), and Erard (1993, 1997). In addition, these estimates indicate that the NRP classification process is successful in flagging for examination many of the more substantial cases of under-reporting with respect to various income components on the return. However, we find that in those cases where auditors choose to examine income components that have not been classified, they sometimes uncover substantial non-compliance, indicating that the classification process alone cannot always identify every issue on a return where non-compliance is present.

Over the course of our analysis, we have found that the yield on ordinary NRP classification-guided face-to-face examinations is not significantly different from the yield from the more comprehensive examinations of a comparable set of returns in the NRP calibration sample. For the calibration sample, auditors were instructed to perform a very thorough examination (more like those undertaken under the predecessor TCMP). This appears to indicate that the NRP approach of guiding audits through a process of classifying mandatory issues for examination, while still allowing examiners the opportunity to examine unclassified issues, may achieve similar results to comprehensive auditing of all issues on all returns. However, the calibration sample size was rather small (1,642 returns), so the results are merely suggestive, not conclusive. Moreover, as discussed previously, examiners are not always able to detect all non-compliance on a return, even with very thorough examinations. So, it remains important to allow for and assess the extent to which non-compliance goes undetected on NRP examinations.

As our preliminary results are still being evaluated by the IRS, we are only able to present a limited set of results that includes statistics on actual audit adjustment rates and predictions of the degree to which non-compliance has been successfully detected with respect to selected income components. We are unable to present the explanatory variables we include in our non-compliance specifications, the parameter estimates associated with those variables, or the implied magnitudes of detected and undetected non-compliance. Once our results have been carefully reviewed by the IRS, we are hopeful we will able to make a fuller set of results public, in a subsequent paper.

The remainder of our chapter is organized as follows. Next, we describe the NRP. This is followed by a discussion of modeling considerations in the subsequent section. We present our model of taxpayer reporting and the NRP classification and examination processes, derive the likelihood functions we estimate, and discuss estimation issues we have encountered and modifications to our base model in the followed section. Next, we present a preliminary set of empirical results, and in the last section we conclude.

National Research Program

For our analysis, we rely on the Internal Revenue Service's National Research Program (NRP). In this important initiative, the IRS gathers data about tax non-compliance through stratified random sample of approximately 45,000 federal individual income tax returns that have been subjected to special examination procedures. An important feature of the data acquisition process is that not all cases follow the same pathway for data collection. There are in particular five features of the data acquisition process that are important for analysis, which we discuss in turn.[2]

First, returns are subject to a classification process. In this process, a classifier examines the filed return and places the return into one of three categories: (i) accepted – meaning the return is accepted as is or with minor adjustments, and, importantly, there is no further contact with the taxpayer (except if the return is then selected into the calibration sample – see below); (ii) correspondence audit – meaning a correspondence will be initiated with the taxpayer regarding a circumscribed set of issues for which adjustments may be made – but there is no planned face-to-face audit; and (iii) audit – a face-to-face audit. The breakdown of cases into these three categories is: approximately 3,400 accepted; 2,600 selected for correspondence audit; and the balance, roughly 39,000, selected for face-to-face audit.

Second, for returns in categories (ii) and (iii) the classifier flags a set of issues for either correspondence, in the case of returns falling in category (ii), or examination during audit, for returns falling in category (iii). Classification may be triggered by a variety of factors. For instance, a classifier will generally assign an issue for audit in cases where a third-party information document indicates the presence of income not reported by the taxpayer. As a second example, in those cases where a taxpayer reports self-employment income, the classifier normally will assign various issues on Schedule C or Schedule F to be investigated, because non-compliance is known to be prevalent on these schedules. We discuss how we model this classification process below in the the followed section.[3]

Third, a subset of cases is chosen for the "calibration sample." The calibration sample includes approximately 470 returns originally assigned to be accepted as filed from the ordinary NRP sample, as well as approximately 1,175 randomly selected returns that were not included in the ordinary NRP sample. Generally, returns assigned to the calibration sample receive a more thorough audit than they were initially assigned to receive. The calibration sample is a stratified random sample covering all three classification categories (returns initially classified as accepted, for a correspondence audit, and for a face-to-face examination). We are in the process of using use the calibration sample to help identify certain parameters in one of our models, but we have not yet completed this work.

Fourth, during a face-to-face audit examiners have the discretion to go beyond the issues that were flagged for examination during the classification process. Indeed, examiners frequently do probe for sources of income not reported on the return, even when these sources have not been classified. Either as a result of such probes or through other information gained during the audit, the examiner may become suspicious of potential non-compliance on an unclassified issue. In such cases, it is not uncommon for the examiner to investigate more deeply and discover significant non-compliance with respect to the issue. Importantly, the NRP data record which issues were examined, which of them were classified, and any adjustments that were made as a result of the examination.

Fifth, with respect to issues examined during a face-to-face audit, the examiner is required to record a zero when he audits an issue but finds no misreporting. This is important in making a clear distinction in the data between issues examined for which no non-compliance is found and issues not examined. By allowing for multiple intensities of interaction with and levels of audit of taxpayers, the

NRP sample design deviates significantly from that of the predecessor Taxpayer Compliance Measurement Program (TCMP), which called for uniformly intensive face-to-face examinations. To properly analyze the NRP, it is therefore necessary to develop and apply new models that account for these differences in sample design and examination procedures.

As explained in the previous section, we focus our analysis on returns that were subject to face-to-face examination. This category accounts for the vast majority of returns in the NRP sample, on which non-compliance appears to be far and away the greatest. In restricting our attention to face-to-face examinations, we exclude approximately 6,000 returns that were subject to a correspondence audit or accepted as filed. When weighted, these returns represent approximately 43 percent of the overall return population. Nonetheless, our analysis of the calibration sample suggests that this portion of the population is responsible for only a very small share of aggregate non-compliance in the population.

Modeling issues

When modeling non-compliance using the NRP, one needs to consider how best to account for variety of issues, including: (i) heterogeneity in reporting behavior, particularly that there are unusually high levels of under-reporting by a small proportion of taxpayers; (ii) the different ways that the examination process can fail to identify all cases of non-compliance; (iii) instances in which an income amount appears to have been overstated; and (iv) the interpretation of non-compliance.

Heterogeneity in reporting behavior

Our models of taxpayer reporting behavior follow our earlier work (see, for example Alm *et al.*, 1996) in specifying reporting non-compliance using a log-normal distribution. The log-normal specification allows for a skewed distribution in which there is a "long tail" to the right of the distribution. This captures the empirical fact that there is a small portion of taxpayers with very high levels of non-compliance. In our specifications, we also account for the non-trivial percentage of taxpayers who fully and accurately report their tax liability. In some cases we break the non-compliance decision into two parts: (i) a simple probit model is used to estimate the probability that an income component has been under-reported, and (ii) a log-normal regression is used to estimate the magnitude of under-reporting conditional on under-reporting having occurred.

Undetected non-compliance

Non-detection arises whenever the examiner fails to detect all non-compliance on a return. In the NRP this may happen for two distinct reasons: (i) the examiner fails to detect all non-compliance on an issue he examines; or (ii) the examiner fails to audit an issue on which non-compliance exists.

We model non-detection of the first kind using the detection-controlled methodology developed by Feinstein (1990, 1991). Other researchers have used this methodology to analyze tax compliance (Alexander and Feinstein, 1987; Erard, 1993, 1997) as well as a variety of applications in other domains, including regulation and health care. We employ in particular the fractional detection model developed in Feinstein (1991).

We model the second form of non-detection using a specification that extrapolates from non-compliance found on returns examined for a specific issue to likely non-compliance for the same issue on returns for which the issue was not examined. As we discuss in our results section this extrapolation is empirically challenging to do in a sensible way, in part because when an examiner chooses to examine an issue that was not classified for examination it is often because he has a lead of some kind that points to potential non-compliance. As a consequence, detected non-compliance on unclassified issues that are ultimately examined tends to be relatively high, and we cannot simply assume that the rate of non-compliance is comparable on returns for which examiners do not have a lead and do not examine the issue. We develop specific modeling strategies to address this problem.

Detected over-reporting

An important issue when accounting for undetected non-compliance is how to treat cases where a return has received a negative adjustment for an income component – in other words, cases where the examiner has assessed that the taxpayer has overstated the amount of that income component on the return. While certainly not trivial, negative audit adjustments are less common and tend to be much smaller, on average, than positive adjustments. The NRP includes a set of sample weights that make the returns broadly representative of the overall return population in tax year 2001. In the NRP, approximately 7 percent of the weighted sample of returns received a negative adjustment to their reported total income amount, while approximately one-third of the weighted sample received a positive adjustment. Among returns with a negative adjustment in the weighted sample, the median reduction in total income was $135. The median increase in total income among positive adjustment cases was $917.

In our econometric analysis, we account for the possibility that examiners do not always fully uncover cases of income under-reporting during their examinations. Should we also account for the possibility that cases of income over-reporting sometimes go undiscovered? We do not do so in this study. Rather, we treat cases with negative adjustments the same as cases with no adjustment; namely, as instances where the examiner has assessed the report to be perfectly compliant.[4] Our reasoning is that, while taxpayers may not have much incentive to reveal instances of under-reporting to the examiner, they (and their representative, if any) do have an incentive to reveal instances of over-reporting. To the extent that taxpayers and their representatives review their returns and related documentation prior to and during the audit, there is a reasonable chance that cases of over-reporting will come to light and be disclosed to the NRP examiner. In addition, the NRP examiners are charged with examining returns with an eye toward finding both instances of under-reporting and instances of over-reporting; their role in the study is to assess the correct amount of tax, neither too much nor too little. Our working assumption is therefore that any detection errors with regard to cases of over-reported income are likely to be modest, and do not justify the substantial additional econometric modeling that would be required to assess them.[5]

Interpreting non-compliance

Our measure of non-compliance for an income component is essentially the difference between the amount of income that the IRS would assess for the component if it were fully aware of all relevant information and circumstances pertaining to the 2001 tax period, and the amount actually reported on the return. Various reviews and checks are built into the NRP to help ensure that examiner assessments are consistent with the IRS' interpretation of tax laws, rules, and procedures. In many instances, the correct amount to report when the underlying facts are known is relatively straightforward to determine, and virtually all reasonable individuals proficient in tax law would agree on this amount. However, there do exist some gray areas of the tax law for which the rules for reporting a given type of income are less clear-cut. With respect to cases involving these areas of the law, experts might reasonably disagree on what amount should be reported. Our estimates are based on what the IRS would deem the appropriate amount to report is in such cases if it were fully aware of the relevant facts and circumstances.

It should be noted that our analysis makes no attempt to infer the motive behind misreporting. In particular, we make no attempt to distinguish among deliberate and unintentional errors.[6]

Models

In this section we present the main models we estimate, which we view as novel and important for analyzing the NRP\null. First we present our model of non-compliance, classification, and detection (Model 1) that is used to analyze non-compliance on income components subject to extensive information reporting, such as wages, interest, and dividends. As discussed in the previous section, this specification allows us to account for the likely possibility that non-compliance with respect to one of these components tends to be larger when the component either has been classified for examination or has not been classified but nonetheless has been examined. Next we present the modified detection-controlled model (Model 2) that we use for income components that are not subject to extensive information reporting. In most cases, such income components are classified for examination whenever they are reported on the return, so it is unnecessary to model the classification decision for these components.

Model 1: non-compliance, classification, and detection

As noted in the previous sections, while certain income items (such as self-employment income) are routinely classified for examination in the NRP, others are not. In particular, for those income items that are subject to substantial third-party information reporting (examples include wages, interest, and dividends), the documents provided by third parties often provide a very strong indication of how much should have been reported on the return. In many cases the amount reported by the taxpayer for such an item is consistent with what is shown on the information documents, obviating the need to perform a detailed examination of the item. Typically, then, such an item is classified for examination only when the reported amount is inconsistent with what is shown on third-party information documents, when those information documents appear to be incomplete or suspicious, or when other available information points to a potential problem with the line item. For such an income item, classification clearly serves as an important screening process. Our first model therefore extends the existing detection controlled estimation methodology (Feinstein, 1991) to account for the role of classification in observed compliance outcomes.

Our model accounts for the interactions among the behavior of three different individuals: the taxpayer, the classifier, and the examiner. Consider an income component, such as wages. We begin by considering the behavior of the taxpayer, who decides how much income to report. If we allow N to represent the true magnitude of non-compliance with respect to this component, then, for any given return in our sample, the value of N might be zero, signifying perfect compliance by the taxpayer, or positive ($N>0$), signifying a positive magnitude of non-compliance.[7]

The first equation in our econometric model provides a specification of the magnitude of non-compliance in the taxpayer's report for the income item:

$$\ln(N^*+h) = \beta_N'x_N + \varepsilon_N. \tag{1}$$

In this expression, N^* is a latent variable describing the taxpayer's propensity to commit non-compliance on this particular income component. (Note that we do not subscript the income component for ease of notation.) The symbol h represents a displacement parameter that allows the distribution of N^* to extend below zero – h is required to be greater than or equal to zero; x_N is a set of variables associated with taxpayer non-compliance, such as filing status, β_N is a vector of coefficients, and ε_N is a random disturbance, discussed further below

The actual level of non-compliance N is determined as:

$$N = \begin{cases} N^* & N^* > 0; \\ 0 & \text{otherwise.} \end{cases} \tag{2}$$

Next, we turn to the behavior of the classifier who has been assigned to review the taxpayer's return. The classifier's decision whether to assign the income component for examination is modeled using the following specification:

$$C^* = \beta_C'x_C + \varepsilon_C, \tag{3}$$

In this expression C^* is a latent variable describing the propensity of the classifier to assign the income component to be examined, x_C is a set of variables associated with the classification decision, β_C is a vector of coefficients, and ε_C is a random disturbance. We observe the classification outcome C, where

$$C = \begin{cases} 1 & C^* > 0; \\ 0 & C^* \leq 0. \end{cases} \tag{4}$$

The outcome $C = 1$ means the income component has been classified for examination. In our empirical specification we include a dummy variable for each classifier who has worked at least 15 returns. We are therefore, able to control for differences in classification styles across classifiers.

Next we turn to the examiner who has been assigned to audit the taxpayer's return. We assume that the examiner always audits the income component if it has been classified for examination. On the other hand, if the component has not been classified, it is possible that the examiner will still elect to audit it. Typically, this will happen when the examiner learns some information over the course of his investigation that leads him to suspect non-compliance with respect to the component. We are able to model whether an unclassified income component is ultimately examined, because the NRP data sample records whether a component has been examined, even when no adjustment has been made for the component. In our econometric model, we specify the probability that an unclassified income component will be examined as:

$$\frac{\exp\{\alpha_0 + \alpha_1 N\}}{1 + \exp\{\alpha_0 + \alpha_1 N\}}. \tag{5}$$

In other words, we allow the examination probability to depend on the magnitude of actual non-compliance.[8] The parameter α_0 in this expression determines the probability that an unclassified income component will be examined when it has been properly reported (i.e., when $N=0$). The parameter α_1 determines the degree to which the probability of an examination changes with the magnitude of non-compliance. If α_1 is positive (the anticipated result), the probability of examination increases with the magnitude of non-compliance. In cases where the income component is neither classified nor examined on a return, the audit adjustment for the component (A) will be equal to zero. If the income component has been properly reported, this adjustment will accurately reflect that the report is fully compliant ($A=N=0$). On the other hand, if the income component has been under-reported on the return, the full amount of the understatement (N) will go undetected.

Now consider the cases where the income component either has been classified for examination, or has not been classified but has been examined anyway.

In such cases, all, some, or none of the non-compliance that is present may be detected. We model the detection process using the fractional detection specification of Feinstein (1991):

$$D^* = \beta_D'x_D + \varepsilon_D. \tag{6}$$

In this specification D^* is a latent variable describing the extent to which non-compliance is detected during the examination. The detection rate (D) represents the actual fraction of non-compliance on the income component that has been detected. It is defined as follows:

$$D = \begin{cases} 1 & D^* \geq 1 & \text{(complete detection)}; \\ D & 0 < D^* < 1 & \text{(partial detection)}; \\ 0 & D^* \leq 0 & \text{(nondetection)}. \end{cases} \tag{7}$$

The term x_D in Equation (6) represents a set of explanatory variables associated with the detection, while β_D is a vector of coefficients, and ε_D is a random disturbance. Among the set of explanatory variables are dummy variables for individual examiners that have audited a sufficient number of returns (typically, 15 or more). This allows us to compare the relative performances of different examiners and to predict the extent to which they have been successful in uncovering any non-compliance that is present with respect to an income component.

Notice that if the income component has been reported properly $(N=0)$, the audit adjustment A will be equal to zero $(A=0)$ regardless of the effectiveness of the examination. In this case, the recorded adjustment will properly reflect the fact that the return is fully compliant with respect to the item. On the other hand, if the income component has not been reported accurately $(N>0)$, the audit adjustment may fully reflect the magnitude of non-compliance $(A=N; N>0)$, only partially reflect the magnitude $(0<A<N)$, or not reflect the magnitude at all $(A=0; N>0)$.

We assume that the error terms, ε_N and ε_C, in our model are bi-variate normally distributed, with zero means, standard deviations of σ_N and 1, respectively, and correlation coefficient ρ. For simplicity, we assume that the error term ε_D is independent of ε_N and ε_C, and that it is normally distributed with mean zero and standard deviation σ_D. The assumption regarding ε_N implies that the propensity to commit non-compliance follows the displaced log-normal distribution. Such a distribution has a long and thin tail, consistent with empirical evidence that tax non-compliance tends to be highly skewed.

Likelihood function for model 1

As discussed in the previous section, there is an important problem that arises in analyzing the NRP and indeed nearly any audit data; namely, not all non-compliance is detected, and we have no direct information about non-compliance that the examiner failed to detect. Our likelihood function thus centers around not the true level of non-compliance N, but rather the audit adjustment A, which is equal to the true level of non-compliance times the detection rate:

$$A = N_* D$$

Thus the likelihood function involves the joint distribution function of the two observable variables A and C, worked out in terms of the underlying model processes and the underlying variables N, D, and C. In carrying out the transformation from the joint distribution of N, D, and C into the joint distribution of A and C, we account for the Jacobian of the transformation $J = 1/D$.[9]

The likelihood function involves five distinct cases: (1) the income component is classified for examination, and there is no detected non-compliance: $C = 1$, $A = 0$; (2) the income component is classified for examination, and some non-compliance is detected: $C = 1$, $A > 0$; (3) the income component is not classified for examination, but the component is examined anyway with no detected non-compliance: $C = 0$, exam, $A = 0$; (4) the income component is not classified for examination, the component is examined anyway, and some non-compliance is detected: $C = 0$, exam, $A > 0$; and (5) the income component is not classified for examination, and the component is not examined: $C = 0$, no exam. We now present the likelihood function for each of the five cases.

Case 1: $C = 1$, $A = 0$

In this case, a return is classified for an examination of the income component, but the examiner does not discover any non-compliance with respect to the component. The likelihood function for this case can be computed as the difference between the marginal probability that $C^* > 0$ (income component classified) and the joint probability that $C^* > 0$, $N^* > 0$, and $D^* > 0$ (income component classified and at least some positive non-compliance detected):

$$L = \Phi\left(\beta_C' x_C\right) - BN\left(\frac{\beta_N' x_N - \ln(h)}{\sigma_n}, \beta_C' x_C, \rho\right)\Phi\left(\frac{\beta_D' x_D}{\sigma_D}\right),$$

where $\Phi(z)$ represents the standard normal cumulative distribution function (c.d.f.) evaluated at Z and $BN(z_1, z_2, \rho)$ represents the standard bi-variate normal c.d.f. evaluated at z_1 and z_2 for correlation coefficient ρ.

Case 2: $C = 1$, $A > 0$

In this case, a return is classified for an examination of the income component, and some positive amount of non-compliance is detected with respect to the component. The likelihood function for this case accounts for the possibilities that non-compliance is either fully or partially detected:

$$L = \frac{1}{\sigma_N(A+h)} \varphi\left(\frac{\ln(A+h)-\beta_N'x_N}{\sigma_N}\right) \Phi\left(\frac{\beta_C'x_C + \rho\left(\frac{\ln(A+h)-\beta_N'x_N}{\sigma_N}\right)}{\sqrt{1-\rho^2}}\right)$$

$$\Phi\left(\frac{\beta_D'x_D - 1}{\sigma_D}\right) + \int_0^1\left[\frac{1}{\sigma_N\sigma_D(A+hD)}\varphi\left(\frac{\ln(A/D+h)-\beta_N'x_N}{\sigma_N}\right)\right.$$

$$\left.\Phi\left(\frac{\beta_C'x_C + \rho\left(\frac{\ln(A/D+h)-\beta_N'x_N}{\sigma_N}\right)}{\sqrt{1-\rho^2}}\right)\varphi\left(\frac{D-\beta_D'x_D}{\sigma_N}\right)\right]dD,$$

where $\phi(z)$ represents the standard normal p.d.f. evaluated at z. The next three cases involve returns for which the income component has not been classified for examination. As discussed previously, when an income component is not classified for examination, we assume that the examiner audits the income component anyway with a probability that depends on the true level of non-compliance N:

$$\frac{\exp\{\alpha_0 + \alpha_1 N\}}{1+\exp\{\alpha_0 + \alpha_1 N\}}$$

The parameter α_0 in the above expression determines the probability that an unclassified return will be examined when the income component is properly reported ($N=0$). The parameter α_1 determines the degree to which the probability of an examination changes with the magnitude of non-compliance. If α_1 is positive (the anticipatedresult), the probability of examination increases with the magnitude of non-compliance.

Case 3: $C=0$, exam, $A=0$

In this case, the income component has not been classified, but the examiner elects to audit it and does not detect any non-compliance. The likelihood function for this case is computed as the sum of two joint probabilities. The first is that the income component is not classified, that it is examined, and that it is non-compliant, but that the non-compliance has gone completely undetected. The second joint probability is that the income component is not classified, that it is examined, and that it is perfectly compliant. Specifically,

$$L = \Phi\left(\frac{-\beta_D'x_D}{\sigma_D}\right)\int_0^\infty\left[\frac{1}{\sigma_N(N+h)}\varphi\left(\frac{\ln(N+h)-\beta_N'x_N}{\sigma_N}\right)\right.$$

$$\left.\Phi\left(\frac{-\beta_C'x_C - \rho\left(\frac{\ln(N+h)-\beta_N'x_N}{\sigma_N}\right)}{\sqrt{1-\rho^2}}\right)\frac{\exp\{\alpha_0+\alpha_1 N\}}{1+\exp\{\alpha_0+\alpha_1 N\}}\right]dN$$

$$+ BN\left(\frac{\ln(h)-\beta_N'x_N}{\sigma_N}, \beta_C'x_C,\rho\right)\left(\frac{\exp\{\alpha_0\}}{1+\exp\{\alpha_0\}}\right).$$

Case 4: C=0, exam, A>0

As with Case 3, we observe this case only when the income component is not assigned by the classifier, but the examiner elects to review the component anyway. In this case, however, the review of the income component uncovers some non-compliance. The likelihood function for this case is somewhat similar to that given earlier for Case 2, which involves detected non-compliance for a classified return:

$$
L = \frac{1}{\sigma_N(A+h)} \varphi\left(\frac{\ln(A+h)-\beta_N'x_N}{\sigma_N}\right) \Phi\left(\frac{-\beta_C'x_C - \rho\left(\frac{\ln(A+h)-\beta_N'x_N}{\sigma_N}\right)}{\sqrt{1-\rho^2}}\right)
$$

$$
\Phi\left(\frac{\beta_D'x_D - 1}{\sigma_D}\right) \left(\frac{\exp\{\alpha_0+\alpha_1 A\}}{1+\exp\{\alpha_0+\alpha_1 A\}}\right) +
$$

$$
\int_0^1 \left[\frac{1}{\sigma_N\sigma_D(A+hD)} \varphi\left(\frac{\ln(A/D+h)-\beta_N'x_N}{\sigma_N}\right) \Phi\left(\frac{-\beta_C'x_C - \rho\left(\frac{\ln(A/D+h)-\beta_N'x_N}{\sigma_N}\right)}{\sqrt{1-\rho^2}}\right)\right.
$$

$$
\left. \varphi\left(\frac{D-\beta_D'x_D}{\sigma_D}\right) \left(\frac{\exp\{\alpha_0+\alpha_1(A/D)\}}{1+\exp\{\alpha_0+\alpha_1(A/D)\}}\right)\right] dD.
$$

Case 5: C=0, no exam

In this case, the income component is not classified, and the examiner elects not to examine the return. The likelihood function for this case takes the form:

$$
L = \int_0^\infty \frac{1}{\sigma_N(N+h)} \varphi\left(\frac{\ln(N+h)-\beta_N'x_N}{\sigma_N}\right) \Phi\left(\frac{-\beta_C'x_C - \rho\left(\frac{\ln(A/D+h)-\beta_N'x_N}{\sigma_N}\right)}{\sqrt{1-\rho^2}}\right)
$$

$$
\left(\frac{1}{1+\exp\{\alpha_0+\alpha_1 n\}}\right) dn + BN\left(\frac{\ln(d)-\beta_N'x_N}{\sigma_N}, -\beta_C'x_C, \rho\right)\left(\frac{1}{1+\exp\{\alpha_0\}}\right).
$$

Model 2: non-compliance and detection

For many of the income components in our analysis, an examination of the component usually takes place whenever a return has reported a non-zero amount for the component. For such income components, we have worked with a simpler model that ignores the decision whether to classify the component for examination. In this model, we focus exclusively on whether non-compliance is present and the extent to which the examiner has been successful in detecting it.

There is a further issue for these types of income components. In particular, while most returns that report a non-zero amount of the component are subject to detailed examination of that component, in most cases for returns that report a zero amount for the component the component is not examined, at least not with the same intensity. Our model therefore employs separate specifications for returns that do and do not report a non-zero amount for each income component.

Specification and likelihood function when non-zero amount reported

For returns that report a non-zero amount for an income component, the specification has two equations:

$$\ln(N*+h) = \beta_N'x_N + \varepsilon_N \tag{8}$$

$$D* = \beta_D'x_D + \varepsilon_D, \tag{9}$$

where the observed level of non-compliance N is related to the latent variable $N*$ as follows:

$$N = \begin{cases} N* & N* > 0; \\ 0 & \text{otherwise.} \end{cases} \tag{10}$$

Similarly, the observed detection rate D is related to the latent variable $D*$ according to:

$$D = \begin{cases} 1 & D* \geq 1 & \text{(complete detection);} \\ D & 0 < D* < 1 & \text{(partial detection);} \\ 0 & D* \leq 0 & \text{(nondetection).} \end{cases} \tag{11}$$

The two parts of this specification are identical with the corresponding parts for Model 1; in particular the specification for non-compliance $N*$ and N are identical to equations (1) and (2), and the specification of the detection process is identical to equations (6) and (7). We maintain the assumptions that ε_N is normally distributed with mean zero and standard deviation σ_N; ε_D is normally distributed with mean zero and standard deviation σ_D; and that ε_N and ε_D are independently distributed.

As before, we work out the likelihood function in terms of assessed non-compliance, $A = N * D$. The likelihood function has two separate cases: $A = 0$ and $A > 0$. We consider each of these cases in turn.

Case 1: $A = 0$
In this case, either the taxpayer is compliant or is non-compliant but no non-compliance is detected. The likelihood function may be computed as one minus the probability that non-compliance is present and is at least partially detected:

$$L = 1 - \Phi\left(\frac{\beta_N'x_N - \ln(h)}{\sigma_N}\right)\Phi\left(\frac{\beta_D'x_D}{\sigma_D}\right)$$

Case 2: $A>0$

In this case, the taxpayer is non-compliant and the non-compliance is either fully or partially detected. Therefore, the likelihood function allows for detection rates ranging from zero to one:

$$L = \frac{1}{\sigma_N(A+h)} \varphi\left(\frac{\ln(A+h)-\beta_N'x_N}{\sigma_N}\right)\Phi\left(\frac{\beta_D'x_D-1}{\sigma_D}\right)+$$

$$\int_0^1 \frac{1}{\sigma_N\sigma_D(A+hD)} \varphi\left(\frac{D-\beta_D'x_D}{\sigma_D}\right)\varphi\left(\frac{\ln(A/D+h)-\beta_N'x_N}{\sigma_N}\right)dD.$$

Specification and likelihood function when zero amount reported

For returns that report a zero amount for the relevant income component, our specification separately addresses the likelihood that the income component is in fact present and the magnitude of that component conditional on it being present. Our specification allows for detection errors both with respect to identifying whether the income component is present and with respect to assessing its magnitude when present. The joint likelihood that the income component is present and the chance that it will be detected if present is modeled as:

$$P^* = \beta_P'x_P + \varepsilon_P \tag{12}$$

$$D^*_P = \beta_{DP}'x_{DP} + \varepsilon_{DP}, \tag{13}$$

where P^* is a latent variable describing the likelihood that some of the income component is present and D^* is a latent variable describing the propensity of the examiner to detect its presence. Unreported income is present if and only if $P^*>0$. Likewise, this income is detected if and only if $D^*_P>0$. We assume that ε_P and ε_{DP} are each normally distributed with zero means and unit standard deviations. For convenience, we also assume that they are independently distributed. The likelihood function for this portion of our model depends on whether the examiner has assessed that some of the income component is present.

Case 1A: Examiner assesses that income component is not present

If the examiner has assessed that the income component is not present, either $P^*<0$ (component really is not present) or $D_{P^*}<0$ (detection error). The likelihood of this can be expressed as one minus the joint probability that $P^*>0$ and $D^*_P>0$:[10]

$$L = 1-\Phi(\beta_P'x_P)\Phi(\beta_{DP}'x_{DP}).$$

Case 2A: Examiner assesses that income component is present
In order for the examiner to assess that at least some of the income component is in fact present, it must be the case that both $P^* > 0$ and $D^*_p > 0$. Therefore, the likelihood function for this case is specified as:

$$L = \Phi(\beta'_p x_p)\Phi(\beta'_{DP} x_{DP}).$$

So far, our model accounts for whether the income component is assessed to be present, but it does not account for the magnitude of the adjustment when the component is deemed to be present. For returns with a positive adjustment for the income component (Case 2A), we assume that the magnitude of the adjustment depends on both the actual amount of the income component that is present and the extent to which it has been detected. More specifically, our specification includes the following two equations:

$$\ln(N) = \beta_N' x_N + \varepsilon_N \tag{14}$$

$$D^* = \beta_D' x_D + \varepsilon_D, \tag{15}$$

where N represents the true magnitude of non-compliance (i.e., the magnitude of the income component that is present but which has been reported as zero), and D^* represents a latent variable for the propensity for non-compliance to be detected. We assume that ε_N is normally distributed with mean zero and standard deviation σ_N. Likewise, we assume that ε_D is normally distributed with mean zero and standard deviation σ_D. Since this portion of model is estimated over returns that are assessed to have at least some of the income component, it must be the case that detection is either partial or complete. The distribution of D^* is therefore truncated to lie above zero. The detection rate D is defined as:

$$D = \begin{cases} 1 & D^* \geq 1 & \text{(complete detection);} \\ D & 0 < D^* < 1 & \text{(partial detection).} \end{cases} \tag{16}$$

Unfortunately, there are relatively few examiners who have audited a sufficiently large number of returns (15 or more) that reported a zero amount of an income component of interest and were found to have a non-zero value for the component. In our analysis, we therefore apply the estimated parameters of the detection equation from our analysis of returns that reported a positive amount for the component. In effect, we are assuming that, once an examiner finds that the income component is present on a return that reports none of the component, his ability to detect the magnitude of non-compliance on that return is comparable to his ability to uncover non-compliance on a return that reports a non-zero amount for the income component.

As in our previous models, the observed assessed level of non-compliance is $A = D * N$. The full likelihood function for Case 2A is:

$$L = \frac{1}{\Phi(\beta_D x_D)} \left[\frac{1}{\sigma_N A} \varphi\left(\frac{\ln(A) - \beta_N' x_N}{\sigma_N} \right) \Phi\left(\frac{\beta_D' x_D - 1}{\sigma_D} \right) \right.$$
$$\left. + \int_0^1 \frac{1}{\sigma_N \sigma_D A} \varphi\left(\frac{D - \beta_D' x_D}{\sigma_D} \right) \varphi\left(\frac{\ln(A/D) - \beta_N' x_N}{\sigma_N} \right) dD \right].$$

Empirical results

In this section we present some summary statistics from our NRP data sample as well as selected results from our analysis. As noted in the introduction to this chapter, due to issues of confidentiality and the need for the IRS to fully review and approve our results for release before making them publicly available, we are unable to report all of our results in this chapter.

Tables 7.1 and 7.2 present statistics for income components estimated using Model 1, which applies to components subject to substantial third party information reporting. We estimate Model 1 for the following components:

1   Wages
2   Taxable interest
3   Taxable state and local tax refunds
4   Dividends
5   Taxable pensions and IRA distributions
6   Gross social security benefits
7   Unemployment insurance.[11]

Table 7.1 presents information about the number of returns in our sample reporting non-zero amounts for each of these items, and the number reporting zero. The raw number of returns, rather than the population-weighted numbers are provided to give the reader a sense of the sample sizes that are available for estimation for each income component. As expected, the majority of households report some wages; the majority also report some interest. Significant numbers report non-zero amounts for each of the other items. The table also presents the percentage of returns reporting non-zero amounts for which the item is classified for examination, and the percentage of returns reporting zero for which the item is classified for examination. These percentages have been weighted to give the reader a sense of the population characteristics. The majority of returns are not classified for examination of a given income component. However, a modest percentage of returns reporting non-zero amounts for a given component are classified, the highest percentages being for interest, dividends, and social security benefits. For returns reporting zero amounts for a given income component, the percentage classified for examination is small; the one exception is interest, for which a non-trivial percentage of returns reporting zero interest income are classified for examination. The last two columns of the table show the number of returns examined for the specified item – both returns that were classified for

Table 7.1 Weighted classification rates by whether non-zero amount reported, Group 1 income components

Income component	Returns with a non-zero report for income component		Returns with a zero report for income component		Raw # total examined returns	
	Raw # returns	Weighted % that were classified	Raw # returns	Weighted % that were classified	Classified	Not classified, but examined
Wages	26,418	12.1	11,452	1.8	2,507	934
Interest	27,937	27.6	9,933	16.3	11,123	688
Dividends	16,692	33.2	21,178	4.5	6,875	397
State and local tax refunds	10,190	11.8	27,680	5.4	2,738	198
Pensions and IRAs	8,076	21.1	29,794	5.4	2,850	217
Gross social security benefits	3,989	36.5	33,881	1.3	1,952	181
Unemployment benefits	1,692	9.6	36,178	0.97	272	30

examination and then examined, and also returns that were not classified for examination but were examined anyway. While most examinations are for returns classified for examination, a non-trivial number of returns are examined for an item which was not classified.

Table 7.2 presents information about adjustments for non-compliance made during examinations for these same items. These numbers are weighted to reflect the filing population. The most striking feature of the table is the cells for which the percentage of cases having a positive adjustment is high. These include certain cells for items for which the household reported zero but the classifier assigned the item for examination – notably wages, interest, dividends, state and local tax refunds, and unemployment benefits. They also include certain cells for items that were not classified for examination but were examined anyway – notably interest, dividends, and state and local tax refunds. In the first group of cases the classifier presumably encountered a signal suggesting that there might be income present, and in the second group the examiner presumably encountered such a signal, even though the classifier had not. It is also interesting to note that for other items these signals are apparently less definitive – the adjustment rates are modest, for example, for social security benefits in cases in which the household repoted zero and the classifier assigned the item for examination, and cases in which this item was not classified for examination but the examiner audited it anyway. Assessment rates for items classified for examination are reasonable but not extraordinarily high, suggesting the classifiers use a fairly low threshold in triggering the decision to classify an item for examination.

Table 7.2 Weighted percentage of examined returns with a positive adjustment by classification and reporting status, Group 1 income components

Income component	Income component classified		Income component not classified, but examined anyhow
	Non-zero report for income component	Zero report for income component	
Wages*	33.3	73.7	24.5
Interest	26.8	92.9	68.0
Dividends	27.3	82.5	67.9
State and local tax refunds	25.0	66.8	65.9
Pensions and IRAs	19.5	48.3	33.8
Gross social security benefits	13.5	14.3	16.9
Unemployment benefits	17.9	82.6	44.9

Note
*Wages variable excludes tip income.

Tables 7.3 and 7.4 present statistics for income components estimated using Model 2. We estimate Model 2 for the following issues/schedules:

1   Net non-farm sole proprietor income (Schedule C)
2   Net farm sole proprietor income (Schedule F)
3   Short-term capital gains
4   Long-term capital gains
5   Net rental and royalty income
6   Net partnership and S-corporation income
7   Other Schedule E income (such as estate and trust income)
8   Supplemental gains reported on Form 4767
9   Other Form 1040 income.

Among the nine income components estimated based on this model, only two (net farm and non-farm sole proprietor income) have a reasonable number of examiners who each audited that component on a sufficiently large number of returns (15 or more) to derive adequate estimates of the variation in detection rates across examiners. For the remaining seven components, we therefore estimated our model for each component jointly, restricting the parameters of the detection equation (with the exception of the constant term) to be common across all components.

Table 7.3 presents results for items (3)–(9) of the list, which are generally subject to partial third-party information reporting. Columns 1 and 3 show the number of returns that report each of these components, and the number that do not. We again note that these numbers are raw numbers from the NRP and are not weighted to reflect the US filer population. As such, they provide the reader a sense of the sample sizes we have to work with for the various income components. The table also shows for each item the percentage of returns among those that report the item for which there is a positive adjustment during the NRP examination process, and the percentage of returns among those that do not report the item for which there is a positive adjustment during the NRP examination process. These percentages have been weighted to reflect the US filer population. As expected, a higher percentage of returns reporting the item have a positive adjustment than of returns not reporting the item. The highest adjustment rate is for households reporting rents and royalties income.

Table 7.4 presents similar information for Schedule C and Schedule F. Here we find that the percentage of returns reporting these items for which there is a positive adjustment during the NRP examination process is rather high, while the percentage of returns not reporting the items for which there is a positive adjustment is quite small.

We note that these tables do not present any information about the magnitude of non-compliance, only the rate. We cannot at present provide information about magnitudes, but hopefully some of this information will be presented in subsequent work.

Table 7.3 Reporting and examiner adjustment statistics, Group 2 income components

Income component	Income component reported		Income component not reported	
	Raw # returns	Weighted % of returns with a positive adjustment	Raw # returns	Weighted % of returns with a positive adjustment
Schedule D short-term gains	7,981	11.1	29,889	1.30
Schedule D long-term gains	13,571	14.7	24,299	2.80
Net rents and royalties	7,400	43.1	30,470	0.54
Net income from partnerships and S-corps	6,339	13.2	31,531	0.11
Other Schedule E income	1,004	14.6	36,866	0.03
Form 4797 gains	2,945	16.8	34,925	0.25
Other income	4,848	10.1	33,022	3.30

Table 7.4 Reporting and examiner adjustment statistics, Group 3 income components*

Type of sole proprietor schedule	Schedule filed		No schedule filed	
	Raw # schedules	Weighted % of schedules with a positive adjustment	Raw # returns	Weighted % of returns with a positive adjustment
Non-farm (Schedule C)	23,943	55.4	17,557	1.70
Farm (Schedule F)	4,830	56.5	33,204	0.01

Note
*Some taxpayers file multiple Schedule C or Schedule F returns; each schedule is counted separately in our statistics and our econometric analysis.

Figures 7.1–7.3 present histograms based on our preliminary estimates of detection rates across examiners for three representative income items: wages, net rents and royalties, and Schedule C net income. For wages, we report results for all returns for which wages were examined, regardless of whether the taxpayer reported a non-zero or zero amount of wages on his return. In the cases of the latter two income components, we report results only for taxpayers who reported a non-zero amount of the component, for which examinations tended to be more thorough.

The histograms illustrate the distribution of detection rates among examiners who have audited the relevant income component on at least 15 different income tax returns. For each of the three components, there is a subset of examiners who are estimated as "near-perfect" detectors – meaning the econometric model has assigned them a detection rate of close to 100 percent. Essentially, these examiners serve as the benchmark against which the other examiners' detection rates are calibrated. The heterogeneity among detection rates is lowest for wages, with a very large subsample of examiners with estimated detection rates exceeding 90 percent.

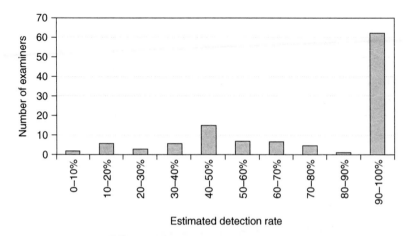

Figure 7.1 Average detection rate for all examiners (wages): 88 percent.

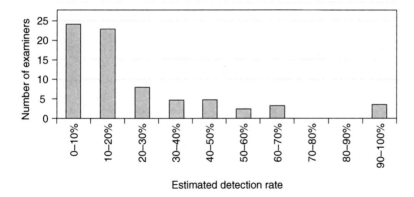

Figure 7.2 Average detection rate for all examiners (rents and royalties): 43 percent.

For both rents and royalties and Schedule C there is substantial heterogeneity, with the majority of examiners estimated as having detection rates below 50 percent, and a substantial number below 30 percent. These results are similar to the findings of our earlier analysis at a more aggregate level, but slightly more extreme. It would be important to explore whether the examiners estimated as perfect are more experienced, and also to check on the allocation of cases across examiners, as this might partly explain the substantial differences in detection rates.

In contrast to our results for examiner detection rates, we have found much less variation in the rate at which a given line item is classified for examination. To some extent, this may reflect common guidelines followed by classifiers for some classification decisions. However, the results might also reflect the fact that the classifiers were generally quite experienced, and therefore may have had similar work patterns.

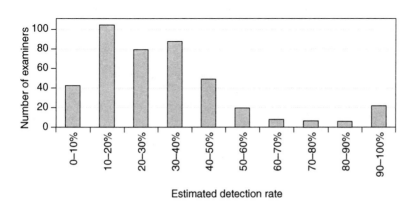

Figure 7.3 Average detection rate for all examiners (Schedule C net income): 32 percent.

Conclusion

In this chapter we have developed an econometric methodology to control for errors in assessments that result from multi-stage audit processes. We have applied our methodology to examine classification, examination, and non-compliance detection on a sample of federal individual income tax returns subjected to audits under the IRS National Research Program. Our models focus on non-compliance with respect to individual income components – the first time detection controlled estimation has been applied at this level of disaggregation.

Overall, we find that we are able to estimate the models successfully, and our preliminary results are broadly comparable to those obtained in previous analyses that have typically relied on more aggregated data. In particular, our initial estimates of non-compliance are broadly consistent with those found in many earlier studies. Our estimates of detection rates indicate substantial heterogeneity across examiners in detection rates for certain income items. We view the results shown here as preliminary and requiring further exploration.

Notes

1　This chapter is based on research performed under contract for the Internal Revenue Service. We thank Charles Bennett, Kim Bloomquist, Robert Brown, Janice Hedemann, Drew Johns, Mark Mazur, Alan Plumley, and Eric Toder for their considerable assistance with understanding the National Research Program data as well as various issues surrounding tax compliance and enforcement. We are also grateful to our discussant, Mark Rider, the editors, and the conference participants for their helpful comments. Any opinions expressed in this chapter are those of the authors and do not necessarily reflect the views of the Internal Revenue Service.

2　A more detailed discussion of the NRP is provided in Brown and Mazur (2003).

3　We note that NRP classifiers had access to "case-building" information when making their decisions. This information was drawn from a variety of sources, both governmental and non-governmental. Some of these sources include third-party information documents, previous year tax returns, IRS activity with respect to the taxpayer over the preceding several years, and a credit history. This information is placed on the NRP data record for the case – though the precise use made of it by the classifier is not recorded. We do make use of the third-party information reports in building our models, but we do not make use of other case-building information. The role of this additional information in the classification and audit process is an area for future research.

4　For the purposes of tax gap estimation, the IRS does net out the amount of income over-reporting discovered on returns from the estimated amount of income under-reporting prior to computing the change in tax liability. However, no adjustment is made to account for possible undiscovered cases of income over-reporting.

5　Refer to Alm *et al.* (1996) and Erard (1997, 1999) for examples of econometric studies that control for income over-reporting.

6　For all issues for which non-compliance is discovered in the NRP, the examiner is supposed to record the reason, as far as he can determine it, for the non-compliance, using a supplied list of reasons and the reason code. We do not use this information in our analysis.

7　As discussed in the previous section (Modeling issues), for purposes of estimation, if a taxpayer overstates his income on the return, we treat this as an instance of perfect compliance ($N=0$).

8 We note that there is a potential identification issue here; in subsequent work, we plan to incorporate the calibration sample to aid in identifying the model.
9 In the course of our work on this project we discovered that Feinstein does not account for this Jacobian term when deriving the likelihood function in his 1991 paper, a lacuna in his analysis.
10 To ensure identification of this portion of our odel, it is desirable that x_P includes at least one continuous variable that is excluded from x_{DP}.
11 There were too few cases involving alimony receipts to include in the analysis.

Bibliography

Alexander, C. and Feinstein, J. S. (1987) "A microeconometric analysis of income tax evasion and its detection", mimeo, Massachusetts Institute of Technology.

Alm, J., Erard, B., and Feinstein, J. S. (1996) "The relationship between state and federal tax audits", in M. Feldstein and J. M. Poterba (eds.) *Empirical Foundations of Household Taxation*, Chicago: University of Chicago Press.

Erard and Associates (2005) "IRS tax gap estimation: Preliminary results of detection controlled analysis", PowerPoint presentation to Internal Revenue Service Office of Research, November 1.

——. (2006) "Preliminary econometric results", Results Summary Report submitted to Internal Revenue Service Office of Research, January 27.

——. (2007). "Detection controlled estimation of tax non-compliance", PowerPoint presentation to Internal Revenue Service Office of Research and U.S. Treasury Office of Tax Analysis, February 5.

Brown, R. E. and Mazur, M. J. (2003) "IRS's comprehensive approach to compliance measurement", *National Tax Journal*, 41(3): 689–700.

Erard, B. (1993) "Taxation with representation: An analysis of the role of tax practitioners in tax compliance", *Journal of Public Economics*, 52(2): 163–97.

——. (1997) "Self-selection with measurement errors: A micro-econometric analysis of the decision to seek tax assistance and its implications for tax compliance", *Journal of Econometrics*, 81(2): 357–93.

——. (1999) "Estate tax under-reporting gap study", Report Prepared for the Internal Revenue Service Research Division, Order No. TIRNO-98-P-00406, March 4.

Feinstein, J. S. (1990) "Detection controlled estimation", *Journal of Law and Economics*, 33(1): 233–76.

——. (1991) "An econometric analysis of income tTax evasion and its detection", *RAND Journal of Economics*,22: 14–35.

——. (1989) "The safety regulation of U.S. nuclear power plants: Violations, inspections, and abnormal occurrences", *Journal of Political Economy*, 109: 360–9.

Internal Revenue Service. (2001) *National Research Program: Program Prospectus.*

——. (2003) *National Research Program: Individual Selection Summary Report*, February.

Part V

Empirical evidence on governance

8 Tax compliance, tax morale, and governance quality

Benno Torgler, Markus Schaffner, and Alison Macintyre[1]

Introduction

Adams' book (1993) begins with the inscription over the entrance to the Internal Revenue Service building: "Taxes are what we pay for a civilized society". An essential question for policy makers is the extent to which individuals are willing to pay this price, given that the probability of being audited by the tax administration is rather low. Allingham and Sandmo's (1972) groundbreaking model assumes that the extent of tax evasion is negatively correlated with both the probability of detection and the degree of punishment, and has since been widely criticized (see, for example, Alm *et al.*, 1992; Graetz and Wilde, 1985). Elffers (2000: 185) points out that "the gloomy picture of massive tax evasion is a phantom". A large share of revenues is collected without a draconian enforcement system. In many countries, the level of deterrence is too low to explain the high degree of tax compliance. Moreover, cooperation in tax compliance experiments is higher than neoclassical models would predict even after controlling for risk attitudes. Thus, the tax compliance literature has shown the necessity of going beyond the neoclassical approach when trying to understand why citizens pay taxes.

What are the reasons behind this puzzle of tax compliance? The literature in the last couple of years has stressed that the social norm of compliance or tax morale may help to explain why people willingly conform. An increasing number of studies have therefore explored which factors shape tax morale in an attempt to gain a broader understanding of this issue. However, there is still a lack of empirical evidence on the link between attitudes and behavior in the tax compliance literature. It is important to address this deficiency because the state and the tax administration have a variety of methods available to influence tax compliance, and traditional approaches such as deterrence can be seen as just one possible instrument. Thus, knowledge about the causes and consequences of tax morale could lead to a better tax policy.

In the first part of the chapter we explore the impact of tax morale on tax evasion or tax compliance using survey, laboratory experimental, and field data. We then take the research a step further and explore the *determinants* of tax morale, with a particular focus on whether governance and institutions matter.

The impact of tax morale on tax compliance

Overview and theoertical considerations

Since the 1990s, the issue of tax morale has increasingly attracted attention. The question of why so many people pay their taxes even though fines and audit probability are low has become a central issue in the tax compliance literature. Erard and Feinstein (1994) stress the relevance of integrating moral sentiments into the models to provide a reasonable explanation of actual compliance behavior, while Andreoni *et al.* (1998: 852) point out that "adding moral and social dynamics to models of tax compliance is as yet a largely undeveloped area of research". Many researchers maintain that a considerable portion of taxpayers are always honest. There are some taxpayers who are "simply predisposed not to evade" (Long and Swingen, 1991: 130), and thus do not even search for ways to cheat at taxes (see Frey, 1999).

Furthermore, Elffers (2000: 187) reasons that not everyone with "an inclination to dodge his taxes is able to translate his intention into action". Many individuals do not have the opportunity or the knowledge and resources to evade. Frey and Schneider (2000: 6) point out that moral costs could act as a disincentive to be active in the illegal sector: "A good citizen has moral qualms to undertake a forbidden activity. These moral costs are closely related to "tax morale" which motivates citizens to pay their dues to the state". An increase in tax morale increases the moral costs of behaving illegally, and therefore reduces the incentives to evade taxes. Spicer and Lundstedt (1976) claim that the choice between tax compliance and evasion is made not only on the grounds of sanctions but also on the grounds of a set of attitudes and norms. Lewis (1982: 165, 177) contends "it could be that tax evasion is the only channel through which taxpayers can express their antipathy ... we can be confident in our general prediction that if tax attitudes become worse, tax evasion will increase".

Polinsky and Shavell (2000), who present a survey of the economic theory of public enforcement of law, draw attention to the issue of social norms for future research. Social norms can be seen as a general alternative to law enforcement in channeling individuals' behavior. The violation of social norms has consequences, including internal sanctions (guilt, remorse) or external legal and social sanctions such as gossip and ostracism. Polinsky and Shavel (2000) explain that there is an expanding literature on social norms because of their influence on behavior, their role as a substitute for and supplement to formal laws, and the possibility that laws themselves can influence social norms.

In literature, we find interesting theories that enable us to integrate moral constraints in a rational taxpayer model. One theory taking an altruistic approach (see, for example, Chung, 1976) involves taxpayers who are not only interested in their own welfare but are also concerned about the general welfare. The decision to evade is constrained by the knowledge that their evasion will reduce the amount of resources available for social welfare. Another theory is the "Kantian" morality approach (see Laffont, 1975; Sugden, 1984). This methodology is broadly related to Kant's definition of morality, and is based on the assumption that a fair tax is a tax which a taxpayer believes to be fair for all other taxpayers to pay. A false declaration will generate anxiety, guilt, or a reduction in the taxpayer's self-image. It is assumed that taxpayers only experience these detrimental effects if they believe that their own tax share is lower than what is defined as fair. If a taxpayer is paying a higher amount, evasion can be seen as a sort of self-defence.

Erard and Feinstein (1994) incorporate shame and guilt directly into the taxpayer's utility. They hypothesize that taxpayers feel guilty when they under-report and escape detection, yet also feel ashamed when they under-report and gets caught. Gordon (1989) modifies the standard model by including non-pecuniary costs of evasion. He appeals to the literature on social customs (see Akerlof, 1980; Naylor, 1989) to provide a reason why utility loss can be incurred by the act of evading. Non-pecuniary or psychic cost increases as evasion increases, and Gordon develops a model which can explain why some taxpayers refuse a favorable evasion game. Furthermore, dishonesty is endogenized as reputation cost. Non-pecuniary costs have a dynamic component, varying inversely with the number of individuals having evaded in the previous period. Interestingly, there is a stable interior equilibrium where evaders and honest individuals coexist. However, non-pecuniary costs are exogenous to the analysis so that they can rationalize, but not explain, differences in tax behavior across consumers or social groups.

Myles and Naylor (1996) state that the model developed by Gordon is a step forward, but lies outside the mainstream of the social custom literature because psychic costs depend on the extent of evasion. They see no reason why such a relation should hold. They argue that if the psychic cost is due to the shame at prosecution then the extent of evasion is irrelevant, or if it is due to the fear of detection then it should be dependent on the detection probability rather than the extent of evasion. Based on the social custom literature, where it is accepted that once a social custom is broken all utility from it is lost, Myles and Naylor suggest a model in which a social custom utility is derived when taxes are paid honestly, but is lost when evasion is undertaken. In their model, taxpayers face a choice between evading or not. If a taxpayer chooses evasion, the standard model of tax evasion becomes operative. Myles and Naylor combine social customs and social conformity with the standard model which represents tax evasion as a choice with risk. Since then, further studies have also modeled this puzzle of tax compliance (see, for example, Schnellenbach, 2006).

Empirical results

We work with a varied set of methodologies to explore the impact of tax morale on tax evasion/compliance. This allows us to see the broader picture and get a better idea regarding the robustness of the results, because each of the techniques has its pros and cons (see Torgler, 2007).

Field/macro evidence

A number of previous studies have investigated the simple correlation between tax morale and the size of shadow in Western societies, transition countries, or Latin America (Alm and Torgler, 2006; *Alm et al.*, 2006; Torgler, 2001, 2005a). These studies report a negative correlation with R values between –0.51 and –0.66. However, these analyses give information only about the raw and not about the partial effects. The observed correlation might be explained in terms of factors that affect the size of the shadow economy. It is important to investigate the causes as a whole with their interdependencies. An investigation that focuses on a simple correlation has a somewhat limited validity. Thus, multiple regressions help us to disentangle the effects of other factors from a possible tax morale effect (for previous studies, see Torgler and Schneider, 2007a, 2007b).

To measure the shadow economy as a percentage of the official GDP, we use the DYMIMIC-method to estimate the parameters for determining the size of the shadow economy. With the help of the Currency Demand Method, we calibrate the estimated coefficients of the DYMIMIC procedure into absolute coefficients. We built a panel with values for the years 1990, 1995, and 2000. The fundamental principle of the database has been elaborated in many previous studies by Friedrich Schneider, and is therefore not further discussed in this chapter (see, for example, Schneider, 2005a, 2005b; Schneider and Enste; 2000, 2002).

In line with the recent literature on tax morale (see Torgler, 2007), we extract the relevant data from the World Values Survey (WVS) 1990–1993, 1995–1997, and 1999–2001 (see Inglehart, 2000). The WVS investigates socio-cultural and political change, and collects comparative data on values and belief systems. It is based on representative national samples of at least 1,000 individuals. The World Values Survey (WVS) is conducted worldwide, and covers quite a large number of countries. The general question posed to assess the level of tax morale is:

> Please tell me for each of the following statements whether you think it can always be justified, never be justified, or something in between: (…) Cheating on tax if you have the chance (% "never justified" – code 1 from a ten-point scale where 1 = never and 10 = always).

The tax morale variable is developed by recoding the ten-point scale into a four-point scale (0 to 3), with the value 3 standing for "never justifiable". The value of 0 is an aggregation of the last seven scale points, which were rarely chosen. The baseline equation has the following form:

$$SHADOW_{it} = \alpha + \beta_1\ CTRL_{it} + \beta_2\ TAXMORALE_{it} + \beta_3\ TD_t + \beta_4\ REGION_i + \varepsilon_{it} \quad (1)$$

where *i* indexes the countries in the sample, and $SHADOW_{it}$ denotes countries' size of the shadow economy as a percentage of the official GDP over the periods 1990, 1995, and 2000. $TAXMORALE_{it}$ is the level of tax morale. In line with Torgler and Schneider (2007a), the regressions also contain several control variables, $CTRL_i$,[2] including factors such as GDP per capita, the share of agriculture in GDP, the share of urban population, the size of the population, the labor force, and the marginal tax rate. To control for time as well as regional invariant factors, we include fixed time, TD_t, and fixed regional effects, $REGION_i$.[3] The error term is denoted by ε_{it}.

Table 8.1 presents the results using two different types of empirical methodology: pooling, and fixed effect regressions. In the pooled estimations, the *beta* or *standardized* regression coefficients compare magnitude, which reveals the relative importance of a variable. To obtain robust standard errors in these estimations, we use the Huber/White/Sandwich estimators of standard errors. We start with an OLS regression that includes only tax morale together with regional and time fixed effects. We observe that tax morale has a strong impact on the size of the shadow economy (high R^2 values); an increase in tax morale leads to a reduction of the size of the shadow economy. In specifications (2) and (3), we add several control variables.

The beta coefficient in specification (2) shows that the quantitative impact of tax morale is comparable to other determinants. In specification (3), we also present results with standard errors adjusted for the clustering on countries to account for unobservable country characteristics. Tax morale is also statistically significant in these estimates. In specifications (4)–(6) we present a fixed effect model, and in specification (6) we also include a proxy for the top marginal tax rate. These results support the overall conclusion that tax morale matters. The last part in Table 8.1 explores potential causality problems. It can be argued that a substantial growth of the shadow economy can lead to a crowding out of the willingness to pay taxes. The more taxpayers believe that others work in the shadow economy, the lower are the moral costs incurred if they behave dishonestly and evade taxes by transferring their own activities into the shadow economy. We therefore present a 2SLS estimation together with the first-stage regression and several diagnostic tests. In the 2SLS regression, we also observe a strong correlation between tax morale and the size of the shadow economy.

In line with previous studies (e.g., Schaltegger and Torgler, 2007; Torgler and Schneider, 2007a), we use a climate proxy as an instrument. Engerman and Sokoloff (1997), Landes (1998), and Sachs (2000) each found a connection between climate and economic development, and the social psychology literature has shown that our instrument of "cloudiness" has a negative impact on individuals' attitudes, well-being, and moods (see, for example, Eagles, 1994; Tietjan and Kripke, 1994). We observe a strong negative correlation between tax morale and cloudiness ($R = -0.414$) and a low correlation between the shadow economy and cloudiness (-0.028). The *F*-test for the instrument exclusion set in the first-stage regression is also statistically significant, in line with the test for instrument relevance (Anderson canonical correlations LR). Overall, Table 8.1 supports the premise that tax morale has a substantial impact on the size of the shadow economy.

Looking at the control variables, we can see that a higher GDP per capita is associated with a smaller shadow economy. We also observe a positive correlation between the share of agriculture in GDP and the shadow economy. On the other

Table 8.1 Determinants of the shadow economy

Dependent variable: shadow economy	OLS^v	OLS^v	OLS Clust. on countries	FE	FE	FE	2SLS	First stage regression
	(1)	(2)	(3)	(4)	(5)	(6)	(7)	
A WILLINGNESS TO PAY								
TAX MORALE	-0.222*** (-3.23)	-0.164** (-2.63)	-5.606*** (-2.24)	-7.605*** (-3.23)	-5.606** (-2.63)	-6.868*** (-2.75)	-32.541** (-2.13)	
B CONTROL VARIABLE								
LOG (GDP PER CAPITA)		-0.578*** (-3.83)	-5.372*** (-2.97)		-5.372*** (-3.83)	-4.536 (-2.58)	-1.514 (-0.51)	0.157*** (2.66)
AGRICULTURE (% OF GDP)		0.252** (2.47)	0.333* (1.88)		0.333** (2.47)	0.565** (2.61)	0.456** (2.14)	0.006 (1.03)
URBANIZATION		0.244*** (3.22)	0.193** (2.21)		0.193*** (3.22)	0.189*** (2.77)	0.005 (0.04)	-0.006** (-2.39)
LOG (POPULATION)		0.803 (1.27)	7.092 (0.83)		7.092 (1.27)	4.695 (0.75)	18.846* (1.78)	0.170 (0.64)
LOG (LABOR FORCE)		-0.962 (-1.52)	-8.583 (-0.97)		-8.583 (-1.52)	-6.670 (-1.06)	-20.286* (-1.91)	-0.155 (-0.58)
TRADE (% GDP)		-0.102 (-1.46)	-0.040 (-1.12)		-0.040 (-1.46)	-0.065** (-2.05)	-0.174** (-2.05)	-0.004*** (-3.23)

TOP MARGINAL TAX RATE

	(1)	(2)	(3)	(4)	(5)	(6)	(7)	(8)
Instrument for tax morale								
Cloudiness						−0.015 (−0.04)		−0.007** (−2.27)
Test of excluded instruments								5.14**
Anderson canon. corr. LR statistic								5.43**
Anderson Rubin test								10.34***
Regional fixed effects	YES	YES	YES	YES	YES	YES	YES	YES
Time fixed effects	YES	YES	YES	YES	YES	YES	YES	YES
Observations	127	127	127	127	127	105	127	127
R^2	0.531	0.749	0.749	0.465	0.714	0.701	0.314	0.439
Prob>F	0.000	0.000	0.000	0.000	0.000	0.000	0.000	0.000

Notes
t-statistics in parentheses. Significance levels: * $0.05 < p < 0.10$, ** $0.01 < p < 0.05$, *** $p < 0.01$.
Regressions with robust standard errors,
a beta coefficients reported.

hand, there is a general tendency for trade (which is transparent and easier to tax) to be negatively correlated with the size of the shadow economy. Thus, the results indicate that sectors which are difficult to tax will report a larger shadow economy. Finally, we also observe a trend towards positive correlation between urbanization and the size of the shadow economy.

Experimental evidence

There are some problems involved with measuring tax evasion and tax compliance. Tax evaders' behavior could be affected by specific circumstances, which are difficult to control. An experimental approach circumvents the problem by generating data in a controlled environment. One possible approach could be to compare the tax compliance results from experiments with a post-experiment questionnaire that assists in gathering information about subjects' attitudes (e.g., Bosco and Mittone, 1997). The main disadvantage of such a method is that behavior during the experiment might influence people's answers to the questions.

In general, laboratory experiments have been criticized as a method that lacks realism. Choices in the laboratory may not accurately reflect the choices in the "outside world", as the setting is too artificial. Thus, tax experimenters try to increase external validity by making the circumstances of the study more realistic. Important factors in the tax compliance experiments, such as audit probability, fine rate, tax rate, etc., have been adapted to real values. Researchers have accordingly done an excellent job in improving the realism of the experiments and trying to analyze cognitive processes that might be similar in reality (see Torgler, 2002). As a result, in this chapter we use the common experimental design structure observed in the literature (see, for example, Alm, 1999; Torgler, 2007).

We conducted experiments in Switzerland, Australia, and Costa Rica between 2002 and 2007 (for a detailed discussion, see Torgler and Schaltegger, 2005; Torgler, 2004; Torgler *et al.*, 2003). All instructions were presented in the same language (English) in each of the three countries. Moreover, the main experimenters (first two authors) were the same in all the trials, to eliminate possible variations arising from uncontrolled procedural differences or uncontrolled personal differences between the experimenters.

In total, 239 subjects took part in the experiments, covering 31 groups or sessions. Participants were aged between 18 and 67 years (mean=25), and 35 percent of these participants were female. Each session lasted either 23 or 25 rounds. Subjects did not know in advance when the experiment would end. Communication was not allowed, except in the situation where discussion was explicitly promoted by the experimenters. The laboratory currency was lab "dollars". The income distribution was either exogenous (subjects received the same income in every period, namely 200 lab dollars) or endogenous. In those experiments where the income distribution was endogenous, subjects were divided into two income categories (200 lab dollars or 400 lab dollars). The income distribution was based on individual performance in a test in which participants were confronted with numerical series following certain numerical patterns.

The experiment lasted about an hour, and participants earned up to around $20 from their accumulated wealth during the experiment.[4] Two endogenous audit selection rules were introduced in the experiment. First, if a subject was audited and found to evade taxes, then the previous four periods were assessed. The evader had to pay all unpaid taxes, plus a penalty on unpaid taxes of the same amount (fine rate=2). Secondly, if the audited subject had reported all income, the previous periods were not examined. Thus, the tax agency went back in time to previous periods' declarations. Furthermore, the audit probability increased from 5 percent to 10 percent, depending on the amount of non-declared income between the present year and the declaration of the year before. In such an experimental design the probability of audit is endogenous, depending on the behavior of taxpayers throughout the experiment.

One experimental design investigated the extent to which the recognition of government services has an effect on tax compliance (see Torgler, 2004). To measure the appreciation of government services, consumers' surplus derived from the government's provision of public goods was changed by varying the group's surplus multiplier (0/1/2 and 3). The resulting amount was then redistributed in equal shares to the members of the group. After a round, subjects' net income in groups 2, 3, and 4 could be calculated as income after taxes plus a share of the multiplied group tax fund. The first group was used as a control group, and thus did not receive any redistribution.

The second experimental design investigated the impact of tax amnesties on tax compliance (see Torgler and Schaltegger, 2005; Torgler *et al.*, 2003). The tax amnesty experiments also implemented a public good structure by doubling taxes on declared income and redistributing the revenue in equal shares to the members of the group. After every round, each subject's net income could thus be calculated as income less taxes plus the share of the group tax fund. The tax rate was held constant at 20 percent. With the exception of a short instruction sheet at the beginning, the experiment was conducted entirely on computers and was programmed with an interactive experimental software named z-Tree (Zurich Toolbox for Readymade Economic Experiments, Fischbacher, 2007). Each subject was informed in every round about the audit probability, the penalty rate, the accumulated income (fortune), and the individual tax redistribution. Before playing 23 or 25 rounds in every session, three practice rounds took place to make sure everybody understood the design. Subjects were informed that the performance in the practice periods did not affect their payments, and were confronted with an explicit tax context language. We used tax terms such as "income to declare", "tax rate", "audit probability", and "fine rate" in order to integrate contextual factors that are important in determining tax reporting behavior. Furthermore, this procedure ensures subjects do not simply perceive the experiment as a mere gamble. Subjects also completed a post-experimental questionnaire, which helped us to investigate the impact of tax morale on tax compliance and to control for other factors (e.g., gender differences) in our econometric estimations.

We use two proxies to investigate the impact of tax morale. The first is the same question we used in our previous macro investigation:

> Please tell me for the following statement whether you think it can always be justified, never be justified, or something in between: Cheat on tax if you have the chance (10=never and 1=always).

The second is an unweighted average value of the scores regarding the following:

1   Given present tax burdens, one can hardly blame tax evaders.
2   Given the easy availability of opportunities to evade taxes, one can hardly blame tax evaders.
3   If in doubt about whether or not to report a certain source of income, I would not report it.
4   Since the government gets enough taxes, it does not matter that some people evade taxes.
5   Taxes are so heavy that tax evasion is an economic necessity for many to survive.
6   If I received $2,000 in cash for services rendered, I would not report it.
7   Cheating on taxes is justifiable in light of the unfairness of the tax system
8   Taxes are something which is taken away from me.
9   Since everybody evades taxes, one can hardly be blamed for doing it.
10 There is nothing bad about under-reporting taxable income on one's tax return.
    (1=strongly disagree; 2=disagree; 3=neutral; 4=agree, 5=strongly agree).

Our two main estimation equations read as:

$$TCit = \alpha + \beta 1 \; CTRLit + \beta 2 \; TAXMORALEit + \beta 3 \; AUDITit$$
$$+ \beta 4 \; TRANSFit + \beta 5 \; WEALTHit + \beta 6 \; EXPi + \beta 7 \; COUNTRi + \varepsilon it \qquad (2)$$

$$TCit = \alpha + \beta 1 \; CTRLit + \beta 2 \; TAXMORALEit + \beta 3 \; AUDITit$$
$$+ \beta 4 \; TRANSFit + \beta 5 \; WEALTHit + \beta 6 \; GROUPi + \varepsilon it \qquad (3)$$

where TC_{it} denotes the tax compliance rate, $CTRL_{it}$ covers the control variables age and gender (female=1), and $TAXMORALE_{it}$ are our two tax morale variables. We measure deterrence ($AUDIT_{it}$) with two different proxies: the first one is a dummy variable equal to 1 if the individual was audited in the previous round and 0 otherwise; the second measures the number of times a subject has been inspected (adjusted after every audit). For simplicity, we are only going to report the results using the second variable; however, both proxies provide similar results. $TRANSF_{it}$ is the amount an individual obtains from the group fund at the end of the previous round, and $WEALTH_{it}$ is the individual's accumulated earnings. In equation (2), we use dummy variables for the experimental design (EXP_i) and country dummy variables ($COUNTR_i$). In equation (3), we go one step further and use dummy variables for each group/session ($GROUP_i$). Because of the presence of the public good, one subject's payoff depends upon the behavior of all other subjects in a group. As a result, it seems reasonable to add group dummy variables, and it also helps to deal with the fact that the number of subjects varies in each session.

Table 8.2 presents the results. In specifications (1) to (4) we begin by reporting Tobit maximum likelihood estimations, since the compliance rate varies between 0 and 1 and there are many observations with the values 0 and 1. Due to the panel structure of the data, we include a random-effects estimation to control for time-specific effects. The random-effects model is appropriate if we assume that the individual specific constant terms are randomly distributed across cross-sectional units.

We add the deterrence variable sequentially (see (1) and (3)) in the specification due to possible causality problems. In specifications (1) and (2) we use the WVS tax morale proxy, and in regressions (3) and (4) we use the index of tax morale. In the next four specifications, (4)–(8), we add random-effects GLS regressions to check the robustness of the results. We include the audit probability in all of these regressions.

In specifications (7) and (8), we use group/session dummy variables instead of country and experimental design dummies. In taking the analysis a step further, we work with OLS models using group and time dummy variables, reporting the *beta* or *standardized* regression coefficients to reveal the relative importance of a variable. Finally, in regressions (11) and (12) we present ordered probit models (3 = full compliance, 1 = zero compliance, 2 = values in between). We also report the marginal effects which indicate the change in the share of taxpayers (or the probability) belonging to a specific tax compliance level, when the independent variable increases by one unit. For simplicity, only the marginal effects for the highest tax compliance level are shown.

Table 8.2 indicates that tax morale has a strong and positive impact on tax compliance, and in all estimations the coefficient was statistically significant at the 1 percent level. The beta coefficient also indicates that the quantitative effect is comparable to the other variables. The ordered probit models indicate that an increase in the tax morale scale by one unit raises the probability of being fully compliant between 2.7 (WVS question) and 11.0 (index) percentage points. Thus, the quantitative effects are quite meaningful.

Looking at the control variables we also observe that females are more compliant than males, and that age is negatively correlated with compliance. In addition, we find that a higher group transfer is positively correlated with tax compliance and that there is tendency for wealth to affect compliance in a negative manner. Higher transfers give subjects a signal that the group on average behaves honestly, and consequently the moral costs of being opportunistic increase. Finally, we observe a negative correlation between deterrence and

Table 8.2 The impact of tax morale on tax compliance in laboratory experiments

Variables	Random-effects Tobit regressions[a]		Random-effects GLS		OLS[b]		Ordered probit[c]	
TAX MORALE WVS	0.039*** (10.75)	0.034*** (9.34)	0.013*** (6.73)	0.011*** (5.77)	0.071*** (5.44)		0.069*** (9.42)	
TAX MORALE INDEX	0.182*** (14.00)	0.157*** (12.11)	0.058*** (8.89)	0.048*** (6.98)		0.092*** (6.91)		0.283*** (10.35)
AUDIT	−0.143*** (−13.04)	−0.134*** (−12.28)	−0.052*** (−9.49)	−0.043*** (−7.83)	−0.124*** (−8.23)	−0.117*** (−7.72)	−0.300*** (−13.78)	−0.285*** (−13.10)
GROUP TRANSFER	0.001*** (4.30)	0.001*** (3.92)	0.0003*** (3.39)	0.0004*** (4.07)	0.068*** (2.95)	0.068*** (2.91)	0.002*** (2.81)	0.002 (2.71)
WEALTH	0.000*** (−2.85)	0.000*** (−3.02)	0.000 (−1.41)	0.000* (−1.77)	−0.202*** (−6.96)	−0.212*** (−7.20)	0.000*** (−4.27)	0.000*** (−4.89)
FEMALE	0.282*** (15.49)	0.271*** (14.89)	0.140*** (15.10)	0.147*** (15.86)	0.210*** (16.61)	0.216*** (17.19)	0.490*** (13.06)	0.523*** (13.92)
AGE	−0.003*** (−2.19)	−0.002 (−1.43)	−0.004*** (−6.08)	−0.004*** (−5.23)	−0.075*** (−4.61)	−0.064*** (−4.04)	0.004* (1.77)	0.008*** (3.33)
COUNTRY DUMMY[d]	YES	YES	YES	YES	NO	NO	NO	NO
EXP. DESIGN DUMMY[d]	YES	YES	YES	YES	NO	NO	NO	NO
TIME DUMMIES	YES	YES	YES	YES	YES	YES	YES	YES
GROUP DUMMIES[e]	NO	NO	NO	YES	NO	NO	YES	YES
Prob>chi²	0.000	0.000	0.000	0.000	0.000	0.000	0.000	0.000
Number of observations	5,719	5,719	5,719	5,719	5,719	5,719	5,719	5,719
R²/Pseudo R²	0.101	0.107	0.168	0.170	0.176	0.179	0.123	0.126

Notes

Dependent variable is the compliance rate. [a] 478 left-censored observations, 2,393 right-censored observations, 2,848 uncensored observations. [b] Beta coefficients reported. [c] Marginal effects. [c] highest tax compliance scale (full compliance). [d] Equation (2) and [e] equation (3). Significance levels: *0.05<p<0.10, **0.01<p<0.05, ***p<0.01. Regressions with robust standard errors. The z-statistics are in bold and marginal effects in italics. Total number of subjects: 239. Number of groups: 31. Number of rounds: 23 or 25.

compliance which is not consistent with an economics-of-crime approach but in line with some other studies (for an overview see Torgler and Schaltegger, 2005). In sum, the experimental results also indicate that tax morale matters.

To check the robustness of the results, we also conducted regressions without the transfer variable. A criticism may be that the variable suffers from endogeneity problems, given that its magnitude depends upon what subjects choose to do. The results show a robust impact of tax morale on tax compliance. The quantitative effects hardly change.

Survey evidence: micro-analysis

To obtain further empirical insights, we work with the Taxpayer Opinion Survey (TOS). In general, surveys provide the opportunity to study a variety of factors, especially attitudes. It is even possible to integrate questions about taxpayers' behavior. However, this approach is not free of biases, because the problem with asking delicate questions lies in knowing whether the answers received are honest. Jackson and Milliron (1986) point out that the technique used to solicit responses and the way questions are framed have an effect on the respondents' answers. One way to deal with this problem is to conduct and evaluate a variety of surveys to get a *general picture* of the main variables. An excellent method would be to conduct panels or to do regular surveys in different countries, similar to the structure of the TOS. In recent years, social researchers have intensively used surveys to investigate the causes and consequences of social capital or compliance behavior. One reason might be that survey research now uses more sophisticated statistical techniques and designs compared to those employed in the earlier years.

We work with the Taxpayer Opinion Survey, collected in the United States in 1987 and providing a broad set of taxpayers' opinions and evaluations of aspects including the tax system, the Internal Revenue Service, tax evasion, and cheating on taxes. Surprisingly, the TOS has not been used by many researchers (see, for example, Sheffrin and Triest, 1992; Smith, 1992). Even if the data set is relatively old, the large number of questions and the fact that not many papers have utilized the data set makes it attractive for newer research projects (see, for example, Forest and Sheffrin, 2002, using the 1990 TOS, or Torgler and Schaffner, 2007). Unfortunately, further data are not available, as the TOS has not been conducted since 1990. The TOS allows separate analysis of two methods of tax evasion (overstating of deduction or expenses and under-reporting income) as the dependent variable. The advantage of the TOS data set is that it poses quite a few questions on tax morale. We use the following scenarios, and ask about their degree of acceptability (scale from 1 to 6, where 6 means not at all acceptable and 1 means perfectly acceptable):

1 Trading or exchanging goods or services with a friend or neighbor and not reporting it on your tax form **(TM 1)**.
2 Reporting your main income fully, but not including some small outside income **(TM 2)**.

3 Being paid in cash for a job and then not reporting it on your tax form **(TM 3)**.
4 Not reporting some earnings from investments or interest that the government would not be able to find out about **(TM 4)**.
5 Stretching medical deductions to include some expenses which are not really medical **(TM 5)**.

The following statements were also used (6=strongly disagree, 1=strongly agree):

6 With what things cost these days, it's okay to cut a few corners on your tax form just to help make ends meet **(TM 6)**.
7 It's not so wrong to hold back a little bit of taxes since the government spends too much anyway **(TM 7)**.
8 Almost every taxpayer would cheat to some extent if he thought he could get away with it **(TM 8)**.
9 In this age of computers, you're bound to get caught if you cheat at all on your taxes **(TM 9)**.
10 The chances of getting caught are so low that it is worthwhile trying to cut corners a little on your taxes **(TM 10)**.
11 When you're not really sure whether or not you deserve a tax deduction, it makes sense to take a chance and take the deduction anyway **(TM 11)**.
12 It's all right to occasionally under-report certain income or claim an undeserved deduction if you are generally a loyal and law-abiding citizen **(TM 12)**
13 When you know you deserve a deduction they won't let you take, it makes sense to take it some other place where they won't catch you on it **(TM 13)**
14 It is not so wrong to under-report certain income since it does not really hurt anyone **(TM 14)**
15 There's nothing wrong with interpreting the ambiguous or gray areas of the tax law to your own advantage **(TM 15)**

Tax evasion was measured with the following two questions:

1 Within the past five years or so, do you think you might have left some reportable income off your federal tax return – even just a minor amount? (1, Definitely have not; 2, Probably have not; 3, Probably have; 4, Definitely have.)
2 Within the past five years or so, do you think you might have overstated any deductions or expenses – like medical, charitable or business deductions, and so forth – even by just a small amount? Would you say you definitely have, probably have, probably have not, or definitely have not overstated any? (1, Definitely have not; 2, Probably have not; 3, Probably have; 4, Definitely have.)

There are pros and cons of using such tax evasion measurements. Looking at the empirical data, the advantage is that we hardly ever find data sets that try to measure the extent of tax evasion in a survey. Lewis (1982: 140) points out:

But why not just ask respondents whether they evade tax or not? If they admit it, ask them how much this amounts to and perhaps even why they do it? What could be simpler? (…) Maybe it is worth a try. But some traditional wisdom (and a smattering of social psychology) recommends a tempering of enthusiasm.

On the other hand, Lewis (1982) is aware of problems with such a procedure. People might refuse to answer or to take part in such a survey, or they may moderate their views to reduce the possibility that information is used non-confidentially – for example, to prosecute taxpayers. As a consequence, such an approach would induce a tendency to *overestimate* tax compliance. Lempert (1992) criticizes the scale used in the TOS to catch over-deduction and under-declarations on the grounds that using terms such as "probably" and "minor amount" encourage individuals to state that they have engaged in tax evasion. Finally, it is difficult to ask people about their behavior five years ago.

We use a common specification that covers socio-demographic and socio-economic variables, risk attitudes, and tax morale, and we also run specifications with the perceived audit probability. Interestingly, the coefficient was found to be not statistically significant. Thus, due to the high number of missing values we have decided not to report the results of the variable in the following tables. In sum, the two main estimation equations are the following:

$$TAXEV1i = \alpha + \beta1 \; SOCIOi + \beta2 \; TAXMORALEi + \beta3 \; RISKi + \varepsilon i \qquad (4)$$

$$TAXEV2i = \alpha + \beta1 \; SOCIOi + \beta2 \; TAXMORALEi + \beta3 \; RISKi + \varepsilon i \qquad (5)$$

where $TAXEV1_i$ and $TAXEV2_i$ denote the tax evasion variables under-declaration and over-deduction; $SOCIO_i$ is a panel of control variables including age, gender, education, income, marital and employment status; and $TAXMORALE_{it}$ are our 15 tax morale variables. In addition, we also measure whether individuals are risk-takers.[5]

We estimate 30 equations with 15 different tax morale variables. This helps check the sensitivity of the relationship between tax evasion and tax morale. Ordered probit equations are estimated to analyze the ranking information of the scaled dependent variables tax evasion. We also use the weighting variable provided by the TOS to get a representative population size. The Tables 8.3 and 8.4 present the results using under-reporting and over-deducting as the dependent variable. Only the marginal effects for the lower tax evasion values are shown, and this explains the sign of the values. The results indicate a strong negative correlation between tax morale and tax evasion. In 29 out of 30 regressions, the coefficient is statistically significant.

Table 8.3 indicates that an increase in tax morale of one point increases the share of persons indicating that they have definitely not under-declared by between 3.0 and 7.5 percentage points. Table 8.4 also shows that the probability of definitely not over-deducting increases by between 0.8 and 6.7 percentage

Table 8.3 Determinants of under-declaration

Weighted ordered probit

Independent variable	TM1	TM2	TM3	TM4	TM5	TM6	TM7	TM8	TM9	TM10	TM11	TM12	TM13	TM14	TM15
TAX MORALE	-0.10***	-0.13***	-0.16***	-0.13***	-0.10***	-0.13***	-0.14***	-0.11***	-0.09***	-0.11***	-0.08***	-0.22***	-0.13***	-0.16***	-0.13***
(TM1–15)	-4.48	-6.08	-7.47	-5.45	-3.72	-5.33	-5.58	-4.69	-3.77	-3.94	-3.53	-8.52	-4.93	-6.02	-5.79
	0.033	0.043	0.054	0.044	0.033	0.044	0.047	0.039	0.030	0.036	0.028	0.074	0.043	0.055	0.045
AGE	-0.01***	-0.01***	-0.01***	-0.01***	-0.01***	-0.01***	-0.01***	-0.01***	-0.02***	-0.01***	-0.01***	-0.01***	-0.01***	-0.01***	-0.01***
	-5.79	-5.06	-4.20	-4.89	-5.61	-5.16	-4.97	-5.13	-6.06	-5.41	-5.87	-4.49	-4.74	-4.48	-5.48
	0.005	0.004	0.004	0.004	0.005	0.004	0.004	0.004	0.005	0.005	0.005	0.004	0.004	0.004	0.005
FEMALE	-0.33***	-0.31***	-0.31***	-0.31***	-0.32***	-0.32***	-0.29***	-0.34***	-0.32***	-0.31***	-0.35***	-0.27***	-0.26***	-0.30***	-0.29***
	-3.71	-3.51	-3.42	-3.46	-3.54	-3.55	-3.24	-3.77	-3.58	-3.46	-3.92	-3.01	-2.92	-3.33	-3.18
	0.110	0.105	0.102	0.105	0.107	0.106	0.096	0.115	0.108	0.105	0.118	0.091	0.088	0.100	0.097
EDUCATION	0.05**	0.06**	0.06**	0.07***	0.05**	0.06***	0.06**	0.06**	0.06***	0.06**	0.06**	0.07***	0.06***	0.06***	0.03
	2.10	2.48	2.52	2.80	2.28	2.71	2.44	2.57	2.63	2.37	2.41	2.83	2.61	2.67	1.27
	-0.017	-0.020	-0.020	-0.023	-0.018	-0.022	-0.020	-0.021	-0.021	-0.019	-0.019	-0.022	-0.021	-0.022	-0.011
MARRIED	0.05	0.07	0.08	0.08	0.04	0.05	0.06	0.07	0.04	0.05	0.06	0.12	0.10	0.09	0.07
	0.64	0.90	0.99	0.97	0.58	0.65	0.76	0.92	0.57	0.61	0.75	1.59	1.21	1.15	0.91
	-0.017	-0.023	-0.026	-0.025	-0.015	-0.017	-0.020	-0.024	-0.015	-0.016	-0.020	-0.041	-0.032	-0.030	-0.024

	C1	C2	C3	C4	C5	C6	C7	C8	C9	C10	C11	C12	C13	C14	C15
INCOME	-0.02	-0.02	-0.02	-0.03	-0.02	-0.02	-0.02	-0.03	-0.02	-0.03	-0.03	-0.02	-0.03	-0.02	-0.03
	-1.20	**-1.07**	**-1.06**	**-1.39**	**-1.14**	**-1.14**	**-1.04**	**-1.44**	**-1.08**	**-1.46**	**-1.38**	**-1.15**	**-1.27**	**-1.20**	**-1.60**
	0.008	0.007	0.007	0.010	0.008	0.008	0.007	0.010	0.007	0.010	0.009	0.008	0.009	0.008	0.011
SELF-EMPLOYED	0.35***	0.35***	0.38***	0.26**	0.31***	0.30**	0.30***	0.31***	0.32***	0.33***	0.30***	0.34***	0.31***	0.31***	0.27**
	3.09	**3.07**	**3.31**	**2.24**	**2.71**	**2.60**	**2.66**	**2.73**	**2.79**	**2.87**	**2.65**	**2.93**	**2.70**	**2.74**	**2.30**
	-0.127	-0.127	-0.137	-0.092	-0.113	-0.106	-0.107	-0.112	-0.115	-0.121	-0.108	-0.121	-0.109	-0.111	-0.095
RISK ATTITUDES	0.16***	0.12**	0.12**	0.13**	0.13**	0.13**	0.16***	0.13**	0.13**	0.13**	0.15***	0.13**	0.14**	0.16***	0.13**
	3.09	**2.22**	**2.41**	**2.56**	**2.59**	**2.49**	**2.98**	**2.50**	**2.56**	**2.46**	**2.82**	**2.42**	**2.54**	**3.03**	**2.49**
	-0.054	-0.039	-0.041	-0.045	-0.045	-0.044	-0.053	-0.046	-0.045	-0.044	-0.051	-0.043	-0.046	-0.053	-0.045
Observations	1,173	1,187	1,189	1,176	1,178	1,192	1,194	1,170	1,176	1,169	1,154	1,182	1,166	1,182	1,137
Prob>>chi²	0.000	0.000	0.000	0.000	0.000	0.000	0.000	0.000	0.000	0.000	0.000	0.000	0.000	0.000	0.000
Pseudo R²	0.055	0.062	0.071	0.057	0.049	0.057	0.059	0.053	0.049	0.050	0.052	0.075	0.052	0.062	0.060

Notes

Dependent variable: tax evasion on a four point scale. The z-statistics are in bold and the marginal effects in italics (lowest tax evasion scale (0)). Significance levels: *$0.05 < p < 0.10$, **$0.01 < p < 0.05$, ***$p < 0.01$.

Table 8.4 Determinants of over-deductions

Weighted ordered probit

Independent variable	TM1	TM2	TM3	TM4	TM5	TM6	TM7	TM8	TM9	TM10	TM11	TM12	TM13	TM14	TM15
TAX MORALE	−0.07***	−0.08***	−0.11***	−0.14***	−0.15***	−0.15***	−0.15***	−0.06**	−0.02	−0.14***	−0.15***	−0.20***	−0.19***	−0.16***	−0.15***
(TM1–15)	**−3.08**	**−3.68**	**−4.93**	**−6.04**	**−6.10**	**−6.30**	**−5.86**	**−2.57**	**−0.99**	**−5.19**	**−6.39**	**−7.52**	**−7.37**	**−5.90**	**−6.36**
	0.021	*0.026*	*0.035*	*0.047*	*0.050*	*0.050*	*0.048*	*0.019*	*0.008*	*0.048*	*0.048*	*0.067*	*0.062*	*0.053*	*0.048*
AGE	−0.01***	−0.01***	−0.01***	−0.01***	−0.01***	−0.01***	−0.01***	−0.01***	−0.01***	−0.01***	−0.01***	−0.01***	−0.01**	−0.01**	−0.01***
	−3.52	**−3.26**	**−2.88**	**−2.71**	**−2.92**	**−2.68**	**−2.74**	**−3.75**	**−3.85**	**−3.38**	**−3.23**	**−2.61**	**−2.47**	**−2.48**	**−2.83**
	0.003	*0.003*	*0.002*	*0.002*	*0.002*	*0.002*	*0.002*	*0.003*	*0.003*	*0.003*	*0.003*	*0.002*	*0.002*	*0.002*	*0.002*
FEMALE	−0.03	−0.02	−0.002	0.01	0.01	−0.01	0.01	−0.05	−0.02	0.00	−0.02	0.04	0.05	0.03	0.07
	−0.34	**−0.24**	**−0.02**	**0.07**	**0.13**	**−0.11**	**0.15**	**−0.61**	**−0.24**	**−0.02**	**−0.26**	**0.42**	**0.50**	**0.37**	**0.71**
	0.010	*0.007*	*0.001*	*−0.002*	*−0.004*	*0.003*	*−0.004*	*0.018*	*0.007*	*0.000*	*0.008*	*−0.012*	*−0.015*	*−0.011*	*−0.021*
EDUCATION	0.08***	0.08***	0.07***	0.09***	0.08***	0.09***	0.08***	0.08***	0.08***	0.08***	0.06**	0.08***	0.09***	0.09***	0.06**
	2.92	**2.97**	**2.84**	**3.50**	**3.14**	**3.41**	**3.22**	**3.09**	**3.04**	**3.02**	**2.41**	**3.19**	**3.37**	**3.35**	**2.18**
	−0.025	*−0.025*	*−0.024*	*−0.030*	*−0.027*	*−0.029*	*−0.028*	*−0.026*	*−0.026*	*−0.026*	*−0.021*	*−0.027*	*−0.029*	*−0.028*	*−0.019*
MARRIED	0.18**	0.21**	0.24***	0.24***	0.17**	0.21**	0.21**	0.21***	0.18**	0.21**	0.20**	0.29***	0.27***	0.24***	0.23***
	2.22	**2.58**	**2.85**	**2.87**	**2.12**	**2.50**	**2.56**	**2.60**	**2.22**	**2.51**	**2.35**	**3.44**	**3.17**	**2.87**	**2.68**
	−0.059	*−0.069*	*−0.076*	*−0.077*	*−0.057*	*−0.066*	*−0.068*	*−0.069*	*−0.059*	*−0.068*	*−0.064*	*−0.092*	*−0.085*	*−0.077*	*−0.073*

INCOME	0.06***	0.06***	0.06***	0.05**	0.06***	0.06***	0.06***	0.06***	0.07***	0.06***	0.06***	0.07***	0.05**	0.06***	0.06***
	2.94	**2.99**	**3.02**	**2.58**	**2.66**	**2.83**	**2.84**	**2.80**	**3.21**	**2.61**	**2.77**	**3.11**	**2.54**	**3.05**	**2.88**
	-0.020	*-0.020*	*-0.021*	*-0.018*	*-0.018*	*-0.019*	*-0.020*	*-0.019*	*-0.022*	*-0.018*	*-0.020*	*-0.021*	*-0.018*	*-0.021*	*-0.020*
SELF-EMPLOYED	0.15	0.16	0.16	0.06	0.14	0.11	0.11	0.12	0.12	0.13	0.07	0.11	0.14	0.11	0.02
	1.31	**1.38**	**1.41**	**0.49**	**1.24**	**1.00**	**1.00**	**1.07**	**1.09**	**1.16**	**0.60**	**0.98**	**1.20**	**1.02**	**0.20**
	-0.050	*-0.053*	*-0.055*	*-0.018*	*-0.048*	*-0.038*	*-0.037*	*-0.041*	*-0.042*	*-0.044*	*-0.022*	*-0.037*	*-0.046*	*-0.038*	*-0.008*
RISK ATTITUDES	0.10*	0.08	0.09*	0.09*	0.09*	0.10*	0.10*	0.10*	0.11*	0.09	0.08	0.08	0.07	0.09*	0.07
	1.79	**1.54**	**1.74**	**1.76**	**1.68**	**1.72**	**1.88**	**1.75**	**1.95**	**1.59**	**1.51**	**1.46**	**1.35**	**1.67**	**1.30**
	-0.032	*-0.027*	*-0.030*	*-0.031*	*-0.029*	*-0.031*	*-0.034*	*-0.032*	*-0.035*	*-0.029*	*-0.028*	*-0.026*	*-0.024*	*-0.030*	*-0.024*
Observations	1,122	1,135	1,134	1,124	1,126	1,138	1,140	1,120	1,124	1,118	1,107	1,135	1,117	1,131	1,083
Prob>chi²	0.000	0.000	0.000	0.000	0.000	0.000	0.000	0.000	0.000	0.000	0.000	0.000	0.000	0.000	0.000
Pseudo R²	0.047	0.048	0.054	0.060	0.058	0.061	0.057	0.046	0.043	0.055	0.060	0.070	0.066	0.057	0.064

Notes

Dependent variable: tax evasion on a four point scale. The z-statistics are in bold and the marginal effects in italics (lowest tax evasion scale (0)). Significance levels: *0.05<p<0.10, **0.01<p<0.05, ***p<0.01.

points when tax morale increases by one unit. Thus, we observe substantial quantitative effects which are also relatively high in relation to the other variables. Thus, tax morale seems to be a key determinant in understanding tax compliance.

Looking at the control variables, we observe that elderly people evade taxes significantly less often than younger individuals. On the other hand, a higher education is positively correlated with tax evasion. The coefficient of the variable "married" has lost its significance. In Table 8.3, married people evade taxes significantly more often than singles. However, the coefficient is not statistically significant in Table 8.4. An income increase enhances the incentive to over-deduct but not to under-declare the income. Interestingly, self-employed people report a higher level of tax evasion than other individuals, and risk-takers are less compliant that risk-averse taxpayers.

Also, here, one could argue that tax morale might be endogenous. It is difficult to find an adequate instrumental variable for tax morale working with the TOS. This is a further reason why it makes sense to explore the question with different data sets and methodologies.

After working with field data at the macro level, tax compliance experiments, and survey data, we can therefore conclude that tax morale is a key factor in determining tax compliance and tax evasion. Thus, to provide further insights it is highly relevant to investigate the determinants of tax morale. The next section will explore the causes of tax morale, focusing in particular on the impact of institutional and governance quality.

The determinants of tax morale

Having found a significant correlation between tax morale and tax evasion, we will now consider tax morale as the dependent variable, thus analyzing the factors that shape tax morale. Although many researchers have pointed out that tax morale influences tax compliance rates, we have found only a couple of studies that specify which characteristics shape tax morale (for an overview, see Torgler, 2007). Surveys allow us to work with a representative set of individuals, which is rarely the case in experimental studies, given that many engage students as participants. We will mainly focus on the impact of institutional/governance quality on tax morale.

It is not only the economic but also the political system which affects formal and informal economic activities. As such, the outcomes in many countries may be attributed to underlying political conditions. Bird *et al.* (2006) stress that countries may tend to achieve an equilibrium position with respect to the size and nature of their fiscal systems that largely reflects the balance of political forces and institutions, and stay at this position until "shocked" into a new equilibrium.

It is worthwhile investigating whether the recent political economy literature on the importance of governance and institutions provides any insight regarding the level of tax morale. If citizens perceive that their interests (preferences) are properly represented in political institutions and they receive an adequate supply of public goods, their identification with the state and their willingness to pay tax increases. On the other hand, in an inefficient state where corruption is rampant the citizens will have little trust in authority, and thus will experience a low incentive to cooperate. A more encompassing and legitimate state increases the citizens' willingness to contribute, yet if the government and the administration hold considerable discretionary power over the allocation of resources, the level of corruption increases.

A sustainable tax system is based on a fair tax system and responsive government, achieved with a strong connection between tax payments and the supply of public goods (Bird *et al.*, 2006)). Agents such as the political elite, administration staff, and legislators wield a discretionary power if institutions are neither credible nor working well. The negative consequence of this situation is that citizens' tax morale is crowded out. In countries where corruption is systemic and the government budget lacks transparency and accountability, it cannot be assumed that the obligation of paying taxes is an accepted social norm. Institutional instability, lack of transparency, and a weak rule of law undermine the willingness of frustrated citizens to be active in the formal economy. There might be a crowding-out effect of morality among the tax administrators when there are large numbers of corrupt colleagues. Citizens will feel cheated if they believe that corruption is widespread, their tax burden is not spent well, and their government lacks accountability, and that they are not protected by the rules of law. This reduces the incentive to pay taxes. Thus, a more encompassing and legitimate state may be an essential precondition for a higher level of tax morale.

To investigate the impact of institutions on tax morale, we use six proxies of the governance indicators developed by Kaufmann *et al.* (2003).[6] The variables measure the process by which governments are selected, monitored, and replaced (voice and accountability, political stability and absence of violence), the capacity of the government to formulate and implement sound policies (government effectiveness, regulatory quality), and the respect of citizens and the state for the institutions that govern economic and social interactions (rule of law and control of corruption). All scores estimated by Kaufmann *et al.* (2003) range between –2.5 and 2.5, with higher scores corresponding to better institutions or outcomes.

We use survey data provided by the European Values Survey (EVS) 1999/2000, which is a European-wide investigation of socio-cultural and political change. The survey assesses the basic values and beliefs of people throughout Europe. The EVS was first carried out from 1981 to 1983, then in 1990 to 1991 and again in 1999 through 2001, with an increasing number of countries participating over time. The EVS methodological approach is explained in detail in the European Values Survey (1999) source book, which provides information on response rates, the stages of sampling procedures, the translation of the questionnaire, and field work, along with measures of coding reliability, reliability in general, and data checks. All country surveys were carried out by experienced professional survey organizations (with the exception of the study conducted in Greece), and were performed through face-to-face interviews among samples of adult citizens aged 18 years and older. Tilburg University coordinated the project and provided the guidelines to guarantee the use of standardized information in the surveys and in the national representativeness of the data. To avoid framing biases, the questions were asked in the prescribed order. The response rate varied from one country to another; in general, the average response rate was around 60 percent.

Because the EVS poses an identical set of questions to people in various European countries, the survey provides a unique opportunity to examine the impact of institutional or governance quality on tax morale. Our study considers 30 representative national samples of at least 1,000 individuals in each country. To assess the level of tax morale from the EVS, we used the same question we employed in the field and experimental study:

> Please tell me for each of the following statements whether you think it can always be justified, it can never be justified, or it falls somewhere in between: ... Cheating on tax if you have the chance.

For this question a ten-scale index of tax morale was used, with the two extremes being "never justified" and "always justified". The scale was recoded into a four-point scale (0, 1, 2, 3), with the value 3 standing for "never justified". Responses 4 through 10 were combined into a value 0 due to a lack of variance.

Our main specifications have the following structure:

$$TM_i = \alpha + \beta_1 \, CTRL_i + \beta_2 \, GOVQ_i + \beta_3 \, COUNTR_i + \varepsilon_i \qquad (6)$$

$$TM_i = \alpha + \beta_1 \, CTRL_i + \beta_2 \, GOVQ_i + \beta_3 \, TRUST_i + \beta_4 \, COUNTR_i + \varepsilon_i, \qquad (7)$$

where TM_i denotes the level of tax morale. $CTRL_i$ is a panel of control variables[7] including age and gender (female$=1$), education, marital status, employment status, and religiosity (church attendance). Previous tax compliance studies demonstrate the relevance of considering socio-demographic and socio-economic variables along with the level of church attendance (see, for example, Torgler, 2007). $GOVQ_i$ corresponds to our six governance quality factors. First, we consider an index of governance quality (unweighted average of all the factors). In the second stage, we explore the impact of all the sub-factors. Finally, $COUNTR_i$ covers our country dummy variables. In equation (7) we also consider two trust variables – namely, trust in the justice system and trust in the parliament.[8] These variables allow us to analyze trust at the constitutional level (e.g., trust in the legal system), thereby focusing on how the relationship between the state and its citizens is established. They also allow us to analyze trust more closely at the current politico-economic level (e.g., trust in the parliament). We do not include income in the reported results. The ten-point income scale in the EVS is based on national currencies, which reduces the possibility of carrying out cross-country comparisons.[9] A proxy for an individual's economic situation could be the self-classification of respondents into various economic classes. Unfortunately this variable has not been collected in all countries; however, the results of testing on this variable indicate that the main findings are robust.

The question of which other factors should be included in the estimations remains an issue. Traditional tax evasion models indicate the relevance of deterrence variables. However, we are not testing a model of tax evasion but a model of tax morale, so it is not obviously necessary to consider deterrence factors. It would only be appropriate to include these factors if tax morale were a good indicator of tax compliance. Several case studies, such as Torgler (2005b), show that deterrence factors are not likely to affect tax morale significantly.

In this estimation, we use an ordered probit model due to the ranking information of the scaled dependent variable. We also calculate the quantitative effects and therefore report the marginal effects. For simplicity, the marginal effects in all estimates are presented for the highest value of tax morale only. Weighted ordered probit estimates are conducted to ensure the samples correspond to the national distribution.[10] Furthermore, answers such as "don't know" and missing values have been eliminated in all estimations.

Table 8.5 presents the first estimated coefficients using two different estimation techniques to identify the effect of the determinants on tax morale. Equations (1) and (2) use robust standard errors with country dummy variables, while equation (3) uses standard errors adjusted for the clustering on 30 countries, which accounts for unobservable country-specific characteristics while also controlling for regional differences. In general, clustering leads to a decrease in the z-values. Consistent with our hypothesis, the estimation results indicate a positive correlation between tax morale and institutional quality. Moreover, the size of the effect is substantial; if the governance quality scale rises by one unit, the percentage of persons reporting the highest tax morale level increases by between 8.4 and 11.2 percentage points.

In specifications (1) and (2), we explore the impact of trust. Each variable has a statistically significant positive effect on tax morale. An increase in trust in the justice system or in the parliament by one unit raises the proportion of persons reporting the highest tax morale by more than 2 percentage points.

Regarding the control variables, older people and women exhibit higher tax morale. Education affects tax morale negatively, but the coefficient is not statistically significant in two out of four estimations. Divorced and separated persons have the lowest tax morale, perhaps because they have become more cynical, or perhaps because persons who are cynical by nature are more likely to get divorced. Self-employed persons have lower tax morale, while church attendance is correlated with higher tax morale. Overall, the results point to the significance of including a broad set of control variables.

To check the robustness, we explore all six sub-factors independently (Table 8.6). In general, the previous results are supported. The strongest effects can be observed for the variables "voice and accountability" and "rule of law". An increase in the voice and accountability (rule of law) scale by one unit raises the probability of reporting the highest tax morale level by 11.6 (9.4) percentage points. Similarly, the trust variables are also statistically significant, with marginal effects between 2.1 and 2.8 percentage points.

Table 8.5 Determinants of tax morale

INDEPENDENT V.	WEIGHTED ORDERED PROBIT — Robust standard errors (1)			WEIGHTED ORDERED PROBIT — Robust standard errors (2)			WEIGHTED ORDERED PROBIT — Standard errors adjusted for clustering on countries (3)		
	Coeff.	z-Stat.	Marg. effects	Coeff.	z-Stat.	Marg. effects	Coeff.	z-Stat.	Marg. effects
INSTITUTION/GOVERNANCE									
INDEX QUALITY OF GOVERNANCE (WB)	0.281***	13.79	0.112	0.264***	12.39	0.105	0.211**	2.00	0.084
TRUST PARLIAMENT				0.070***	6.74	0.028	0.068***	3.76	0.027
TRUST JUSTICE SYSTEM				0.053***	5.33	0.021	0.055***	3.36	0.022
Demographic factors									
AGE 30–39	0.130***	5.27	0.051	0.127***	5.00	0.050	0.104***	2.97	0.041
AGE 40–49	0.245***	9.39	0.096	0.242***	9.01	0.095	0.230***	5.78	0.091
AGE 50–59	0.331***	11.71	0.129	0.328***	11.22	0.128	0.305***	6.63	0.119
AGE 60–69	0.388***	10.92	0.150	0.376***	10.27	0.145	0.332***	5.28	0.129
AGE 70+	0.526***	12.82	0.199	0.501***	11.71	0.190	0.446***	5.80	0.171
WOMAN	0.152***	10.06	0.061	0.147***	9.38	0.058	0.133***	6.30	0.053
EDUCATION	0.001	0.98	0.001	0.001	0.35	0.0002	-0.006*	-1.86	-0.002
Marital status									
WIDOWED	-0.018	-0.63	-0.007	-0.031	-1.02	-0.012	-0.045	-1.35	-0.018
DIVORCED	-0.152***	-5.57	-0.061	-0.146***	-5.16	-0.058	-0.165***	-5.23	-0.066
SEPARATED	-0.142**	-2.58	-0.057	-0.130**	-2.28	-0.052	-0.131***	-2.88	-0.052
NEVER MARRIED	-0.096***	-4.38	-0.038	-0.092***	-4.06	-0.037	-0.088**	-2.29	-0.035

Employment status

	(1)			(2)			(3)		
PART-TIME EMPLOYED	-0.021	-0.74	-0.008	-0.027	-0.95	-0.011	-0.094***	-3.01	-0.038
SELF-EMPLOYED	-0.146***	-4.51	-0.058	-0.152***	-4.62	-0.061	-0.131**	-2.99	-0.052
UNEMPLOYED	0.139***	4.75	0.055	0.138***	4.56	0.054	0.132***	3.64	0.052
AT HOME	0.019	0.64	0.008	0.006	0.20	0.003	0.010	0.19	0.004
STUDENT	-0.019	-0.56	-0.008	-0.035	-0.97	-0.014	-0.057	-1.10	-0.023
RETIRED	-0.045	-1.54	-0.018	-0.033	-1.11	-0.013	-0.044	-1.04	-0.017
OTHER	0.013	0.24	0.005	-0.013	-0.24	-0.005	0.000	-0.01	-0.0001
Religiosity									
CHURCH ATTENDANCE	0.023***	6.83	0.009	0.020***	5.75	0.008	0.036***	3.21	0.014
REGION	NO			NO			YES		
COUNTRY	YES			YES			NO		
Pseudo R^2	0.046			0.046			0.027		
Number of observations	35,588			33,166			33,166		
Prob>chi^2	0.000			0.000			0.000		

Notes

The dependent variable is tax morale measured on a four point scale from 0 to 3. The reference group consists of AGE <30, MAN, MARRIED, FULL-TIME EMPLOYED. Significance levels: * $0.05 < p < 0.10$, ** $0.01 < p < 0.05$, *** $p < 0.01$. We report the marginal effects of the highest tax morale score (3).

Table 8.6 The impact of institutions on tax morale

WEIGHTED ORDERED PROBIT	Coeff.	z-Stat.	Marg. effects	Coeff.	z-Stat.	Marg. effects	Coeff.	z-Stat.	Marg. effects	Coeff.	z-Stat.	Marg. effects	Coeff.	z-Stat.	Marg. effects	Coeff.	z-Stat.	Marg. effects
		(4)			(5)			(6)			(7)			(8)			(9)	
INDEPENDENT V.																		
Voice and accountability	0.291***	11.38	0.116															
Political stability				0.223***	6.93	0.089												
Government effectiveness							−0.089***	−4.59	−0.035									
Regulatory quality										0.214***	12.13	0.085						
Rule of law													0.237***	12.39	0.094			
Control of corruption																0.108***	6.14	0.043
TRUST PARLIAMENT	0.070***	6.74	0.028	0.070***	6.74	0.028	0.070***	6.74	0.028	0.070***	6.74	0.028	0.070***	6.74	0.028	0.070***	6.74	0.028
TRUST JUSTICE SYSTEM	0.053***	5.33	0.021	0.053***	5.33	0.021	0.053***	5.33	0.021	0.053***	5.33	0.021	0.053***	5.33	0.021	0.053***	5.33	0.021
OTHER VAR. INCLUDED	Yes			Yes			Yes			Yes			Yes			Yes		
COUNTRY	Yes			Yes			Yes			Yes			Yes			Yes		
Number of observations	33,166			33,166			33,166			33,166			33,166			33,166		
Prob>chi²	0.046			0.046			0.046			0.046			0.046			0.046		

Notes
The dependent variable is tax morale measured on a four point scale from 0 to 3. The reference group consists of AGE <30, MAN, MARRIED, FULL-TIME EMPLOYED. Significance levels: * 0.05<p<0.10, ** 0.01<p<0.05, *** p<0.01. We report the marginal effects of the highest tax morale score (3).

We run further robustness checks in Table 8.7. First, we use an index out of the variables trust in the justice system and trust in the parliament (INDEX TRUST STATE[11]). In a next step, we deal with the concern that the index might be endogenous. We therefore present in Table 8.7 a 2SLS estimation together with the first-stage regression. We use as an instrument a variable that we label as CONCERNED IN HUMANKIND.[12] The instrument satisfies the two key properties: it affects the potential endogenous trust variable, as can be seen in the first-stage regression an in the diagnostic tests, and it also affects the dependent variable via its impact on trust. The instrument has no impact on tax morale, and the F-tests for the instrument exclusion set in the first-stage regression are statistically significant at the 1 percent level. In addition, Table 8.7 also reports a test for instrument relevance using the Anderson canonical correlations LR for whether the equation is identified. The test shows that the null hypothesis can be rejected, indicating that the model is identified and the instrument is relevant. The Anderson-Rubin test suggests that the endogenous variable is statistically significant. Such a test is robust to the presence of a weak instrument.

Conclusions

Our primary intention in this chapter was to verify the correlation between tax compliance and tax morale. A central question in the tax compliance literature is why so many people pay their taxes even though fines and audit probability are low. One key determinant might be tax morale – i.e., the intrinsic motivation to pay taxes. Interestingly, tax morale is not often discussed in the tax compliance literature, and is seen as a residual explanation without referring to the factors that shape tax morale. We have used a variety of methodologies to explore this aspect in detail. This allows us to take into account the fact that every method has its pros and cons, especially when investigating tax evasion, which by its nature is concealed. The results are very consistent. Tax morale has a strong positive effect on tax compliance regardless of which methodology is used. Thus, if tax morale seems to be a key determinant in enhancing tax compliance, there are a variety of policies besides coercion that will help to increase tax compliance. Therefore, to derive some policy recommendation from these results it was necessary to go a step further and explore the determinants of tax morale. We focused predominantly on the impact of governance quality. Our results show that the quality of political institutions has a strong observable effect on tax morale. It is clear that not only the overall index but also the sub-factors of voice and accountability, rule of law, political stability and absence of violence, regulatory quality, and control of corruption exercise a strong influence on tax morale. Moreover, trust in the justice system and the parliament also has a highly significant positive effect on tax morale.

In general, our analysis highlights the relevance of extending the standard economic theory of tax evasion, which is based on the narrow principle of *homo*

Table 8.7 Robustness check

	Coeff.	z-Stat.	Marg. effects	Coeff.	t-Stat.	Coeff.	t-Stat.
	WEIGHTED ORDERED PROBIT (10)			2SL (11)		First stage regression	
INSTITUTION/GOVERNANCE							
INDEX TRUST STATE	0.122***	11.20	0.049	1.223***	7.05	0.089***	7.21
INDEX QUALITY OF GOVERNANCE (WB)	0.264***	12.37	0.105	0.200***	6.56		
Demographic factors							
AGE 30–39	0.127***	5.01	0.050	0.130***	4.11	0.001	0.09
AGE 40–49	0.243***	9.03	0.095	0.260***	7.90	0.004	0.29
AGE 50–59	0.328***	11.26	0.128	0.296***	8.12	0.037**	2.24
AGE 60–69	0.376***	10.29	0.146	0.356***	8.11	0.039*	1.91
AGE 70+	0.502***	11.72	0.190	0.342***	6.14	0.143***	6.03
WOMAN	0.147***	9.35	0.058	0.152***	8.00	0.007	0.81
EDUCATION	0.001	0.39	0.000	-0.001	-0.34	0.001	1.01
Marital status							
WIDOWED	-0.031	-1.02	-0.012	-0.023	-0.66	-0.010	-0.56
DIVORCED	-0.146***	-5.16	-0.058	-0.095**	-2.59	-0.060***	-3.70
SEPARATED	-0.130**	-2.28	-0.052	-0.029	-0.41	-0.101***	-3.24
NEVER MARRIED	-0.092***	-4.05	-0.037	-0.092***	-3.28	-0.008	-0.63

Employment status							
PART-TIME EMPLOYED	-0.027	-0.95	-0.011	-0.015	-0.41	-0.009	-0.53
SELF-EMPLOYED	-0.152***	-4.61	-0.060	-0.131***	-3.32	-0.026	-1.45
UNEMPLOYED	0.138***	4.58	0.055	0.129***	3.66	0.001	0.03
AT HOME	0.006	0.21	0.003	-0.022	-0.59	0.015	0.90
STUDENT	-0.036	-0.98	-0.014	-0.170***	-3.40	0.112***	5.79
RETIRED	-0.034	-1.12	-0.013	0.015	0.40	-0.057***	-3.23
OTHER	-0.013	-0.24	-0.005	-0.013	-0.19	-0.003	-0.10
Religiosity							
CHURCH ATTENDANCE	0.020***	5.77	0.008	-0.013*	-1.90	0.030***	15.48
COUNTRY	YES			YES		YES	
Instrument for INDEX TRUST STATE							
CONCERNED IN HUMANKIND				0.048***	11.94		
Test of excluded instrments				142.54***			
Anderson canon. corr. LR statistic				184.986***			
Anderson Rubin test				89.810***			
Number of observations	33,166			32,402			

Notes

The dependent variable is tax morale measured on a four point scale from 0 to 3. The reference group consists of AGE <30, MAN, MARRIED, FULL-TIME EMPLOYED. Significance levels: * $0.05<p<0.10$, ** $0.01<p<0.05$, *** $p<0.01$. We report the marginal effects of the highest tax morale score (3).

economicus. The concept of tax morale provides answers about the taxpayer's personal decision on whether, and to what extent, they evade their own taxes. We have shown that the political economy literature provides an appropriate basis for understanding the determinants of tax morale.

Further empirical work is needed to better understand the causes and consequences of tax morale. For example, an excellent method would be to collect a panel of data that allows the exploration of shocks and inter-temporal aspects. In general, the results and conclusions obtained in tax morale research are of considerable importance. First, they can provide insight into a more efficient way of raising revenues, since the interaction between the taxpayer and the tax authority is taken into account. Second, this research points to a broader understanding of tax compliance using a rich set of theories and methodologies to systematically evaluate the puzzle of tax compliance.

Notes

1 We would like to thank participants of the Tax Compliance and Tax Evasion Conference at the Andrew Young School of Policy Studies, Georgia State University in Atlanta (October 2007) for helpful comments and suggestions.
2 Variables are taken for the WDI (per capita GDP, trade volume in relation to the GDP, share of agriculture in GDP, population size, and urbanization), except the top marginal tax rate where we use the top marginal tax rate (and income threshold at which it applies) provided by the Economic Freedom of the World data base.
3 We differentiate between developed, Asian, and developing or transition countries.
4 It should be noted that the experiments in Australia were not conducted with monetary incentives.
5 Question: In order to get ahead in this world a person has to be willing to risk taking some chances (4 = strongly agree, 3 = mildly agree, 2 = mildly disagree, 1 = sharply disagree).
6 Aggregate Governance Indicators 1998.
7 The demographic variables are age, gender, and education. As a proxy for education, we use the answers to the following question: At what age did you complete or will you complete your full time education, either at school or at an institution of higher education? Please exclude apprenticeships. As a measure of religiosity, we use answers to the following question: Apart from weddings, funerals and christenings, how often do you attend religious services these days? More than once a week, once a week, once a month, only on special religious days, once a year, less often, practically never or never (8 = more than once a week to 1 = practically never or never.)
8 These variables depend on responses to the following two questions, respectively. "Could you tell me how much confidence you have in the justice system: Do you have a great deal of confidence, quite a lot of confidence, not very much confidence or no confidence at all? (4 = a great deal of confidence to 1 = no confidence at all.". "Could you tell me how much confidence you have in the parliament: Do you have a great deal of confidence, quite a lot of confidence, not very much confidence or no confidence at all? (4 = a great deal of confidence to 1 = no confidence at all)".
9 Moreover, income is coded on a scale from 1 to 10, and these income intervals are not fully comparable across countries.
10 The weighting variable is provided by the EVS.
11 The index is developed using the mean of both questions.
12 To what extent do you feel concerned about the living condition of humankind? (4 = very much, 1 = not very much).

Bibliography

Adams, C. (1993) *For Good and Evil: The Impact of Taxes on the Course of Civilization*, London, UK: Madison Books.

Akerlof, G. A. (1980) "A theory of social custom of which unemployment may be one consequence", *Quarterly Journal of Economics*, 94: 749–95.

Allingham, M. G. and Sandmo, A. (1972) "Income tax evasion: A theoretical analysis", *Journal of Public Economics*, 1: 323–38.

Alm, J. (1999) "Tax compliance and administration", in W. B. Hildreth and J. A. Richardson (eds.), *Handbook on Taxation*, New York, NY: Marcel Dekker.

Alm, J. and Torgler, B. (2006) "Culture differences and tax morale in the United States and Europe", *Journal of Economic Psychology*, 27: 224–46.

Alm, J., McClelland G. H., and Schulze, W. D. (1992) "Why do people pay taxes?", *Journal of Public Economics*, 48: 21–48.

Alm, J., Martinez-Vazquez, J., and Torgler, B. (2006) "Russian attitudes toward paying taxes – before, during, and after the transition", *International Journal of Social Economics*, 33: 832–57.

Andreoni, J., Erard, B., and Feinstein, J. (1998) "Tax compliance", *Journal of Economic Literature*, 36: 818–60.

Bird, R., Martinez-Vazquez, J., and Torgler, B. (2006) "Societal institutions and tax effort in developing countries", in J. Alm, J. Martinez-Vazquez, and M. Rider (eds.), *The Challenges of Tax Reform in the Global Economy*, New York, NY: Springer.

Bosco, L. and Mittone, L. (1997) "Tax evasion and moral constraints: Some experimental evidence", *KYKLOS*, 50: 297–324.

Chung, P. (1976) "On complaints about high taxes: An analytical note", *Public Finance*, 31: 36–47.

Eagles, J. M. (1994) "The relationship between mood and daily hours of sunlight in rapid cycling bipolar illness", *Biological Psychiatry*, 36: 422–4.

Elffers, H. (2000) "But taxpayers do cooperate!", in M. Van Vught, M. Snyder, T. R. Tyler, and Anders Biel (eds.), *Cooperation in Modern Society: Promoting the Welfare of Communities, States and Organizations*, London, UK: Routledge.

Engerman, S. and Sokoloff, K. (1997) "Factor endowments, institutions and differential paths of growth among the new world economics", in S. Haber (ed.), *How Latin America Fell Behind*. Stanford, CA: Stanford University Press.

Erard, B. and Feinstein, J. S. (1994). "The role of moral sentiments and audit perceptions in tax compliance", *Public Finance*, 49: 70–89.

Fischbacher, U. (2007) "z-Tree: Zurich toolbox for ready-made economic experiments", *Experimental Economics*, 10: 171–8.

Forest, A. and Sheffrin, S. M. (2002) "Complexity and compliance: An empirical investigation", *National Tax Journal*, 55: 75–88.

Frey, B. S. (1999) *Economics as a Science of Human Behaviour*, Dordrecht: Kluwer Academic Publishers.

Frey, B. S. and Schneider, F. (2000) "Informal and underground economy", in Ashenfelter, O. (ed.), *International Encylopedia of Social and Behavioral Science, Bd. 12, Economics*, Amsterdam: Elsevier Science Publishing Company.

Gordon, J. P. F. (1989) "Individual morality and reputation costs as deterrents to tax evasion", *European Economic Review*, 33: 797–805.

Graetz, M. J. and Wilde, L. L. (1985) "The economics of tax compliance: Fact and fantasy", *National Tax Journal*, 38: 355–63.

Inglehart, R. (2000) *Codebook for World Values Survey*, Ann Arbor, MI: Institute for Social Research.

Jackson, B. and Milliron, V. C. (1986) "Tax compliance research: Findings, problems, and prospects", *Journal of Accounting Literature*, 5: 125–65.

Kaufmann, D., Kraay, A., and Mastruzzi, M. (2003) "Governance matters III: Governance indicators for 1996–2002", Washington, DC: World Bank, June, 30.

Laffont, J. J. (1975) "Macroeconomic constraints, economic efficiency and ethics: An introduction to Kantian economics", *Economica*, 42: 430–7.

Landes, D. (1998) *The Wealth and Poverty of Nations: Why Some Are So Rich and Some So Poor*, New York, NY: Norton.

Lempert, R. (1992) "Commentary of the paper: Smith, K. W. (1992) "Reciprocity and fairness: Positive incentives for tax compliance", in Slemrod, J. (ed.), *Why People Pay Taxes: Tax Compliance and Enforcement*, Ann Arbor, MI: University of Michigan Press.

Lewis, A. (1982). *The Psychology of Taxation*, Oxford, UK: Martin Robertson.

Long, S. and Swingen, J. (1991) "The conduct of tax-evasion experiments: Validation, analytical methods, and experimental realism", in P. Webley, H. Robben, H. Elffers, and D. Hessing (eds.), *Tax Evasion: An Experimental Approach*, Cambridge, UK: Cambridge University Press.

Myles, G. D. and Naylor, R. A. (1996) "A model of tax evasion with group conformity and social custom", *European Journal of Political Economy*, 12: 49–66.

Naylor, R. A. (1989) "Strikes, free riders and social customs", *Quarterly Journal of Economics*, 104: 771–805.

Polinsky, M. A. and Shavell, S. (2000) "The economic theory of public enforcement of law", *Journal of Economic Literature*, 38: 45–76.

Sachs, J. (2000) "Tropical underdevelopment", NBER Working Paper, No. 8119.

Schaltegger, C. A. and Torgler, B. (2007) "Government accountability and fiscal discipline: A panel analysis with Swiss data", *Journal of Public Economics*, 91: 117–40.

Schneider, F. (2005a) "Shadow economies of 145 countries all over the world: What do we really know?", CREMA Working Paper 2006–01, Basel, Center for Research in Economics, Management and the Arts.

Schneider, F. (2005b) "Shadow economies around the world: What do we really know?", *European Journal of Political Economy*, 21: 598–642.

Schneider, F. and Enste, D. (2000) "Shadow economies: Size, causes, and consequences", *Journal of Economic Literature*, 38: 77–114.

Schneider, F. and Enste, D. H. (2002) *The Shadow Economy: An International Survey*, Cambridge, UK: Cambridge University Press.

Schnellenbach, J. (2006) "Tax morale and the taming of leviathan", *Constitutional Political Economy*, 17: 115–30.

Sheffrin, S. M. and Triest, R. K. (1992) "Can brute deterrence backfire? Perceptions and attitudes in taxpayer compliance", in J. Slemrod (ed.), *Why People Pay Taxes: Tax Compliance and Enforcement*, Ann Arbor, MI: University of Michigan Press.

Smith, K. W. (1992) "Reciprocity and fairness: Positive incentives for tax compliance", in J. Slemrod (ed.), *Why People Pay Taxes: Tax Compliance and Enforcement*, Ann Arbor, MI: University of Michigan Press.

Spicer, M. W. and Lundstedt, S. B. (1976) "Understanding tax evasion", *Public Finance*, 31: 295–304.

Sugden, R. (1984) "Reciprocity: The supply of public goods through voluntary contributions", *Economic Journal*, 94: 772–87.

Tietjen, G. H. and Kripke, D. F. (1994) "Suicides in california (1968–1977) – Absence of seasonality in Los Angeles and Sacramento counties", *Psychiatric Research*, 53: 161–72.

Torgler, B. (2001) "Is tax evasion never justifiable?", *Journal of Public Finance and Public Choice*, XIX: 143–68.

Torgler, B. (2002) "Speaking to theorists and searching for facts: Tax morale and tax compliance in experiments", *Journal of Economic Surveys*, 16: 657–84.

Torgler, B. (2004) "Cross culture comparison of tax morale and tax compliance: Evidence from Costa Rica and Switzerland", *International Journal of Comparative Sociology*, 45: 17–43.

Torgler, B. (2005a) "Tax morale in Latin America", *Public Choice*, 122: 133–57.

Torgler, B. (2005b) "Tax morale and direct democracy", *European Journal of Political Economy*, 21: 525–31.

Torgler, B. (2007) *Tax Compliance and Tax Morale: A Theoretical and Empirical Analysis*, Cheltenham, UK: Edward Elgar.

Torgler, B. and Schaffner, M. (2007) "Causes and consequences of tax morale: An empirical investigation", CREMA Working Paper series, 2007-11, Center for Research in Economics, Management and the Arts (CREMA).

Torgler, B. and Schaltegger, C. A. (2005) "Tax amnesties and political participation", *Public Finance Review*, 33: 403–31.

Torgler, B. and Schneider, F. (2007a) "Shadow economy, tax morale, governance and institutional quality: A panel analysis", CREMA Working Paper series, 2007-02, Center for Research in Economics, Management and the Arts (CREMA).

Torgler, B. and Schneider, F. (2007b) "The impact of tax morale and institutional quality on the shadow economy", CREMA Working Paper series, 2007-01, Center for Research in Economics, Management and the Arts (CREMA).

Torgler, B., Schaltegger, C. A., and Schaffner, M. (2003) "Is forgiveness divine? A cross-culture comparison of tax amnesties", *Swiss Journal of Economics and Statistics*, 139: 375–96.

9 Tax evasion, corruption, and the social contract in transition

Eric M. Uslaner[1]

Introduction

In 1997, a Russian civil servant asked the Swedish political scientist Bo Rothstein how the Russians could solve the widespread problem of tax evasion. Almost all Swedes were honest in reporting and paying their taxes, while Russians regularly cheated the state (Rothstein, 2001: 477):

> First, [Russian citizens] rightly did not believe that all "the other" taxpayers where paying their taxes properly, so it was really no point in being "the only one" who acted honestly. The goods (public, semi-public or private) that the government was going to use the money to produce, would simply not be produced because there were too little taxes paid in the first place. Secondly, they believed that the tax authorities were corrupted, so that even if they paid their taxes, a significant part of the money would never reach the hospitals or schools, etc. Instead, the money would fill the pockets of the tax bureaucrats.

Tax evasion is an endemic problem in Russia – and most other transition countries – especially in comparison with the West. Easter (2007: 234–9), Hanousek and Palda (2007: 332), Ott (2007: 292–3), and Owsiak (2007) detail the extent of tax evasion in Russia, the Czech Republic, Croatia, and Poland, respectively, and the figures are distressingly high – often as great as 40 percent of the total economy.

Tax evasion is part of a more general syndrome of corruption, impotent legal systems, shaky economies, and, especially, inefficient governments that fail to provide essential services. New democratic institutions did not ensure smoothly functioning states and reduced corruption. Parliamentary elections and promises of the rule of law did not turn Romania or Russia into Sweden (Uslaner and Badescu, 2004). When people believe that public officials steal their tax payments – and especially when they believe that they don't receive high quality services for their taxes (Hanousek and Palda, 2004) – they are more likely to evade paying their taxes.

Tax compliance is thus a social contract between ordinary citizens and the government rather than a contract among people based upon trust, as Rothstein

(2001) argued. Scholz (2007) and Smith (1992) argue that there is a basic expectation of reciprocity: if you don't believe that others will pay their taxes, then you too will withhold your tax payments. Yet an explanation based upon reciprocity – you pay your taxes because you believe that others will also pay theirs – doesn't explain why others pay their taxes (Uslaner, 2007).

People obey the law – generally and, more specifically, by paying their taxes – when they believe that they will be treated fairly and equitably. A fair judicial system is more important than an efficient one (Tyler, 1990; Uslaner, 2008: Chs 2, 4). Throughout transition countries, people believe that the law is *not* fair, and that the rich and powerful can get away with corruption and tax evasion (Uslaner, 2008: Ch. 4). Wealthy people can pay off the courts and avoid prosecution. If they are nevertheless indicted, they can pay off the judges to fix their trials. If they are somehow convicted, they can appeal and ensure that they never serve time in jail. In 2003, the Russian government of Vladimir Putin arrested billionaire Mikhail Khodorkovsky for tax evasion and extortion and argued that no one, no matter how rich, was above the law (even though most viewed Khodorkovsky's arrest and ultimate jailing as a move to quash his political aspirations).

I argue, with Hanousek and Palda (2004), that the quality of government services is a key factor in tax compliance. Corruption also matters. When people believe that their taxes will go toward public services, and not into the pockets of politicians, they will be more likely to pay their fair share. Where there is widespread corruption and an unfair (as well as weak) legal system, tax compliance will be lower. Belief in the honesty of officials is a key component of why people trust the government in both Western and transition countries (Uslaner, 2008: Ch. 5). Performance, however, is just as critical. In the West, evaluation of how well the government manages the economy is the key to understanding why people trust that government (Citrin, 1974). In transition countries, the provision of basic services seems to be more critical than simple economic performance (Uslaner, 2008: Ch. 5). This is not such a critical concern in the West, where routine services are routinely provided. Trust in government is a key factor in explaining tax compliance in Romania (Uslaner, 2007), but the surveys of businesspeople (described below) that I employ have no direct question regarding trust in government. I can only establish a direct linkage from the quality of services to tax compliance, rather than a causal chain from service provision to trust in government to paying taxes.

There is mixed support for the claim that enforcement matters. Beron *et al.* (1992), Smith (1992), and Scholz (2007) find that the likelihood of detection is a key factor in tax compliance in the United States, while Hanousek and Palda (2004) find it to be insignificant in the Czech Republic, as do Feld and Frey (2007) in Switzerland.

I provide support for the claims that tax compliance in transition countries reflects perceptions of the quality of services and the level of corruption, both in the tax administration offices and throughout government and society, using the 2002 and 2005 surveys of business people, the BEEPS (Business Enterprise and

Environment Performance Surveys), conducted for the World Bank and the European Bank for Reconstruction and Development. BEEPS 2002 and 2005 encompassed 28 and 27 transition countries, respectively. Turkmenistan was not included in the 2005 survey, and I excluded respondents from Turkey (which is not a transition country) in both years.

The BEEPS surveys do not tell us anything about compliance by ordinary citizens. However, they contain an excellent set of questions both on tax compliance and on levels of corruption (as reflected in gift payments to officials), the fairness of the legal system, the structure of firms, and expectations of audits. Approximately 7,500 respondents were surveyed in 2002 and 9,500 in 2005, with samples stratified by location, sector, size, whether the firms were exporters, and locus of control (domestic versus foreign). Business people are different from ordinary citizens. They are considerably less likely to see corruption and unfairness than the mass public (Uslaner, 2008: Chs 5, 6). Thus, the results I present here may even *underestimate* the importance of corruption and the quality of services. This may be less of an issue than it first seems, since businesses depend even more than the mass public on government services. In countries with unfair legal systems and many "grabbing hands", business people are more likely to be personally affected by corruption than are ordinary citizens.

The 2002 BEEPS survey involved respondents from 6,667 firms and the 2005 survey involved respondents from 9,655 firms, in 27 nations – including Turkey. Both surveys included respondents from Turkey.[2] As my focus is on formerly Communist nations, I have excluded the Turkish respondents. I have used the surveys to estimate models of: (i) the perceived share of income reported by firms for tax purposes for the 2002 BEEPS; (ii) gift payments to tax collectors in the 2005 BEEPS; (iii) taxes reported in the 2005 BEEPS; (iv) reported taxes in the 2005 BEEPS, with gift payments to tax collectors as endogenous using instrumental variables; and (v) income reported for taxes across the countries in the 2005 BEEPS (in an aggregate model). Overall, I have found strong support for the claim that the quality of government services and the level of corruption matter greatly. Clearly, other factors also matter, including the size and ownership of the firm, the fairness of the legal system, the level of competition, the tax rate, the quality of the bureaucracy, and the expectation of audits. The quality of services and the level of corruption stand out as critical factors shaping tax compliance.

Taxes, services, corruption, and transition

Rothstein is correct: tax compliance in transition countries is essentially the same problem as it is elsewhere. Torgler and his associates (Alm *et al.*, 2004; Torgler, 2003, 2007; Torgler and Schneider, 2006) argue that trust in government and trust in the legal system are the key factors in explaining "tax morale" in both transition and Western European countries. Tax morale is the belief that people ought not to cheat on their taxes. It is a good surrogate for tax compliance, since asking people directly whether they have paid their taxes may not elicit truthful information.

While the dynamics of compliance (and evasion) may be the same in the West and the transition countries, there is likely to be far less obedience to the law in the formerly Communist countries. Tax morale in transition nations is rather low – in the former Soviet Union, less than half the public (an average of 42.6 percent) held that tax evasion is never justifiable in the 1995–1997 World Values Survey, and barely more than half (54.2 percent) made the same judgment in Central and Eastern Europe (Torgler, 2003: 362). Over 60 percent in the West held that tax cheating was never acceptable. The tax morale question uses a scale from 1 (never acceptable) to 10 (always acceptable). The mean score in the 1995–1997 World Values Survey was 3.06 for respondents from countries with a legacy of Communism, and 2.13 for people from other nations ($t=48.90$, $p<0.00001$). Clearly, tax morale is weaker in the former Communist nations.

Torgler (2007: 159–60), echoing Rothstein, and Hanousek and Palda, argues,

> Taxes can be seen as a pride paid for government's positive actions.... If the government tries to generate trust with well functioning institutions, cooperation can be initiated or increased ... when taxpayers are satisfied with the way they are treated, the cooperation is enhanced. If the outcome received from the government is judged to be fair in relation to the taxes paid, no distress arises.

Corruption both robs the treasury of available resources for public projects and destroys people's faith in governing authorities (Torgler, 2007: 161; Uslaner, 2008: Chs 2, 4). Highly corrupt governments such as Zaire (now the Congo) and Haiti are often called "kleptocracies". Transfer payments, social insurance, and health spending are lower where corruption is high (Mauro, 2002: 349) – all reinforcing inequality. Not only is there less money to spend on social programs such as health and education, but also, where corruption is rampant, the poor will likely have to make extra "gift" payments to receive routine services – thus imposing extra costs on people who are least able to afford them (Gupta *et al.*, 2002: 255). Corruption and weak legal systems have deleterious effects on perceived service delivery for water supplies, phone services, and power outages (Uslaner, 2008: Ch. 4). This forms a vicious circle: poor service delivery and corruption make people less willing to pay taxes. When government cannot provide essential services, people rely upon the informal sector, and this means that the state is robbed of taxes on hidden income (Torgler, 2007: 157–8; Uslaner, 2008: Ch. 4). The greater the share of the economy beyond the reach of the state, the more difficult it will be for a government to marshall the resources to gain public confidence that the state can provide essential services.

Not only is tax morale lower in transition countries than in other nations, especially the West, but the shadow economy is also much greater – twice as large as in the West, according to estimates by the World Bank (2004). Even the best-performing economies, Slovakia and the Czech Republic, had almost 20 percent of their revenue off the books (using data from Schneider, 2003). Three countries had the majority of their revenue in the informal sector (Ukraine,

Azerbaijan, and Georgia), and 15 of 21 countries for which there are data had at least a third of their income in the shadow economy. Even more distressing is that 16 of the 18 countries for which there are data experienced increases in the shadow economy from 1989 (the time of transition) to 2000 of between 10 and 42 percent; only one country (Hungary) had a (very slight) decrease, while another (Slovenia) experienced no change. Overall, the average share of the shadow economy more than doubled from 1989 to 1999–2000, from 17 percent to 38 percent.

Corruption is also far worse in the transition countries than in the West. The Transparency International Corruption Perceptions Index ranges from 1 (completely corrupt) to 10 (completely honest). The transition countries in 2006 averaged 3.45, while the Western nations averaged 7.94. The legal system is also largely viewed as unfair. A measure of legal fairness from the Economist Intelligence Unit ranges from 1 (unfair) to 5 (completely fair); see Uslaner (2008: Ch. 3) for a discussion of the index. Western nations averaged 4.30, compared to 2.39 for transition nations. Barely more than a quarter of respondents in the 2005 BEEPS survey argued that the courts are uncorrupt and that they are fair.

Rothstein suggested that Russians could reduce corruption and build trust by creating a stronger legal system, but they seemingly paid him little heed. In 2005, over 1,400 "takeover artists" seized control of Russian private businesses, owned by locals and foreigners alike, by forging sales agreements, voting out the rightful owners, and often using violence to take over factories. By either bribing authorities or stealing the ownership documents, these con men are outside the reach of the law (Kramer, 2006). Starbucks, Kodak, Forbes, Audi, and the HandM clothing chain have all been the targets of trademark "squatters", who have registered the company names and extorted up to $60,000 from the rightful owners to reclaim their brands as the courts stood idly by. The Starbucks brand name was far more coveted, with an asking price of $600,000 (Kramer, 2004: Chs 1, 4).

This lawlessness – as reflected in the power of organized crime – makes doing business hazardous. In the BEEPS 2005 survey, 41 percent of respondents said that the Mafia was an obstacle to doing business, ranging from 15 percent in prosperous Slovenia – which had long had access to Western markets, even when it was part of the Soviet Union – to 83 percent in Albania. Street crime is also an obstacle to business – slightly greater at 45 percent, and prominent in the same countries. Of the respondents who said that the Mafia was an obstacle to business, 83 percent also worried about street crime ($\varphi=0.662$, Yule's $Q=0.924$). In countries where there is little respect for the rule of law, paying taxes for protection one doesn't receive, or even paying taxes at all, may seem fruitless.

Ordinary people often face a justice system biased against them. A Russian court convicted a railway worker in a closed trial in 2006 after his car was hit from behind by a vehicle carrying one of the country's most prominent politicians, causing an accident that ended in the death of the official. The court ruled that the worker should have seen the leader's car coming, and sentenced him to four years' hard labor, provoking widespread protests (Finn, 2006).

The public in transition countries see corruption as a long-term, insoluble problem. In a 2005 survey, just 8 percent of Russians held that corruption can be eliminated "if dishonest leaders are replaced with honest ones", while 26 percent held that "Russia has always been characterized by bribery and embezzlement, and nothing can be done about it" (Popov, 2006; cf. Karklins, 2005: 59 for a more general statement on transition countries).

Under Communism, people had to resort to informal connections – petty corruption – to get by in daily life; using them to stand in line for food or to help run errands, or using a friend or relative to cut through the bureaucracy was common practice under Communism (Flap and Voelker, 2003; Ledeneva, 1998). This system persists, as people must make "gift payments" for many routine services, such as seeing a doctor, avoiding traffic fines, or achieving decent grades in school or acceptance into good schools or universities. Barely more than a third of Hungarians see a moral problem when doctors demand "gratitude payments" for medical services (Kornai, 2000: 3, 7, 9). This system of "gift giving" is so widespread that almost all doctors accept "gratitude money"; 62 percent of physicians' total income came off the books. A majority of public officials in the Czech Republic, Slovakia, Bulgaria, and Ukraine in 1997–1998 found it acceptable to receive extra payments from clients. Between 11 and 39 percent of citizens of those countries (in that order) reported offering a "small present" to officials, and between 6 and 24 percent offered "money or an expensive present" (Miller *et al.*, 2001: 217, 241).

Two-thirds of respondents to a Polish survey said that giving gift payments was inevitable, more than half said that such extra charges were simply signs of respect, and little more than a third would refuse to give a bribe. However, over two-thirds said that both giving and receiving such payments was morally reprehensible (Kolarska-Bobinska, 2002: 323–4). State Department surveys of attitudes toward corruption in Bulgaria, the Czech Republic, Hungary, Poland, Romania, and Slovakia found that between 75 and 86 percent of their publics said that "accepting a bribe in the course of a person's duties" was never justified – comparable to (or even greater than) corresponding shares of the public in Britain, France, Germany, and Italy (Office of Research, 1999: 9). This strong disapproval of corruption, together with the pervasiveness of malfeasance in transition countries, makes people less trusting of their public officials – and thus more likely to evade paying taxes.

It is hardly surprising that business people in transition countries rate the quality of basic services poorly. In the 2005 BEEPS, only 24 percent of entrepreneurs said that the government was run efficiently.[3] The judiciary fared worse (19 percent), and survey respondents were generally negative about the legislature (16 percent favorable), roads and public works (18 percent), public health (20 percent), the police (25 percent), and education (30 percent). Some other services and institutions fared better, with banks and the military at 40 percent, and water, telephone, postal, and electricity services gaining positive ratings from 45 percent to 51 percent of respondents. No basic service received substantial support from the business people. These entrepreneurs do not see that they are getting much value for their tax payments.

There are other reasons for tax evasion in transition countries. Under socialism's command economy, most people didn't pay taxes; taxes came largely from the big state enterprises. After transition, many entrepreneurs were able to hide their income in a barter (underground) economy that escaped state control. Moreover, the tax administrations left over from the socialist systems were as inefficient as other public bureaucracies (Alm *et al.*, 2004: 9; Easter, 2007; Torgler, 2003: 359).

Tax compliance may be enhanced by several factors related to company structures and practices. Large firms will find it more difficult to hide assets and thus should be more likely to comply with tax laws (Gehlbach, 2006). Firms that have substantial state or foreign ownership should also be more likely to pay their taxes. State ownership, like size, will make it difficult to hide assets. Foreign-owned firms may face greater scrutiny by tax authorities. Their foreign investors/owners may also have greater "tax morality" if, as is likely, tax evasion is viewed less favorably in their home countries. Firms that have a larger number of competitors will also be more likely to pay taxes, since they may worry that the tax authorities have a ready basis for comparison of company assets and profits. More frequent audits should also lead to greater compliance – although "gift payments" to tax collectors might work to enhance evasion.

My account has paid scant attention to an issue that has become central to transition economies: growing economic inequality. Elsewhere, I have focused on how inequality has grown in these nations. The Rosser *et al.* (2000) data on income distribution show an increase in economic inequality from 1989 to the mid-1990s for every transition country save one (Slovakia). The more recent WIDER estimates[4] indicate substantial increases in inequality – an average change of 78 percent from 1989 to 1999 – for each of 21 countries. In Uslaner (2008: Chs 2, 4–6), I argue that corruption rests upon a foundation of economic inequality and leads in turn to greater wealth disparities, forming an "inequality trap" that is difficult to escape. Even though the transition countries have historically had lower levels of inequality, the transition to a market economy has led to growing divisions between the new rich and the new poor.

In transition countries (as well as others), growing inequality is linked to the rise in the shadow economy (greater in 2000 than in 1989 in every country except Hungary), greater corruption, unfair legal systems, and state failure more generally, including poor public services. Inequality lies at the heart of transition problems, especially growing corruption and declining generalized trust, yet there is no evidence that it leads to greater tax evasion (cf. Hanousek and Palda, 2004: 246). No other measure of inequality was found to have significant country-level effects on tax reporting in the individual-level analysis or in the aggregate model. Inequality – specifically the change in the unequal distribution of income from 1989 to the present as estimated by WIDER, the World Institute for Development Economics Research of the United Nations University (see endnote 3) – is an important determinant of how often business people make gift payments to tax collectors.

Tax compliance in transition

What drives tax compliance in transition countries? I used the 2002 and 2005 BEEPS to examine the share of sales that firms believe that "the typical firm in your area of business reports for tax purposes". While this is not the same question as the share of sales that the respondent's firm reported, asking about "typical" behavior is an acceptable surrogate for illicit behavior (Tavits, 2005). Most respondents reported great compliance with the law among themselves and their peers. The mean share of revenue expected to be reported was 89.4 percent, ranging from 75 percent quarters in Albania and Macedonia to 97 percent in Estonia, which has the least corrupt government among all transition countries in the Transparency International rankings (a rating of 6.7 on the 10-point scale). Armenia and Uzbekistan also had very high means, 95 and 97 percent, respectively – which may either reflect idiosyncratic survey results or dynamics other than those I consider here.

I use both the 2002 and 2005 BEEPS to show that similar dynamics apply over time – and as a source of replication. I estimate regression models for the perceived share of income reported in both surveys, as well as a model for how common (on a six-point scale) it is to give "gifts" to tax collectors, and then an instrumental variables regression of the expected share of sales reported for tax purposes with gifts to tax collectors as endogenous. In Tables 9.3 and 9.4, I include aggregate measures as additional predictors, clustering the standard errors at the country level. For the 2002 BEEPS, no country-level effects were significant. Finally, I use aggregated data from BEEPS 2005 to examine variations across countries of the share of sales reported. The analyses strongly confirm the expectations I have laid out above.

I begin with summaries of the dependent variables – the share of a firm's sales reported for taxes – and one of the central independent variables, the share of a firm's sales paid in extra "gift" payments in 2002 and 2005 (see Table 9.1). Three things stand out in this table. First, the rates of reporting appear rather high for countries with high levels of corruption, if not by the standards of Western market economies: in 2002, the average share of income reported was 82 percent, rising to 89 percent in 2005. By 2005, only Albania and Macedonia had average rates of reporting below 80 percent. Some figures seem anomalously high, such as the 95.4 percent for Azerbaijan and 97 percent for Uzbekistan in 2005. Second, most business people report only small shares of sales paid as "gift" payments – an average of 3.2 percent in 2002 and 1.7 percent in 2005. Third, tax compliance became more common and gift payments less frequent in the three-year period between 2002 and 2005. Whether this was due to the maturation of the transition or to variations in the samples it is difficult to tell. The samples show very large gains in tax compliance for Serbia (14 percent), Bosnia (21 percent), and Georgia (24 percent), which seems implausible. Outside of these three countries, the average increase in tax compliance is 4.8 percent, which is just outside sampling error.

While these data are thus far from perfect, they do offer the opportunity to examine tax compliance cross-nationally in countries with weak legal systems

Table 9.1 Descriptive data from the BEEPS surveys by country

	Sales reported to tax authorities 2002	Share of sales in gift payments 2002	Sales reported to tax authorities 2005	Share of sales in gift payments 2005
Albania	77.5	3.1	77.0	6.2
Armenia	90.8	3.6	95.4	0.9
Azerbaijan	86.9	3.8	84.4	4.3
Belarus	91.9	2.7	92.8	1.0
Bosnia	67.5	3.1	88.2	0.5
Bulgaria	82.8	3.0	86.5	3.3
Croatia	87.3	2.6	92.4	0.7
Czech Republic	90.2	3.2	86.9	1.8
Estonia	92.7	2.9	96.9	0.5
Georgia	64.3	4.2	89.1	0.6
Hungary	88.5	2.8	88.1	2.5
Kazakhstan	82.7	3.2	93.5	1.7
Kyrgyzstab	73.9	3.5	85.4	2.2
Latvia	87.4	2.6	92.9	1.7
Lithuania	85.3	3.1	89.7	2.0
Macedonia	63.8	3.1	76.5	1.8
Moldova	79.5	3.5	88.2	0.6
Poland	90.2	2.7	89.5	1.0
Romania	86.6	3.2	93.7	0.7
Russia	82.0	3.2	84.5	2.0
Serbia	74.0	2.5	87.7	1.4
Slovakia	86.9	3.1	95.5	1.9
Slovenia	82.0	2.9	92.8	0.5
Tajikistan	72.2	–	91.0	1.1
Ukraine	85.4	3.7	89.3	1.8
Uzbekistan	89.5	3.6	97.0	1.4

and a great deal of economic uncertainty. Before transition, service delivery was not a high priority for Communist regimes – and infrastructure is still lacking. Many of these countries have been marked by political instability, with governments falling regularly, and no coherent party system for voters to hold regimes accountable. What, then, drives tax compliance in these systems? I first estimate a regression analysis of the 2002 BEEPS (see Table 9.2). The three most powerful factors (as determined by the t ratios) all reflect structural aspects of the firm: the size of the firm (which Gehlbach (2006) found to be the strongest predictor of hidden taxes in the 1999 BEEPS), the share of the firm owned by foreigners, and the size of the tax bill. The share owned by the state is also a significant predictor of the share of income respondents believe that most firms report, as is the number of competitors. Each of these structural factors promotes tax compliance, though there is no additional impact from the total sales of a firm or whether a firm sells to customers abroad.

Surprisingly, *neither how common gift payments to tax collectors are nor the overall share of a firm's income going to gift payments are significant in this*

Table 9.2 Regression model of perceived share of income reported by firms for tax purposes: BEEPS 2002 survey (transition countries)

Variable	Coefficient	Std error	t ratio
Size of tax bill	3.193****	0.761	4.20
Gift payments to tax collectors	0.486	0.598	0.81
Percent of income in gift payments	0.195	0.656	0.30
Quality of education	2.147****	0.606	3.54
How much influence firm has on ministry	−1.526**	0.812	−1.88
Size of firm (employees)	9.068****	1.209	7.50
Total sales of firm	−0.431	0.331	−1.30
Number of competitors	3.659***	1.379	2.65
Share owned by state	0.130***	0.043	3.00
Share owned by foreigners	0.149****	0.029	5.23
Firm sells to customers abroad	0.709	1.743	0.41
Constant	16.427*	7.487	2.19
RMSE = 28.901, R^2 = 0.107, n = 1,411			

Notes
** $p < 0.05$, **** $p < 0.0001$ (all tests one tailed except for constants).
Model estimated with robust standard errors.

estimation. Both are highly significant in the 2005 estimation, however. Firms that believe they have influence on ministries will be *less likely* to estimate high shares of revenue reported. Only one measure of services – the quality of education – is significant, but since education is such a fundamental function of government, this result is reassuring.

The model for the 2005 BEEPS is more in accord with my theoretical expectations (see Table 9.3). There is no measure of firm size in the 2005 BEEPS, so I cannot control for firm size (or ownership). There is no simple question on tax rates, but the perception that the tax rate is an obstacle to doing business has a strong (negative) impact on expectations for reporting income. Government subsidies are not significant, neither is auditing (inspections carried out). There are strong effects for gift payments – both how common these extra payments are to tax collectors, and the overall share of sales spent on gift payments (in sharp contrast to the 2002 results). The more firms have to pay extra for routine services, and to tax collectors, the less they believe is reported for taxes. The payments to tax collectors are likely made so that firms do not have to report their full income, as investments in lower taxes.

Equally strong or even stronger are effects of the quality of government service on perceived tax compliance. Respondents whose firms see telecommunications as an obstacle to doing business or have experienced power outages in the past year are substantially less likely to perceive strong tax compliance. Telecommunications and reliable power are essential to any firm doing business, so failure in either of these arenas may lead firms to underpay their taxes.

The legal environment and the political culture are also critical to tax compliance. Respondents who believe that the legal system is fair are substantially more likely to believe that most income is reported, but those who say that they have lost significant business to crime are slightly less prone to say that firms report their fair share. However, in countries where people have frequent inter-action with the courts, tax compliance is lower. Raiser, Rousso, and Steves (2004) argue that the share of sales on credit is a good proxy for trust in econo-mies where people have long had little faith in strangers–and just as little experi-ence in extending credit. Firms that give a substantial share of their business on credit are no more likely to say that revenue is reported accurately. However, an aggregate measure of trust from the Life in Transition Survey of the European Bank for Reconstruction and Development[5] is significant: business people living in countries with higher shares of trusting citizens report a larger share of their sales for tax purposes. People rely on the courts when trust is lacking, not when it is strong (Uslaner, 2002: 43–6), so the contrary effects of trust and interaction with the courts on tax compliance make sense.

The frequency of gift payments to tax collectors is a major factor shaping tax compliance, and bears examination in its own right. I thus estimate a model for gift payments to tax collectors in Table 9.4. The story of gift payments is straightforward: they do not reflect service quality, and there is little reason to expect them to do so (as reflected in the insignificant effect for power outages). They do reflect a variety of measures of (dis)honesty in government and on the street, as well as corruption-based quality of government institutions. A key determinant of the frequency of gift payments to tax collectors is the overall share of sales going to all gift payments. Beyond that are two measures of judi-cial corruption: whether courts are uncorrupt, and whether the judiciary is an obstacle to doing business. The expectation that contracts will be enforced is not significant. As with corruption more generally, what matters most is the *fairness*

Table 9.3 Regression model of share of sales reported for tax purposes: BEEPS 2005 survey (transition countries)

Variable	Coefficient	Std error	t ratio
Gift payments to tax collectors	−1.795****	0.383	−4.68
Percentage of sales in gift payments	−0.940****	0.195	−4.83
Tax rate obstacle to doing business	−1.223****	0.314	−3.89
Court system is fair	0.873***	0.279	3.13
Share of sales lost to crime over past 3 years	−0.240*	0.157	−1.53
Share of sales on credit	0.007	0.009	0.73
Telecommunications obstacle to doing business	−1.247****	0.288	−4.32
Experienced power outage in last year	−0.036****	0.005	−6.72
Inspection carried out by tax inspector last year	0.636	0.892	0.71
Subsidies from national govt. last 3 years	−1.222	1.369	−0.89
Trust (LITS survey)	4.460**	2.288	1.95
Frequency of interaction with courts (LITS)	−98.372****	30.990	−3.17
Constant	91.024****	6.969	13.06
RMSE = 18.148, R^2 = 0.109, n = 4,592			

Notes
* $p<0.10$, ** $p<0.05$, *** $p<0.01$, **** $p<0.0001$ (all tests one tailed except for constants).
Standard errors clustered by country (26 countries).

Table 9.4 Regression model of regression model of gift payments to tax collectors: BEEPS 2005 survey (transition countries)

Variable	Coefficient	Std error	t ratio
Percentage of sales in gift payments	0.090****	0.019	4.78
Contracts will be enforced	–0.034	0.029	–1.15
Courts uncorrupt	–0.068****	0.013	–5.04
Judiciary an obstacle to doing business	0.077****	0.019	4.02
Street crime an obstacle to doing business	0.060**	0.028	2.19
Mafia an obstacle to doing business	0.070**	0.028	1.73
Share of sales pay for security services	0.036***	0.013	2.76
Service interruption: Power outage	0.001	0.002	0.62
World Bank Corruption Control (2004)	–0.300****	0.087	–3.44
Sharp economic decline (Failed States)	–0.098***	0.030	–3.24
WIDER Change in Gini 1989–present	0.484***	0.170	2.84
Constant	1.233**	0.333	3.71
RMSE=1.129, R^2=0.151, n=3,107			

Notes
*$p<0.10$, **$p<0.05$, ***$p<0.01$, ****$p<0.0001$ (all tests one tailed except for constants).
Standard errors clustered by country (19 countries).

of the judicial system rather than its efficiency (Uslaner, 2008: Ch. 3). When firms cannot rely upon the courts, they depend upon bribery. When the Mafia and street crime are obstacles to doing business, and when businesses must spend a large share of their revenue on security, respondents have lower expectations of tax compliance.

The three country-level measures in the model confirm the findings at the individual level. The greater the degree of corruption, as measured by the World Bank control of corruption measure for 2004 (Kaufmann *et al.*, 2005), the more common gift payments to tax collectors are. And firms are more likely to make extra payments when the economy is fragile, as represented by the Failed States 2006 indicator of sharp economic decline in a country. Sharp economic decline makes people worry about the future, and thus they are more concerned with protecting their assets and keeping assets away from the grip of the state. Gift payments are also more common in countries where the level of economic inequality has increased since transition. Tax collection was simpler under Communism, since there was little private income. In the new market economies, the wealthy become the target of tax collectors because they have greater resources – and also because they are perceived as more likely to avoid taxation. As inequality grows, the wealthy will be more likely to be targeted because of public pressure, but they will also be better situated to avoid taxation by making gift payments to tax collectors. Gift payments to tax collectors depend upon a shaky legal environment and high levels of corruption both in high places and on the street.

Gift payments to tax collectors are clearly endogenous, so I estimate an instrumental variables regression (two-stage least squares) of the share of sales reported. The instruments I use for gift payments to tax collectors are the percentage of all sales in gift payments, whether the judiciary is an obstacle to business, the share of sales devoted to security services, and whether the court system is uncorrupt (as in the hierarchical linear model in Table 9.5). I present the instrumental variables regression in Table 9.5. The story is much the same as in Table 9.4: the instrument for gift payments to tax collectors has by far the highest t ratio, and there is a modest additional effect for the share of sales lost to crime in the past three years. There are also strong effects, as in Table 9.4, for whether telecommunications is an obstacle to business and whether the respondent's firm had experienced power outages in the last year. As in the previous estimation, the (dis)honesty of officials, street-level crime, and the quality of government services shape the expected share of sales reported for tax purposes. So, in this estimation, does the strong arm of the law: in contrast to previous estimations, there is now a powerful effect for whether tax inspectors carried out an audit in the previous year.

Finally, I estimate an aggregate model across the 26 countries for the expected share of sales reported for tax purposes in the 2005 BEEPS. The results largely confirm the individual-level analyses (see Table 9.6). One key difference is that the greatest effect comes from an estimate of the time respondents spent with public officials interpreting laws in the past year. The greater the time spent with officials, the lower the expected rate of reporting – suggesting that this variable may be tapping something beyond bureaucratic meetings. Where meetings consume the most time, respondents expect 11.5 percent less of revenues to be reported than when the fewest meetings occur.

Gift payments overall also matter: where they are most prevalent, respondents believe that revenue will be unreported by an additional 5 percent (and their effect is slightly stronger at 5.7 percent when Armenia and Uzbekistan are excluded). The quality of electricity services also matters strongly: expected revenue reporting is almost 9 percent greater where public utilities are evaluated most positively

Table 9.5 Instrumental variable estimation of share of sales reported for tax purposes: BEEPS 2005 survey (transition countries)

Variable	Coefficient	Std error	t ratio
Gift payments to tax collectors	−7.844****	0.966	−8.26
Share of sales lost to crime over past 3 years	−0.289*	0.199	−1.45
Telecommunications obstacle to doing business	−1.092***	0.343	−3.18
Experienced power outage in last year	−0.021***	0.008	−2.68
Inspection carried out by tax inspector last year	3.082****	0.638	4.83
Constant	97.322****	4.800	20.27
$F=42.77$ RMSE$=20.18$ $n=4,175$			

Notes
*$p<0.10$, **$p<0.05$, ***$p<0.01$, ****$p<0.0001$ (all tests one tailed except for constants)
Standard errors clustered by country (26 countries).
Instruments for gift payments to tax collectors: Percentage of sales in gift payments, the judiciary is an obstacle to the operation and growth in your business, the share of sales revenue paid for security services, court system is uncorrupt.

Table 9.6 Aggregate regression: share of sales reported for tax purposes: BEEPS 2005 survey (transition countries)

Variable	Coefficient	Std error	t ratio
Percentage of sales in gift payments	−1.867**	1.017	−1.84
Electricity obstacle to doing business	−11.631****	3.178	−3.66
Time with public officials interpreting laws last year	−1.178****	0.267	−4.41
Constant	114.325****	4.540	25.18
RMSE = 2.870, R² = 0.733, n = 26			

Note
**$p<0.05$, ****$p<0.0001$ (all tests one tailed except for constants).

than when they are viewed most negatively. All of these are significant effects, since the mean expectation of reported revenue is almost 90 percent. And overall, both the quality of services and the honesty of officials shape tax compliance more than any other factor (save firm size in the 2002 BEEPS).

Summary

Transition countries are marked by high levels of corruption and weak government services. People pay taxes and expect that the money they give to the state will go for public purposes – not into the pockets of public officials. When corruption is widespread and public services, especially those critical for business, are poor, people will be more likely to evade taxes. While there are sporadic effects of enforcement in the models I have estimated, the problem with tax enforcement in transition countries is that the bureaucrats who enforce the laws may well be corrupt themselves. The arm of the law seems to be bent rather than strong – as reflected in the powerful negative effect of time spent with bureaucrats on expected tax compliance in the aggregate results.

Business elites see far less corruption than do ordinary citizens, so the results I have presented likely underestimate tax avoidance. My findings are similar to those of Hanousek and Palda (2004; cf. Uslaner, 2007) for the Czech Republic using more direct measures of tax compliance for the general public. So the lesson seems clear: people pay taxes when they believe that they are getting something for their money. The social contract underlying tax collection is not among citizens, but between citizens and the state.

I cannot estimate a more complex model incorporating company structure, corruption, and the quality of government services. The 2002 BEEPS has good measures of company structure and the 2005 BEEPS has better indicators of corruption and the quality of services. The models I have estimated suggest that all three sets of factors matter. Potential reformers who wish to achieve greater compliance with tax laws should promote policies that foster greater liberalization, more transparency, and, especially, better provision of government services. Foreign investment clearly leads to greater tax compliance. Larger firms pay larger shares in taxes, so economic policies that promote the establishment of large firms with substantial foreign investment will lead to greater tax compliance. So will less corruption – though how to make the polity more honest is not so straightforward (see Uslaner, 2008, especially Chapter 7). Perhaps the best advice that one can give a reformer is: make the government work. It's not just that people get what they pay for; they pay for what they get.

Notes

1 This chapter draws on Uslaner (2007) and especially Uslaner (2008). I am grateful for the sustained comments on my research from Bo Rothstein, Gabriel Badescu, Mark Lichbach, and Jong-sung You. I am also grateful to the General Research Board of the University of Maryland–College Park for generous released time.
2 On the BEEPS surveys, see www.ebrd.com/country/sector/econo/surveys/be ps.htm. For the sampling in 2002 and 2005, respectively, see www.ebrd.com/country/sector/econo/surveys/beeps02r.pdf and www.ebrd.com/country/sector/econo/surveys/beeps05r.pdf.
3 These figures are based on ratings of 1 or 2 on a six-point scale.
4 The WIDER data are available at www.wider.unu.edu/wiid/wiid.htm.
5 The trust measure is a six-point scale of the standard question, "Generally speaking, do you believe that most people can be trusted or can't you be too careful in dealing with people?" I am grateful to Franklin Steves of EBRD for making the data available to me. Details of the EBRD survey are at www.ebrd.com/pubs/econo/lits.pdf.

Bibliography

Alm, J., Martinez-Vazquez, J., and Torgler, B. (2004) "Russian attitudes toward paying taxes – before, during, and after the transition", Unpublished paper, Andrew Young School of Public Policy, Georgia State University.

Beron, K., Tauchen, H. V., and Witte, A. D. (1992) "The effect of audits on reporting behavior," in J. Slemrod (ed.), *Why People Pay Taxes*, Ann Arbor, MI: University of Michigan Press.

Citrin, J. (1974) "Comment: The political relevance of trust in government", *American Political Science Review*, 68: 973–88.

Easter, G. M. (2007) "Taxation and state re-formation in Russia: Policy, capacity, compliance", in N. Hayoz and S. Hug (eds.), *Tax Evasion, Trust, and State Capacities*, Bern, Switzerland: Peter Lang.

Feld, L. P. and Frey, B. S. (2007) "Tax evasion in Switzerland: The roles of deterrence and tax morale", in N. Hayoz and S. Hug (eds.), *Tax Evasion, Trust, and State Capacities*, Bern, Switzerland: Peter Lang.

Finn, P. (2006) "For Russians, Car Wreck is a Case Study in Privilege", *Washington Post*, February 13: A1, A18.

Flap, H. and Voelker, B. (2003) "Communist societies, the velvet revolution, and weak ties: The case of East Germany", in G. Badescu and E. M. Uslaner (eds.), *Social Capital and the Transition to Democracy*, London, UK: Routledge.

Gehlbach, S. (2006) "The consequences of collective action; an incomplete-contracts approach", *American Journal of Political Science*, 50: 802–23.

Gupta, S., Davoodi, H. R., and Tiongson, E. R. (2002) "Corruption and the provision of health care and education services", in G. T. Abed and S. Gupta. (eds.), *Corruption and Economic Performance*, Washington, DC: International Monetary Fund.

Hanousek, J. and Palda, F. (2004) "Quality of government services and the civic duty to pay taxes in the Czech and Slovak Republics, and other transition countries", *Kyklos*, 57: 237–52.

——. (2007) "The evolution of tax evasion in the Czech Republic: A Markov chain analysis", in N. Hayoz and S. Hug (eds.), *Tax Evasion, Trust, and State Capacities*, Bern, Switzerland: Peter Lang.

Karklins, R. (2005) *The System Made Me Do It: Corruption in Post-Communist Societies*, Armonk, NY: M.E. Sharpe.

Kaufmann, D., Kray, A., and Mastruzzi, M. (2005) "Governance matters IV: Governance indicators for 1996–2004", Washington, DC: World Bank, retrieved from www.worldbank.org/wbi/governance/pubs/govmatters4.html.

Kolarska-Bobinska, L. (2002) "The impact of corruption on legitimacy of authority in new democracies", in S. Kotkin and A. Sajo (eds.), *Political Corruption in Transition: A Skeptic's Handbook*, Budapest, Hungary: CEU Press.

Kornai, J. (2000) "Hidden in an envelope: gratitude payments to medical doctors in Hungary", retrieved from www.colbud.hu/honesty-trust/kornai/pub01.PDF.

Kramer, A. (2004) "He doesn't make coffee, but he controls 'Starbucks' in Russia", *New York Times*, Washington edition (October 12): C1, C4.

——. (2006) "From Russia with dread: American faces a truly hostile takeover attempt at his factory", *New York Times*, Washington edition (May 16): C1, C4.

Ledeneva, A. (1998) *Russia's Economy of Favours*, Cambridge, UK: Cambridge University Press.

Mauro, P. (2002) "The effects of corruption on growth and public expenditure", in A. Heidenheimer and M. Johnston (eds.), *Political Corruption*, 3rd edn, New Brunswick, NJ: Transaction.

Miller, W. L., Grodeland, A. B., and Koshechkina, T. Y. (2001) *A Culture of Corruption: Coping with Government in Post-Communist Europe*, Budapest, Hungary: CEU Press.

Office of Research. (1999) "On the take: Central and East European attitudes toward corruption", Washington, DC: Department of State.

Ott, K. (2007) "What do state capacity and trust have to do with the evolution of the informal economy and tax evasion in Croatia?", in N. Hayoz and S. Hug (eds.), *Tax Evasion, Trust, and State Capacities*, Bern, Switzerland: Peter Lang.

Owsiak, S. (2007) "Taxes in post-communist countries – old and new challenges", in N. Hayoz and S. Hug (eds.), *Tax Evasion, Trust, and State Capacities*, Bern, Switzerland: Peter Lang.

Popov, N. (2006) "To give and take", retrieved from www.indem.ru/en/publicat/Popov/GiveandTake.htm.

Raiser, M., Rousso, A., and Steves, F. (2004) "Measuring trust in transition: Preliminary findings from 26 transition economies", in J. Kornai, B. Rothstein, and S. Rose-Ackerman (eds.), *Creating Social Trust in Post-Socialist Transition*. New York, NY: Palgrave Macmillan.

Rosser, J. B., Rosser, M. V., and Ahmed, E. (2000) "Income inequality and the informal economy in transition countries", *Journal of Comparative Economics*, 28: 156–71.

Rothstein, B. (2001) "Trust, social dilemmas, and collective memories: On the rise and decline of the Swedish model", *Journal of Theoretical Politics*, 12: 477–99.

Scholz, J. T. (2007) "Contractual compliance: Tax institutions and tax morale in the US", in N. Hayoz and S. Hug (eds.), *Tax Evasion, Trust, and State Capacities*, Bern, Switzerland: Peter Lang.

Smith, K. W. (1992) "Reciprocity and fairness: positive incentives for taxpayer compliance", in J. Slemrod (ed.), *Why People Pay Taxes*, Ann Arbor, MI: University of Michigan Press.

Tavits, M. (2005) "Causes of corruption: testing competing hypotheses," paper presented at the Joint Sessions of Workshops, European Consortium for Political Research, Nicosia, Cyprus, April, 2005 retrieved from www.nuffield. ox.ac.uk/Politics/papers/2005/Tavits%20Nuffield%20WP.pdf.

Torgler, B. (2003) "Tax morale in transition countries", *Post-Communist Economies*, 15: 357–81.

——. (2007) "Tax morale in Central and Eastern European countries", in N. Hayoz and S. Hug (eds.), *Tax Evasion, Trust, and State Capacities*, Bern, Switzerland: Peter Lang.

Torgler, B.and Schneider, F. (2006) "What shapes attitudes toward paying taxes? Evidence form multicultural European countries", Institute for the Study of Labor, IZA DP No. 2117, Bonn, Germany.

Tyler, T. R. (1990) *Why People Obey the Law*. New Haven, CT: Yale University Press.

Uslaner, E. M. (2002) *The Moral Foundations of Trust*, New York, NY: Cambridge University Press.

——. (2007) "Tax evasion, trust, and the strong arm of the law", in N. Hayoz and S. Hug (eds.), *Tax Evasion, Trust, and State Capacities*, Bern, Switzerland: Peter Lang.

——. (2008) *Corruption, Inequality, and the Rule of Law: The Bulging Pocket Makes the Easy Life*, New York, NY: Cambridge University Press.

Uslaner, E. M. and Badescu, G. (2004) "Honesty, trust, and legal norms in the transition to democracy: Why Bo Rothstein is better able to explain Sweden than Romania", in J. Kornai, S. Rose-Ackerman, and B. Rothstein (eds.), *Creating Social Trust: Problems of Post-Socialist Transition*, New York, NY: Palgrave.

World Bank (2004) *Doing Business in 2004: Understanding Regulation*, Washington, DC: World Bank retrieved from www.doingbusiness.org/Documents/DB2004-full-report.pdf.

10 Procedural justice and the regulation of tax compliance behavior

The moderating role of personal norms

Kristina Murphy[1]

Introduction

The aim of regulatory enforcement is to gain future compliance from offenders. At the same time, enforcement practices should not result in the alienation of those they come into contact with. In an area such as taxation, like in many other regulatory contexts, the behavior being regulated is continuous and fundamental to the long-term health of the community. In such a regulatory context, the goal should therefore be to secure long-term voluntary compliance. This chapter will present an argument for why deterrence-based enforcement strategies might be counterproductive in meeting these goals, especially if emphasized in the first encounter between a regulator and regulatee. Using survey data collected from a group of 652 tax offenders, it will be suggested that a process-based model of regulation – one which places persuasion and fair treatment in the foreground of a regulatory enforcement encounter – offers much promise in the regulation of taxpayer behavior.[2]

In particular, the present study builds upon existing research in two ways. It first seeks to replicate and extend those findings which suggest that procedural justice (i.e., persuasion and fair treatment from regulators) is effective in shaping tax compliance behavior. Second, it seeks to test whether personal norms moderate the effect of procedural justice on compliance behavior, as they do for deterrence effects. As will be evident from the research summarized below, the relationships between procedural justice and compliance, and between norms and compliance, have previously been explored. However, no studies in the taxation context have sought to test the conditions under which procedural justice is more or less effective in nurturing compliance. The present study therefore seeks to examine whether personal norms moderate the effect of procedural justice on self-reported compliance behavior. Before proceeding to discuss the findings from the present study, however, the following sections first review the literature on tax compliance.

Deterrence and tax compliance

When reviewing the literature on tax compliance, by far the most common approach to explaining taxpayer behavior is the rational actor approach and its corresponding regulatory strategy of deterrence. The rational actor approach argues that people are motivated entirely by profit-seeking. They assess opportunities and risks, and disobey the law when the anticipated fine and probability of being caught are small in relation to the profits to be made through non-compliance (see, for example, Allingham and Sandmo, 1972). In the case of the regulation of people's behavior, the rational choice model focuses upon the ability of expected losses associated with law-breaking to lessen the likelihood that people will break the law (Nagin and Paternoster, 1991). This regulatory model is referred to as the social control model, or deterrence model. According to advocates of this approach, taxpayers should be deterred from tax non-compliance when they perceive the chance that their non-compliance will be detected to be high, and the consequences and penalties to be severe and costly.

The deterrence model has tended to dominate the formulation of public policy in areas as diverse as criminal justice, welfare policy, and taxation. But does it work? Indeed, some research does support the suggestion that variations in the perceived certainty and severity of punishment do shape people's compliance with the law (see Grasmick and Bursik, 1990) and, more specifically, their tax-paying behavior (see Andreoni *et al.*, 1998; Fischer *et al.*, 1992; Franzoni, 2000). For example, evidence of the effects of audit or detection probability has been found using actual taxpayer data (e.g., Witte and Woodbury, 1985), in experimental studies (e.g., Alm *et al.*, 1992, 1995), and in survey research (e.g., Kinsey and Grasmick, 1993; Varma and Doob, 1998). Similarly, there is evidence for the positive effects of sanction severity on tax compliance (e.g., Alm *et al.*, 1995; Wenzel, 2004a). It should be noted, however, that other studies have yielded inconsistent findings (e.g., Dubin and Wilde, 1988; Dubin *et al.*, 1987; Elffers *et al.*, 1987; Webley and Halstead, 1986).

Although research supports the basic premise of the deterrence model and its ability to deter people from breaking the law, research also suggests that estimates of the likelihood of being caught and punished have, at best, a minor influence on people's law-related behavior. Some studies suggest that such estimates do not independently influence behavior when the influence of other factors is considered. For example, in a longitudinal study of juvenile delinquents, Paternoster and Iovanni (1986) found that numerous other factors, such as fear of informal sanctions from peers or family, also contribute to the deterrence of crime. In the taxation context, Scott and Grasmick (1981) reported survey findings showing that legal sanctions had a greater deterrence effect on tax evasion for respondents who perceived the tax system as unjust, and were thus presumably more motivated to evade tax. In an Australian tax study, Wenzel (2004a) also found that perceived deterrence was less effective for respondents who identified strongly as Australians. Wenzel argued that this finding may have been due to "strong identifiers" being less motivated by individual self-interest than by the collective good. These research findings suggest that compliance with the law may, at best, be only weakly linked to the risks associated with law-breaking behaviors.

Not only has the deterrence model been used to deter would-be non-compliers from breaking the law (i.e., as a general deterrent); it has also been used as a specific deterrent to those who have already been detected and caught breaking the law. The deterrence model makes the assumption that by handing out harsh punishment and penalties to rule-breakers this will deter them from committing *future* acts of non-compliance. Evidence to suggest such an approach can work comes from a recent tax study conducted in Australia. Williams (2001) analyzed tax return data from 528 taxpayers who had previously been prosecuted for failing to lodge their tax returns with the Australian Taxation Office. His results showed that prosecutions were successful in obtaining subsequent lodgement compliance, but he qualified this by showing that lodgement rates reduced significantly in subsequent years once the initial threat of deterrence had subsided.

A growing body of research suggests that deterrence-based enforcement strategies with offenders can sometimes be counterproductive in the long term (see, for example, Ayres and Braithwaite, 1992; Blumenthal *et al.*, 1998; Kagan and Scholz, 1984). In fact, research into reactance has shown that the use of threat and legal authority, particularly when perceived as illegitimate, can produce the opposite behavior from that sought; these actions are more likely to result in further non-compliance (Brehm and Brehm, 1981; Murphy and Harris, 2007; Williams, 2001), creative compliance (McBarnet, 2003), criminal behavior, or overt opposition (Fehr and Rokenbach, 2003; Frey, 1997; Kagan and Scholz, 1984; Unnever *et al.*, 2004). Kagan and Scholz (1984) further argue that unreasonable behavior by regulators during an enforcement experience generates resistance to compliance. They suggest that unreasonableness may involve disrespect for citizens, or arbitrary refusal to take their concerns into account in the enforcement process. They suggest that citizen response to such unreasonableness is likely to be weakened respect for compliance with the law.

An analysis of compliance that is patterned on the deterrence model provides an important starting point for thinking about tax compliance. However, although there is evidence to support this regulatory framework, it nonetheless represents only one piece of the tax compliance phenomenon. Behavior is multifaceted and is influenced by many different factors, including taxpayer disposition toward authority, ethics, morals, norms, and the perceived fairness of the tax system and the way in which enforcement is used. Given the potential problems that deterrence strategies may pose for subsequent compliance behavior, a number of scholars have therefore suggested that these additional factors need to be considered when managing non-compliance (Braithwaite, 2002; Kagan and Scholz, 1984; Tyler, 1990). These scholars argue that the core motivation of a regulator should be not to punish an evil, but to repair the harm done and to secure future compliance (see also Black, 2001).

A process-based model of regulation

The limits of the deterrence model suggest the importance of developing a broader regulatory model to explain compliance behavior. One such model has been proposed by Tyler (1990). According to Tyler (1990), people's compliance behavior is strongly linked to views about justice and injustice. In particular, he suggests that procedural justice plays an important role in people's decision to comply with rules and regulations.

Procedural justice concerns the perceived fairness of the procedures involved in decision-making and the perceived treatment one receives from a decision maker during an enforcement experience (referred to by Feld and Frey, in Chapter 5 of this volume, as procedural justice and interactional justice, respectively). The procedural justice literature demonstrates that people's reactions to their personal experiences with authorities are rooted in their evaluations of the fairness of procedures those agencies use to exercise their authority (Lind and Tyler, 1988; Tyler and Blader, 2000). There is empirical evidence to show that people who feel they have been treated in a procedurally fair manner by an authority will be more likely to trust that authority (Murphy, 2004b), and will be more inclined to accept its decisions and follow its directions (Lind and Tyler, 1988; Tyler and DeGoey, 1996). Furthermore, Tyler and Huo (2002) suggest that procedurally fair regulation also lessens defiance and hostility. In fact, a number of scholars have found that people are more likely to challenge a situation collectively when they believe that the procedures an authority uses are unfair (Greenberg, 1987; Murphy, 2003; Smith and Stalans, 1994).

The procedural justice literature specifically highlights the importance of an authority's trustworthiness, interpersonal respect, and neutrality in its dealings with others (Tyler, 1997). Research has shown that if people believe that an authority has tried to be fair with them, that they have been treated with respect, and that they have been dealt with in an impartial way, then these three factors enhance feelings of fairness. In fact, the research suggests that this is the case both for general encounters with authorities and for enforcement encounters where the offender has been penalized in some fashion. Hence, Tyler and Huo (2002) suggest that instead of relying purely on deterrence-based strategies, regulators should adopt what they refer to as a process-based model of regulation. According to Tyler and Huo, a more effective regulatory strategy would be to encourage the judgment that a regulator is using fair procedures in exercising authority, and to develop the public's trust in the motives of legal authorities. Tyler and Huo refer to this as process-based regulation because such a strategy is based on seeking to gain the cooperation and consent of members of the public through the fair, respectful behavior of regulatory authorities. Tyler and Huo (2002) show that process-based regulation offers several advantages. As mentioned earlier, it has been shown to lessen defiance and hostility, making it easier for regulators to gain acceptance for their decisions from the public. Second, because people are accepting the decisions of authorities more voluntarily, there is a greater likelihood of them adhering to those decisions over time. Tyler and Huo suggest that when people unwillingly give way to coercive and deterrence-based strategies, their compliance does not develop from internal motivations. Once the immediate threat of punishment is lessened, people revert to their prior behaviors (as is evidenced by Williams' (2001) tax study presented earlier). This is why they suggest regulators often have to revisit problems and people over and over again to remind them of the possibility of sanctioning.

Procedural justice and tax compliance

Advocates of the deterrence approach would have us believe that economic self-interest factors dominate taxpayers' actions. However, a growing number of research studies have found that procedural justice can in fact be more effective in shaping compliance than instrumental factors such as judgments about gain and losses or about fear of punishment (e.g., Feld and Frey, 2002; Magner *et al.*, 1998; Murphy, 2005a; Wenzel, 2002a, 2006). For example, in a Swiss study, Feld and Frey (2002) presented empirical evidence to suggest that actual tax compliance increased when taxpayers were treated as trustworthy in the first instance by tax authorities; a major principle of procedurally fair regulation. In a study of Australian taxpayers, Wenzel (2002b) also studied the impact of justice perceptions on self-reported tax compliance. Using a survey methodology, Wenzel found that taxpayers reported being more compliant when they thought that they had been treated fairly and respectfully by the Australian Taxation Office (ATO).

More recently, Wenzel (2006) studied the effectiveness of different reminder letters that prompt business taxpayers about their requirements to file their quarterly business activity statements with the ATO. Taxpayers in his study were all non-compliant taxpayers, as they had all failed to file their business activity statements with the ATO by the required date. Working with the ATO, Wenzel tested three different letters on subsequent filing compliance. The first was the ATO's standard reminder letter, which made penalties and punishment salient. The other two letters focused on principles of procedural fairness. The first of these procedural justice letters emphasized consideration and respect for taxpayers (i.e., interpersonal fairness), while at the same time communicating to the taxpayers that they had not fulfilled their taxation obligations under the tax code because they had not filed their activity statement by the due date. The second letter provided taxpayers with information about their obligations, and provided justifications for the ATO's decision to pursue them further (i.e., informational justice). Each of the three letters was sent to a random sample of taxpayers (N=2,052). It was found that both the informational and the interpersonal letter yielded greater subsequent filing compliance from individuals compared to the standard ATO letter. In other words, small business owners were more likely subsequently to file their late activity statements promptly after receiving the procedural justice letters. Importantly, it was also found that fewer complaints and excuses were made to the ATO from taxpayers who received informational and interpersonal letters (Wenzel, 2002a).

Finally, I myself have published research into the effectiveness of procedural justice with taxpayers who have had personal experience with the ATO's enforcement procedures. Using longitudinal survey data collected from 652 tax offenders, I found that taxpayers who perceived their enforcement experience with the ATO to be procedurally unfair were significantly more likely to report having evaded their taxes again two years later (Murphy, 2005a; see also Murphy, 2003, 2004b). Coupled with the other studies in the procedural justice literature, these tax studies in general suggest that individuals do not react to authorities primarily or exclusively in terms of what they do or do not receive from those authorities; instead, they react to how they are treated. It is therefore proposed here that an enforcement model that utilizes procedural justice principles may prove particularly effective in nurturing the long-term voluntary compliance of taxpayers.

The present study

The previous section presented empirical evidence to suggest that a process-based model of regulation may prove particularly useful to regulators in the management of tax non-compliance. The findings in general establish a relationship between treating taxpayers with procedural justice and subsequent tax compliance behavior. However, the conditions under which procedural justice may be more or less effective have not yet received much attention in the taxation literature. For example, is it possible that procedural justice may be more effective in shaping compliance behavior for some taxpayers than for others? Specifically, would regulatory strategies that rely on procedural justice principles be ineffective for those who hold weak personal norms about obeying the law? If we are to support a process-based model of regulation in the taxation context, we would hope to find that procedural justice can be used effectively with offenders who have little respect for the law.

The moderating role of personal norms?

In addition to being influenced by their judgments about the behavior of regulatory agencies they encounter during an enforcement experience, people's willingness to comply with the law has also been found to be shaped by their personal norms. If we look at the criminology literature, for example, we can see that one view on why people comply with legal directives is what Skogan and Frydl (2004) refer to as "substantive morality" – that is, compliance is motivated by personal norms and values. If one's personal norms or values are consistent with the law, cooperation and compliance will be voluntarily extended.

Various studies have demonstrated the important role that personal norms play in predicting taxpaying behavior. In a classic study conducted by Schwartz and Orleans (1967), for example, it was found that appeals to taxpayers' personal conscience could increase their tax compliance behavior more so than deterrent threats. A number of other studies produced similar findings of personal norms increasing tax compliance (e.g., Bosco and Mittone, 1997; Erard and Feinstein, 1994; Reckers et al., 1994; Wenzel, 2004a, 2004b). A particularly interesting pattern of results, however, has shown that personal norms can actually delimit the relevance of deterrence. Wenzel (2004a) found that personal norms of tax honesty were negatively related to self-reported tax evasion, and moderated the effects of perceived sanction severity. In other words, Wenzel's findings showed deterrence effects only when personal norms regarding taxation compliance were weak.

Such findings have important implications about the role that norms might play in the procedural justice–compliance relationship. As suggested by Wenzel (2004a: 549), "deterrence should only be relevant where people's ethics do not discard non-compliance as one such option altogether." If this assertion is indeed correct, then we may also expect to see that taxpayers' personal norms moderate the effect that procedural justice has on compliance behavior. For a process-based model of regulation to be widely supported, we should also expect to find that procedural justice is effective in shaping the tax behavior of those who hold questionable norms about paying tax.

Method

Participants and procedure

The 652 taxpayers who participated in the present study had all been caught and punished by the Australian Taxation Office (ATO) for investing in illegal tax avoidance schemes. All schemes that were used by the taxpayers under study were financially structured in a similar way. Hence, the taxpayers in the present study form a homogenous group in terms of the offense they had been accused of. What makes this case study particularly interesting is the fact that many of the taxpayers who invested in these illegal tax avoidance schemes did so on the advice of their tax agents. Many claimed that they were therefore the victims of aggressive marketing and bad financial advice. This is important, because it means that not all those who "broke the law" by investing in these schemes did so for the dominant purpose of cheating the tax system. One would therefore expect there to be a mixture of people in the surveyed group who hold both strong and weak norms about paying tax.

With assistance from the ATO, a nationwide random sample of 1,250 tax offenders was sent a 28-page survey. Taxpayers were invited to participate in a study that was interested in taxpayers' views of the ATO and their enforcement processes. Taxpayers were informed that their responses would be kept confidential and would not be used against them by the ATO. Non-respondents were followed up over time using an identification number that was affixed to each survey booklet, which was in turn linked to the sample name. A total of four mailings were made, and after a period of approximately three months a total of 652 usable surveys were received. When adjusting for people who had moved address, had died, or were incapable of completing the survey ($N = 146$), the response rate was 60 percent.

Respondents in the final sample were between 25 and 76 years of age ($M = 50.43$, $SD = 9.00$), 83 percent were male, 46 percent had received a University education, and their average personal income was approximately AUS$79,000 ($SD = AUS$59,000$; at the time of writing the average equated to approximately US$65,000, or €47,700). Using the limited amount of demographic data provided by the ATO (i.e., state of residence and sex), the sample proved to be representative of the overall scheme offender population ($N = 32,493$).

Measures used in the present study

The survey contained in excess of 200 questions designed to test respondents' attitudes towards the Australian tax system, the Australian Taxation Office, and paying taxes. A number of questions were also designed with the aim of assessing investors' self-reported tax compliance behavior, and their views about their enforcement experience. For the purposes of the present study, however, only those questions relevant to three categories of variables were used: (1) procedural justice, (2) personal norms about taxpaying honesty, and (3) self-reported tax compliance variables. The Appendix to this chapter lists all individual questions used to construct each scale.

Procedural justice

The eight-item procedural justice measure was based on previous research conducted by Tyler (1990). Specifically, the items used to construct the procedural justice scale assessed Tyler's three concepts of trustworthiness, respect, and neutrality. As was noted in the introduction to this chapter, these three concepts are commonly used in the literature to define procedural justice. Taxpayers were asked to think back and reflect on the ATO's treatment of them during their enforcement experience. They were then presented with a series of questions, each measured on a 1 (strongly disagree) to 5 (strongly agree) scale, and each designed to assess whether respondents felt they had received procedural justice from the ATO during their enforcement encounter (sample item: "The ATO tries to be fair when making its decisions"). The factor analysis presented in Table 10.1 shows that the eight items loaded strongly onto only one factor, and the Cronbach reliability coefficient revealed the scale to be strong (see Table 10.2). The scale was constructed by summing and averaging respondents' scores to all eight items. The overall scale was coded in the present study so that those scoring higher on this scale were more likely to see the ATO as having used procedurally fair methods. As can be seen in Table 10.2, the average score on this scale fell below the midpoint of the scale, suggesting that the majority of respondents were not happy about the treatment they had received from the ATO.

Personal norms

The three-item personal norms scale was based on previous research conducted by Wenzel (2004a, 2004b). The scale was designed to assess whether taxpayers' moral values about tax evasion were at odds with the ATO's tax laws. Specifically, taxpayers were asked about their views regarding the cash economy and making false claims on tax returns (sample item: "Do you think you should honestly declare cash earnings on your tax return?"). Again, respondents were asked to indicate how supportive they were of these statements on a 1 (strongly disagree) to 5 (strongly agree) scale. And again the scale was constructed by summing and averaging respondents' scores to all three items. Two items of the scale were reverse scored so that those scoring high on this measure were deemed to have strong personal norms that paying tax is the right thing to do. As can be seen from Table 10.2, respondents' personal norms were on average quite strong. Further, the Cronbach alpha reliability coefficient revealed that the scale was reliable.

Tax compliance

In order to assess tax compliance, taxpayers were asked a series of six questions about how they thought their enforcement experience had subsequently affected their taxpaying behavior. Taxpayers were asked to indicate whether they believed the experience had made them more defiant towards the ATO, whether they now go out of their way to avoid tax, and whether they use the tax system in a negative way to recoup the financial losses they incurred as a result of their enforcement experience. Each question was measured on a 1 (strongly disagree) to 5 (strongly agree) scale (sample item: "I now try to avoid paying as much tax as possible"). All responses to the six items were reverse scored, summed, and averaged to form the tax compliance scale. A higher score on this scale indicates greater compliance. As can be seen from Table 10.2, self-reported compliance was quite high, and the compliance scale was extremely reliable (as indicated by the Cronbach coefficient).

Factor analysis

A principal components analysis was conducted to test for the dimensionality of the items, and the eigenvalues (5.08, 3.39, 1.38, 0.83, 0.76) and scree plot[3] of this analysis suggested that three factors should be extracted. Inspection of the rotated factor structure (see Table 10.1) shows that the three factors extracted in the analysis support the scales that are described in the measures section. Factor 1 comprised eight items that measured procedural justice, Factor 2 comprised six items that measured tax compliance, and Factor 3 comprised three items that measured personal norms. While one item in Factor 2 ("I no longer declare all my income") was found to cross-load weakly with items in Factor 3, it was decided to retain this item in the tax compliance scale. The reason for this was twofold. First, a separate regression analysis without this single item included produced the same findings and conclusions as the analysis that did include the item. Second, it is perhaps not surprising that a weak cross-loading was apparent between this item and the Factor 3 items. The tax compliance item measures self-reported behavior to do with declaring cash income. Two of the personal norm items ask participants about their views on paying tax on cash income. Given that one set of items measures personal norms and the other set of items measures behavior, it could therefore be reasonably argued that the two sets of items are conceptually distinct from one another despite there being a substantial relationship between them.

Table 10.1 Factor analysis differentiating variables used in the analysis

Item	Factor		
	1	*2*	*3*
1 Procedural justice			
ATO is concerned with respecting rights	0.84		
ATO cares about position of taxpayers	0.83		
ATO tries to be fair in decision-making	0.81		
ATO respects individual's rights	0.78		
ATO considers citizen's concerns when making decisions	0.77		
ATO is generally honest with people	0.73		
ATO gives equal consideration to all	0.72		
ATO gets information to make informed decisions	0.53		
2 Tax compliance			
Use tax system in negative way (r)		0.82	
Look for ways to purposefully cheat (r)		0.77	
Now more defiant towards ATO (r)		0.68	
Look for many ways to recoup losses (r)		0.68	
Try to avoid paying as much tax as possible (r)		0.67	
No longer declare all my income (r)		0.63	0.30
3 Personal norms			
Working for cash is trivial offence (r)			0.77
Should honestly declare cash		0.76	
Acceptable to overstate deductions (r)			0.76
Eigenvalues	5.08	3.39	1.38
Explained variance (%)	30	20	8

Note
Principle-components analysis, with varimax rotation. Only factor loadings >0.30 are displayed.

Study limitations

Before proceeding to discuss the findings of the study, several limitations of the present study should first be mentioned. First, given the cross-sectional nature of the survey data, it is impossible to make definitive conclusions about the causal direction of any relationships that are found. For example, it is impossible to ascertain whether the tax offenders studied held strong or weak personal norms about taxpaying prior to investing in tax schemes, or whether it was their enforcement experience that led to their currently held norms. Accordingly, this study will limit itself to identifying the presence of relationships, which are valuable in themselves, rather than attempting to draw inferences about their direction. Second, due to the widespread taxpayer resistance exhibited towards the ATO's decision to punish scheme investors, the ATO was forced to defend its position to punish taxpayers in court.[4] It could be the case, therefore, that the taxpayers who participated in the present study were particularly angry with the ATO's handling of the situation, and responded to survey questions with hostility. Hence, the data may be biased towards those with particularly negative views and attitudes toward the ATO, the tax system, and paying tax. Third, it is also important to note that a self-report measure of tax compliance was used as the measure of repeat offending in the present study. A method that relies on the honesty of the surveyed participants to disclose dishonest behavior is obviously vulnerable to a challenge to its validity. However, participants were made aware that their responses would be kept confidential, and a strong tradition of research in criminology supports the validity of using self-report data in such circumstances (Maxfield and Babbie, 2008; Thornberry and Krohn, 2000).

Results

As noted earlier, this study is interested in assessing the relationship between perceptions of procedural justice, personal norms, and tax compliance behavior. It is interested in addressing whether a process-based model of regulation might be effective in nurturing compliance for taxpayers who have both strong and weak norms about complying with the law. Specifically, this study is interested in whether personal norms moderate the effect of procedural justice on compliance behavior. Table 10.2 presents the means, standard deviations, and Cronbach alpha reliability coefficients for all scales measured in the present study. It also details the bi-variate correlations between each scale. As can be seen from Table 10.2, procedural justice is positively correlated with compliance, suggesting that respondents who felt they received procedurally fair treatment from the ATO were more likely to be compliant. Further, and as expected, personal norms were also correlated with compliance. This finding suggests that those who hold strong personal norms about doing the right thing by the law are also more likely to be compliant.

Regression analysis

In order to test whether personal norms moderate the effect of procedural justice on self-reported compliance behavior a hierarchical regression analysis was performed. All variables were centerd prior to analysis. To identify the unique contribution offered by the two predictor variables of interest, "personal norms" was entered separately into the regression model at Step 1, followed by "procedural

Table 10.2 Means and standard deviations for each scale, and bi-variate correlations among all scales in the study. Figures in parentheses are Cronbach alpha reliability coefficients.

Variables	Mean	SD	1	2	3
1 Procedural justice	2.27	0.72	(0.89)		
2 Personal norms	3.94	0.75	−0.04	(0.69)	
3 Tax compliance	4.00	0.71	0.23***	0.34***	(0.80)

Notes
*$p < 0.05$, **$p < 0.01$, ***$p < 0.001$; all scales measured on a 1 to 5 scale (1=strongly disagree, 2=disagree, 3=neither, 4=agree, 5=strongly agree).

justice" at Step 2. The "procedural justice" × "personal norms" interaction term was entered into the model at Step 3. Table 10.3 displays the results for this analysis. First, it can be seen that 19 percent of the overall variation in compliance behavior could be explained by all three steps of the regression. It was found that 12 percent of the variation in compliance could be explained by one's personal norms, an additional 6 percent by perceptions of procedural justice, and 1 percent by the interaction between these two variables.

From Step 3 of Table 10.3, it can be seen that both "personal norms" and "procedural justice" were found to have significant main effects on self-reported "tax compliance behavior". Like the bi-variate correlation results, as expected, these regression findings indicate that taxpayers who expressed a strong personal norm of tax honesty reported being more compliant, and those who felt they had been treated in a procedurally fair manner by the ATO during their enforcement experience reported being more compliant. While tax authorities have little influence over people's personal norms, the latter finding is important, as it indicates that tax authorities can do something themselves to shape people's compliance behaviors. By treating people with procedural justice, they can shape their compliance behavior in a positive way.

More interestingly, the interaction between procedural justice and personal norms was also found to be significant. The negative interaction suggests that procedural justice has a different effect upon compliance behavior depending upon one's personal norms. To probe the meaning of the interaction effect, simple slope effects of procedural justice over compliance at -1 and $+1$ standard deviation of personal norms were calculated (Aiken and West, 1991). The simple slope analyses indicate that procedural justice always had a significant influence upon compliance levels, but that it had a stronger effect in nurturing tax compliance behavior among those with weaker personal norms of tax honesty ($\beta = 0.35$, $p < 0.001$). Procedural justice significantly affected compliance levels in a positive way for those with strong personal norms ($\beta = 0.15$, $p < 0.01$), but

Table 10.3 Hierarchical regression model for the effect of procedural justice and personal norms on self-reported tax compliance behaviour

Predictor	Step		
	1	*2*	*3*
Personal norms	0.34***	0.35***	0.34***
Procedural justice (PJ)		0.25***	0.25***
PJ × Personal norms			−0.10**
R^2	0.12	0.18	0.19
R^2 change	0.12	0.06	0.01
F change	84.53***	46.72***	7.67**
Df	636	635	634

Note
Predictor entries are standardised regression coefficients (β). **$p < 0.01$; ***$p < 0.001$.

the influence was found to be weaker. These results reveal that personal norms do moderate the effect of procedural justice on compliance behavior, and the implications of these findings will be discussed in the next section. The interaction effect is depicted graphically in Figure 10.1.

Discussion

As discussed in the introduction to this chapter, taxation researchers have found that regulatory enforcement strategies that rely solely on deterrence principles can be used to deter people from breaking the law. However, a growing body of research has revealed that deterrence-based enforcement strategies used with offenders can sometimes generate future resistance to compliance and, under extreme conditions, can encourage game-playing and blatant disrespect for the law (see, for example, Ayres and Braithwaite, 1992; Blumenthal *et al.*, 1998; Brehm and Brehm, 1981; Fehr and Rokenbach, 2003; Frey, 1997; Kagan and Scholz, 1984; McBarnet, 2003; Murphy and Harris, 2007; Unnever *et al.*, 2004; Williams, 2001). Given these limitations, the aim of the present study was to examine whether a process-based model of enforcement – one that relies on treating offenders with procedural justice in the first instance – would be more effective in nurturing long-term voluntary compliance with the spirit of the law.

A number of empirical studies have now demonstrated that taxpayers' perceptions of procedural justice can affect their compliance behavior; those taxpayers who see a tax authority acting with procedural fairness are more willing to comply with their taxation obligations (e.g., Feld and Frey, 2002; Murphy, 2005a; Wenzel, 2002a, 2006). Such findings point to the value of adopting a process-based enforcement model. Up to now, however, none of this earlier

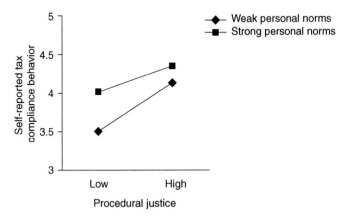

Figure 10.1 Interaction between procedural justice and personal norms on self-reported tax compliance behavior.

Note
The standardized simple slopes are depicted here for −1 and +1 standard deviations of each predictor variable.

research has attempted to understand the conditions under which procedural justice may be more or less effective in shaping tax compliance behavior. The present study attempted to rectify this oversight. Specifically, it examined whether taxpayers' personal norms could moderate the effect of procedural justice on self-reported compliance behavior.

The study yielded a couple of interesting and important findings. Using a sample of tax offenders, it was found that procedural justice was related to self-reported tax compliance behavior, thus supporting prior research. Those taxpayers who were more likely to feel that the ATO used procedural justice during their enforcement experience were more likely to report that they had complied with their taxation obligations two years later. As expected, it was also found that norms predicted compliance behavior. Not surprisingly, taxpayers with stronger norms about taxpaying honesty were more likely to report that they had complied with their tax obligations. Of specific interest to the present study was the significant interaction between perceptions of procedural justice and personal norms on compliance behavior. It was found that taxpayers with weaker norms about taxpaying honesty were in fact more sensitive to procedural justice effects. Their compliance behavior was affected more positively by procedurally fair treatment than was the compliance behavior of taxpayers who held strong personal norms about taxpayer honesty.

The interesting thing about this particular finding is that it parallels those obtained by Wenzel (2004a) in his examination of the effect that norms play in the relationship between deterrence and compliance. Wenzel found that taxpayers who had weak norms about taxpaying honesty were more strongly affected by the threat of deterrence; they were more likely to indicate they would comply with the law when there was the threat of severe sanctions. In contrast, Wenzel found only weak deterrent effects for those taxpayers who held strong norms about taxpaying honesty. He argued that this was most likely the case because people with strong norms about doing the right thing are likely to comply with the law regardless of what penalties or sanctions may be apparent; deterrence does not become a factor to these people because they would not consider breaking the law to begin with (see also Carroll, 1987; Grasmick and Green, 1980). None of the taxpayers surveyed by Wenzel, however, had been previously punished for tax non-compliance. It was therefore unclear from Wenzel's study whether offenders are affected by deterrence differently from non-offenders.

In the present study, all taxpayers surveyed had been caught and punished for engaging in tax non-compliance. Here, the question is not about how to deter non-compliance in the first place, but how an authority can best regulate offenders to ensure long-term voluntary compliance with the spirit of the law. Many authorities believe that people who do the wrong thing are bound to be bad people, and need to be treated like the villains that they are. In other words, when dealing with a "difficult customer" (i.e., someone with weak norms about doing the right thing), it is generally believed that a hard line and aggressive stance in the first instance will exert power, authority, and legitimacy, and will therefore be more effective in bringing people to compliance. As Braithwaite

(2003b: 35) notes, however, "from the perspective of the tax authority, part of dealing with an individual's non-compliance is to ensure that it will not happen again, and part is to show the community that compliance standards are high and will be maintained". Braithwaite argues that the challenge for tax administrators is to play a two-handed game: to deal with the wrongdoing today, while nurturing consent for tomorrow. What the findings of the present study show is that a process-based model of enforcement may in fact offer some promise in the long term with non-compliant taxpayers, and particularly for those who hold weaker norms about paying tax. While the present study has discussed the virtues of adopting a process-based model in enforcement situations, it should be noted that a process-based approach should also be adopted in tax authorities' everyday encounters with the public. As discussed at the beginning of this chapter, general perceptions of the ATO's use of procedural justice have been found to be effective in shaping the general public's tax compliance behavior (see Wenzel, 2002b). Feld and Frey (2002; see also Chapter 5 of this volume) and Kirchler (2007) also advocate such an approach with the general public.

Of course, the skeptic may question whether a process-based approach to dealing with offenders will be accepted by the general community. For example, Margaret Levi's (1988, 1997) research into taxation suggests that citizens are more likely to trust a government that ensures that others do their part. In particular, Levi (1998: 91) argues that "one's willingness to pay taxes quasi-voluntarily often rests on the existence of the state's capacity and demonstrated readiness to secure compliance of the otherwise non-compliant". Some may view a process-based model as going soft on tax offenders, and hence it will not demonstrate to the public that offenders' non-compliance is being dealt with effectively. The concern expressed by some is that this may alter the general public's behavior toward paying tax. I would argue, however, that a process-based model should not do this. The argument that I have presented in this chapter is not about letting an offender "get away" with an offense. Rather, I argue that punishment should be administered, but in a manner that can be judged by both offenders and the community to be procedurally fair; an enforcement approach which allows dialogue between the offender and the tax authority, and one which ensures the tax authority treats the offender with the dignity and respect that he or she deserves during the enforcement process. By administering punishment in this manner, it is hoped that future compliance will be borne out of an internal motivation to do the right thing, rather than purely due to the fear of being caught and punished.

Research to suggest that such an approach would in fact be accepted by the general public has been conducted by myself and colleagues from the Centre for Tax System Integrity, The Australian National University (see Wenzel *et al.*, 2004). In 2002, we surveyed 965 taxpayers from the general population in Australia. We presented numerous questions designed to assess how the public feels tax evasion can be best brought under control. It was found that 71 percent of taxpayers believed that tax offenders deserve respectful treatment from the Tax Office, and 74 percent believed that the Tax Office should consider the personal needs and well-being of the offender during the enforcement process. More importantly, taxpayers were found to favor a dialogic approach (discussions between the offender, tax office personnel, and tax agents; 71 percent) over a punitive approach (through enforcing strict rules and disciplining the guilty; 63 percent). In fact, 78 percent believed that a dialogic approach should be attempted first, with stricter enforcement of rules being applied if the problem cannot be resolved. Such findings therefore demonstrate that a process-based model of regulation would be accepted by the public.

The virtues of procedural justice: a social distancing framework

This study has found that procedural justice can be particularly effective in shaping compliance behavior among those taxpayers who hold weak norms about taxpaying. But why should this be the case? This section attempts to provide a possible theoretical explanation for this particular finding.

There could be a couple of possible explanations for why procedural justice may be more effective in nurturing compliance among tax offenders who hold weak norms about taxpaying. The first explanation for the results is simply a methodological one. As can be seen from Figure 10.1, compliance levels among those taxpayers who held stronger personal norms about doing the right thing were particularly high, even when they perceived procedural justice to be low. It is therefore possible that a ceiling effect could have masked the positive effects of procedurally fair treatment for this particular group of taxpayers. So rather than procedural justice truly being more effective in changing compliance for those with weak norms, it could be the case that a failure to find a stronger effect in the "strong personal norms" group was an artefact of a ceiling effect.

Let us assume, however, that the results are not due to a ceiling effect, but are in fact due to some real underlying process. Valerie Braithwaite's (2003b) theory of motivational posturing and social distancing offers a possible theoretical explanation for the results. Braithwaite (2003b) suggests that motivational postures capture the way people position themselves in relation to regulatory authority. She argues that individuals evaluate authorities in terms of what they stand for and how they perform, and that, as such evaluations are made, revised, and shared with others over time, these people develop a position in relation to the authority. A concept central to such positioning is social distance. Social distance, as was conceived by Bogardus (1928), refers to the degree to which individuals (or groups) have positive feelings for other individuals or groups and ascribe status to those groups. In the regulatory context, social distance relates to the liking one has for a regulator and the ascription of status one gives to that regulatory authority. When people or groups decide how much they want to align themselves and be associated with an authority, or how much they want to remain at a distance from that authority, they are indicating the social distance they wish to place between themselves and the regulator.

Braithwaite (2003b) goes on to suggest that the social distance a regulatee places between themselves and a regulator may be intuitive at first, but does not remain so for long. It is argued that individuals go on to articulate their beliefs, develop rationalizations for their feelings, and use values and ideologies to justify the way they position themselves in relation to the authority (Bersoff, 1999; Sykes and Matza, 1957; Thurman, St John and Riggs, 1984). These beliefs and attitudes are what Braithwaite calls "motivational postures".

Hence, in the context of taxation, for example, posturing captures the manner in which taxpayers see themselves as they relate to the tax system and the tax authority, and particularly the amount of social distance they wish to place between themselves and the tax authority. Braithwaite (2003b) has shown that taxpayers can adopt five different motivational postures toward a tax authority. These postures are commitment, capitulation, resistance, disengagement, and game-playing. Those who adopt a posture of commitment or capitulation place less social distance between themselves and the regulator, and have been shown to be more inclined to comply with the law. Those who adopt a resistant, disengaged, or game-playing posture, in contrast, place greater social distance between themselves and the regulator, and have been shown to be less compliant with the law.

Braithwaite further argues that how taxpayers are treated by a tax authority during an encounter can change their motivational postures in either a positive or a negative manner. Tyler (1990) argues that procedurally fair treatment conveys status and communicates to people that they are valued members of society. Harsh and insensitive treatment from an authority during an enforcement process is therefore likely to encourage further psychological distancing between the two sides, because taxpayers see themselves as undervalued citizens. Braithwaite argues that if regulators are prepared to first engage in dialogue and fair treatment with those they regulate, then this will serve to encourage a more committed posture by the regulatee. This follows that procedurally fair treatment will reduce the social distance between the two sides.

In utilizing this theoretical approach to explain the findings of the present study, therefore, procedural justice may be particularly effective at nurturing subsequent compliance behavior among those with weaker taxpaying norms (see Table 10.3 or Figure 10.1) because it can be assumed that this group has more opportunity for procedural justice to effect the social distance they place between themselves and the tax authority; there is more chance that they can move from a posture of disengagement or resistance to one of commitment. People with strong norms about doing the right thing, in contrast, may be more likely to comply with the law regardless of what treatment they receive. One could reasonably assume that such people are likely to be more committed to the tax system to begin with, so procedural justice may be less likely to change their stance toward the tax authority. In other words, there is little room to improve the social distance between the two sides. However, it should be noted that in the present study procedural justice did still have a positive effect on changing compliance for this group.

Empirical evidence to suggest that procedural justice can in fact reduce or change the social distance between a regulatee and regulator comes from an earlier study I conducted (see Murphy, 2005b). Using panel data obtained from the same group of taxpayers studied in the present study, I found that the motivational posture of resistance changed over time if the tax offender had perceived their treatment by the ATO over the previous two years to be procedurally fair. Taxpayers were asked to indicate how resistant they were toward the ATO in 2002. They were then asked again in 2004 about their level of resistance toward the ATO. Changes in resistance levels over time were found to be a function of procedural justice; those who felt they had received procedural justice during the intervening period became less resistant over time. In a recently published study (Murphy et al., 2008), I have also found that motivational postures are related to one's views about the law; in other words, people place greater social distance between themselves and authority when they question the law (i.e., have weak norms about compliance). These studies, taken together, add further support to the suggestion that social distancing theory may offer a useful framework in which to explain the results of the present study, although further empirical work in this area is needed.

Conclusion

As noted at the beginning of this chapter, the aim of regulatory enforcement is to gain future compliance from offenders. The findings of the present study have shown that a regulatory enforcement strategy that places persuasion and fair treatment of the taxpayer in the foreground shows much promise in doing just that. In fact, the findings also suggest that a process-based enforcement approach may be particularly effective for those who have weaker respect for the law than for those who have a strong commitment to do the right thing. A social distancing framework was presented to offer a possible theoretical explanation for these results.

Appendix

Contained here is a complete list of the measures used in the analysis of this study. Items denoted with (r) represent items that were reverse scored.

Procedural justice

- The ATO respects the individual's rights as a citizen
- The ATO is concerned about protecting the average citizen's rights
- The ATO gives equal consideration to the views of all Australians
- The ATO considers the concerns of average citizens when making decisions
- The ATO cares about the position of taxpayers
- The ATO gets the kind of information it needs to make informed decisions
- The ATO tries to be fair when making its decisions
- The ATO is generally honest in the way it deals with people

Personal norms about taxpaying honesty

1   Do you think you should honestly declare cash earnings on your tax return?
2   Do you think it is acceptable to overstate tax deductions on your tax return? (r)

3   Do you think working for cash-in-hand payments without paying tax is a trivial offense? (r)

Tax non-compliance

Below are some statements that describe how your experience may have affected your taxpaying behavior.

* I now look for ways to purposefully cheat the tax system (r)
* I now use the tax system in a negative way to recoup the financial losses I have incurred (r)
* I no longer declare all of my income (r)
* I am now more defiant towards the ATO (r)
* I now look for many ways to recoup my financial losses (r)
* I now try to avoid paying as much tax as possible (r)

Notes

1 The present research was supported by the Australian Research Council (Grants Numbers: DP0666337 and DP0987792). I would like to thank, Benno Torgler, James Alm, Jorge Martinez-Vazquez, and Luc Noiset for their helpful comments on an earlier draft of this chapter.
2 Through the introduction of the Taxpayer Compliance Model, the Australian Taxation Office (ATO) has recently recognized the value of such an approach for regulating taxpayers. While a discussion of this model and its application to tax administration is beyond the scope of this chapter, readers interested in the Australian Taxation Office's new approach to taxpayer enforcement are directed to Braithwaite (2003a, 2003b, 2007), Job *et al.* (2007), and Murphy (2004a).
3 A scree plot is a statistical technique that can tell the data analyst how many factors should be extracted from the data. A scree plot essentially plots the eigenvalues which are produced in the analysis.
4 A number of court cases were conducted and, in general, ruled in favor of the Australian Taxation Office's interpretation of the law (see, for example, Howland-Rose and Ors vs Federal Commissioner of Taxation (2002) FCA 246, (2002) 49 ATR 206, 2002 ATC 4200; Puzey vs Federal Commissioner of Taxation (2002) FCA 1171, 50 ATR 595; Vincent vs Federal Commissioner of Taxation (2002) FCA 656, 50 ATR 20).

Bibliography

Aiken, L. and West, S. (1991) *Multiple Regression: Testing and Interpreting Interactions*, Newbury Park, CA: Sage.

Allingham, M. and Sandmo, A. (1972) "Income tax evasion: A theoretical analysis", *Journal of Public Economics*, 1: 323–38.

Alm, J., Sanchez, I., and De Juan, A. (1995) "Economic and noneconomic factors in tax compliance", *Kyklos*, 48: 3–18.

Alm, J., McClelland, G. H., and Schulze, W. D. (1999) "Changing the social norm of tax compliance by voting", *Kyklos*, 52: 141–71.

Andreoni, J., Erard, B., and Feinstein, J. (1998) "Tax compliance", *Journal of Economic Literature*, 36: 818–60.

Ayres, I. and Braithwaite, J. (1992) *Responsive Regulation: Transcending the Deregulation Debate*, New York, NY: Oxford University Press.

Bersoff, D. M. (1999). "Why good people sometimes do bad things: Motivated reasoning and unethical behavior", *Personality and Social Psychology Bulletin*, 25: 28–39.

Black, J. (2001) "Managing discretion", unpublished manuscript, London School of Economics.

Blumenthal, M., Christian, C., and Slemrod, J. (1998) "The determinants of income tax compliance: Evidence from a controlled experiment in Minnesota", *National Bureau of Economic Research Working Paper No. 6575*, Massachusetts, USA.

Bogardus, E. (1928) *Immigration and Race Attitudes*, Boston, MA: DC Heath and Company.

Bosco, L. and Mittone, L. (1997) "Tax evasion and moral constraints: Some experimental evidence", *Kyklos*, 50: 297–324.

Braithwaite, J. (2002) *Restorative Justice and Responsive Regulation*, New York, NY: Oxford University Press.

Braithwaite, V. (2003a) "A new approach to tax compliance", in V. Braithwaite (ed.), *Taxing Democracy: Understanding Tax Avoidance and Evasion*, Aldershot, UK: Ashgate Publishing.

——. (2003b) "Dancing with tax authorities: Motivational postures and non-compliant actions", in V. Braithwaite (ed.), *Taxing Democracy: Understanding Tax Avoidance and Evasion*, Aldershot, UK: Ashgate Publishing.

——. (2007) "Responsive regulation and taxation: Introduction", *Law and Policy*, 29: 3–10.

Brehm, S. S. and Brehm, J. W. (1981) *Psychological Reactance: A Theory of Freedom and Control*, New York, NY: Academic Press.

Carroll, J. (1987) "Compliance with the law: A decision-making approach to taxpaying", *Law and Human Behavior*, 11: 319–35.

Dubin, J. and Wilde, L. (1988) "An empirical analysis of federal income tax auditing and compliance", *National Tax Journal*, 16: 61–74.

Dubin, J., Graetz, M., and Wilde, L. (1987) "Are we a nation of tax cheaters? New econometric evidence on tax compliance", *American Economic Review*, 77: 240–5.

Elffers, H., Weigel, R. H., and Hessing, D. J. (1987) "The consequences of different strategies for measuring tax evasion behavior", *Journal of Economic Psychology*, 8: 311–37.

Erard, B. and Feinstein, J. (1994) "The role of moral sentiments and audit perceptions in tax compliance", *Public Finance*, 49: 70–89.

Fehr, E. and Rockenbach, B. (2003) "Detrimental effects of sanctions on human altruism", *Nature*, 422: 137–40.

Feld, L. and Frey, B. (2002) "Trust breeds trust: How taxpayers are treated", Centre for Tax System Integrity Working Paper No. 32. Canberra: The Australian National University.

Fischer, C., Wartick, M., and Mark, M. (1992) "Detection probability and taxpayer compliance: A review of the literature", *Journal of Accounting Literature*, 11: 1–46.

Franzoni, L. (2000) "Tax evasion and tax compliance", in B. Bouckaert and G. DeGeest (eds.), *Encyclopedia of Law and Economics*, Vol. 4, Cheltenham, UK: Edward Elgar.

Frey, B. (1997) "A constitution for knaves crowds out civic virtue", *The Economic Journal*, 107: 1043–53.

Grasmick, H. and Bursik, R. Jr (1990) "Conscience, significant others, and rational choice: Extending the deterrence model", *Law and Society Review*, 24: 837–61.

Grasmick, H. and Green, D. (1980) "Legal punishment, social disapproval and internalisation as inhibitors of illegal behavior", *Journal of Criminal Law and Criminology*, 71: 35–335.

Greenberg, J. (1987) "Reactions to procedural injustice in payment distributions: Do the ends justify the means?", *Journal of Applied Psychology*, 72: 55–61.

Job, J., Stout, A., and Smith, R. (2007) "Culture change in three taxation administrations: From command-and-control to responsive regulation", *Law and Policy*, 29: 84–101.

Kagan, R. A. and Scholz, J. T. (1984) "The criminology of the corporation and regulatory enforcement strategies", in K. Hawkins and J. M. Thomas (eds.), *Enforcing Regulation*, Boston, MA: Kluwer-Nijhoff Publishing.

Kinsey, K. and Grasmick, H. (1993) "Did the tax reform act of 1986 improve compliance? Three studies of pre- and post-TRA compliance attitudes", *Law and Policy*, 15: 239–325.

Kirchler, E. (2007) *The Economic Psychology of Tax Behavior.* Cambridge, UK: Cambridge University Press.

Levi, M. (1988) *Of Rule and Revenue.* Berkeley, CA: University of California Press.

—— (1997) *Consent, Dissent and Patriotism.* New York, NY: Cambridge University Press.

—— (1998) "A state of trust", in V. Braithwaite and M. Levi (eds.), *Trust and Governance*, New York, NY: Russell Sage Foundation.

Lind, E. A. and Tyler, T. R. (1988) *The Social Psychology of Procedural Justice.* New York, NY: Plenum Press.

Magner, N., Sobery, J. S., and Welker, R. B. (1998) "Tax decision making in municipal governments: Citizens' reactions to outcomes and procedures", *Journal of Public Budgeting, Accounting and Financial Management*, 9: 552–70.

Maxfield, M. G. and Babbie, E. (2008) *Research Methods for Criminal Justice and Criminology*, 5th edn, Belmont, CA: Thomson Wadsworth.

McBarnet, D. (2003) "When compliance is not the solution but the problem: From changes in law to changes in attitude", in V. Braithwaite (ed.), *Taxing Democracy: Understanding Tax Avoidance and Evasion*, Aldershot, UK: Ashgate.

Murphy, K. (2003) "Procedural justice and tax compliance", *Australian Journal of Social Issues*, 38: 379–407.

—— (2004a) "Moving forward towards a more effective model of regulatory enforcement in the Australian Tax Office", *British Tax Review*, 6: 603–19.

—— (2004b) "The role of trust in nurturing compliance: A study of accused tax avoiders", *Law and Human Behavior*, 28: 187–210.

—— (2005a) "Regulating more effectively: The relationship between procedural justice, legitimacy, and tax non-compliance", *Journal of Law and Society*, 32: 562–89.

—— (2005b) "Turning resistance into compliance: Evidence from a longitudinal study of tax scheme investors", Centre for Tax System Integrity Working Paper No. 77. The Australian National University.

Murphy, K. and Harris, N. (2007) "Shaming, shame and recidivism", *British Journal of Criminology*, 47: 900–17.

Murphy, K., Tyler, T. R., and Curtis, A. (2009) "Nurturing regulatory compliance: Is procedural justice effective when people question the legitimacy of the law?", *Regulation and Governance*, 3: – 26.

Nagin, D. and Paternoster, R. (1991) "The preventive effects of the perceived risk of arrest: Testing an expanded conception of deterrence", *Criminology*, 29: 561–87.

Paternoster, R. and Iovanni, L. (1986) "The deterrent effect of perceived severity: A re-examination", *Social Forces*, 64: 751–77.

Reckers, P., Sanders, D., and Roark, S. (1994) "The influence of ethical attitudes on tax-payer compliance", *National Tax Journal*, 47: 825–36.

Schwartz, R. and Orleans, S. (1967) "On legal sanctions", *University of Chicago Law Review*, 34: 274–300.

Scott, W. and Grasmick, H. (1981) "Deterrence and income tax cheating: Testing inter-action hypotheses in utilitarian theories", *Journal of Applied Behavioral Science*, 17: 395–408.

Skogan, W. G. and Frydl, K. (2004) *Fairness and Effectiveness in Policing: The Evidence*, Committee to Review Research on Police Policy and Practices. Committee on Law and Justice, Division of Behavioral and Social Sciences and Education, National Research Council, The National Academies Press, Washington, DC.

Smith, K. and Stalans, L. (1994) "Negotiating strategies for tax disputes: preferences of taxpayers and auditors", *Law and Social Inquiry*, 19: 337–68.

Sykes, G. M. and Matza, D. (1957) "Techniques of neutralization: A theory of delin-quency", *American Sociological Review*, 22: 664–70.

Thornberry, T. P. and Krohn, M. D. (2000) "The self-report method for measuring delin-quency and crime", in D. Duffee (ed.), *Measurement and Analysis of Crime and Justice: Criminal Justice 2000*, Vol. 4, Washington DC: US Department of Justice.

Thurman, Q. C., St John, C., and Riggs, L. (1984) "Neutralization and tax evasion: How effective would a moral appeal be in improving compliance to tax laws", *Law and Policy*, 6: 309–27.

Tyler, T. R. (1990) *Why People Obey the Law*. New Haven, CT: Yale University Press.

—— (1997) "The psychology of legitimacy: A relational perspective on voluntary defer-ence to authorities", *Personality and Social Psychology Review*, 1: 323–45.

Tyler, T. R. and Blader, S. (2000) *Cooperation in Groups*. Philadelphia, PA: Psychology Press.

Tyler, T. R. and Degoey, P. (1996) "Trust in organisational authorities: The influence of motive attributions on willingness to accept decisions", in R. Kramer and T. R. Tyler (eds.), *Trust in Organisational Authorities*, Beverly Hills, CA: Sage.

Tyler, T. R. and Huo, Y. (2002) *Trust in the Law*, New York, NY: Russell Sage Found.

Unnever, J., Colvin, M., and Cullen, F. (2004) "Crime and coercion: A test of core theo-retical propositions", *Journal of Research in Crime and Delinquency*, 41: 219–43.

Varma, K. and Doob, A. (1998) "Deterring economic crimes: The case of tax evasion", *Canadian Journal of Criminology*, 40: 165–84.

Webley, P. and Halstead, S. (1986) "Tax evasion on the micro: Significant simulations or expedient experiments?", *Journal of Interdisciplinary Economics*, 1: 87–100.

Wenzel, M. (2002a) "Principles of procedural fairness in reminder letters: A field experi-ment", Centre for Tax System Integrity Working Paper No. 42. Canberra: The Austral-ian National University.

——. (2002b) "The impact of outcome orientation and justice concerns on tax com-pliance: The role of taxpayers' identity", *Journal of Applied Psychology*, 87: 629–45.

——. (2004a) "The social side of sanctions: Personal and social norms as moderators of deterrence", *Law and Human Behavior*, 28: 547–67.

——. (2004b) "An analysis of norm processes in tax compliance", *Journal of Economic Psychology*, 25: 213–28.

——. (2006) "A letter from the Tax Office: Compliance effects of informational and interpersonal justice", *Social Justice Research*, 19: 345–64.

Wenzel, M., Murphy, K., Ahmed, E., and Mearns, M. (2004) "Preliminary findings from 'The what's fair and what's unfair survey' about justice issues in the Australian tax context", Centre for Tax System Integrity Working Paper No. 59. Canberra: The Australian National University.

Williams, R. (2001) "Prosecuting non-lodgers: To persuade or punish?", Centre for Tax System Integrity Working Paper No. 12. Canberra: The Australian National University.

Witte, A. D. and Woodbury, D. F. (1985) "The effect of tax laws and tax administration on tax compliance: The case of the US individual income tax", *National Tax Journal*, 38: 1–15.

Part VI
Case studies

11 Tax non-compliance among the under-30s

Knowledge, obligation, or skepticism?

Valerie Braithwaite, Monika Reinhart, and Michael Smart[1]

Introduction

Relatively consistently across taxpaying jurisdictions, younger people are found to be less compliant than middle-aged and older people (Andreoni *et al.*, 1998; Jackson and Milliron, 1986; Mason and Calvin, 1978; Orviska and Hudson, 2002; Wearing and Headey, 1997). The finding has prompted some tax authorities, like the Australian Taxation Office, to tailor their advisory services to young taxpayers through a special purpose online site (Commissioner of Taxation, 2004), while others, like the Swedish Tax Agency, have launched extensive advertising campaigns to educate younger people about the benefits of paying taxes (Wittberg, 2006). Both interventions have research findings to support them. Younger taxpayers are known to be less knowledgeable about tax matters (McKerchar, 2002; Niemirowski and Wearing, 2006a), they have been shown to have a less well developed sense of moral obligation or law abidingness to pay tax (Orviska and Hudson, 2002; Wearing and Headey, 1997), and they are more likely to be skeptical about government authority (Inglehart, 1997; Putnam, 2000; Watts, 1999).

This chapter examines whether the lower compliance levels of younger taxpayers are associated with lack of knowledge, less moral obligation or greater skepticism regarding government authority. In the first set of analyses, those under 30 years of age are compared with those in middle-aged and older age groups in terms of (a) tax evasion; (b) knowledge and resources; (c) moral obligation and deterrence; and (d) skepticism as measured by motivational postures in relation to authority. Knowing that age groups differ on these qualities, however, does not mean that all these differences are implicated in non-compliance. Thus, a logistic regression analysis is used to find out which of these factors – knowledge and resources, moral obligation and deterrence, or motivational posturing to authority – explain the relationship between age and tax evasion. Before investigating these relationships using a national survey of Australian taxpayers – the *Community Hopes, Fears and Actions Survey* – a brief review is undertaken of previous work that underpins expectations of a systemic reason for why younger generations are less compliant.

Lack of knowledge of youth non-compliance

A number of theoretical models of voluntary compliance recognize the importance of capacity – that is, the importance of a person or group knowing what an authority expects, and being able to deliver on such expectations (Carver and Scheier, 1998; Kagan and Scholz, 1984; Mitchell, 1994). Yet such knowledge in the field of taxation is not so readily accessible, particularly to the uninitiated.

A body of research has been critical of the complexity of tax systems and the problems this poses for achieving high rates of compliance (Andreoni *et al.*, 1998; Brand, 1996; Tanzi and Shome, 1994). A significant portion of supposed tax evasion has been shown as unintentional, resulting from lack of knowledge, misunderstanding, and ambiguous interpretation of tax law (Hasseldine and Li, 1999; Long and Swingen, 1991). Fear of unintentional non-compliance is experienced by taxpayers: a high proportion use tax agents to lodge their returns, and their ideal tax agent overwhelmingly is one who is honest and will do their tax without fuss and risk (Hite and McGill, 1992; Sakurai and Braithwaite, 2003; Tan, 1999). It is likely that newcomers to the tax system, with lower levels of income, uncomplicated tax returns, and less obvious gain through use of a tax agent, will be at risk of non-compliance. McKerchar (2002) and Niemirowski and Wearing (2006a) have reported that the tax knowledge of younger people is significantly less than that of older taxpayers. If young people are unsure of what the tax authority expects of them and are not connected with a tax agent who can provide them with appropriate advice, they may be considerably disadvantaged in their capacity to comply with tax law, particularly in a self-assessment tax system. Thus:

> *Hypothesis 1 (a): The under-30s are less knowledgeable about tax office expectations, and also may be less likely to have access to expert advice on tax matters;* and

> *Hypothesis 1 (b): Less knowledge and access to knowledge among the under-30s explains higher non-compliance.*

Low moral obligation and youth non-compliance

"Know-how" is one factor in models of voluntary compliance; feeling that one "ought to" do the right thing is another (Kagan and Scholz, 1984). There is evidence that paying tax can initially be met with resistance: people need time to become socialized into taxpaying norms (Kirchler, 1999). The criminological literature provides further support for the thesis that younger people are more likely to question their moral obligation to pay tax than older people. They tend to be less likely to feel the constraints of law or convention, and are less risk averse (Gottfredson and Hirschi, 1990; Sampson and Laub, 1993). Wearing and Headey (1997) have argued that younger people risk being socially marginalized within the taxpaying community. The networks that young taxpayers belong to are unlikely to encourage them to identify with or internalize the standards of honest taxpayers.

Not only is moral obligation weaker in younger taxpayers; it is also one of the most stable predictors of tax evasion (see Andreoni *et al.* (1998) and Richardson and Sawyer (2001) for reviews). With Bruno Frey and Lars Feld (Feld and Frey 2007; Frey 1997; Frey and Feld 2001), Torgler has reinvigorated interest in how cultures instigate a process that leads to an internal motivation to pay tax – a state described by these researchers as "tax morale" (see, for example, Alm and Torgler, 2004; Torgler, 2001, 2003). Torgler (2003) has used the World Value Survey to show that younger people are more likely than older age groups to think it is justified to cheat on their tax if they have a chance.

Tax morale and tax obligation do not exist in a social vacuum. The legal sanctioning system is not irrelevant. Tax obligation is correlated positively with perceptions of the likelihood of being caught (Grasmick and Bursik, 1990; Scholz and Pinney, 1995). In other words, those who express high moral obligation to pay their tax believe that the chances of being caught if they do not pay are high. Thus:

Hypothesis 2 (a): The under-30s have less moral obligation to be honest and are less fearful of being caught for tax cheating; and

Hypothesis 2 (b): Low scores on moral obligation and fear of being caught among the under-30s explain higher non-compliance.

Skepticism and youth non-compliance

The above explanations attribute tax non-compliance among the young to transitional states of inexperience or poor socialization. The expectation is that younger taxpayers will "age-out" of non-compliance or defiance as they gain greater understanding of the processes and grow into acceptance of their taxpaying role. Their lower compliance is a function of their disadvantage as newcomers: they lack the "how to" knowledge and the "ought to" sentiment that would make them honest.

A different way of approaching the problem posits no "ageing-out" effect, but instead a changing taxpaying culture that disproportionately affects younger taxpayers. Less certainty, greater need for individual adaptability, greater awareness of individual rights, and the desire for individual freedom have all been hallmarks of responding to a globalized world. Younger generations have been notably more enthusiastic in embracing individualism and expressing skepticism about government agendas (Inglehart 1997; Putnam, 2000). The central proposition of social change theorists is that experiences in the formative years play a profoundly important role in how each successive generation negotiates the life-course. This means that younger taxpayers may resist becoming well-socialized into the customs established by older generations: Instead, they will be setting new standards that reflect adaptation to the world as they are experiencing it.

The importance of culture, particularly the quality of democratic governance, has emerged as an important theme in the taxpaying literature. Feld and Frey (2007) refer to a psychological contract between an individual and the state – people are more likely to cooperate with a tax authority if that tax authority is respectful of and responsive to the public and what citizens expect of government. Through acknowledging a relational element in taxpaying, Feld and Frey make room for some individuals having a more satisfying and mutually supportive relationship with their tax authority than others. Frey and Feld (2001) have presented a strong argument for why quality of democratic governance should be appreciated more widely as a factor shaping willingness to comply with tax laws – a position supported by Braithwaite (2010). As the perceived quality of governance changes, so does the taxpaying culture and tax compliance.

One way in which the changing relationship between government and its people can be understood is through motivational posturing theory (Braithwaite, 2003; Braithwaite *et al.*, 2007). This theory maintains that individuals see themselves as being in a relationship with their government that can be defined by liking and by deference. Liking refers to positive feelings. Deference refers to accepting authority – that is, assigning oneself to a position of subservience vis-à-vis government. Both liking and deference are regarded as indicators of the social distance that individuals choose to place between themselves and the authority (Bogardus, 1928).

Social distance increases when authorities are seen as a threat to an individual's identity – that is, authorities threaten an individual's freedom or capacity to generate wealth as desired. Threat is expressed in the guise of motivational postures that wax and wane as authorities behave in ways that are seen as acceptable and unacceptable. Five types of motivational postures have been identified to represent social distance from authority. The postures that reflect least social distance of the actor from the authority are commitment (believing in the cause that the regulator is protecting, the tax system in this instance) and capitulation (recognizing the power of the authority to enforce compliance and caving in to pressure). The postures that reflect most social distance are resistance (opposing the authority's demands), disengagement (cutting oneself off from the authority's demands), and game playing (challenging and outsmarting the authority) (see the Appendix to this chapter for measures of the postures). Commitment, capitulation, and resistance define a dimension that reflects liking for the authority. Disengagement and game playing reflect a dimension defined by refusal to defer to the authority (Braithwaite, 2003). Thus:

Hypothesis 3 (a): The under-30s will maintain greater social distance from authority; they will be more resistant, more disengaged and more prone to game playing, and less committed and less open to capitulation.

Hypothesis 3 (b): Greater social distance in the under-30s explains higher non-compliance.

Method

In 2000, a national survey, the *Community Hopes, Fears and Actions Survey (CHFAS)*, was conducted. The 2,040 respondents who completed the survey were among a sample of Australians whose names were drawn from the publicly available electoral rolls by means of a stratified random sampling frame. The purpose of the survey was to find out what Australians thought of their tax system. Self-completion questionnaires were posted to respondents with a reply-paid envelope. Completed and returned surveys represented 29 percent of the targeted sample. While this was lower than desirable, it is consistent with the response rates obtained by other survey researchers who have focused on the issue of taxation (Kirchler, 1999; Kirchler *et al.*, 2006; Pope *et al.*, 1993; Walls-chutzky, 1996; Webley *et al.*, 2002). In order to assess the bias associated with the participating sample, a number of comparative analyses have been conducted (Braithwaite and Reinhart, 2005; Mearns and Braithwaite, 2001). The findings support the conclusion that the *CHFAS* provides a broad cross-section of the population, and is suitable for uncovering and explaining relationships among variables in a general population sample.

The *CHFAS* contained questions that were designed to measure self-reported tax evasion, knowledge and resources, moral obligation and deterrence, and motivational posturing in relation to authority. For the most part they comprise multi-item scales. All have been used in previous publications and have been shown to have acceptable levels of reliability and validity (measures are described in detail in Braithwaite 2001, 2003). For ease of interpretation, the survey questions associated with each of the measures will be reviewed as the findings are presented below.

Also included in the *CHFAS* were demographic variables, including age in years, sex (0=female, 1=male), higjest educational attainment[2] (1=primary or less, 2=some secondary, 3=completed secondary, 4=trade, diploma, 5=tertiary). The age of respondents in the *CHFAS* in 2000 was used to form three groups for sub-sequent analyses: those under 30 years of age (the younger group), those between 30 and 55 (the middle-aged group), and those older than 55 (the older group). Respondents were included in the groups only if they had answered questions about their taxpaying behavior in the financial year prior to the survey (*n*=1,528). There were 201 respondents in the younger group, 934 in the middle-aged group, and 393 in the older group. These groups formed the base for testing the hypotheses.[3]

Are young taxpayers more likely to evade tax?

Respondents were asked to report on how much of their income they had declared in their last tax return, and how likely it was that they had claimed false deductions when they lodged the return. Respondent also were asked if they had worked in the cash economy in the last 12 months.

Undeclared income: This index comprised a general question, "As far as you know, did you report all the money you earned in your 1998–1999 income tax return?", and seven specific measures requiring respondents to run down a checklist and consider whether they had reported all or just some of the income derived from the following sources: (a) salary and wages; (b) honorariums, tips, allowances, bonuses, director's fees; (c) eligible termination payments; (d) Australian government allowances; (e) Australian government pensions; (f) interest; and (g) dividends.

Over-claiming deductions: This index was formed through aggregating responses to two questions: "How much did you exaggerate the amount of deductions or rebates", and "How confident are you that the claims were legitimate".

Cash economy income: This was measured through a single question: "Have you worked for cash-in-hand payments in the last 12 months? By cash-in-hand we mean cash money that tax is not paid on." Responses were scored 0 for "no" and 1 for "yes."

For present purposes, these measures were used together to form a single dichotomous measure of evasion versus non-evasion (see Ahmed and Braithwaite (2005) for details). If a respondent failed to comply on any of the 11 questions on tax evasion, they were coded as an evader. If they were compliant on every question, they were coded as a non-evader. The measure proved to be particularly suitable for younger people, who tend to have more limited opportunities for evasion (Ahmed and Braithwaite, 2005).

Of the under-30 year olds, 44 percent evaded tax in the *CHFAS*, compared with 30 percent of the middle-aged and 28 percent of the older age group (chi-square test of independence $(df=2) = 18.43, p<0.001$).

Are young taxpayers less able to comply?

The potential of young taxpayers to be compliant may be compromised if they are less knowledgeable about tax office expectations than other taxpayers. Compensating for such deficits may be the capacity to access those with knowledge. Two questions measured support from others when lodging a tax return. Young taxpayers may be less aware of or have less access to sources of sound tax advice.

Deficit in knowledge of what is expected: Respondents were asked the following questions: "When preparing for the lodgement of your income tax return, how well did you understand what the tax office expected of you? Was your understanding of what was required (a) extremely good, (b) good, (c) reasonable, (d) partial, or (e) poor?". The scores ranged from 1 for extremely good to 5 for poor.

The younger group was significantly less confident that they had a good understanding of what the tax office expected (M(SD)=2.89 (1.09), compared with M(SD)=2.74 (1.01) for middle-aged and M(SD)=2.56 (1.07) for older age groups $(F(d,f)=7.64, p<0.001)$. The difference, however, was only significant when the comparison was made with older respondents. Middle-aged respondents and younger respondents were not significantly different.

Support network: Respondents reported who they relied upon in preparing their 1998–1999 tax return: (a) family member or close friend; (b) tax agent or adviser; (c) business partner; (d) tax office; (e) industry association; and (f) work employee. Only two sources of help were important – family/friends and tax agents/tax advisers. All others were endorsed by less than 7 percent of respondents.

Younger respondents relied on family and friends more than other age groups to complete their tax returns (41 percent compared with 19 percent among the middle-aged and 16 percent among the over-55s; chi-square test of independence ($df=48.53, p<0.001$). They were significantly less likely than other groups to rely on tax agents or advisers (58 percent compared with 79 percent among the middle-aged and 79 percent among the over-55s; chi-square test of independence ($df=2)=42.24, p<0.001$).

Hypothesis 1(a) was partially supported. Younger taxpayers were unsure of what the tax office expected of them, as hypothesized. Yet, they had support. They were more likely than other age groups to rely on family and friends for help. They were less likely, however, to use tax agents, possibly because their tax affairs were relatively uncomplicated. The taxpaying situation young people find themselves in is one where informal networks are almost as important as formal networks for learning about taxation. This is not likely to be a problem, providing the informal advice is sound. With the middle-aged group expressing comparable uncertainty to the younger age group with regard to tax office expectations, doubts might be raised about the soundness of informal-sector advice. Younger people may be more in need than most of the feedback and advice that the formal network of tax agents and advisers can offer.

Are young taxpayers less deterred and obligated?

The extent to which younger people lagged behind in developing a moral obligation to pay tax was inferred from two measures: (a) their ethical taxpaying norm about being honest and law abiding; and (b) holding as an ideal a tax adviser who advocated an honest and no-fuss approach. The third measure was awareness of the external constraints that were in place should they stray – specifically, the deterrence measure of being caught. Perceived deterrence sets boundaries on actions that are not acceptable, so that even if ethical norms for taxpaying have not been internalized, there is awareness that such norms are considered desirable and that taxpaying standards are enforced. The higher risk-taking of younger people suggested that they could be oblivious to the consequences of tax evasion.

Ethical taxpaying norm: The scale that was used to measure a person's taxpaying norm was similar to that used by Wenzel (2004), and was formed by averaging rating scale responses (no!! (1) through yes!!(5)) to the following items: (a) Do YOU think you should honestly declare cash earnings on your tax return?; (b) Do YOU think it is acceptable to overstate tax deductions on your tax return? (reverse scored); (c) Do YOU think working for cash-in-hand payments without paying tax is a trivial offense? (reverse scored); (d) Do YOU think the government should actively discourage participation in the cash economy? Scores ranged from 1 to 5, with 5 representing a strong ethical taxpaying norm.

Ideal of an honest, no-fuss tax adviser: Respondents were asked about their ideal tax adviser (Sakurai and Braithwaite, 2003). If honest taxpaying norms are internalized, the ideal is likely to be "someone who will do your return for you honestly with the minimum of fuss" and "someone who does not take risks and only claims for things that are clearly legitimate". Responses to these two items were averaged. Scores ranged from 1 for low priority to 4 for top priority.

Perceptions of being caught: Respondents were asked to report on how likely it would be for them to be caught should they do the following: (a) fail to declare $5,000 in income; and (b) over-claim $5,000 in deductions. In each case, they were given a scale ranging from 0 to 100 percent. The deterrence index comprised the average of the chances of being caught in the two scenarios. Higher scores indicated greater recognition of the likelihood of being caught. For purposes of analysis, scores were collapsed into a 1 to 5 rating scale.

One-way analyses of variance were used to compare younger, middle-aged, and older groups in term of moral obligation and deterrence (see Table 11.1). Table 11.1 shows strong support for the hypothesis that younger age groups were lagging behind the middle-aged group in their moral obligation to pay tax, and the middle-aged group, in turn, were lagging behind the over-55s. The under-30s displayed a weaker taxpaying ethical norm than other age groups, and showed less interest in having an honest, no-fuss tax adviser. Perceptions of the likelihood of being caught were lowest among the under-30s, increasing for the middle-aged group, and increasing again for the over-55s. The data supported Hypothesis 2(a). Together these variables show lower tax morale among younger age groups. These findings are consistent with those appearing in the tax and criminological literatures (Torgler and Valev, 2006). Younger people are less committed to being law abiding, and are less fearful of consequences.

Table 11.1 A comparison of the under-30s, the middle-aged, and the over-55s on moral obligation and deterrence: means, standard deviations and F-statistics

Moral obligation and deterrence	Under-30s (n = 201)	Middle-aged ("M") (n = 934)	Over-55s ("O") (n = 393)	F-value
Ethical taxpaying norm	3.30 M,O (0.64)	3.52 O (0.73)	3.79 (0.64)	36.90***
Ideal is honest, no-fuss adviser	3.08 M,O (0.69)	3.27 O (0.62)	3.37 (0.59)	12.88***
Likelihood of being caught	3.00 M,O (1.01)	3.31 O (1.05)	3.64 (1.00)	27.09***

Notes
*$p < 0.05$; ** $p < 0.01$; ***$p < 0.001$.
"M" signifies that the under-30s are significantly different ($p < 0.05$) from the middle-aged, "O" that they are significantly different ($p < 0.05$) from the over-55s.

Are young taxpayers more socially distant?

The items used to measure the motivational postures of commitment, capitulation, resistance, disengagement, and game playing appear in the Appendix to this chapter. Each item was rated on a five-point rating scale. Scale scores were formed through averaging ratings for each scale; the higher the score, the stronger the posture.

The mean scores for the three age groups were compared using one-way analyses of variance (see Table 11.2). Only partial support could be found for Hypothesis 3(a). On the cooperative postures of commitment and capitulation, the under-30s had lower scores. The younger age group was significantly weaker on commitment than both the middle-aged and older groups. On capitulation, the under-30s were significantly weaker than the older group but no different from the middle-aged group.

In terms of the defiant postures, the differences that emerged showed that the under-30s were more likely to challenge the authority of the tax office. The younger group was no different from the other age groups on resistance, the posture communicating dislike, but not lack of deference. In contrast, on the postures of game playing and disengagement, the under-30s were relatively higher, suggesting a reluctance to defer to tax authority. The under-30s were significantly more attracted to game playing than the middle-aged group, but, surprisingly, not more so than the older group. The under-30s were significantly more disengaged than others, and the middle-aged group more so than the over-55s (see Table 11.2).

Table 11.2 A comparison of the under-30s, the middle-aged, and the over-55s on the motivational postures: means, standard deviations and *F*-statistics

Motivational postures	Under-30s (n = 201)	Middle-aged ("M") (n = 934)	Over-55s ("O") (n = 393)	F-value
Commitment	3.68 M,O	3.83 O	3.97	20.80***
	(0.55)	(0.56)	(0.46)	
Capitulation	3.27 O	3.34 O	3.52	10.85***
	(0.46)	(0.54)	(0.52)	
Resistance	3.16	3.20 O	3.13	2.94*
	(0.48)	(0.55)	(0.52)	
Game-playing	2.45 M	2.37 O	2.47	4.51***
	(0.59)	(0.62)	(0.63)	
Disengagement	2.44 M,O	2.29	2.26	9.03***
	(0.51)	(0.50)	(0.49)	

Notes
*$p<0.05$; **$p<0.01$; ***$p<0.001$.
"M" signifies that the under-30s are significantly different ($p<0.05$) from the middle-aged, "O" that they are significantly different ($p<0.05$) from the over-55s.

Logistic regression analysis predicting tax evasion

The question addressed is the following: Do differences in knowledge, moral obligation and deterrence, and motivational posturing translate into behavioral differences in tax evasion, and in particular, can these factors explain why younger people are more likely to evade tax? Hierarchical logistic regression analyses were used to examine whether the effect of age in the prediction of evasion (0 = no, 1 = yes) became non-significant when knowledge, moral obligation and deterrence, and motivational posturing were entered into the regression models. Three separate analyses tested for the effects of each set of explanatory variables. The two steps involved in the analyses were entering age as a dummy variable on the first step of the analysis along with the social demographic control variables of sex and education (Model 1), and on the second step adding the explanatory variables (Model 2). Tables 11.3–11.5 show the changes in B coefficients that occurred when the explanatory variables were added to the predictors of age and the social demographic controls. The expectation was that all three – knowledge and resources, moral obligation and deterrence, and motivational posturing – would be risk factors that predispose young people to evasion.

The first hierarchical logistic regression model tested the importance of knowledge of tax authority expectations and access to a support network (family and a tax adviser), after age and the social demographic control variables had been entered into the model. Table 11.3 shows age as significant in Model 1, with membership in the younger age group increasing the likelihood of evasion. Sex

Table 11.3 B Coefficients, R^2, and significant tests in an hierarchical logistic regression analysis predicting tax evasion from age, social demographic controls, knowledge and resources ($n = 1,232$)

Predictor variables	B coefficients	
	Step 1	*Step 2*
Age		
Under-30s (18–29)	1.00***	0.76***
Middle-aged (30–55)	0.32	0.23
Social demographic controls		
Sex (0 = female, 1 = male)	0.32*	0.40**
Education	−0.01	0.08
Knowledge and resources		
Deficit in knowledge		0.32***
Support – family, friends		0.63***
Support – tax adviser		0.08
Nagelkerke R^2	3%	8%
Chi-square	25.98***	67.73***

Note
*$p < 0.05$; ** $p < 0.01$; ***$p < .001$.

was also a significant predictor, with the likelihood of tax evasion being higher for men than women. In Model 2, age and sex remained significant, with knowledge and support from family and friends becoming complementary predictors of evasion. Uncertainty over tax office expectations and reliance on family and friends increased the likelihood of evasion. Reliance on a tax adviser neither increased nor decreased prospects for evasion. What is of note here is that knowledge did not satisfactorily explain the relationship between age and tax evasion. Membership in the younger age group remained significant. Thus, knowledge is important in its own right as a predictor of evasion, without fully explaining greater evasion among the under-30s. Hypothesis 1(b) is not supported. A further important finding is that reliance on family and friends did not improve tax compliance as hypothesized; instead it decreased.

Table 11.4 tests the importance of having an ethical taxpaying norm, holding as an ideal an honest, no-fuss tax adviser, and believing in being caught, once age was entered into the model. Table 11.4 shows that when the set of variables relating to tax obligation and deterrence was entered into the model, age became insignificant as a predictor. The likelihood of evasion was greater if individuals had a weaker ethical taxpaying norm, and were less enthused by the ideal of an honest, no-fuss tax adviser, and less convinced of being caught should they cheat on tax. These data are supportive of Hypothesis 2(b). It remains a plausible hypothesis that younger people are more likely to evade tax because they have a less developed sense of moral obligation and less conviction about being caught by authorities. Further work is required before any claims can be made about directions of causality.

Table 11.4 B coefficients, R^2, and significant tests in an hierarchical logistic regression analysis predicting tax evasion from age, social demographic controls, moral obligation and deterrence ($= 1,430$)

Predictor variables	B coefficients	
	Step 1	*Step 2*
Age		
Under-30s (18–29)	0.90***	0.28
Middle-aged (30–55)	0.26	−0.08
Social demographic controls		
Sex (0=female, 1=male)	0.28*	0.26*
Education	−0.02	0.04
Moral obligation and deterrence		
Ethical taxpaying norm		−0.86***
Ideal is honest, no-fuss adviser		−0.47***
Perception of being caught		−0.13*
Nagelkerke R^2	2%	16%
Chi-square	24.33***	170.43***

Note
*$p<0.05$; **$p<0.01$; ***$p<0.001$.

Table 11.5 introduces the social distance measures of motivational postures. Those who were stronger on game playing and disengaged postures – that is, were not deferential to tax authority – had a greater likelihood of engaging in tax evasion. Age remained a significant predictor of evasion after the postures were entered into the hierarchical logistic regression model. The younger age group remained more likely to evade tax. Hypothesis 3(b), therefore, is not supported.

Interestingly, in Table 11.5, sex was no longer a significant predictor of evasion when the postures were added to the equation. Deference to authority, while not important in explaining age differences, is possibly one factor that contributes to explaining the greater compliance commonly observed among women (Andreoni *et al.*, 1998; Richardson and Sawyer, 2001).

Integration of findings

The above analyses point to moral obligation and deterrence as the most plausible determinants of youth non-compliance. Skepticism about authority assessed through the motivational postures did not seem promising as an explanation of why younger people were more likely to evade tax. Similarly, knowledge did not appear to provide a satisfactory explanation. The absence of significant findings raised the question of whether the relationships among the explanatory variables were more complex than had been supposed. In particular, was the effect of one masked by the effect of the others?

Table 11.5 B coefficients, R^2, and significant tests in an hierarchical logistic regression analysis predicting tax evasion from age, social demographic controls and motivational postures ($n=1,502$)

Predictor variables	B coefficients	
	Step 1	Step 2
Age		
Under-30s (18–29)	0.84***	0.69***
Middle-aged (30–55)	0.22	0.18
Social demographic controls		
Sex (0=female, 1=male)	0.28*	0.19
Education	–0.04	0.01
Motivational Postures		
Commitment		–0.13
Capitulation		–0.01
Resistance		0.22
Disengagement		0.44***
Game playing		0.33***
Nagelkerke R^2	2%	7%
Chi-square	23.03***	74.46***

Note
*$p<0.05$; **$p<0.01$; ***$p<0.001$.

A path model was built using the structural equation modeling program, AMOS (Version 6.00) (Arbuckle, 1999). The motivational postures did not appear to play much of a role in accounting for why younger people evaded tax, and therefore were dropped from the model-building exercise. In order to simplify the process, only one of the two moral obligation variables were taken forward: ethical taxpaying norms. The path model was built around knowing what the tax authority expected, ethical taxpaying norms, perceived likelihood of being caught, and compliance.

The path model representing the relationships among these variables is depicted in Figure 11.1. Age was directly and positively linked to knowledge, moral obligation, and believing in the likelihood of getting caught. All three variables were then linked to tax evasion, but, in the case of knowledge and being caught, only weakly. Interestingly, however, knowledge had a strong association with moral obligation. According to the model in Figure 11.1, moral obligation, the most important predictor of tax evasion, can be strengthened by making it clearer to taxpayers what the tax authority expects. More extensive testing with longitudinal data would provide a more definitive test of the proposed direction of causality. The model in Figure 11.1 explained 11 percent of variance in evasion. Indicators of the fit between the data and the model were all satisfactory (chi-square ($df=2$)=0.487, $p<0.784$; GFI=1.00; AGFI=0.999; RMSEA=0.000).

Discussion

Previous research has consistently reported that younger taxpayers are less positively disposed to taxpaying than others. This chapter has examined three likely explanations and tested them empirically; separately in the first instance, and subsequently in conjunction with each other. The idea that young people lack knowledge is pitted against low moral obligation and little fear of being caught,

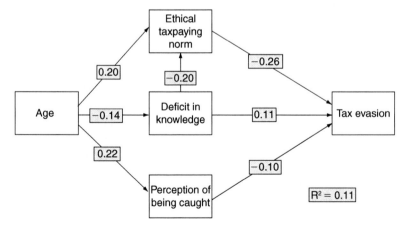

Figure 11.1 A path model representing the relationships among age, knowledge, moral obligation, perception of being caught, and tax evasion.

and both are pitted against skepticism about tax authority as measured through motivational postures.

The data are cross-sectional in nature, and therefore do not allow for the drawing of causal inferences about why young people are less compliant. The outcome is an assessment of different explanations in terms of their relative plausibility and worthiness of further investigation with longitudinal data. The most plausible explanations are likely to be those that not only differentiate young from middle and older age groups, but also relate to non-compliance, and do so in a way that renders the age relationship insignificant.[4]

Taxpayers under 30 years of age were more likely to self-report tax evasion than those who were middle-aged or older: 44 percent of the younger group (compared with 30 percent of the middle-aged group and 28 percent of the older group) admitted that they may have over-claimed deductions, or earned money in the shadow (sometimes called cash or black) economy, or not declared all their income. Having established a pattern of non-compliance among the under-30s, the expectation was that we would be able to identify a core set of variables, such as lack of knowledge, lower moral obligation and perceived deterrence, or motivational posturing, that would explain the pattern. Knowledge and postures (with the exception of resistance) were related to age, but not to tax evasion in such a way as to explain why younger taxpayers were less compliant. Lower levels of moral obligation and less fear of being caught, however, did explain, in a statistical sense, the higher levels of evasion among the under-30s. Tax obligation appears to be the most plausible explanation of tax non-compliance among younger taxpayers, and most worthy of further causal analysis.

While knowledge and posturing were not important variables in explaining the age–tax evasion relationship, a path analysis was able to demonstrate that knowledge at least indirectly contributed to the pathway linking age to moral obligation. Older individuals were clearer about what the tax authority expected of them, and clarity of understanding was associated with greater moral obligation. Intuitively, it makes sense that people need to know what an authority expects before they feel an ethical obligation to obey.

These findings are consistent with previous researchers who have argued that younger people age through non-compliance as they become socialized into the expectations of authority and the practices of their older peers. That said, it is noteworthy that the variance accounted for in tax evasion by age is very small. These data challenge the assertion that the under-30s represent a cohort that is distinctive in its outlook from other age groups (Mackay, 1997), at least as far as taxpaying is concerned. On a number of variables, the under-30s were not so different from the middle-aged group (deficit in knowledge, capitulation, resistance), and were on occasion just like the older group (game playing). Earlier work showed that younger people were distinctive neither in their beliefs about the fairness of the system, nor in their assessment of their competence, or in the priority they placed on tax (Braithwaite *et al.*, 2006).

Possibly the introduction of a new tax system managed to blur some of the distinctiveness associated with age in so far as everyone was a newcomer to the system. Perhaps at another time age would prove to be a more important predictor of evasion than it has been in this particular study. Even so, it is of note that others have observed that younger taxpayers are not so different from the middle-aged group, even if the difference from the older-aged group reaches statistical significance (Torgler, 2003). From available data, it seems that younger taxpayers do not undergo a dramatic change of identity post-30 to join the ranks of honest taxpayers. Borrowing from the criminological tradition (in particular, Matza, 1964), it may be more applicable to think of younger taxpayers as not being trapped in an enclave of tax evasion, but rather just drifting in and out of compliance with slightly greater frequency than older age groups. As their financial or personal situation becomes more "mainstream", they may be more inclined to access tax practitioners for advice and become less reliant on family and friends. Networks may place limits on how much drift is possible as taxpayers develop a tax "history" and "routine" that shapes the way in which they deal with tax in their later years. The data seem most consistent with the drift interpretation, and suggest that it is quite plausible that, with time, the under-30s will become like the over-55s, but not perhaps without facing a few tax demons in their middle years.

Others have reached similar conclusions favoring the "ageing-out" perspective. Wearing and Headey (1997) concluded that younger age groups were marginalized as taxpayers both in terms of their personal dispositions to paying tax and the networks that were likely to influence them. This chapter supports Wearing and Headey's findings. Torgler and Valev (2006), in their comparison of cohort and developmental trends for the related subject of corruption, favor the developmental interpretation. As individuals become older, they assess corruption as less justifiable.

In suggesting that we are getting closer to closure on the role of age in tax evasion, it is worthwhile to take a bigger picture and point out that a pro-tax sensibility is a more important focus for intervention by tax authorities worried about the sustainability of their system than is age. The results were compelling in demonstrating how age pales into insignificance as a threat to the tax system compared with the erosion across age groups of moral obligation, the desire for an honest tax adviser, and commitment to the tax system. This conclusion supports the claims of Frey and colleagues (see, for example, Feld and Frey, 2007; Frey, 1997; Frey and Feld, 2001). Their Swiss-based research reveals the importance of governments investing in the building and maintenance of tax morale, if democratic societies are to maintain sustainable, healthy taxpaying systems. In return for citizens' accepting the obligation to pay taxes, governments are required to show respect for democratic principles, and to be responsive to the needs and expectations of citizens. Scholz and Lubell (1998a, 1998b) have a similar understanding of tax compliance, with a body of empirical data to support their argument.

While this is the primary message for tax authorities, there are insights into where there are opportunities for hastening younger people's maturation as far as honest taxpaying is concerned. Unexpectedly, the support of family and friends was related to non-compliance. A recent and well-documented finding to emerge in the Australian taxation context is that taxpayers have poor knowledge and understanding of the tax system (McKerchar, 2002; Niemirowski and Wearing, 2006b). Add to this Niemirowski and Wearing's (2006a) finding that younger people perform less well on a tax knowledge task than older people, and the picture emerges of an age cohort with imperfect knowledge, some doubts about what the tax office wants, and reliance on family and friends who also have imperfect knowledge. The work of Wearing and Headey (1997) and Niemirowski and Wearing (2006b) points to the value of examining how tax knowledge is derived and shared through work, family, and other networks. Possibly, improving younger taxpayers' access to tax practitioners is a way of fast-tracking the development of commitment and obligation as far as taxpaying is concerned. This presupposes tax practitioners who are sympathetic to the cultivation of a pro-tax sensibility among younger people.

Conclusion

Taken together, the findings of this study provide some interesting insights into possibilities for the erosion of Australia's self-assessment tax system across time and across generations. There is evidence that older generations are better socialized into taxpaying. Perhaps younger generations will follow in their footsteps, but if this is so, it is of some practical significance to realize that the socialization process promises to be a lifelong experience for taxpayers: the middle-aged group have more in common with the under-30s than they do the over-55s. The middle-aged group does not show signs of being the ideal role models for moving younger generations quickly into "compliant and cooperative mode".

With this in mind, there are glimpses in the data of cultural movements that present a challenge to a sustainable voluntary taxpaying culture. Game playing among older age groups suggests a pocket of defiance among a group that have been traditional tax system supporters. The role that reliance on friends and family plays in undermining compliance also warrants some consideration, as does the general standard of tax ethics in the community. Loss of tax ethics, lack of knowledge about what is required, interest in game playing with the tax authority, reliance on family and friends, and low likelihood of being caught for evasion all play a role in weakening the normative fabric of the taxpaying culture.

Addressing these considerations in the community at large is as important, if not more so, than addressing youth non-compliance. Policies that rest on the argument that the non-compliance of youth is a passing fad appear to be gaining support. At the same time, there is good reason for policy makers to think more systemically and question the assumptions that underlie this position. For instance, is the taxpaying culture that younger people pass into rich in tax morale? Any hope of young people becoming good taxpayers through socialization must rely first and foremost on role models; role models who exemplify the high standards of a community that openly promotes taxpayer honesty and commitment to the tax system. In this fundamental way, the sustainability of the tax system rests less on the tax morale of the young and more upon the tax morale of the society as a whole.

Appendix: motivational posture scales

Commitment (alpha reliability coefficient=0.82; homogeneity ratio=0.43)

Paying tax is the right thing to do.
Paying tax is a responsibility that should be willingly accepted by all Australians.
I feel a moral obligation to pay my tax.
Paying my tax ultimately advantages everyone.
I think of taxpaying as helping the government do worthwhile things.
Overall, I pay my tax with good will.
I resent paying tax. (reversed)
I accept responsibility for paying my fair share of tax.

Capitulation (alpha reliability coefficient=0.63; homogeneity ratio=0.27)

If you cooperate with the Tax Office, they are likely to be cooperative with you.
Even if the Tax Office finds that I am doing something wrong, they will respect me in the long run as long as I admit my mistakes.
The Tax Office is encouraging to those who have difficulty meeting their obligations through no fault of their own.
The tax system may not be perfect, but it works well enough for most of us.
No matter how cooperative or uncooperative the Tax Office is, the best policy is to always be cooperative with them.

Resistance (alpha reliability coefficient=0.68; homogeneity ratio=0.31)

As a society, we need more people willing to take a stand against the Tax Office.
It's important not to let the Tax Office push you around.
The Tax Office is more interested in catching you for doing the wrong thing, than helping you do the right thing.
It's impossible to satisfy the Tax Office completely.
Once the Tax Office has you branded as a non-compliant taxpayer, they will never change their mind.
If you don't cooperate with the Tax Office, they will get tough with you.

Disengagement (alpha reliability coefficient=0.64; homogeneity ratio=0.27)

If I find out that I am not doing what the Tax Office wants, I'm not going to lose any sleep over it.
I personally don't think that there is much the Tax Office can do to me to make me pay tax if I don't want to.

I don't care if I am not doing the right thing by the Tax Office.
If the Tax Office gets tough with me, I will become uncooperative with them.
I don't really know what the Tax Office expects of me and I'm not about to ask.

Game playing (alpha reliability coefficient=0.69; homogeneity ratio=0.32)

I enjoy talking to friends about loopholes in the tax system.
I like the game of finding the gray area of tax law.
I enjoy the challenge of minimizing the tax I have to pay.
I enjoy spending time working out how changes in the tax system will affect me.
The Tax Office respects taxpayers who can give them a run for their money.

Notes

1 This research was undertaken while the authors were part of the Centre for Tax System Integrity at the Australian National University, and was subsequently supported by the Regulatory Institutions Network (RegNet), Australian National University. The Centre for the Tax System Integrity received funding from the Australian Taxation Office. The views expressed in this chapter do not represent those of the Office or its Commissioner.
2 Education was treated as a quasi-interval variable in the logistic regression analysis.
3 A parallel set of analyses were carried out for the full sample to address part (a) of the three hypotheses. The findings were substantively the same for the full sample and the sample who reported on taxpaying behavior.
4 It is conceivable that an age-related explanatory factor, such as cynicism, does not trigger non-compliance concurrently, but rather makes its presence felt a number of years later as such individuals learn the ropes and understand how they might manipulate the system. We could catch a glimpse of such an effect with cross-sectional data through testing interaction terms. With the data set used in this study, interaction terms involving age and the explanatory variables were not significant.

Bibliography

Ahmed, E. and Braithwaite, V. (2005) "A need for emotionally intelligent policy: Linking tax evasion with higher education funding", *Legal and Criminological Psychology*, 10: 1–19.

Alm, J. and Torgler, B. (2004) "Culture differences and tax morale in the United States and in Europe", CREMA Working Paper No. 2004-14, Basel.

Andreoni, J., Erard, B., and Feinstein, J. (1998) "Tax compliance", *Journal of Economic Literature*, 36: 818–60.

Arbuckle, J. (1999) *AMOS 6.0 User's Guide*, Chicago, IL: SPSS.

Bogardus, E. S. (1928) *Immigration and Race Attitudes*, Boston, MA: D. C. Heath and Co.

Braithwaite, V. (2001) "The *Community Hopes, Fears and Actions Survey*: Goals and measures", Centre for Tax System Integrity Working Paper No. 2, The Australian National University.

Braithwaite, V. (2003) "Dancing with tax authorities: Motivational postures and non-compliant actions", in V. Braithwaite (ed.), *Taxing Democracy: Understanding Tax Avoidance and Evasion*, Aldershot, UK: Ashgate.

Braithwaite, V. (2010) *Defiance in Taxation and Governance: Resistance and Dismissiveness to Authority in a Democracy*, Cheltenham, UK: Edward Elgar (in press).

Braithwaite, V. and Reinhart, M. (2005) "Preliminary findings and codebook for the *Australian Tax System-Fair or Not Survey (ATSFONS)*", Centre for Tax System Integrity Working Paper No. 79, The Australian National University.

Braithwaite, V., Murphy, K., and Reinhart, M. (2007) "Threat, motivational postures and responsive regulation", *Law and Policy*, 29(1): 137–58.

Braithwaite, V., Smart, M., and Reinhart, M. (2006) "Why young people are less compliant on tax: enduring or transient defiance?" Regulatory Institutions Network (RegNet) Occasional Paper No. 11, The Australian National University.

Brand, P. (1996) "Compliance: A 21st century approach", *National Tax Journal*, 49: 413–19.

Carver, C. S. and Scheier, M. F. (1998) *On the Self-regulation of Behaviour*, Cambridge, UK: Cambridge University Press.

Commissioner of Taxation (2004) *Commissioner of Taxation Annual Report 2003–2004*, Canberra, ACT: Australian Government.

Feld, L. P. and Frey, B. S. (2007) "Tax compliance as the result of a psychological tax contract: The role of incentives and responsive regulation", *Law and Policy*, 29(1): 102–20.

Frey, B. S. (1997) *Not Just for the Money: An Economic Theory of Personal Motivation*, Cheltenham, UK: Edward Elgar.

Frey, B. S. and Feld, L. P. (2001) "The tax authority and the taxpayer: An exploratory analysis", paper presented at the Second International Conference on Taxation, Centre for Tax System Integrity, The Australian National University, Canberra, 10–11 December, 2001.

Gottfredson, M. and Hirschi, T. (1990) *A General Theory of Crime*, Stanford, CA: Stanford University Press.

Grasmick, H. G. and Bursik, R. J. (1990) "Conscience, significant others, and rational choice: Extending the deterrence model", *Law and Society Review*, 24: 837–61.

Hasseldine, J. and Zhuhong L. (1999) "More tax evasion research required in new millennium", *Crime, Law and Social Change*, 31: 91–104.

Hite, P. A. and McGill, G. (1992) "An examination of taxpayer preference for aggressive tax advice", *National Tax Journal*, 45: 389–403.

Inglehart, R. (1997) *Modernization and Postmodernization: Cultural, Economic, and Political Change in 43 Societies*, Princeton, NJ: Princeton University Press.

Jackson, B. R. and Milliron, V. C. (1986) "Tax compliance research: Findings, problems and prospects", *Journal of Accounting Literature*, 5: 125–65.

Kagan, R. A. and Scholz, J. T. (1984) "The criminology of the corporation and regulatory enforcement strategies", in K. Hawkins and J. M. Thomas (eds.), *Enforcing Regulation*, The Hague, The Netherlands: Kluwer-Nijhoff Publishing.

Kirchler, E. (1999) "Reactance to taxation: Employers' attitudes toward taxes", *Journal of Socio-Economics* 28: 131–8.

Kirchler, E., Niemirowski, P., and Wearing, A. (2006) "Shared subjective views, intent to cooperate and tax compliance: Similarities between Australian taxpayers and tax officers", *Journal of Economic Psychology*, 27: 502–17.

Long, S. and Swingen, J. (1991) "The conduct of tax-evasion experiments: Validation, analytic methods, and experimental realism", in P.Webley, H. Robben, H. Elffers, and D. Hessing (eds.), *Tax Evasion: An Experimental Approach*, Cambridge, UK: Cambridge University Press.

Mackay, H. (1997) *Generations – Baby Boomers, their Parents and their Children*, Sydney, NSW: Pan Macmillan.

Mason, R. and Calvin, L. D. (1978) "A study of admitted income tax evasion", *Law and Society*, 13: 73–89.

Matza, D. (1964) *Becoming Deviant*, Englewood Cliffs, NJ: Prentice-Hall.

McKerchar, M. (2002) "The effects of complexity on unintentional non-compliance for personal taxpayers in Australia", *Australian Tax Forum*, 17(1): 131–8.

Mearns, M. and Braithwaite, V. (2001) *"The Community Hopes, Fears and Actions Survey*: Survey method, sample representativeness and data quality", Centre for Tax System Integrity Working Paper No. 4, Australian National University, Canberra.

Mitchell, R. B. (1994) *Intentional Oil Pollution at Sea: Environmental Policy and Treaty Compliance*, Cambridge, MA: MIT Press.

Niemirowski, P. and Wearing, A. "Tax competence and younger Australian taxpayers' ability to meet tax compliance obligations", paper presented at the IAREP/SABE Congress, Pantheon-Sorbonne University, Paris, 5–7 July, 2006a.

Niemirowski, P. and Wearing, A. (2006b). "Do ATO staff and compliant taxpayers identify with tax from the same perspective or are there significant degrees of separation?" *Journal of Australian Taxation*, 9(2): 119–71.

Orviska, M. and Hudson, J. (2002) "Tax evasion, civic duty and the law abiding citizen", *European Journal of Political Economy*, 19: 83–102.

Pope, J., Fayle, R., and Chen, D. (1993) *The Compliance Costs of Employment-Related Taxation*, Sydney, NSW: Australian Tax Research Foundation.

Putnam, R. (2000) *Bowling Alone: The Collapse and Revival of American Community*, New York, NY: Simon and Schuster.

Richardson, M. and Sawyer, A. J. (2001) "A taxonomy of the tax compliance literature: Further findings, problems and prospects", *Australian Taxation Forum*, 16: 137–320.

Sakurai, Y. and Braithwaite, V. (2003) "Taxpayers' perceptions of practitioners: Finding one who is effective and does the right thing?" *Journal of Business Ethics*, 46: 375–87.

Sampson, R. J. and Laub, J. H. (1993) *Crime in the Making: Pathways and Turning Points through Life*, Cambridge, MA: Harvard University Press.

Scholz, J. T. and Lubell, M. (1998a) "Adaptive political attitudes: Duty, trust and fear as monitors of tax policy", *American Journal of Political Science*, 42: 903–20.

Scholz, J. T. and Lubell, M. (1998b) "Trust and taxpaying: Testing the heuristic approach to collective action", *American Journal of Political Science*, 42: 398–417.

Scholz, J. T. and Pinney, N. (1995) "Duty, fear and tax compliance: The heuristic basis of citizenship behavior", *American Journal of Political Science*, 39: 490–512.

Tan, L. M. (1999) "Taxpayers' preference for type of advice from tax practitioner: a preliminary examination", *Journal of Economic Psychology*, 20: 431–47.

Tanzi, V. and Shome, P. (1994) "A primer on tax evasion", *International Bureau of Fiscal Documentation* June/July: 328–37.

Torgler, B. (2001) "What do we know about tax morale and tax compliance?" *International Review of Economics and Business (RISEC)*, 48(3): 395–419.

Torgler, B. (2003) "Tax morale and institutions", CREMA Working Paper No. 2003-09, Basel.

Torgler, B. and Valev, N. T. (2006) "Corruption and age", *Journal of Bioeconomics*, 8: 133–45.

Wallschutzky, L. (1996) "Issues in research methods: with reference to income tax research", unpublished manuscript, University of Newcastle, Australia.

Watts, M. W. (1999) "Are there typical age curves in political behavior? The "age invariance" hypothesis and political socialization", *Political Psychology*, 20(3): 477–99.

Wearing, A. and Headey, B. (1997) "The would-be tax evader: A profile", *Australian Tax Forum*, 13: 3–17.

Webley, P., Adams, C., and Elffers, H. (2002) "VAT compliance in the United Kingdom", Centre for Tax System Integrity Working Paper 41, The Australian National University, Canberra.

Wenzel, M. (2004) "The social side of sanctions: Personal and social norms as moderators of deterrence", *Law and Human Behavior*, 28: 547–67.

Wittberg, L. "Communication", paper presented at "Managing and Maintaining Compliance: Closing the Gap between Science and Practice," a conference hosted by the Dutch Tax and Customs Administration and the Netherlands Institute for the Study of Crime and Law Enforcement, Leiden University, Netherlands, 9–11 April, 2006.

12 The economic psychology of value added tax compliance

Paul Webley and Julie Ashby

VAT: the background

Economic psychologists have shown a sustained interest in the psychology of taxation for 25 years. The progress made in the field is evident if one compares Lewis's (1982) *The Psychology of Taxation* to Kirchler's (2007) *The Economic Psychology of Tax Behaviour*. Whilst Lewis (1982) had to work hard to find enough material to describe and analyze, Kirchler (2007) had the opposite problem of having a vast amount of material to deal with. Much of this work has been on tax compliance, and there has been a wide range of empirical research, from qualitative studies, through surveys to experiments, and the development of a large number of psychological theories and approaches to evasion and compliance (see, for example, Braithwaite, 2003; Elffers, 1991). However, the focus of this research has been personal income tax: business tax compliance in general and value added taxation (VAT) compliance in particular have been seriously neglected (see Webley, 2004). This focus does not derive from the financial significance of personal income tax evasion compared to business tax evasion. Instead, it seems more likely to be a consequence of the fact that psychology is well equipped, both methodologically and theoretically, to deal with the individual, and less able to cope with the explanation of behavior in institutions. That said, it is notable that work in economics on tax compliance (see Andreoni *et al.*, 1998) has a similar bias towards investigating personal income tax, and again has many models that explain the behavior of individuals, rather than institutions.

We will argue in this chapter that in order to understand VAT compliance, one needs to move away from these individualistic approaches. In particular, occupational group membership and identity appear to be very relevant to tax-paying situations. We conducted a series of studies in both the UK and Australia using a mix of quantitative (surveys) and qualitative (interviews and focus groups) methods and techniques to determine and to demonstrate the relevance of a social identity approach to tax evasion generally and to VAT evasion specifically.

Details matter: in the UK, a customer not paying VAT on a bill presented by a decorator is not breaking the law (the decorator is), whereas in Italy the customer is deemed to be colluding with the decorator and so is also committing an offense. This particular detail significantly changes the nature of the act. As details matter, we will begin with a description of VAT and then move on to discuss what is involved in complying with this tax, before outlining some studies into VAT compliance and then considering how best to interpret the findings of these studies. Finally, we will present the findings from a series studies exploring the role of occupational taxpaying cultures in taxpaying behavior and attitudes, and consider the way in which they speak to issues in VAT research.

What is VAT?

VAT is a tax on consumer expenditure, collected on business transactions and assessed on the value added to goods and services. It applies, with some exceptions (for example, to young children's clothes and shoes in the UK), to all goods and services that are bought and sold. VAT is a general tax (as it applies, in principle, to all commercial activities) and a consumption tax (as it is paid ultimately by the final consumer). It is not actually a tax on business, though some business owners do see it that way. In fact, whilst VAT is paid to the tax authorities by the seller of the goods or services, the tax is paid by the buyer to the seller as part of the tax and so, in essence, businesses are acting as unpaid tax collectors.

VAT was first introduced in France in 1954, and subsequently has been extended, through a series of directives, to cover the whole of the European Union (EU). The system in the EU is now reasonably standardized, although different rates of VAT apply in different EU member states. The minimum standard rate in the EU is 15 percent, though lower rates are applied to certain services. Some goods and services are exempt from VAT throughout the EU (e.g., postal services, insurance, betting).

In addition to spreading throughout Europe (member states are required to introduce VAT, so the increase in membership of the EU has inevitably increased the number of countries that use this system), VAT has also been introduced in a large number of other countries, notably China (Yeh, 1997), and India (after many delays) in 2005, so that now over 130 countries world-wide operate VAT. In the Caribbean, for example, Belize, Dominica, Guyana, and Antigua have all introduced VAT in the past two years. Other countries have introduced taxes that are classified as value added taxes, such as Australia, which now operates a General Sales Tax (GST). The introduction of VAT has been the major tax reform around the world in the past 25 years, and VAT is now of global significance and impact (Ebrill *et al.*, 2001).

How VAT works

VAT is charged on most transactions, whether these are sales to consumers or to other businesses. However, a business can credit the VAT it is charged on the items and materials it buys ("input VAT") against the VAT it must charge on its sales ("output VAT"). An example should make the operation of VAT clear.

A builder who has carried out some construction work may charge the homeowner $10,000. On top of that (assuming a standard VAT rate of 20 percent), the homeowner would pay $2,000 VAT. So the total bill to the homeowner is $12,000, of which the tax authorities will receive $2,000. Let's assume that the builder had to buy $5,000 worth of bricks from Yellow Brick Road Supplies and $1,000 worth of fittings from a company called Nice-space. These will cost him $6,000 and $1,200 respectively. Yellow Brick Road Supplies will issue the builder a VAT invoice of $1,000, and Nice-space a VAT invoice of $200. These invoices provide the evidence that is needed to claim an input tax credit. So when the builder submits his VAT return to the tax authorities, he will list the VAT he has charged (in this case $2,000) and the VAT he is reclaiming (in this case $1,200), and the difference between the two is the amount ($800) he has to pay in tax (which is based on the value he has "added" to the raw materials).

Ultimately it is the homeowner who is paying all the VAT, but the money has been collected at different stages, and three companies (the builder, Yellow Brick Road Supplies, and Nice-space) have acted as tax collectors.

Not all transactions are charged at the standard rate. In the UK at the moment, for example, the standard rate which applies to most goods and services is 17.5 percent. In addition there is a reduced rate of 5 percent, which applies to, among other things, domestic fuel and power, and children's car seats, and a zero rate, which applies to food (but not meals in restaurants), books, and children's clothing. Some goods and services are exempt from VAT, such as insurance and education. Exemption and zero-rating are not the same. If a company sells zero-rated goods, since they are taxable, it can recover the VAT it has paid to its suppliers; however, an institution (such as a university) that is exempt cannot register for VAT or reclaim the VAT it has paid.

It is quite possible for a VAT-registered company to be claiming back VAT from the tax authorities. This is quite common in the first year of a company's business, because set-up costs may well exceed earnings. If a company continues to claim back VAT over a sustained period it is liable to get a tax inspection, as this situation suggests either that the company is not sustainable, or that there is some fraudulent activity.

The extent of VAT evasion

It used to be thought that VAT was less vulnerable to evasion than other forms of taxation, but there has been a growing concern this century about the size of this problem, especially in the EU. The European Commission (2004), for example, reported that revenue losses were as much as 10 percent of VAT receipts in some EU countries, though it is not at all clear what the basis for these figures is. There has only been a limited number of published studies, but from these it is evident that VAT evasion is widespread, though the extent varies greatly across countries. Agha and Haughton's (1996) review, based on studies from five countries in Europe and two in Asia, suggests that revenue losses vary from a low of 3 percent (France, United Kingdom) to a high of 40 percent (Italy). Bergman and Nevarez's (2006) figures from Latin America are within this range, with revenue losses being about 22 percent in Chile and roughly double this in Argentina. There are two points worth making about these figures. First, even the low figure represents a very large sum of money (equivalent to $3 billion dollars for France). Second, relatively low revenue losses in percentage terms hide the fact that a high proportion of businesses are probably involved in some non-compliance. So a study of Dutch businesses found that 34 percent of firms had evaded VAT (Cnossen, 1981), and Duverne (1990) reports that 66 percent of French VAT taxpayers audited had understated the value of taxable sales, and 40 percent had overstated the value of taxable inputs.

The most thorough analysis of the extent of VAT non-compliance is provided by Keen and Smith (2006). They summarize the official estimates provided in the UK by HM Revenue and Customs (HMRC), and the work on estimated VAT evasion rates in ten EU countries by Gebauer and Parsche (2003). HMRC has approached the problem of assessing the extent of VAT non-compliance in two ways. First, they have used a "top-down" approach, where national statistics on consumer spending are used, with appropriate adjustments, to estimate the amount of VAT revenue expected. This can then be compared with the actual revenue obtained to get a measure of the gap between expected and actual revenue. Second, they have used a "bottom-up" approach, where operational data are used to "guesstimate" the amount of VAT evasion in various categories. These guesstimates are based on a variety of sources, including audits, and the regular visits made to businesses by HMRC officers.

HMRC has been using the "top-down" approach since 1992, and over these 15 years the gap between expected and actual revenue has increased from just under 10 percent of expected revenue to about 15 percent – which equates to approximately 11 billion pounds. The "bottom-up" approach gives a broadly similar kind of figures, with the estimate of the tax gap being between 10 and 14.5 percent of expected tax revenue. This approach also allows estimates to be made on the sources of this loss. A large proportion (2.5–3.9 percent of expected revenue) comes from missing-trader or so-called "carousel" fraud, which exploits the fact that exports are zero-rated for VAT. Non-registration for VAT accounts for losses of 0.6–0.7 percent of expected revenue.

Gebauer and Parsche's (2003) work, also using a top-down approach, gives rather different figures for the size of the tax gap in the UK (a three-year average of 3.8 percent for 1991–1993), which presumably reflects different judgments about the nature and size of the adjustments that are necessary. This gives an indication of how difficult it is to make such estimates, and how large the margin of error must be. Gebauer and Parsche's (2003) work also shows, like that of Agha and Haughton (1996), striking differences between countries. Italy is estimated to have the highest tax gap of the ten countries analyzed, at 34.5 percent – Greece's is lower, but still very substantial, at 20.2 percent, and France's is estimated at 8.8 percent.

How to evade VAT

It is important to understand how businesses can evade VAT. A thorough account is provided by Keen and Smith (2006); here, we will discuss only the more common and simple methods. Perhaps the most obvious is not to register. Small businesses that operate below the threshold (currently £67,000 in the UK; HM Revenue and Customs, 2008) do not pay VAT – this saves them tax and also the compliance costs. If turnover increases over the threshold there is a clear incentive not to register, and to maintain the competitive advantage that not being registered gives them over registered businesses. So-called "ghosts", small traders who are unknown to the tax authorities, may also be able to evade income taxes. A very common form of non-compliance is to under-report sales, particularly for those businesses providing personal services (decorators, hair-dressers, builders working for private customers), as in this case the value added at the point of sale is very large. The customer may realize that the sale is being made without VAT and may share some of the gains from the fraud, as when a decorator offers a different quotation for a job depending on whether it is settled through a cash payment ("cash-in-hand") or through an invoice and check or other traceable payment method. Another common method, when traders have goods that are liable to different rates, is to exaggerate the proportion of sales of goods in the lower tax rates. For example, cafés that sell food and drink to be consumed both on and off the premises might report more food being sold as takeaways (cold take-away food and drink is zero-rated in the UK).

These forms of evasion are equally possible with a sales tax, but there are some forms of fraud that are distinctive to VAT. The most important of these is probably the submissions of false claims for refunds. Bird (1993) puts this succinctly: "a VAT invoice [is] a check written on the government". These can be either completely bogus (forged invoices), or exaggerated purchases. According to Bergman and Nevarez (2006), the use of fake invoices is the most popular way of evading VAT in Argentina, and a whole industry exists to provide these in areas such as "research and development endeavors" and "representation expenses". Since exports are zero-rated, fraudulent claims to have exported goods are a particular difficulty for VAT systems, and have led to much concern about carousel fraud in the EU. Carousel fraud involves transactions between companies in member states, where the goods go from one country to another and back (the "carousel") and VAT goes missing.

Current approaches to VAT non-compliance

Studies of VAT non-compliance

There have been very few published studies of VAT non-compliance. We stress the term *published*, as we know from conversations with officers from tax authorities in a number of countries that there are a number of internal reports on VAT compliance, which are kept confidential on operational grounds. We have been able to trace three different sources of studies: those carried out in Exeter, UK (Adams, 2002; Adams and Webley, 2001; Webley *et al.*, 2006), which use interview, survey, and experimental techniques; experimental studies carried out in Trento, Italy (Mittone, 2001); and a study of the impact of audits using individual tax return information from Argentina and Chile (Bergman and Nevarez, 2006). We will consider each of these in turn.

The Exeter work on VAT compliance was part-funded by HMRC, and there was a particular focus on small businesses and VAT. The research was not strongly theoretically driven; the aim was to test the relevance of psychological factors identified as playing an important causal role in income tax evasion to VAT evasion.

A number of different methodological approaches were used, but the most notable was the combination of survey data with compliance classifications provided by the HMRC. Two studies of this type were carried out (Adams, 2002; Webley *et al.*, 2006). For each, HMRC provided the names and addresses of the owners of catering and flooring/furnishing businesses with a turnover of less than £1 million. These sectors were chosen to be contrasting groups: HMRC believed the flooring/furnishing sector to be generally compliant, with non-compliance being more common in the catering business. The businesses were sorted by HMRC into four compliance groups: A=new businesses that had not been audited; B=visited in past three years by HMRC and found to be compliant; C=visited and found to be mildly non-compliant; D=visited and found to be seriously non-compliant. Questionnaires, color-coded to indicate each compliance group, were sent to respondents. These differed in the two studies, but both included a range of questions about attitudes, knowledge, and behavior in respect of VAT. These included direct questions about compliance behavior ("How often over the past five years have you been involved in cash transactions so as to reduce VAT payments?") and hypothetical questions about compliance (e.g., "If you had the opportunity to pay less VAT than you should do and you believed that there was absolutely no chance of getting caught, would you do so?"). The response rate was relatively low (13.5 percent in the first study, 18 percent in the second), though this is not unusual in survey research on tax issues (see Wallschutsky, 1996).

There were no significant differences in self-reported compliance between the two types of businesses in either study. However, in both studies there were differences in related variables. Those in the catering business were less likely to believe that people were honest, more likely to believe that under-declaring VAT would help profits, less likely to think that the VAT system was fair, and less likely to apply any decrease in VAT to their prices. This provides some support for the HMRC view of the differences between these two sectors.

More strikingly, there were only limited differences in psychological and other variables between the HMRC compliance categories, which can be summed up in two sentences. Group D (the serious non-compliers) had had significantly more penalties for late payment than the other groups. The non-compliers (Groups C and D) were younger, had been in business for less time, and had a higher turnover.

However, there were a large number of differences between individuals classified according to their responses to a variety of questions (some mentioned above) as self-reported compliers or non-compliers. Compliers were older, were more community-minded than non-compliers, and were more likely to believe that VAT was a source of general taxation, that VAT evasion was wrong, and that their reputation would suffer if they were discovered to have been non-compliant. Compliers were also more likely to believe that the paying of taxes was a moral responsibility of being a good citizen and that the VAT system was fair, and more likely to feel guilty if they underpaid VAT.

The interview study reported by Adams and Webley (2001) fleshes out the picture painted by these survey studies. Interviews were carried out with 27 people from three sectors (catering, flooring/furnishing, and building). They were not asked directly about their own behavior in respect of VAT; compliance was raised indirectly, often by using a hypothetical question. Four interesting themes emerged from these interviews: fairness, sanctions, morality, and "mental accounting". Many people perceived inequities at some level: some felt that the VAT burden was particularly heavy on small businesses, some felt that it was unfair because of competition from unregistered businesses, and some (especially builders) resented having to do unpaid work for the government. There was a belief that HMRC had very strong powers and did not hesitate to use them, which contributed to a widespread belief that any evasion would be detected and punished. Morality was notable by its absence. There was a recognition that taxes are required to maintain our society, but few people saw taxpaying as a moral issue. For them, minimizing tax payments is good business practice that overshadows what might be considered to be good social practice. These themes (fairness, sanctions, and morality) are all familiar from the psychological literature on income tax evasion. The final theme, "mental accounting", is not. What this refers to is that the majority of respondents saw the VAT that they collected as being their own money, and they begrudged paying it. A typical comment is "VAT takes about £12,000 a year from my business so *I pay* just as much in VAT as what I earn" [our emphasis]. Contrast this with a much less typical comment: "It's not a cost to the business, we're just looking after the money for the government. There's no point is worrying about paying. It's their money." The fact that so many participants felt a sense of ownership about VAT monies they collect clearly adds a new dimension to VAT compliance.

The experiments on VAT compliance carried out by Adams (2002) provide further support for the notion that inequity and mental accounting are crucial in encouraging VAT evasion. Adams created a web-based restaurant simulation in which participants had to make a number of decisions – for example, on the kinds of meals to be offered and their pricing, on advertising and on staffing – across a two-year period. Pricing and other decisions were taken each month, VAT returns made each quarter, and income tax returns made each year. Taxpaying was therefore just one decision among many that the participants had to make (unlike many tax compliance experiments, where it is very evident that tax is the focus of the study).

Adams used two samples – one of restaurant owners, the other of catering and management students – in addition to participants recruited over the web. The results showed that those who evaded tax were more egoistic, saw VAT as unfair, and tended to see VAT as coming from their business funds. This confirms the qualitative and survey findings, and suggests that the role of mental accounting in the compliance process for those taxes where businesses collect the tax on behalf of the government is an important one.

Mittone's (2001) four experiments on VAT evasion are of a rather more traditional design. They are based on the classic competitive market experiment described by Bergstrom and Miller (1997). In this market, which is implemented on a computer network, there are several buyers and sellers, each of whom is given a reservation price. Participants are each allocated the role of either a buyer or a seller, which they keep throughout the experiment. Every period (round) of the experiment, the sellers offer their good at a price of their choosing, and the buyers can choose from the list of offers that appears on their computer screen. Thus far this is a very standard market experiment. What makes these experiments distinctive is that sellers and buyers can attempt to collude with a potential partner by clicking on a "collusion" button. The potential partner then has the choice of either accepting or refusing this offer of collusion. If he or she accepts, both the buyer and seller benefit; however, if they are caught by the tax authorities, both are liable to pay a fine. If the offer of collusion is refused, then VAT is paid on the transaction. In one of the experiments sellers were able to expropriate the VAT collected from the buyers, and in this case only the sellers would be fined if they were caught evading.

Mittone's (2001) results are instructive. In the "expropriation" experiment, the main effect was to produce a generalized reduction in prices. Sellers appeared to use the ability to expropriate VAT so as to compete on price – which means that they were implicitly sharing with the buyers the advantage of expropriation, even though they alone run the risk of sanctions if they are caught. In the other three experiments, it appears as if sellers interpreted making a collusion proposal as a competitive mechanism, and buyers saw it as a way of saving money. What is interesting is that the task of proposing collusion became associated with a given role (buyer or seller) within each experiment, but was different across experiments. In other words, there were emergent norms about who should offer collusion. Related to this, there are clear reputation effects, where buyers show loyalty to particular sellers – this, of course, makes particular sense where collusion in illegal activities is involved.

Bergman and Nevarez' (2006) study of the impact of audits on VAT compliance uses a very different kind of methodology. They used individual tax return data from two groups of Argentine and Chilean taxpayers. The experimental group had been audited – the control group consisted of taxpayers who matched individuals in the audited group for location, trade, and level of tax payments. The dependent measure used was the debit/credit (D/C) ratio, where debits were the total VAT charged when goods or services were sold, and credits were the VAT already paid by the taxpayer. The lower the D/C ratio, the more likely it is that an individual is being non-compliant, though the type of industry and size of the company have to be taken into account in benchmarking these figures. Thus, a service company with a D/C ratio of less than 1.5 would be considered as very likely to be non-compliant, whereas this ratio for a food-processing company would indicate a profitable and compliant company.

The results of the analysis show that, in the period prior to the audit, the D/C ratio for audited taxpayers in both Chile and Argentina was lower than in the control group (e.g., it was 90 percent of the median figure for the control group). This is to be expected, as those selected to be audited would have been chosen by the tax authorities on the basis that they were probable evaders. Compliance for the audited groups in both countries increased during the year of the audit (to 104 percent in Chile), and afterwards returned to previous levels or an even lower figure (to 89 percent in Chile). This increase in compliance is largely a result of a reduction in credits – probably the consequence of people using fewer fake invoices. A more detailed analysis reveals that whilst audits have no or even a deleterious impact on those who were found to be non-compliant, they do increase post-audit compliance for those who were audited and found to be compliant.

Individualistic interpretations of VAT non-compliance

The results reported in the previous section, despite using a wide range of methods and both psychological and economic theories, are all interpreted by their authors using individualistic approaches. Webley et al. (2006), for example, use a combination of the Australian Tax Office model (Braithwaite, 2003) and Elffer's (1999) WBAD (Willing – Being Able – Daring) model to interpret their findings. This essentially categorizes individuals into types of taxpayers (for instance, those who are unwilling to evade taxes) and identifies the appropriate approach for the tax authorities to use with this group of taxpayers (in this case, to rely on self-regulation, education, and communication). Individuals may fall into particularly categories because of their personalities or approach to life (such as being community-minded), or because they are deterred by financial and reputational risk. Webley et al. (2006) suggest that individuals may move from one group to another (so those who are in the daring group may be moved down to the "being able" group through appropriate punishment and then deterrence), so this model is not entirely static. Social groups are notable by their absence however, and there are really only two players in this model – the individual and the tax authorities.

Though Mittone (2001) sees VAT evasion through very different lenses (in his case, the prism of the standard Allingham and Sandmo (1972) model of tax evasion), explicitly recognizes three parties in VAT transactions (the seller, the buyer, and the government), and acknowledges the essentially social nature of taxpaying, he too takes a very individualistic approach. Tax evasion is analyzed as a straightforward decision based on the expected values of the alternatives. Thus, the social act of collusion is reduced to a judgment about the costs of benefits of offering (or accepting) collusive proposals.

Bergman and Neverez (2006) do not outline a particular theoretical approach, beyond commenting that standard game-theoretic approaches to tax evasion predict no effect of audits on compliance; their approach is implicitly individualistic, with particular types of taxpayers being characterized (e.g., as "entrenched cheaters", "small group of free-riders", and "honest taxpayers"). They do, however, conclude that social context and norms matter – although they do not model this at all. For us, this raises the question of whether it is possible to explain VAT compliance using a more avowedly social approach – something we will explore in the next section.

An alternative approach to explaining VAT non-compliance

Although some models (and, as noted above, researchers) recognize the role that social factors such as social and personal norms play in taxpaying behavior (see, for example, Hessing *et al.*, 1988; Myles and Naylor, 1996), they tend to be treated in a simplistic and reductionist way. Also, in relation to VAT, research studies often treat small-business individuals as a single homogenous group. In so doing, the importance of certain group memberships and norms has been overlooked. Small-business individuals (and individual taxpayers, come to that) are members of many different groups, and so may be exposed to a range of cultures (and subcultures) with varying (and sometimes conflicting) norms, values, and behaviors. In particular, research suggests that different occupational sectors have very different traditions and norms (i.e., cultures) when it comes to tax compliance (e.g., Sigala *et al.*, 1999).

Taxpaying is unusual in that is something we only start *consciously* engaging in as adults (for example, although everyone pays tax when they purchase goods from shops, they would not necessarily think about this as taxpaying). Research shows that the concept of tax is something few young people, even those aged 15 years, fully grasp (Furnham, 2005). This means that even though individuals are likely to have experience of dealing with other rules and regulations, many embark on their careers as tax novices and could become acculturated into their sector's taxpaying culture. Carroll (1992) suggests that a taxpayer could be late completing a return, overstate deductions, report the wrong type of deductions (e.g., mix business and personal), or even refuse to pay tax because they are following common practices in their occupational group. In line with this, Sigala *et al.*'s (1999) qualitative study revealed that "cash-in-hand" payments are very common amongst tradesmen in the UK construction industry. As one of their respondents, a plumber, articulated (Sigala, 1999: 240): "Everybody in that sort of business that I'm in they talk about accepting cash. It's a sort of everyday thing. It is accepted in the plumbing industry." Also, in an Australian interview study focusing on builders, Shover *et al.* (2003) report that weekend work is routinely paid in cash and then not declared as income.

On the theme of cash-in-hand payments, in an Australian qualitative study (with business individuals, the general public, and tax officials), Noble (2000) found that cash jobs are generally seen as socially acceptable and encouraged by industry peers. Despite their contribution, these particular studies are limited by their small sample size, and unclear definitions of culture. Also, although they look at occupational group membership, the focus of research has not, on the whole, been on occupational group norms (or values) per se, but on the norms and values of friends, people taxpayers know, and fellow citizens (e.g., Walls-chutzky, 1984). Some of this research suggests that perceptions (as well as knowledge) of social norms do influence people's taxpaying behaviors (e.g., Alm et al., 1999; Bosco and Mittone, 1997; Cullis and Lewis, 1997; De Juan et al., 1994; Porcano, 1988; Sigala, 1999; Vogel, 1974; Webley et al., 1988) and attitudes (e.g., Torgler, 2005). Consequently, social norms have been incorporated into models of tax compliance by economists who recognize the significance of social variables (Alm and Martinez-Vazquez, 2003).

When investigating norms and values of this kind, it is worth bearing in mind that findings from past social norm research have not always been consistent. Whilst some studies show that if a person believes non-compliance is widespread he or she is more likely not to comply, others do not. For example, Wenzel's (2005a) experimental research both in the lab and the field, and a survey commissioned by the ATO (Artcraft Research, 1998, cited in Wenzel, 2005a) revealed that whilst Australian taxpayers think that fellow Australians engage in and endorse tax non-compliance, they personally regard it as inappropriate. Wenzel (2005a) suggests that the process of pluralistic ignorance (see Allport, 1924; O'Gorman, 1986; Prentice and Miller, 1996) – where group members privately reject a group norm but believe others accept it – might be responsible for this norm misinterpretation.

These inconsistent findings could be partly due to definitional and measurement issues. Researchers have used a diverse range of conceptualizations and definitions of social norms (Kirchler, 2007). Indeed, reaching a singular definition of culture is problematic, since it is a word that has different meanings depending on who or which domain is using it (e.g., anthropology, sociology, psychology; Sackmann, 1989). Schein (1996: 236) defines culture as "a set of shared, taken for granted implicit assumptions that a group holds and determines how it perceives, thinks about and reacts to its various environments". Deal and Kennedy (1982: 15) describe culture as "a system of informal rules that spells out how people are to behave most of the time". For them, norms (a set of attitudes and/or behaviors prescribed or proscribed by an individual's group membership; Livingstone and Haslam, 2008; see also Sherif, 1936; Turner, 1991) and values (what is desirable, that is, the accepted principles or standards of a group; Morris, 1956) represent the key elements of culture, and this is the working definition that we use.

As well as definitional and measurement issues, the inconsistent findings could also be related to the fact that the role norms play in behavior and attitudes is complex. A social identity framework aims to "unpack" some of this complexity, and offers a more nuanced analysis of taxpaying norms and values. It is only in the past few years that this approach has been explored as a potential framework for tax research (see Taylor, 2003; Wenzel, 2002, 2004, 2005a, 2005b, 2007). The use of a social identity approach sits well with Akerlof and Kranton's (2000) advocacy for the importance of identity in economic models of behavior.

A social identity approach

Taxpayers are members of many different groups. A social identity approach suggests that whilst taxpayers may think of themselves as individual and unique in comparison with others, in certain contexts they may think of themselves as belonging to some social category (i.e., common ingroup, Turner, 1991). This is in comparison to an outgroup – i.e, a category to which they do not belong. It should be recognized that self and other categories can exist at different levels of abstraction, with higher levels being more inclusive (Turner *et al.*, 1994). The level of category abstraction is a relative concept, and so for any one person, more than one level of social self-category will be available – it is argued that no one level is inherently more useful or appropriate than another and none is more fundamental to who a person is (Turner *et al.*, 1994). For example, people may categorize themselves as individuals, as members of a country, as members of an organization, or as members of an occupational group.

Taylor (2003) suggests that if individuals categorize themselves as a group member in a taxpaying situation (and this group membership is meaningful), then what is good for the group collectively is likely to motivate behavior. However, if they categorize themselves as an individual, then personal self-interest (rather than a sense of what is good for the group) may motivate behavior. Which self-categorization is salient in a particular context depends on situational and perceived factors (Turner *et al.*, 1994; Wenzel, 2004). Taylor (2003) suggests that it is when social identity is salient, where greater similarity to ingroup others and greater dissimilarity to outgroup others is perceived, that attitudes and behavior become more in line with ingroup norms (Turner, 1991).

One important question is, which identities are taxpayers likely to spontaneously adopt in taxpaying situations? In a survey study, Wenzel (2005b) attempted to address this question by coding participants' responses to the question "Can you describe the sort of people who you think of as being in the same boat as you when it comes to tax?" The findings revealed that taxpayers perceived themselves in terms of a large range of social categories. However, the most frequent self-categories referred to participants' employment status, economic status and occupational group – and, given that people pay tax on the money that they earn whilst working, this is perhaps unsurprising.

Subscribing to a social identity line of thinking suggests that taxpayers should be more influenced by social norms when they identify with the group to whom the norms are ascribed. If identification is weak, social norms should be less effective or even ineffective. This is what Wenzel (2004) found in his study focusing on national (Australian) identity and the social norm of what "most others" think that they should do in relation to tax. When there was a norm to pay tax, those who identified strongly with fellow Australians displayed a greater level of self-reported compliance. However, for those who only identified weakly, this norm was ineffective and, in some cases, counterproductive. Since in this study only a relatively small proportion of participants were weak identifiers, Wenzel (2004, 2005a) advises a regulatory strategy where tax authorities make reference to social norms and widely shared views about the importance of paying one's taxes honestly.

Wenzel (2004, 2007) and Taylor (2003) also suggest that it is conducive to tax compliance if tax authorities are included within this national self-concept – that is, authorities are seen as acting on behalf of national citizens (i.e., as ingroup members) rather than in opposition to them (i.e., as outgroup members). Authorities are only likely to be thought of as ingroup members if they are perceived as both fair and legitimate. However, as mentioned above, findings show that taxpayers often perceive the tax system to be unfair, and see themselves as having a difficult relationship with the tax office (e.g., Adams and Webley, 2001; Noble, 2000; Wenzel, 2002). Also, Wenzel (2005a) found that the more power tax authorities are perceived to have, the less legitimate they are seen to be. However, those who identified highly with fellow Australian citizens (and presumably saw the tax office as included in this national self-concept) considered a powerful tax office to be more legitimate than did those who identified less highly with fellow citizens (see Wenzel, 2005a).

However, although making reference to national group membership and widely shared norms about the importance of tax honesty might be conducive to tax compliance, tax authorities have a *limited ability* to determine which identity is salient in a given tax context. Occupational group membership and identity, however, appear to be very relevant to taxpaying situations (Carroll, 1992; Sigala et al., 1999; Wenzel, 2002, 2004, 2005b, 2007), and in the next section we consider the findings of our studies in these areas, how they speak to issues in VAT research, and their implications for tax authorities.

Examples of the social identity approach applied to empirical work

Ashby and Webley's (2008) in-depth interview study set out to build a detailed picture of one occupational group's taxpaying culture: the hairdressing and beauty sector. The findings of this study (with 19 self-employed hairdressers and beauticians from the UK) indicate that factors which could affect taxpaying behaviors and attitudes (such as a reliance on accountants/tax advisors, the notion of an acceptable level of cash-in-hand payments, and the use of different mental accounts for different types of income) are tied to occupational group membership, as they are socially constructed within occupational groups and are a key component of the group's taxpaying culture. For example, there is a norm amongst hairdressers and beauticians that occasional cash-in-hand payments are acceptable. This and similar norms appear to be sustained through talking to fellow colleagues and clients. In line with this idea, Haslam et al. (1998) suggest that group-based interactions foster consensus within groups. This could mean that in using cash-in-hand payments hairdressers and beauticians are acting in accordance with their group's shared norm, rather than making an individual decision arising from a cost–benefit analysis.

Although some of the factors that emerged in this and our other studies (in particular, mental accounting, fairness, sources of tax advice, and tax as a legal rather than a moral obligation) have already arisen in the small business literature (see Adams and Webley, 2001; Ahmed and Sakurai, 2001; McKerchar, 1995), they have often been couched in relatively individualistic terms. Next, by drawing on the findings from our studies, we will explore how previous findings in relation to (a) mental accounting (b) sources of tax advice, and (c) fairness and taxpaying as a legal (rather than a moral) obligation, can be interpreted in a less individualistic way.

As well as the interview study described above (see Ashby and Webley, 2008), we will draw on the findings from a UK self-report survey (with 46 hairdressers) and two other qualitative studies: a UK focus group study with 20 taxi driver and hairdresser participants, and an Australian in-depth interview study with 15 hairdressers (for more details of these studies, see Ashby, 2007). It might be noted that there is a particular focus on hairdressers in these studies. This approach – of focusing on one occupational sector – was favored because it is a way of obtaining detailed well-characterized information. It is also especially suited to the study of occupational taxpaying cultures, which are complex and under-researched. The rationale behind selecting the hairdressing sector was twofold. First, hairdressers have opportunities to make cash-in-hand payments, and as such are targeted by tax authorities (e.g., Australian Tax Office, 2004). Second, practically speaking, compared to other groups (such as builders), hairdressers are accessible (since in the UK and Australia each city or town center has a number of salons) and relatively easy to recruit. Also, that the data comes from two different countries strengthens our overall arguments, in so much as it provides evidence of the same "processes" in both countries. However, although this allowed for continuity and an in-depth understanding of one sector, this narrow focus does mean that there is a case for further research to be conducted with a wider range of occupational groups.

(a) Mental accounting

In both the UK and Australia, not declaring two sources of extra income (money from out-of hours payments and tips) seems to be acceptable in the hairdressing sector. Part of the reason for this appears to stem from how this money is conceptualized. That is to say, this extra money is placed in a different mental account to ordinary taxable income, earmarked as "mine to spend as I wish". Participants felt a sense of ownership over this extra money, in a way that they did not with ordinary income – where they recognized that some of it belonged to the tax office. As Holly, an Australian hairdresser, said: "if you want to give me a 10-dollar tip, you just give it to me and I put it in my pocket". Tips in particular tended to be seen as a gift. Will, a UK salon-owner who participated in the focus group study, articulated this:

> If you were to have said do we agree with the fact that we should have our tips taxed, then you would have a major uproar, we would all be ranting and raving, screaming at you because we have to declare our tips and they get taxed okay, the very word gratis is, is, it's obviously in Latin and it's a grateful, it's a

gratitude, it's a thanks, it's like a present, so it's like saying to somebody I'm giving you ten pounds for your birthday, that is a present ok, somebody saying to me I'm giving you three pounds fifty for doing my hair as a present.

Although, for the hairdressers, taxing tips was an emotive subject, overall the taxi drivers (at least in our focus group study; see Ashby, 2007) seemed to have a more pragmatic attitude towards tips being taxed and did not perceive such a sense of ownership of this money. Their conversations around tax and tipping primarily focused on the way in which they organized their finances. Tips were conceptualized as just another part of their income, with one taxi driver, Sharon, "bunging" her takings from taxi fares together with her tips, and declaring all of it to the tax office. Similarly, another taxi driver, Pat, asked her accountant to ensure that any income she declares includes her tips.

Our findings suggest that the way in which different types of money are conceptualized (or, in other words, the mental account they are placed in) depends, at least to some extent, on the occupational group an individual belongs to, and the norms of this group. In relation to VAT, Adams and Webley (2001) found that some of their participants conceptualized VAT money as "mine", whereas others conceptualized it as "theirs" (the tax office's). What the present findings indicate is that the way in which VAT money is conceptualized varies as a function of occupational group. So whilst builders, for example, might see this money as "mine", another group who organize and think about their money differently might see it as the tax office's. The challenge for tax authorities is to pinpoint groups that hold this "it's mine" conceptualization. Through interacting with trainees, possibly by holding training workshops, they could try to change how this money is organized and thought of. This fits nicely with a UK tax official's statement that "The trick is to stop thinking of it as 'your' money" (Revenue Auditor, n.d., cited by Chartered Institute of Taxation, n.d.).

(b) Sources of advice

Although the tax office might see financial book-keeping as an important part of being an occupational group member (as it affects how tax forms are filled in), for the most part our hairdressing (and taxi driver) participants did not appear to see it (or dealing with taxes) as particularly tied to, or a large part of, being a hairdresser (or a taxi driver) per se. Interestingly, though, they did see other rules and relations (such as those relating to health and safety) as more occupation-specific. As Rhonda, an Australian hairdresser, put it, "It's [book-keeping and taxes] not hairdressing". Tax laws are complex, and the skills required to maintain books and manage finances are not necessarily the skills that attract people to run small businesses or become self-employed. This means that many small-business individuals seek tax or financial book-keeping advice.

Hairdressers (more than taxi drivers) cited fellow colleagues as a source of advice. In relation to VAT, Sue, a hairdresser in our UK interview study, discussed registering for it with her friends, who had advised her not go over the

VAT threshold (see Ashby and Webley, 2008). This is noteworthy, because it is through discussions with colleagues that certain taxpaying values and norms are likely to be transmitted (Sigala, 1999). Although there is likely to be variation between individuals, certain occupational groups may openly discuss tax practices more than others.

Although friends were one source of advice, it was accountants that acted as the primary source of tax advice for the majority of participants in all of our studies. For some (although not all) hairdressers, having an accountant appeared to be tied to their own and others' perception of them as "not good with figures" or "not that bright". As Grace, a salon-owner from our focus group study, said, "unless you know how to fill out your own tax return, which I don't think most hairdressers could, then they [hairdressers] bloody better have an accountant". Tracy, who participated in our UK interview study, echoed this sentiment: "I think it's always advisable to have an accountant, especially when you're not sort of mathematically minded, as I'm not really [laughs]" (see Ashby and Webley, 2008). However, although nearly all of the taxi drivers (from the focus group study) also had an accountant, one of the main reasons for getting one was not because they could not do it, but because they felt that the tax office might question the way they filled in their tax returns.

Overall, our findings fit with previous ones that small business individuals struggle to complete tax forms, and often rely on an accountant. However, our studies do more than reproduce past findings. Specifically, they add depth to previous research by suggesting that decisions – such as whether or not to get an accountant – can be tied to occupational group membership. That is to say, hairdressers, for example, may get an accountant because they do not equate their occupation with being good at book-keeping. The findings also suggest that dealing with taxes is not necessarily an important part of being an occupational group member. This, and the confusion surrounding taxes, could be tied to the fact that hairdressers, like many other groups, do not learn about taxes or book-keeping during their training. In the UK, although the self-employed can attend free courses run by the tax office, these courses are not occupation-specific, and people need to actively seek them out. This does not seem to be an ideal strategy. Instead, it might be beneficial for authorities to run tax workshops (focusing on VAT and income tax) in occupational colleges or universities, as well as encourage such institutions to include occupation-specific tax material in their syllabuses. In so doing they could help dispel some of uncertainty surrounding tax forms and book-keeping, as well as make tax a more relevant part of being an occupational group member. Doing so would seem to be particularly important in light of the findings (from our UK survey study) that when tax was relevant to occupational group membership, respondents were more likely to think that they should cooperate with tax authorities.

(c) Fairness and taxpaying as a legal (not moral) obligation

As Richard Lambert, Director-General of the Confederation of British Industries said (*The Times*, 2007: 1): "It is important that the tax system is fair". Although, as mentioned, past research illustrates the importance of fairness, legitimacy, and treatment by tax authorities, our findings suggest that, at a national level, tax authorities (in the UK and Australia) are not included in the national self-concept. That is to say, authorities are not seen as acting on behalf of citizens but in opposition to them. Similarly, at an occupational level there was a sense of an "us" (occupational group members) and "them" (the tax office) relationship. As one hairdresser from the UK focus group study said, "The tax inspector will do anything, he will bend over and he will pull out his back teeth to find one [a mistake]". A number of our participants (in the UK and Australia) were unhappy with the taxpayer–tax office (or government) exchange. According to Paul (a hairdresser in the focus group study), his clients "don't think their tax comes back to them, they're not paying tax to benefit themselves they're paying tax to feed the government". There was also the perception (amongst some) that smaller businesses were targeted whereas "the big boys are getting away with blue murder"(Liz, Australian interview study).

These findings are consistent with previous studies which indicate that taxpayers tend to have a difficult relationship with the tax office and perceive the tax system as unfair (e.g., Coleman and Freeman, 1994; Noble, 2000). The following tax joke, featured on the Chartered Institute of Taxation website (CIOT, n.d.), captures the nature of this difficult relationship, and indicates how ingrained negative perceptions of the tax office and its inspectors are:

Question: How can you tell when a tax inspector is trying to trap you into a confession?
Answer: When his lips are moving.

It is worth noting that not all regulators are thought of in this negative way. In particular, for the most part, hairdressers in (Australia and the UK) tended to see the Health and Safety Department (another regulator) as there to "help them out" rather than "catch them out". As George, an Australian hairdresser, articulated, "I don't think they [health and safety] come in just to give you headache, no, I think they're just part of the regulations, they're nice, they will advise you". It therefore appears that the tax office needs to work to improve the public image of itself, and of taxpaying more generally. This is not an easy task, as they need to strike a balance between being perceived as fair and approachable, and being thought of as having a "big stick" which they can use when necessary.

At present, it appears that they may have the "big stick" at the expense of being fair and approachable. Indeed, Ross, a salon owner (from our UK interview study) who said he had been "had" by her Majesty's Customs and Excise (which since 2005 has been HMRC) in the past, described them as "the police", saying, "the VAT office could walk in here now and shut me" (see Ashby and Webley, 2008). Also, as Will (a hairdresser from the UK focus group study) articulated, the perception of the tax office as powerful and having "threat value" is ingrained in British culture.

One first step in achieving this balance between fairness and power is to treat taxpayers in a fair and understanding manner (see, for example, Braithwaite,

2003; Tyler, 1990). Although this suggestion is by no means original, what our findings indicate is that tax authorities would be better equipped to treat taxpayers in this way if they had a better understanding of different occupational cultures. This is because it would prevent them from unduly targeting groups that already have a compliant or cooperative occupational taxpaying culture, and which might react negatively to being threatened with coercive tactics.

The suggestion to manage different occupational groups in different ways (that are appropriate for them) might seem commonsensical. However, whilst in recent years tax authorities in the UK, US, Australia, France, and Sweden have begun to conceptualize and treat taxpayers less like "robbers" and more like clients (Kirchler, 2007), and the ATO has adopted a responsive approach to compliance (see Braithwaite 2003), there is still a tendency for authorities (especially in the UK) to manage occupational groups in a very similar manner.

However, beliefs that the tax office is "there to catch you out" appear to be quite ingrained, and although treating groups in ways that are appropriate for them is beneficial in the sense that taxpayers receive fairer treatment, it can only do so much. Another suggestion would be to have more positive "tax" stories in the media. Thus, rather than just reporting on tax rises, tax office mistakes, or tax evaders, the media could be encouraged to report on the way tax money is used to fund different public services (such as health care, the police) which benefit everyone. Although the issue of how tax money is spent is a contentious one, such stories might go some way to convincing taxpayers that all tax money is not wasted.

Stories about the way tax money is used could also help to promote taxpaying as a moral as well as a legal obligation. This is important because if taxpaying is seen as "morally right," a feeling of shame might act as a stronger deterrent to tax evasion or avoidance (Grasmick and Bursick, 1990). In line with previous VAT research, the present findings suggest that many taxpayers (in the UK and Australia) actually see taxpaying primarily as a legal rather than a moral obligation. An example of this can be seen in an Australian hairdresser's statement that "culturally [taxpaying's] not a moral issue". This is a very current issue, with a global religious authority, Pope Benedict XVI, calling for tax evaders to be condemned as "socially unjust" (Owen, 2007).

Concluding remarks

Thus far, we have sought to make a case that the findings from research into VAT compliance can be interpreted in a less individualistic light. With our social identity framework and focus on occupational taxpaying cultures, we move away from rational and individualistic approaches. This chapter has concentrated on research with small businesses rather than medium or large ones. However, large and medium businesses in particular are organizations, and need to be understood as such (Webley, 2004). Although researchers with a specific interest in business crime recognize this (e.g., Braithwaite, 1989; Clarke, 1990; Delaney, 1994), those working in this area have produced little in the way of theory

(Webley, 2004). This means that applying a social identity framework to research with medium and large businesses could be fruitful – especially given that Braithwaite's (1989: 141) comment that "much thinking about corporate crime ... adopts an overly economically rational conception of the organization; it excessively downplays the corporation's role as a choosing collective agent with organizational policies and values about social responsibility" is still true of much research today.

Although in this chapter we recognize that, when taxpayers' personal identities are salient, personal self-interest may be more likely to motivate behavior, we reject the traditional economic conception that *all* taxpayers are rational utility maximizers all the time. Instead, for future research, we suggest a broader conceptualization of taxpaying behavior and attitudes in which economic, and social and cultural, variables are seen as linked in the sense that economic variables (such as personal norms or perceptions of deterrence and fairness) can be tied to occupational group membership and shaped by group norms.

However, more research is required to develop a full model that clarifies and elaborates the interplay between occupational identity, occupational taxpaying culture, and more economic variables in taxpaying attitudes and behaviors. Nonetheless, our take-home message is that attention to occupational group membership and, in particular, to different group's taxpaying cultures can help improve our understanding of why people hold certain tax attitudes and why they do (or do not) pay VAT.

Bibliography

Adams, C. J. (2002) "The economic psychology of VAT compliance", Unpublished thesis, University of Exeter, UK.

Adams, C. J. and Webley, P. (2001) "Small business owners' attitudes on VAT compliance in the UK", *Journal of Economic Psychology*, 22: 195–216.

Agha, A. and Haughton, J. (1996) "Designing VAT systems: some efficiency considerations", *Review of Economics and Statistics*, 78: 303–8.

Ahmed, E. and Sakurai, Y. (2001) "Small business individuals: What do we know and what do we need to know?" Working Paper No. 27, Canberra: Australian National University, Centre for Tax System Integrity.

Akerlof, G. A. and Kranton, R. E. (2000) "Economics and identity", *The Quarterly Journal of Economics*, 115: 715–53.

Allingham, M. G. and Sandmo, A. (1977) "Income tax evasion: A theoretical analysis", *Journal of Public Economics*, 1: 323–38.

Allport, E. H. (1924) *Social Psychology*, Boston, MA: Houghton Mifflin.

Alm, J. and Martinez-Vazquez, J. (2003), "Institutions, paradigms and tax evasion in developing and transition countries", in J. Martinez-Vazquez and J. Alm (eds.), *Public Finance in Developing and Transitional Countries*, Cheltenham, UK: Edward Elgar.

Alm, J., McClelland, G. H., and Schulze, W. D. (1999) "Changing the social norm of tax compliance by voting", *Kyklos*, 52: 141–71.

Andreoni, J., Erard, B., and Feinstein, J. (1998) "Tax compliance", *Journal of Economic Literature*, 36: 818–60.

Ashby, J. (2007) "Occupational taxpaying cultures: A social identity approach", Unpublished thesis, University of Exeter, UK.

Ashby, J. S. and Webley, P. (2008) "But everyone else is doing it: A closer look at the occupational taxpaying culture of one business sector", *Journal of Community and Applied Social Psychology*, 18: 194–210.

Australian Taxation Office (2004). *Cash Economy: Practical Tax Audit*. Canberra, ACT: Author.

Bergman, M. and Nevarez, A. (2006) "Do audits enhance compliance? An empirical assessment of VAT enforcement", *National Tax Journal*, 59: 817–32.

Bergstrom, T. C. and Miller, J. H. (1997). *Experiments with Economic Principles*. New York, NY: McGraw Hill.

Bird, R. M. (1993) "Review of Principles and practice of value added taxation: lessons for developing countries", *Canadian Tax Journal*, 41: 1222–5.

Bosco, L. and Mittone, L. (1997) "Tax evasion and moral constraints: Some experimental evidence", *Kyklos*, 50: 297–324.

Braithwaite, J (1989) *Crime, Shame and Reintegration*. Cambridge, UK: Cambridge University Press.

Braithwaite, V. (2003) "A new approach to tax compliance", in V. Braithwaite (ed.), *Taxing Democracy: Understanding Tax Avoidance and Evasion*, Aldershot, UK: Ashgate.

Carroll, J. S. (1992) "How taxpayers think about their taxes: Frames and values", in J. Slemrod (ed.), *Why People Pay Taxes: Tax Compliance and Enforcement*, Ann Arbor, MI: Michigan University Press.

Chartered Institute of Taxation (n.d.) *Tax Jokes and Quotes*, retrieved September 4, 2007, from www.tax.org.uk/showarticle.pl?id=1256.

Clarke, M. (1990). *Business Crime: Its Nature and Control*. Oxford, UK: Polity Press

Cnossen, S. (1981) "The Netherlands", in J. Aaron (ed.), *The Value Added Tax: Lessons from Europe*, Washington, DC: The Brookings Institute.

Coleman, C. and Freeman, L. (1994). The development of strategic marketing options directed at improving compliance levels in small businesses. *Australian Tax Forum*, 11: 347–67.

Cullis, J. G. and Lewis, A. (1997) "Why people pay taxes: From a conventional economic model to a model of social convention", *Journal of Economic Psychology*, 18: 305–21.

Deal, T. and Kennedy, A. (1988) *Corporate Cultures: The Rites and Rituals of Corporate Life*, Harmondsworth, UK: Penguin Books.

De Juan, A., Lasheras, M. A., and Mayo, R. (1994) "Voluntary tax compliant behavior of Spanish income tax payers", *Public Finance*, 49: 90–105.

Delaney, K. J. (1994). The organizational construction of the bottom line. *Social Problems*, 41: 497–518.

Duverne, D. (1990) "Coordinate audits of income tax and VAT", paper presented at the Conference on Administrative Aspects of a Value-Added Tax. Washington, DC, October 1990.

Ebrill, L., Keen, M., Bodin, J.-P., and Summers, V. (2001) *The Modern VAT*, Washington, DC: International Monetary Fund.

Elffers, H. (1991) *Income Tax Evasion: Theory and Measurement*, Amsterdam, The Netherlands: Kluwer.

Elffers, H. (1999) "But taxpayers do cooperate!", in M. van Vugt, A. Biel, M. Snyder, and Tom Tyler (eds.), *Collective Helping in Modern Society: Dilemmas and Solutions*, London, UK: Routledge.

Furnham, A. (2005) "Understanding the meaning of tax: Young people's knowledge of the principles of taxation", *Journal of Socio-Economics*, 34: 703–13.

Gebauer, A. and Parsche, R. (2003) "Evasion of value-added taxes in Europe: IFO approach to estimating the evasion of value-added taxes on the basis of national accounts data (NAD)", *CESifo DICE Report No 2*: 40–4.

Grasmick, H. G. and Bursik Jr, R. J. (1990) "Conscience, significant others, and rational choice: Extending the deterrence model", *Law and Society Review*, 24: 837–61.

Haslam, S. A., Turner, J. C., Oakes, P. J. *et al.* (1998) "The group as a basis for emergent stereotype consensus", *European Review of Social Psychology*, 8: 203–39.

Hessing, D. J., Kinsey, K. A., Elffers, H., and Weigel, R. H. (1988) "Tax evasion research: Measurement strategies and theoretical models", in W. F. van Raaij, G. M. van Veldhoven, and K. E. Warneryd (eds.), *Handbook of Economic Psychology*, Dordrecht, The Netherlands: Kluwer.

HM Revenue and Customs (2008). *Supplement to Notices 700/1 and 700/11*. Retrieved July 12, 2008, from http://customs.hmrc.gov.uk.

Keen, M. and Smith, S. (2006), "VAT fraud and evasion: What do we know and what can be done?", *National Tax Journal*, 59: 861–87.

Kirchler, E. (2007) *The Economic Psychology of Tax Behaviour*, Cambridge, UK: Cambridge University Press.

Lewis, A. (1982), *The Psychology of Taxation*. Oxford, UK: Martin Robertson.

Livingstone, A. and Haslam, S. A. (2008), "The importance of social identity content in a setting of chronic social conflict: The case of intergroup relations in Northern Ireland", *British Journal of Social Psychology*, 47: 1–21.

McKerchar, M. (1995) "Understanding small business taxpayers: Their sources of information and level of knowledge of taxation", *Australian Tax Forum*, 12: 25–41.

Mittone, L. (2001). "VAT evasion: An experimental approach", University of Trento: Technical Report 5, Department of Economics (available through University of Trento e-prints). Trento, Italy: University of Trento.

Morris, R. C. (1956) "Typology of norms", *American Sociological Review*, 21: 610–13.

Myles, G. D. and Naylor, R. A. (1996) "A model of tax evasion with group conformity and social customs", *European Journal of Political Economy*, 12: 49–66.

National Audit Office (1994) *HM Customs and Excise: Costs to Business of Complying with VAT Requirements*, London, UK: HMSO.

Noble, P. (2000), "Qualitative research results: The New Zealand cash economy – a study of tax evasion amongst small and medium businesses", paper presented at the Centre for Tax System Integrity first international conference, Canberra, Australia.

O'Gorman, H. J. (1986) "The discovery of pluralistic ignorance: An ironic lesson", *Journal of the History of the Behavioral Sciences*, 22: 333–47.

Owen, R. (2007) "Pope set to declare income tax evasion socially unjust", *The Times*, August.

Porcano, T. M. (1988) "Correlates of tax evasion", *Journal of Economic Psychology*, 9: 47–67.

Prentice, D. A. and Miller, D. T. (1996) "Pluralistic ignorance and the perpetuation of social norms by unwitting actors", in M. Zanna (ed.), *Advances in Experimental Social Psychology*, San Diego, CA: Academic Press.

Sackmann, S. (1989) "The framers of culture: The conceptual views of anthropology, organizational theory, and management", paper presented at the Academy of Management Annual Meeting. Washington, August.

Schein, E. H. (1996) "Culture: The missing concept in organizational studies", *Administrative Science Quarterly*, 41: 229–40.

Sherif, M. (1936). *The Psychology of Social Norms*, New York, NY: Harper.

Shover, N., Job, J. and Carroll, A. (2003), "The ATO compliance model in action: A case study of building and construction", in V. Braithwaite (ed.), *Taxing Democracy: Understanding Tax Avoidance and Evasion*, Aldershot, UK: Ashgate.

Sigala, M. (1999) "Tax communication and social influence: Evidence from a British Sample", unpublished doctoral thesis, University of Exeter, UK.

Sigala, M., Burgoyne, C., and Webley, P. (1999) "Tax communication and social influence: Evidence from a British sample", *Journal of Community and Applied Social Psychology*, 9: 237–41.

Taylor, N. (2003) "Understanding taxpayer attitudes through understanding taxpayer identities", in V. Braithwaite (ed.), *Taxing Democracy: Understanding Tax Avoidance and Evasion*, Aldershot, UK: Ashgate.

The Times (2007) "Quote of the day", *The Times*, September 12, p. 1.

Torgler, B. (2005) "Tax morale in Latin America", *Public Choice*, 122: 133–57.

Turner, J. C. (1991) *Social Influence*, Buckingham, UK: Open University Press.

Turner, J. C., Oakes, P. J., Haslam, S. A., and McGarty, C. (1994) "Self and collective: cognition and social context", *Personality and Social Psychology Bulletin*, 20, 454–63.

Tyler, T. (1990) *Why People Obey the Law*, New Haven, CT: Yale University Press.

Vogel, J. (1974) "Taxation and public opinion in Sweden: An interpretation of recent survey data", *National Tax Journal*, 27: 499–513.

Wallschutzky, I. G. (1984) "Possible causes of tax evasion", *Journal of Economic Psychology*, 5: 371–84.

Wallschutzky, I. G. (1996) "Issues in research methods: With reference to income tax Research", unpublished manuscript, University of Newcastle, Australia.

Webley, P. (2004) "Tax compliance by businesses", in H. Sjögren and G. Skogh (eds.), *New Perspectives on Economic Crime*, Cheltenham, UK: Edward Elgar.

Webley, P., Robben, H., and Morris, I. (1988) "Social comparison, attitudes and tax evasion in a shop simulation", *Social Behaviour*, 3: 219–28.

Webley, P., Adams, C. J., and Elffers, H (2006) "Value added tax compliance", in E. J. McCaffery and J. Slemrod (eds.), *Behavioral Public Finance: Toward a New Agenda*, New York, NY: Russell Sage.

Wenzel, M. (2002) "The impact of outcome orientation and justice concerns on tax compliance: The role of taxpayers' identity", *Journal of Applied Psychology*, 87: 629–45.

Wenzel, M. (2004) "An analysis of norm processes in tax compliance", *Journal of Economic Psychology*, 25: 213–28.

Wenzel, M. (2005a) "Misperception of social norms about tax compliance: From theory to intervention", *Journal of Economic Psychology*, 26: 862–83.

Wenzel, M. (2005b) "The multiplicity of taxpayer identities and their implications for tax ethics", Working Paper No. 78, Canberra: Australian National University, Centre for Tax System Integrity.

Wenzel, M. (2007) "The multiplicity of taxpayer identities and their implications for tax ethics", *Law and Policy*, 29: 31–50.

Yeh, C. M. (1997) "On the reform of mainland China's value added tax system", *Issues and Studies*, 33: 64–86.

13 Tax evasion, the informal sector, and tax morale in LAC countries

James Alm and Jorge Martinez-Vazquez

Introduction

It is well accepted that most people do not like to pay taxes, and, for this funda-mental reason, it is hard for tax administrations to levy and collect taxes, any-where and any time. However, taxing certain kinds of activities, sectors, or individuals – the so-called "informal sector" – is an additional challenge for tax administrations in both developing and developed countries, and the "fiscal gap" that arises from the failure to tax this sector can be quite large. This issue is especially pressing in Latin America and Caribbean (LAC) countries, where often over half of the workforce is found in the informal sector.

In this chapter we examine taxation and tax compliance in LAC countries and beyond, focusing on several main questions: What is meant by the "informal sector"? What is the size of informal sector in LAC countries? What are some effects from an informal sector, including the size of the "fiscal gap"? What are the reasons for this fiscal gap? What can be done to address these various issues? Using the size of the informal sector as a proxy for the amount of tax evasion, we find that tax evasion is quite prevalent in LAC countries – a prevalence that is due both to tax administrative problems and to a societal culture that often generates low tax morale. Measures to combat evasion include administrative improvements consistent with the punishment paradigm and also with the service paradigm views of compliance, as well as changes in societal institutions that address tax morale.

Basic structural features of LAC tax systems and economies

We begin with an overview of the tax systems in LAC countries, in particular the basic structural features of personal income taxes (PIT), corporate income taxes (CIT), and value-added taxes (VAT) or other general consumption taxes. There is a great variety of approaches as to what is taxed, what is exempted, what the rate structures are, and so on.

In the case of the PIT, for example, Bolivia has a flat rate tax, while Colombia has a multiplicity of progressive rates (132 in all) ranging from 0.26 percent to 35 percent. Chile also has a very progressive schedule, with eight brackets, and minimum and maximum rates of 5 percent and 40 percent, respectively. On the other hand, Uruguay has no PIT. In the area of exemptions, most income from capital is exempt in Argentina (although Argentina imposes a wealth tax on gross asset values, with rates ranging from 0.5 percent to 0.75 percent), while most other LAC countries tax capital income; however, realized capital gains are often either fully or partially exempt. Other forms of diversity in personal income taxation are provided by Mexico's low-income tax credit, which no other country in the LAC region uses. Diversity is also shown by the fact that several countries provide partial or total credit for VAT paid.

There is more uniformity in the structure of the CIT, especially in the definition of the tax base, but even here the rates imposed vary considerably, ranging from 10 percent to 38.5 percent. In the case of the VAT, most LAC countries operate with a single rate but again there are significant differences in rates, ranging from 5 percent in Panama to 23 percent in Uruguay. Although most countries zero-rate exports, there are wide differences in the scope of exempted commodities.

Diversity in tax structure is accompanied by diversity in typical tax processes (for example, time spent preparing taxes, number of payments for tax purposes, and so on), the overall level of taxation as a percentage of GDP, and the composition of tax revenues (e.g., the direct/indirect tax revenue shares). Information on these variables is presented in Appendix Table 13A.1. For example, the average number of payments that the typical taxpayer across the LAC region has to make is 41, but it is as high as 68 in the case of Colombia and as low as 8 for Ecuador. The average business spends 430 hours in filing and paying taxes, but there are wide variations, ranging from 2,600 hours in Brazil to 224 hours in El Salvador and 198 hours in Suriname. The ratio of tax revenue to GDP in LAC countries is relatively low, at 11.85 percent as an average for the period 1995–2005. This figure is fairly representative of the countries in the region, but there are some outliers. For example, the tax revenue to GDP ratio was as high as 17.80 percent in Uruguay, and as low as 9.54 percent in Guatemala.[1] On average, taxes on domestic good and services are twice as important (as a percent of total revenues) as taxes on income, profits, and capital gains. Of course, there are again significant variations across countries. The share of indirect domestic taxation in total revenues is 58 percent in Mexico and 56 percent in Guatemala, but only 9 percent in Panama. Many countries in the LAC region still rely quite significantly on taxes on international trade. For example, during the period 1995–2005, Argentina received on average over 15 percent of its revenues from taxes on international trade.

There is also diversity across LAC countries by size of GDP, its composition, and the level of GDP per capita (Appendix Table 13A.1). GDP per capita in Argentina over 1995–2005 averaged roughly $12,000, while in Bolivia per capita GDP was $2,400 and in Nicaragua it was $3,210. However, both Bolivia and Nicaragua had, during that period, significantly higher tax revenue to GDP ratios than Argentina. The composition of GDP, which likely affects the ability to raise taxes and the overall elasticity of tax revenues, also differed markedly across LAC countries. For example, value added from agriculture was only 6.18 percent in Chile and 7.02 percent in Argentina, while it reached 23.16 in Guatemala and 24.20 percent in Paraguay.

Given the existing statutory tax structures and the economic environments of each of the countries in the LAC region, the actual level of tax revenues raised in each country depends on the ability and willingness to administer the existing taxes. There is some evidence that the overall effectiveness in using the existing tax structure differs significantly across LAC countries. For example, VAT productivity (defined as the yield of each percent point of the VAT rate as a share of GDP) ranges from a high of 0.64 in Chile to a low of 0.17 in Guatemala.[2]

A conventional way to look at the performance of tax systems is to ask whether the country's tax effort is "in line" with other countries of the same level of development and general economic characteristics. Although it is clear that there is no definitive way to establish how high taxes should be in a country, comparison with international practice allows us to know how far a particular country's taxes may be below or above the international norm. If the level of such "tax effort" is low relative to the international norm, then this would be an indication that less than the adequate level of public services and infrastructure may be being provided, and that tax effort could increase without it appearing to be a "high tax" country to potential foreign direct investors.[3]

However, different countries may differ in their ability to collect taxes because of different economic structures. To control for these differences, regression analysis is typically used to estimate the average capacity to collect taxes for a sample of countries, controlling for GDP per capita and other proxies for the ability to collect taxes, such as value added in agriculture as a share of GDP (Bahl, 1971; Bird, 1976). These regressions are then used to generate the level of "predicted taxes" that, on average, each country would be able to collect, given the per capita income and other characteristics of the given country. A comparison of "actual taxes" of the country versus its "predicted taxes" (expressed as a ratio) then gives a measure of "tax effort". If actual taxes are greater than predicted taxes, then the country is said to have a relatively high tax effort; if actual taxes are less than predicted taxes, then tax effort is relatively low.

There are many different specifications that can be used in estimating tax effort across countries. Here, we estimate tax effort for two different periods: the 1990s and the 2000s (through 2005), using a simple specification that has worked well in numerous previous studies. Our specification has the ratio of actual tax collections to GDP as the dependent variable; explanatory variables include per capita GDP in US dollars as a proxy for greater ability to collect taxes, the ratio of agricultural value added to GDP as a negative and unfavorable tax handle, and the rate of population growth as an indicator of tax base growth. All these variables have shown to be mostly significant in previous studies. The data used for the estimation are from the International Monetary Fund's *Government Finance Statistics (GFS) Yearbook* and the World Bank's World Development Indicators. Due to missing data, only 105 countries (out of 219) are used for the 1990s regression, and 98 countries for the 2000s regression.[4]

The implied tax effort results for LAC countries (denoted "index") from these regressions are reported in Table 13.1. (More detailed, alternative regression results are presented later in several other tables.) These results for tax effort show that, with the general exception of the Caribbean area, tax effort in LAC countries is below par relative to international experience. However, there are some significant variations. For example, Chile and Nicaragua are close to an average international tax effort, but countries such as Guatemala and others are well below the expected international norm. There appears to be a generalized increase in tax effort in LAC countries between the 1990s and the 2000s, although this tendency is weak.

There can be multiple causes behind the relatively low tax efforts. First, as we emphasize in later discussion, a major source of difficulties is the existence of sizable underground economies and informal sectors. Second, the overall level of tax compliance is low because of a high level of tax evasion and a poor performance of the tax administration. Third, tax policy itself could have been contributing to lackluster collections by allowing excessive deductions and

Table 13.1 Tax effort in selected LAC countries in the 1990s and early 2000s

Country	Average 1990s			Average 2000–2004		
	Actual	Forecast	Index	Actual	Forecast	Index
Argentina				12.176	15.297	0.796
Belize	19.819	17.119	1.158			
Brazil	10.995	16.246	0.677			
Chile				16.285	16.242	1.003
Colombia	12.039	17.123	0.703	13.148	14.231	0.924
Costa Rica	13.479	17.337	0.777	13.020	16.308	0.798
Dominican Republic				15.143	16.443	0.921
El Salvador	22.741	19.273	1.180	10.967	15.195	0.722
Grenada						
Guatemala	8.165	13.820	0.591	10.159	13.445	0.756
Jamaica	23.541	19.446	1.211	24.507	17.447	1.405
Mexico	11.041	17.536	0.630	11.650	16.159	0.721
Nicaragua	16.149	14.549	1.110	14.104	14.727	0.958
Panama	12.155	21.440	0.567	9.730	17.939	0.542
Paraguay	9.984	14.871	0.671	9.974	14.109	0.707
Peru	12.616	16.296	0.774	12.624	14.141	0.893
Trinidad and Tobago	22.440	19.984	1.123			
Uruguay	17.822	17.355	1.027			
St Kitts and Nevis	19.805	20.949	0.945	23.480	17.787	1.320
St Vincent and the Grenadines	22.286	19.182	1.162			
Venezuela	14.279	17.601	0.811	11.888	15.041	0.790

Source: Calculations by authors.

Notes
"Forecast" values are based on OLS regressions using data from World Development Indicators, World Bank (2006). "Index" values are calculated as actual taxes (as a percent of GDP) divided by Forecast revenues (as a percent of GDP).

exemptions in the major taxes. Fourth, the overall buoyancy of the tax systems may have been low over time – for example, because of tariff/trade reforms and subsequent difficulties in recovering the revenue losses from the customs tariff with domestic taxes.[5] Fifth, different tax systems tend to show different abilities to adapt to the changes in economic structure. In many countries, the area of services continues to expand while manufacturing shrinks, but service firms are more difficult to tax than manufacturing businesses. Sixth, the overall level of tax effort in a country also depends directly on the revenue performance of sub-national governments, when these jurisdictions are charged with raising their own revenues and have some degree of discretion in doing so. Seventh, there may be political reasons for keeping the level of tax effort more or less constant.[6] Countries may tend to achieve an equilibrium position with respect to the size and nature of their fiscal systems that largely reflects the balance of political forces and institutions, and countries may leave that position only after a significant institutional shock.[7]

The taxation performances in LAC countries, partial and in many ways unsatisfactory as they are, suggest several general patterns:

- Relatively low levels of taxation in most LAC countries are not a recent phenomenon. Over the past few decades, taxes have not gone up in LAC countries. Although some rates have risen, mainly for the VAT, other rates (mainly for income taxes) have declined, leading to positive but small changes in tax effort over time.
- National patterns of taxation have been persistent over time. Countries that had relatively high taxes at the end of the 1970s continued to be above the regional average in the 1990s and 2000s, and countries that depended more on income than on consumption taxes continued on the whole to do so over the decades.
- Despite the relative constancy in both tax levels and composition of tax structures across and within countries, many changes have taken place in tax policy across LAC countries over the past few decades. Economic and political circumstances have changed dramatically at times in some countries, and sometimes tax systems have changed with them.

In the following sections we explore reasons for this generally low tax effort.

Weak tax enforcement capacity and corruption in the LAC region

Although the data are not generally available to know with certainty, there appears to be weak enforcement capacity across the LAC region, especially with regard to audit systems, which tend to be outdated and underfunded. There is more recent survey information that tax administrations in LAC countries also suffer from corruption and bribery problems, and that the prevalence of some of these problems is worse in the LAC region than in other regions of the world.

Before we look at the evidence on enforcement capacity, we discuss some of the survey evidence on corrupt practices in tax administration.

Appendix Table 13A-2 presents some recent survey evidence of significant levels of bribery in tax administration practices across LAC countries, and also some indirect evidence on under-reporting and evasion. These data are based on the World Bank's Enterprise Surveys 2005–2006. Regarding the existence of under-reporting, the average for the sample of LAC countries represented in Appendix Table 13A-2 indicates that the sales amount reported by a typical firm for tax purposes was just above three-fourths of "true" sales. However, there were significant differences across countries, with the typical firm in Chile reporting over 98 percent of sales, while that figure was 67 percent in Brazil, and 66 percent in Nicaragua. By comparison with other regions of the world, only countries in East Asia and the Pacific average a lower percent of sales reported; notably, the survey reveals a slightly higher percentage of sales reported in Sub-Saharan Africa countries than in the LAC region.

Regarding the presence of bribery in tax administration practices, the World Bank's Enterprise Surveys ask questions about the practice of "paying bribes to get things done", or "firms expected to give gifts in meetings with tax inspectors". The results by country in Appendix Table 13A-2 show significant variations across LAC countries. In general, corrupt practices have a higher presence in LAC countries vis-à-vis countries in other regions of the world.

Despite the data limitations, there is evidence that LAC countries are far from homogenous in their ability to collect taxes. This theme is well developed by Bergman (2003), who compares the success of Chile and the failure of Argentina to collect taxes over the past several decades. These two countries differ considerably in their ability to enforce taxes. As reported by Bergman (2003), tax evasion in Argentina is close to twice that in Chile, although the tax structures and the tax administration apparatus of the two countries are roughly similar. Bergman (2003) also argues that factors beyond tax administration capacity determine the different levels of compliance in both countries, such as the ability of government to create a permanent credible threat of being caught and punished. Since the 1970s both Argentina and Chile have undergone the modernization of their tax administration agencies, involving collection and audit schemes and other measures of punitive capacity. Where these two countries have differed is in the ability of the governments to sustain these reforms over time and to "...build a strong and autonomous tax administration capable of deterring tax evaders" (Bergman, 2003: 613.) Chile has been successful in creating improved tax compliance on a sustained basis, while Argentina and other major countries in Latin America (e.g., Colombia, Mexico, Peru, and Bolivia) have not. Bergman (2003) emphasizes especially that the difference in the performances of Chile and Argentina lies in the very significant disparities in the subjective perception of being caught cheating in each country, and, ultimately, in the credibility of sanctions. While sociological and cultural factors play a role, these are largely endogenously determined by efficient, non-corrupt, and credible government institutions, especially the tax administration. This is a theme to which we return later.

A digression on the theoretical foundations of individual compliance behavior

In the context of penalties and other sanctions, the standard economic approach to the analysis of tax compliance has relied upon the economics-of-crime methodology first applied to tax compliance by Allingham and Sandmo (1972).[8] This approach gives the sensible result that compliance depends upon enforcement. However, it is essential to recognize that this approach also concludes that an individual pays taxes because – and only because – of the economic consequences of detection and punishment. Again, this is a plausible and productive insight, with the obvious implication that the government can encourage greater tax compliance by increasing the audit and penalty rates. The many extensions of this economics-of-crime approach considerably complicate the theoretical analyses, and generally render clear-cut analytical results impossible. Nevertheless, they retain the basic approach and the basic result: individuals focus exclusively on the financial incentives of the evasion gamble, and they pay taxes solely because they fear detection and punishment.

However, it is clear to many observers that compliance cannot be explained entirely by such financial considerations, especially those generated by the level of enforcement (Elffers, 1991; Graetz and Wilde, 1985; Smith and Kinsey, 1987). For example, the percentage of individual income tax returns that are subject to a thorough tax audit is generally quite small in most countries – often less than 1 percent of all returns – and typically much lower in LAC countries. Indeed, the puzzle of tax compliance behavior is why people pay taxes, not why they evade them (Alm et al., 1992). This observation suggests that the compliance decision must be affected in ways not captured by the basic economics-of-crime approach.

The limited ability to incorporate many relevant factors, or to incorporate them in a meaningful way, has meant that the standard theoretical analysis of the compliance decision is largely unable to explain the level of tax reporting, even when it has more success in explaining the change in reporting in response to policy innovations. Consequently, most of the theoretical analyses that economists have produced in the context of developed economies give limited help in understanding the problem of tax evasion in LAC countries. As Alm and Martinez-Vazquez (2003) argue, a meaningful study of tax compliance requires recognition of the important, perhaps decisive, role of societal institutions in the tax compliance decision. It is in this context that "tax morale" plays an especially important role, as discussed in more detail later.

The presence of the "informal sector"

The starting point here must be to define precisely the "informal sector" and its participants. Are these individuals who mainly operate in small- and medium-sized enterprises? Are they mainly self-employed professionals, individual proprietors, or farmers? There is no single definition that is universally accepted.

Indeed, all taxpayers are hard to tax in one way or another. However, there is a group of taxpayers that it is considerably more difficult to tax than the rest. Who are they, and how do we identify them?

No precise and widely accepted definition exists of the informal sector – sometimes also referred to as the "hard-to-tax" (HTT) sector – but there are various notions. As noted by Terkper (2003) and Das-Gupta (1994), these are taxpayers who often fail to register voluntarily. Even when they do register, they generally fail to keep appropriate records of their earnings and costs, they frequently do not file their tax returns promptly, and they tend to be tax delinquent.

Independently of the right definition, there is considerable consensus in the tax literature regarding the identity of those in the informal sector. Terkper (2003) and Engelschalk (2003) identify these agents as those running small-and-medium-sized firms, professionals, and farmers. Similarly, Tanzi and de Jan-scher Casanegra (1989) identify them mainly as individual proprietorships, farmers, and professionals

The so-called HTT includes taxpayers in both the informal and the formal sectors of the economy. In the informal sector, the hard-to-tax may include unregistered merchants and professionals who are involved in cash transactions or even barter (Terkper, 2003). In the formal sector, the HTT may include professionals with a college education, as well as small manufacturing firms and commercial farms who are capable of keeping accounts and who often do so for purposes other than paying taxes. Thus, both types of the HTT may or may not operate in a cash economy, and they may or may not be capable of providing the tax authorities with relevant information, but are always unwilling to do so; therefore, the tax authorities have a hard time extracting the information from them (Bird and Oldman, 1990).

The idea of the informal sector is closely related to several other important concepts, including the shadow economy and tax evasion. Indeed, in terms of their economic base, individuals in the informal sector are likely to be quite similar to those who operate in the shadow economy.[9] As with the informal sector, most authors trying to measure the "shadow economy" face the difficulty of how to define it. Smith (1994) defines it as "market-based production of goods and services, whether legal or illegal, that escapes detection in the official estimates of GDP". A more commonly used working definition is all currently unregistered economic activities that contribute to the officially calculated and observed GNP or GDP (Feige, 1989; Frey and Pommerehne, 1984; Schneider, 2002; Schneider and Enste, 2000, 2002).

Of course, all estimates of the informal sector and the shadow economy are subject to significant data limitations, and their interpretation is subject to important caveats. Regardless, we use measures of the shadow economy to measure the informal sector, and also to measure the amount of tax evasion – that is, the proxy measures that we use for the size of the informal sector are estimates of the shadow economy and of tax evasion in different countries around the world, generated from the work of Schneider (2002) and Schneider and Enste (2000, 2002). The next section presents these estimates.

What is the size of the informal sector in LAC countries and beyond?

Schneider (2002) and Schneider and Enste (2000, 2002) have used various methods and time periods to estimate the size of the shadow economy for single countries and groups of countries. These estimates are presented in Figure 13.1, which summarizes the LAC country estimates. The physical input (electricity) method, the currency (money) demand, and the model (or DYMIMIC) approach are used for the estimates for developing countries.

The results for 17 LAC countries for 1999/2000 showed the average size of the shadow economy of these countries to be 41.0 percent of official GNP. The largest shadow economy was in Bolivia (67.1 percent), followed by Panama (64.1 percent) and Peru (59.9 percent); the smallest shadow economies were in Chile (19.8 percent) and Argentina (25.4 percent).

Overall, the average sizes of the shadow economies of South and Latin America and of Africa are generally similar, and somewhat larger than in Asia. The sizes of the shadow economies in Africa are typically quite large. For example, the average size of the shadow economy in Africa was 41 percent of GNP for the year 1999/2000. As for other countries, the average size of the shadow economy for transition countries relative to official GNP was 38 percent for the year 1999/2000. OECD countries typically have a smaller shadow economy than the other country groupings; in European OECD countries in 1999/2000 it was 18 percent, while in the remaining OECD countries it was 13.5 percent.

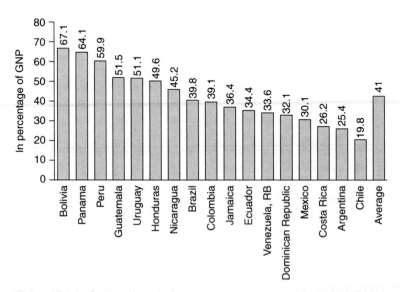

Figure 13.1 Latin America – shadow economy as percent of GNP, 1999/2000.

What are some effects from an informal sector, including the size of the "fiscal gap"?

Despite their limitations, these estimates of the shadow economy are used in the rest of the chapter as a proxy measure of the informal sector, in order to quantify various aspects and effects of the informal sector.

A first issue is the determinants of the size of the informal sector, and Table 13.2 presents some simple correlations between size and possible causes. The relative importance of the informal sector is likely to vary across countries and over time, and to vary according to some obvious determinants. A priori, there should be a larger relative presence when there are more taxpayers unprepared to keep books of accounts and where the tax administration lacks the means both to help and to audit those other taxpayers who can keep their accounts but refuse to do so. Thus, the problem of the informal sector is likely to decrease in importance with the level of development. This hypothesis receives some support from the simple correlation coefficient between our proxy for the informal sector and GDP per capita in Table 13.2.

The problem of the informal sector could also be seen as becoming more serious when the public sector is trying to raise more taxes, exercising a higher tax effort. Perhaps surprisingly, however, this hypothesis is not supported by the correlation coefficient between the size of the informal sector and tax effort in Table 13.2; this result may reflect the fact that tax effort is highly correlated with GDP per capita.

For the same level of general economic development, as measured by GDP per capita, we would expect the size of the informal sector to increase with the relative share of agriculture in GDP and decrease with the share in GDP of manufacturing.[10] The positive correlation coefficient for the share of agriculture in Table 13.2 supports the notion of higher incidence of the informal sector with a larger relative presence of agriculture, although we do not control for the level of development in these simple correlations.

We would also expect the problems of the informal sector to become more acute in societies with higher levels of corruption. We measured the latter through the corruption index from Amnesty International, which "...relates to perceptions of the degree of corruption as seen by business people, risk analysts and the general public, and ranges between 10 (highly clean) and 0 (highly corrupt)". This hypothesis is supported by the negative correlation coefficient in

Table 13.2 Correlation coefficients between the shadow economy and selected variables

	GDP per capita	Tax revenue/ GDP	Manufacturing value added/ GDP	Agriculture/ GDP	Corruption index
Shadow economy/GNP	−0.50	−0.26	0.02	0.45	−0.60

Source: Calculations by authors.

Table 13.2. Thus, the shadow economy seems highly complementary with corruption: a less corrupt economy (and so an economy with a higher corruption index) tends to be an economy with a smaller informal sector.

Dabla-Norris *et al.* (2005) identify the determinants of the size of the informal sector, including tax and regulation burdens, financial market development, and the quality of the legal system. They find evidence that practically all the factors previously identified in the literature play a role in explaining the presence of informality. They particularly emphasize the role played by the quality of the legal system. Similarly, Loayza *et al.* (2005) find that a heavier regulatory burden in product and labor markets leads to the higher presence of informality. Schneider and Enste (2000) find that increasing taxation and social security contributions, rising state regulations, and corruption all lead to a higher incidence of informality.

On this last point, there is a growing empirical literature linking corruption to informality (Dreher *et al.*, 2005; Friedman *et al.*, 2000; Johnson *et al.*, 2000). Also, there is some evidence of differential effects of corruption – effects that depend upon the level of income in the country. According to Dreher and Schneider (2006), corruption may cause larger (smaller) informal shadow economies in low (high)-income countries.

As for some effects of the informal sector on taxation, an obvious and immediate effect of the presence of a large informal sector is to reduce the revenue potential of any given tax structure; that is, the existence of an informal sector increases the size of the "fiscal gap". In addition, however, we argue that the presence of the informal sector also affects the choice of tax structure (e.g., the composition of taxes).

Measuring the fiscal gap – indeed, measuring tax evasion more generally – is notoriously difficult. Still, there is widespread evidence that tax evasion is extensive and commonplace in nearly all countries. For the United States, the most recent estimates from the Internal Revenue Service suggest that the amount of unpaid federal individual and corporate income taxes totaled $345 billion for 2000, with an annual growth rate of 10 percent since 1973. There is also some limited evidence for other countries, based on examination of individual tax returns, on tax effort/tax capacity estimations, on survey methods, on discrepancies between tax-related information and national income accounts, or between income and consumption in the national income accounts, and the like.

To our knowledge, there exists very limited direct information on the revenue losses implied by the informal sector per se. For the United States, Kenadjian (1982) reports on the findings of a 1979 IRS study that estimated total unreported legal sector income of $75 billion in 1976, of which self-employment income was $33 billion; a considerable share of unreported self-employment income could be considered as belonging to the hard-to-tax group. Also, Terkper (2003) states that developing countries lose tax revenue from the informal sector in proportionally greater amounts than do developed countries, because small and medium traders (e.g., the hard-to-tax) tend to thrive in underground economies.

There are at least two possible ways that we can examine the impact of the informal sector on tax revenues. First, we can explore how its presence affects the overall tax effort in any country. As discussed earlier, there is a fairly extensive literature regarding the determination of tax effort, as well as on its limitations. Despite these limitations, our hypothesis is that a greater presence of the informal sector will reduce the tax effort in any country. The regression in Table 13.3 explores the effects of the relative size of the informal sector/shadow economy on a measure of tax effort, defined as total tax revenues in 2000 divided by GNP for the same year. We follow the literature on tax effort in our basic specification. We include as separate control variables GDP per capita, and the ratio of the shadow economy to GNP. We also introduce an interaction term with these two variables, which allows for a differential impact of the informal sector on tax effort at different levels of development. In particular, higher-income countries may have better coping mechanisms in tax enforcement to deal with the problems presented by the informal sector. Finally, we include the ratio of taxes on internal trade to GDP, as a measure of a tax handle.

The impact of the informal sector on tax effort in Table 13.3 indicates that the intensity of the informal sector reduced the overall tax effort for a sample of developed and developing countries in 2000. However, this impact on tax effort is dampened with increases in the level of economic development.[11]

The second approach to examining the impact of the informal sector on tax revenues is to estimate directly the revenue losses induced by this group. To do this, we continue to make use of the assumption that the tax base of the informal sector can be approximated by the size of the shadow economy, and we also assume that the effective average tax rate in the formal (non-shadow) economy is also the effective average tax rate that would apply to the hard-to-tax. Both

Table 13.3 Determinants of tax effort

Independent variable	Coefficient (t-statistic)
GDP per capita	−0.01
	(−2.69)
Shadow economy/GNP	−0.23
	(−2.59)
(Shadow economy/GNP) × GDP per capita	9.17E-05
	(3.42)
Taxes on internal trade/GDP	−1.1E-05
	(−0.46)
Constant	0.24
	(5.94)
Observations	41
R^2	0.34

Source: Calculations by authors.

Notes
The dependent variable is total tax revenue divided by GNP in year 2000. White corrected t-statistics are in parentheses. The equations are estimated by OLS methods.

assumptions are open to question, and so our approach is only a suggestion. Indeed, our estimates of the revenue loss from the informal sector seem likely to be upper-boundary estimates, for several reasons. First, the actual size of the hard-to-tax may be smaller than the underground economy. Second, the effective average tax rate that would apply to activities in the informal sector is likely to be lower than that of the regular formal economy.

Table 13.4 shows the summary statistics for the losses in revenue for two groups of developing and developed countries, with the losses in revenue expressed as a percentage of potential tax revenue, where potential tax revenues are derived from the estimates in Table 13.3 and losses in revenues are calculated as the difference between potential tax revenue and actual tax revenue. Revenue losses tend to be considerably higher (in relative terms) in developing countries than in developed countries; they also tend to show higher dispersion in developing countries. The estimates of losses can represent up to 40 percent of total potential revenues in developing countries.

There is also some work that examines the role of societal institutions on tax effort. For example, governance, corruption, the rule of law, trust in government, and similar factors seem likely to affect estimates of tax effort. In this regard, Bird et al. (2006) have studied the role of demand factors such as societal institutions in explaining relative revenue performance in developing countries. Their basic premise is that although traditional "supply factors", such as the availability of tax handles and the structure of tax bases, clearly matter in explaining tax effort, there is also a need to account for citizen attitudes in response to government performance as shaped by societal institutions. To account for such "demand factors", or societal institutions, they study the explanatory power of variables such as a quality of governance index, regulation of entry, inequality in income and wealth distribution, fiscal decentralization, tax morale, and the shadow economy. Their empirical results strongly suggest that institutions play a significant role in the determination of the level of tax effort of developing and transition countries. Although the conventional supply factors play a robust and significant role, demand factors also clearly matter.

The informal sector may also affect the structure of the tax system itself, given the constraints imposed by economic structure, administrative capabilities, and taxpayer voluntary compliance on the choice of tax structure. Clearly, a higher presence of the informal sector in developing countries and also in developed countries may constrain the optimal choice of the tax mix. A heavy

Table 13.4 Ratio of revenue loss from the hard-to-tax to potential tax revenue

Sample	Observations	Mean	Standard deviation	Minimum	Maximum
Developing	57	0.25	0.07	0.11	0.40
Industrialized	19	0.15	0.05	0.08	0.22
Full sample	76	0.22	0.07	0.08	0.40

Source: Calculations by authors.

presence of informal activity leaves less room for sophisticated taxes requiring more reporting by taxpayers and more complex auditing by tax administrators. Thus, we hypothesize that a larger informal sector should be associated with more reliance on indirect taxes (especially excises), on taxes on international trade, and on natural resource extraction.

We can approximate the tax mix in a variety of ways. Five possible measures, or dependent variables, are as follows:

1   Ratio of Direct Taxes to Indirect Taxes:

$$Dependent\ 1 = \frac{\text{Taxes on Income, Profit, and Captial Gains}}{(\text{Domestic Taxes on Goods and Services } + \text{ Taxes on International Trade})}$$

2   *Ratio of Direct Taxes to Indirect Domestic Taxes:*

$$Dependent\ 2 = \frac{\text{Taxes on Income, Profit, and Captial Gains}}{\text{Domestic Taxes on Goods and Services}}$$

3   *Ratio of Special Taxes to Total Tax Revenue:*

$$Dependent\ 3 = \frac{(\text{Exises} + \text{Taxes on Income, Profit, and Captial Gains})}{\text{Domestic Taxes on Goods and Services}}$$

4   *Ratio of Direct Taxes to Total Tax Revenue:*

$$Dependent\ 4 = \frac{\text{Taxes on Income, Profit, and Captial Gains}}{\text{Domestic Taxes on Goods and Services}}$$

5   *Ratio of Domestic Taxes on Goods and Services to Total Tax Revenue:*

$$Dependent\ 5 = \frac{\text{Taxes on Income on Goods and Services}}{\text{Total Tax Revenue}}$$

Table 13.5 shows the results of simple OLS regressions explaining the variation across the sample of countries in tax mix, measured in the above five possible ways; independent variables include the relative size of the informal sector (again measured by the share of the shadow economy in GDP), as well as several control variables, including GDP per capita, the share of the manufacturing sector in GDP, and the openness of the economy.[12]

The results in Table 13.5 are generally supportive of the hypothesis that, after controlling for the level of economic development and other factors, a larger informal sector leads to a heavier reliance on indirect taxation. As expected, the coefficient for the shadow economy is negative and statistically significant for dependent variables 1, 2, and 4, and positive and significant for variable 5. Note

Table 13.5 Shadow economy effects on tax composition (2000)

Explanatory variable	Dependent 1	Dependent 2	Dependent 3	Dependent 4	Dependent 5
GDP per capita	0.21	−0.02	−0.02	0.001	0.005
	(0.92)	(−1.55	(2.36)	(0.29)	(3.08)
Shadow economy /GNP	−1.48	−2.71	−0.04	−0.34	0.41
	(−2.34)	(−1.85)	(−0.24)	(−2.15)	(2.94)
Manufacturing valued added/GDP	−0.01	−0.05	−0.002	−0.001	−0.005
	(−0.51)	(−0.81)	(−0.56)	(−0.30)	(−1.17)
Openness	−0.004	−0.006	−0.001	−0.002	0.001
	(−2.04)	(−1.62)	(−1.56)	(−2.41)	(1.55)
Constant	1.72	3.38	0.44	0.52	0.29
	(2.03)	(1.70)	(3.46)	(3.96)	(2.61)
Observations	41	42	38	43	42
R^2	0.11	0.10	0.24	0.21	0.19

Source: Calculations by authors.

Notes
The dependent variables are defined as:
Dependent 1 = ratio of direct taxes to indirect taxes
Dependent 2 = ratio of direct taxes to indirect domestic taxes
Dependent 3 = ratio of special taxes to total tax revenue
Dependent 4 = ratio of direct taxes to total tax revenue
Dependent 5 = ratio of domestic taxes on goods and services to total tax revenue.
See the text for detailed discussion. White corrected t-statistics for the OLS regressions are in parentheses.

that the shadow economy coefficient for dependent variable 3 is negative, the opposite of what was expected, but it is not statistically significant. The shadow economy should be much harder to reach through direct taxation than through indirect taxation. Not surprisingly, the openness of the economy also leads to a heavier reliance on indirect taxation. It is, however, surprising that higher levels of GDP per capita, after controlling for other factors, seem to lead to greater reliance on indirect taxation.

What are the reasons for the fiscal gap?

There are many suggested reasons for the high informality, the fiscal gap, and/or tax evasion. The most obvious is poor tax administration (for example, weak enforcement technology or capture of the tax administration by elites). There is much casual, and also some systematic, evidence that suggests that enforcement capacity, with the exception of Chile, is very low throughout the LAC region (Bergman, 2003; Taliercio, 2004; Tanzi and Shome, 1993). In particular, tax auditing systems tend to be outdated and underfunded. Because smaller firms are particularly costly to monitor, there tends to be a high concentration of tax collection on a small number of large firms (Gallagher, 2004). At the same time, larger firms usually have the political leverage to affect tax policy in ways that benefit them.

Some (for example, Frey, 1997) have also suggested that the intrinsic motivation to pay taxes – what is sometimes termed "tax morale" – may differ across countries, for reasons related to tax administration and enforcement but also to such factors as cultural norms. If taxpayer values are influenced by cultural norms, with different societal institutions acting as constraints and varying between different countries, then tax morale may be an important determinant of taxpayer compliance and other forms of behavior. However, isolating the reasons for these differences in tax morale is notoriously difficult.

Torgler (2005) presents information on tax morale in LAC countries, based on survey evidence from the World Values Survey (WVS) and the Latinobarómetro. The WVS is a worldwide investigation of socio-cultural and political change that collects comparative data on values and belief systems among peoples around the world. It is based on representative national samples of at least 1,000 individuals in a country, and has been conducted in more than 80 countries over multiple waves (or time periods). All surveys are done via face-to-face interviews at the respondents' homes and in their respective national languages. The sampling design consists of a multi-stage, random selection of sampling points, with a number of individual observations drawn from all administrative regional units, after stratification by region and by degree of urbanization. The survey results can be weighted to represent national population parameters.[13] The Latinobarómetro is a similar survey that focuses on 17 LAC countries for 1998. Both ask an identical question to all individuals in the sampled countries that can be used to derive an estimate of tax morale. Both surveys also ask a range of other questions on individual economic and demographic characteristics, as well as questions regarding societal attitudes about religion, and culture.

The general question to assess the level of tax morale is:

> Please tell me for each of the following statements whether you think it can always be justified, never be justified, or something in between: ... Cheating on tax if you have the chance ("never justified", code 1 from a ten-point scale where 1 = never and 10 = always).

The natural cut-off point is at the survey response of 1, because many respondents assert that cheating on tax is "never justified". The aggregate averages of tax morale in the 17 countries in the Latinobarómetro are given in Table 13.6.

Torgler (2005) finds that individuals who say that they know or have heard that others practice tax avoidance have significantly lower tax morale than others. He also finds lower tax morale in South America and Mexico than in the Central American or Caribbean regions; individuals in South America have a lower tax morale than those in Central America, by 10 percentage points, and individuals in Mexico have an especially lower tax morale (20 percentage points) than those in Central America. Also, Torgler (2005) finds that if individuals say that they trust that others will obey the law, say that they have trust in government officials, and say that they have "pride" in their country, then tax

Table 13.6 Tax morale in Latin America and the Caribbean, 1998

Country	Tax morale
Argentina	2.266
Bolivia	2.044
Brazil	2.165
Colombia	2.214
Costa Rica	2.100
Chile	2.209
Ecuador	1.910
El Salvador	2.205
Guatemala	2.556
Honduras	2.159
Mexico	1.732
Nicaragua	2.395
Panama	2.228
Paraguay	2.373
Peru	2.058
Uruguay	1.948
Venezuela ·	2.310

Source: Latinobarómetro.

Notes

"Tax Morale" is calculated as the simple average of individual responses in a country, scaled from 0 to 3, where 3 is the highest tax morale score (e.g., tax evasion is "never justified").

morale increases significantly. Individuals who are older, married, self-employed, salaried, and heads of a household tend to have higher tax morale. Of special importance, individuals who are more supportive of democratic government also have higher tax morale. More importantly, from the perspective of this chapter, Torgler (2005) finds that there is a significant positive correlation between tax morale and the size of the shadow economy. Tax policy or the structural features of the tax system can also be important determinants of the fiscal gap: what is taxed (e.g., income, consumption, wealth), what is exempted from taxation, and what are the rate structures of the various taxes? Some taxes are inherently harder to collect than others, and individuals are more resistant to some taxes (and some rate structures) than others.

What can be done to address the problem?

Methods to address tax evasion fall into several main categories.

First, there clearly is scope for improving tax administration systems in the traditional three areas of taxpayer registration, taxpayer audit, and collections. For example, taxpayer registration can be increased via better use of third-party information (e.g., cross-references between tax reporting, social security records, and data from the financial system). Audits can be made more effective via adoption of modern audit technology, including more systematic selection of returns for audit. There are fairly recent good examples of this in a number of countries, such as Chile (Bergman, 2003) and Spain (Martinez-Vazquez and Sanz, 2007). Collections could be increased by adding interest income to the tax base for the income tax, even if at reduced rates with a schedular treatment (Owens, 2006); by applying non-harsh penalties often and consistently (1999); by facilitating payments through the banking system; by allowing for simple cross-tax deductions (e.g., of interests payments on loans or mortgages); and by relying more heavily on source-withholding (Tanzi and Zee, 2000). These approaches are consistent with the traditional approach to taxpayer compliance, in which the taxpayer is seem mainly as a potential criminal who must be deterred from criminal activities; Alm and Martinez-Vazquez (2003) have termed this the "punishment paradigm" of tax compliance, and it has long been recognized by tax administrators and practitioners in an extensive list of country studies.

It is also – and increasingly – the case that tax administration reforms are not limited to these traditional enforcement mechanisms and have started to see the taxpayer more as a client in need of services. This alternative approach to tax administration reforms leads to a different set of policies, which emphasize the provision of taxpayer services via such things as:

- promoting taxpayer education and developing taxpayer services to assist taxpayers in every step of their filing returns and paying taxes
- broadcasting advertisements that link taxes with government services
- simplifying taxes and the payment of taxes
- promoting voluntary compliance by lowering the costs for taxpayers associated with filing their taxes
- ensuring relative stability of the tax system
- adopting the general principle of self-assessment
- promoting a taxpayer – and a tax administrator – "code of ethics".

Alm and Martinez-Vazquez (2003) term this approach the "service paradigm" of tax compliance. This second paradigm recognizes the role of enforcement, but also emphasizes the role of tax administration as a facilitator and a provider of services to taxpayer-citizens. As discussed later, this new paradigm for tax administration fits squarely with the perspective that emphasizes the role of a "social norm" in tax compliance; that is, government can change tax compliance by changing the social norm of tax compliance.

Second, the modernization and greater autonomy and specialization of tax administrations may facilitate their reorientation from the punishment paradigm to the service paradigm. The use of "semi-autonomous revenue authorities" and "large taxpayer units", with a more service-oriented approach to tax enforcement, has been shown in several countries to improve tax administration (Baer *et al.*, 2002; Mann, 2004; Silvani, 1992; Taliercio, 2004).

Third, there is scope for changes in tax structure (e.g., rates and bases) that can encourage more compliance. There is some evidence that lower tax marginal tax rates provide an incentive for greater payment of taxes (Alm *et al.*, 1991,

1993a; Gorodnichenko *et al.*, 2008). The effect of broader tax bases on incentives to comply is not known.

Fourth, more generally, and as suggested by our earlier discussion of the difficulties of the standard economics-of-crime approach to tax compliance, we believe that societal institutions, broadly defined, have a major impact on tax evasion. Here we highlight two such institutions.

One institution is what might be termed the "social norm" of compliance – what we have discussed above as tax morale. Although difficult to define precisely, a social norm can be distinguished by the feature that it is process-oriented, unlike the outcome orientation of individual rationality (Elster, 1989). A social norm therefore represents a pattern of behavior that is judged in a similar way by others, and that therefore is sustained in part by social approval or disapproval. Consequently, if others behave according to some socially accepted mode of behavior, then the individual will behave appropriately; if others do not so behave, then the individual will respond in kind.[14]

The existence of a social norm suggests that an individual will be more likely to comply as long as he or she believes that compliance is the social norm. Conversely, if non-compliance becomes pervasive, then the social norm of compliance disappears.[15] It is also likely, though not without controversy, that the social norm of compliance differs significantly across countries. If we take tax morale as a measure of this social norm, then there is much evidence that tax morale differs, and differs systematically, across countries.

This perspective also suggests that if government can affect the social norm of compliance, then such government policies represent a potentially significant tool in its battle with tax evaders. Of course, policies to change the social norm of compliance are difficult to determine in theory. There is some evidence from various social sciences that suggests that these norms can be affected by government institutions and policies.

The role of process in individual and group decisions is becoming increasingly recognized. For example, there is much behavioral science evidence that implies that greater individual participation in the decision process will foster an increased level of compliance, in part because participation implies some commitment to the institution, and such commitment in turn requires behavior that is consistent with words and actions. This notion implies that one dimension by which social norms can be affected is via individual participation in the decision process – for example, by voting. Also, survey evidence suggests that compliance is higher when taxpayers feel that they have a voice in the way their taxes will be spent. Under such circumstances, they are likely to feel more inclined to pay their taxes.

Another dimension by which social norms may be affected by government actions is related to the level of popular support for the government program. Widespread support tends to legitimize the public sector, and so imposes some social norm to pay taxes. Consequently, it seems likely that there will be more tax compliance when the public good provided to a community is popular. Survey evidence is largely consistent with this hypothesis.

Still another dimension by which social norms can be changed is the government's commitment to enforcing the tax laws. In fact, it seems likely that there is a constant interaction between social norms and tax administration. If the perception becomes widespread that the government is not willing to detect and penalize evaders, then such a perception legitimizes tax evasion. The rejection of sanctions sends a signal to each individual that others do not wish to enforce the tax laws, and that tax evasion is in some sense socially acceptable, so the social norm of compliance disappears. Such an outcome is common in many countries, such as those in the LAC region, where it seems to be accepted that tax evasion is the norm. The introduction of a tax amnesty may also affect the social norm of compliance. A tax amnesty gives individuals an opportunity to pay previously unpaid back taxes without being subject to the penalties that the discovery of evasion normally brings. Such amnesties may reduce compliance if honest taxpayers resent the forgiveness given to tax cheats (and if individuals believe that the amnesty may be repeated again).

We believe that there is considerable intuitive appeal regarding the potential importance of social norms in tax compliance behavior.[16] There is strong evidence that countries with roughly the same fiscal system exhibit far different patterns of compliance – see, for example, Bergman (2003) for a comparison of Argentina and Chile. There is also much survey evidence from many countries that indicates that compliance is strongly affected by the strength and commitment to the social norm of compliance.[17] These surveys conclude, among other things, that those who comply view tax evasion as "immoral", that compliance is higher if a "moral appeal" to taxpayers is made by government, that the low social standing of tax evaders can be an effective deterrent, that individuals with tax evaders as friends are more likely to be evaders themselves, and that compliance is greater in communities with stronger social cohesion. Other survey evidence suggests that some people will not pay their taxes if they dislike the way their taxes are spent, if they feel they have no say in the decision process, if they feel that government is unresponsive to their wishes, or if they feel that they are treated unfairly by government. There is also some empirical, simulation, and, especially, experimental evidence that compliance is affected by the collective decision process, at least in democratic countries (Alm *et al.*, 1993b, 1999; Frey and Torgler, 2007; Pommerehne *et al.*, 1994; Torgler, 2005; Torgler and Schaltegger, 2005; Traxler 2006). Such sentiments may play an important – perhaps a dominant – role in tax compliance.[18]

In summary, to the extent that these norms are influenced by the responsiveness of government to citizens' needs and the effectiveness of government institutions, including the tax administration, the scope of government policies to combat tax evasion is significantly broader than implied by the standard economic approach. It should not come as a surprise to many government officials in LAC countries that controlling tax evasion will require improving overall governance and delivering value for money to taxpayer citizens.

A second and obvious institution is, as noted above, the "tax administration machinery" of the government tax agency. Indeed, much of the literature on tax administration reform for developing countries (Bagchi *et al.*, 1995; Bird and Casanegra de Jantscher, 1992; Silvani and Baer, 1997; Tanzi and Pellechio, 1995) has emphasized the service paradigm of the role of tax administration, as a facilitator and a provider of services to taxpayer citizens. Some recent administrative reforms around the world have also embraced this new paradigm with great success. One of the best examples is provided by Singapore's tax administration reform in the 1990s (Bird and Oldman, 2000). The main tenet of Singapore's reform is service-oriented, and includes: the conversion from a hard-copy filing system to a paperless imaging system, the extensive use of electronic filing, a one-stop service to answer inquiries about any type of tax, the ability for filers to see the entire tax form with any corrections before it is submitted, the use of interest-free installment plans for paying taxes with direct deduction from bank accounts, separate functional areas within the tax administration with little opportunity for corruption, and a changed attitude of officials toward taxpayers. During the 1990s, the tax administration service of Singapore went from being the lowest rated government agency regarding public satisfaction to one that 90 percent of the taxpayers found to provide courteous, competent, and convenient services. Of course, most countries, especially LAC countries, will not be able to fully imitate Singapore's reforms anytime soon. Nevertheless, there is much to be gained in improved tax compliance by reforming the tax administrations along the lines of the service paradigm.[19]

Note that the criminalization of certain tax offenses (e.g., by their inclusion in penal codes) is not uncommon around the world, having been legislated also in many developing countries. What is more unusual is the developing world is its actual application. For example, Pakistan has criminalized certain tax offenses, but these statutes do not appear to have ever been used.[20] On the other hand, the criminalization of tax offenses and the effective use of the new statutes in combination with a modernized tax administration agency have been credited as playing a key role in Spain's success in the late 1970 and 1980s in drastically reducing tax evasion and eventually doubling the tax revenue to GDP ratio.[21]

Conclusions: how can tax evasion in LAC countries and beyond be reduced?

Tax evasion is among the most vexing problems in LAC countries. Our motivation for this chapter has been to examine what we have learned from the analyses of tax evasion, and to indicate what we can apply from these lessons to reducing the problem of tax evasion in LAC countries. Our general conclusion is simple and basic. Institutions matter everywhere, but they are especially decisive in developing countries, where their quality is generally lower than in developed countries. Because of the crucial role of such institutions, improving tax compliance requires focusing primarily upon improving societal institutions, especially the social norm of compliance (or tax morale) and tax administration itself. Indeed, from a policy viewpoint, it would appear that it may be as important in

LAC countries to strengthen the social norms of compliance as it is to improve and modernize a service-oriented tax administration.

In this regard, recent work by Gould (1996) emphasizes that it is grossly misleading to represent a complex system by a single, so-called representative agent, who behaves in some average or typical way. Instead, most systems have incredible variety – or a "full house" of individual behaviors – and the proper understanding of any system requires recognition of this basic fact. Indeed, Gould (1996) argues that the way in which a system changes over time is attributable largely to changes in the amount of variation within the system, rather than to changes in some largely meaningless "average" behavior across its individual members.

This lesson is especially apt for tax compliance. People exhibit a remarkable diversity in their behavior. There are individuals who always cheat and those who always comply, some who behave as if they maximize the expected utility of the tax evasion gamble, others who seem to overweight low probabilities of being caught cheating, individuals who respond in different ways to changes in their tax burden, some who are at times cooperative and at other times free-riders, and many who seem to be guided by such things as social norms, moral sentiments, and tax equity. Any government approach toward tax compliance must address this "full house" of behaviors in devising policies to ensure compliance. Consequently, a government compliance strategy based only on detection and punishment may well be a reasonable starting point for tax administration, but is not a good end point. Instead, what is needed is a multifaceted approach that emphasizes enforcement, but that also highlights the much broader range of actual motivations that explain why people pay taxes.

Table 134.1 Indicators for paying taxes, tax revenue collections, and GDP per capita for LAC countries in recent years

Tax indicators	LAC	Argentina	Bolivia	Brazil	Chile	Colombia	Costa Rica	Ecuador	El Salvador	Guatemala
Paying taxes[a]										
Payments (number)	41.3	34	41	23	10	68	41	8	66	50
Time (hours)	430	615	1,080	2,600	432	456	402	600	224	294
Total tax rate (% profit)	49.10	116.80	80.30	71.70	26.30	82.80	83.00	34.90	27.40	40.90
Tax rates (% of managers surveyed ranking this as a major business constraint)[b]	–	–	–	84.50	–	–	–	38.10	22.60	56.50
Time to prepare and pay taxes (hours)[a]	549	580	1,080	2,600	432	432	402	600	224	260
GDP[c]										
GDP per capita, PPP (constant 2000 international $)	7,048.92	11,981.74	2,400.15	7,278.55	9,333.64	6,460.84	8,161.34	3,468.34	4,547.62	3,888.33
GDP per capita, PPP (current international $)	7,118.37	12,080.46	2,423.98	7,350.50	9,462.92	6,518.93	8,258.69	3,504.46	4,591.70	3,925.32
Agriculture value added (% of GDP)	7.70	7.02	15.65	8.69	6.18	13.62	10.49	11.10	11.45	23.16
GNI per capita, PPP (current international $)	6,892.83	11,648.18	2,350.91	7,116.36	8,982.73	6,323.64	7,893.64	3,310.91	4,500.00	3,879.09
Mining and quarrying value added (current 000,000 US$)	–	6033	526	–	6,837	4,734	–	–	–	–
GDP (current 000,000 US$)	1,928,444	229,670	8,128	644,181	79,807	93,327	15,535	24,097	13,138	21,222
Tax Revenue[c]										
Tax revenue (% of GDP)	11.85	12.18	13.75	11.65	1,6.24	13.23	12.64	–	10.95	9.54
Taxes on goods and services (% of revenue)	39.55	27.84	39.08	22.34	47.57	31.29	38.37	–	40.77	56.04
Taxes on goods and services (% value added of industry and services)	–	5.51	12.29	6.76	11.71	7.00	10.05	–	7.60	7.38
Taxes on income, profits, and capital gains (% of revenue)	17.28	15.99	6.69	18.79	20.20	32.70	12.87	–	21.01	23.01
Taxes on income, profits, and capital gains (% of total taxes)	–	21.65	11.26	38.45	26.62	43.87	21.68	–	30.22	24.36
Taxes on international trade (% of revenue)	6.17	15.30	3.41	2.74	3.72	5.73	7.00	–	7.17	13.85
Total tax payable by businesses (% of gross profit)	54.47	97.90	64.00	147.90	46.70	75.10	54.30	33.90	32.20	53.40

Paying taxes[a]

Payments (number)	41.3	45	48	49	64	59	33	53	17	41	68
Time (hours)	430	288	424	552	240	560	328	424	198	300	864
Total tax rate (% profit)	49.10	44.20	51.40	37.10	66.40	52.40	43.20	40.80	27.80	27.60	51.90
Tax rates (% of managers surveyed ranking this as a major business constraint)[b]	–	16.70	35.60	–	34.70	–	–	–	–	–	–
Time to prepare and pay taxes (hours)[a]	549	288	424	536	240	424	328	424	–	300	864
GDP[c]											
GDP per capita, PPP (constant 2000 international $)	7,048.92	4,071.05	2,547.51	8,574.87	3,210.33	6,071.70	4,616.90	4,838.29	–	8,575.75	5,730.67
GDP per capita, PPP (current international $)	7,118.37	4,107.32	2,567.75	8,668.38	3,241.48	6,147.80	4,642.62	4,892.48	–	8,639.57	5,761.87
Agriculture value added (% of GDP)	7.70	33.98	16.89	4.69	21.30	7.51	24.30	9.71	11.85	7.98	4.72
GNI per capita, PPP (current international $)	6,892.83	3,799.09	2,484.55	8,444.55	3,055.45	5,823.64	4,657.27	4,730.00	–	8,449.09	5,626.36
Mining and quarrying value added (current 000,000 US$)	–	94	86	6941	32	–	31	–	66	48	15,934
GDP (current 000,000 UUS$)	1,928,444	719	5,866	533,376	3,889	11,637	7,842	58,886	949	17,851	98,513
Tax Revenue[c]											
Tax revenue (% of GDP)	11.85	–	–	10.87	13.74	11.00	10.28	13.16	–	17.80	13.12
Taxes on goods and services (% of revenue)	39.55	–	–	58.27	45.81	8.91	36.53	42.82	–	40.25	28.71
Taxes on goods and services (% value added of industry and services)	–	–	–	9.76	13.37	2.64	7.76	9.10	–	11.74	6.70
Taxes on income, profits, and capital gains (% of revenue)	17.28	–	–	31.92	11.84	18.12	12.26	19.71	–	10.84	24.92
Taxes on income, profits, and capital gains (% of total taxes)	–	–	–	42.21	18.56	39.07	19.14	26.16	–	17.11	38.29
Taxes on international trade (% of revenue)	6.17	–	–	4.06	6.41	8.57	12.55	7.95	–	3.91	7.37
Total tax payable by businesses (% of gross profit)	54.47	20.70	43.20	31.30	54.30	32.90	37.90	50.70	–	80.20	48.90

Source: The World Bank, and calculations by authors.

Notes
a Data are for 2005
b Data are averages for 2002–2005
c Data are averages for 1995–2005.

Table 13.4.2 Bribery in tax administration: survey evidence for selected LAC countries (2005–2006)

Indicators	LAC	Brazil	Chile	Costa Rica	Ecuador	El Salvador	Guatemala	Guyana	Honduras	Nicaragua
Informality										
Sales amount reported by a typical firm for tax purposes (% of sales)	76.51	67.35	98.24	71.63	79.76	76.95	77.83	73.82	68.4	66.42
Bribery and tax administration										
Unofficial payments for typical firm to get things done (% of sales)	1.2	–	0.31	2.25	2.83	1.14	2.56	0.43	1.72	1.77
Firms expected to give gifts in meetings with tax inspectors (% firms)	30.4	9.93	1.59	0	1.44	0.82	17.5	5.41	4.35	12.79
Pays bribes to get things done (% firms)	36.3	–	10.38	33.8	56.18	29.97	48.57	20	45.93	31.72
Firms expected to give gifts to get an import license (% firms)	14.6	4.98	1.12	–	9.09	6.56	9.02	8.33	8.96	6.12
Value of gifts for tax inspector (% sales)	0	–	–	–	0	0	0	0	0	0.01
Average time firms spent in meetings with tax officials (days)	3.5	–	1.69	0.53	5.91	3.61	3.12	1.3	2.53	5.51

Source: The World Bank, Enterprise Surveys 2005–2006, www.enterprisesurveys.org/.

Notes

1 Although the ratio of tax revenue to GDP changes over time for some countries, it is possible to divide the LAC countries into three categories of relatively high, intermediate, and relatively low ratios. Gomez Sabaini (2005) categorizes as relatively high-ratio countries Brazil, Uruguay, and Argentina; as relatively low, Paraguay, Mexico, Ecuador, Venezuela, Guatemala, and Haiti; and as intermediate all other countries in the region.
2 Estimates of VAT productivity are as follows:

Country (year)	VAT or GST Rate (2006, as percent)	VAT productivity (as percent of GDP)
Argentina (2004)	21	35
Bolivia (2004)	15	21
Brazil (2004)	15	43
Chile (2004)	18	64
Colombia (2003)	16	26
Costa Rica (2004)	13	38
Dominican Republic (2003)	12	18
Ecuador (2003)	12	54
Guatemala (2004)	12	17
Honduras (2002)	12	45
Mexico (2004)	15	24
Nicaragua (2003)	15	20
Panama (2003)	5	30
Paraguay (2004)	10	49
Peru (2003)	19	35
Uruguay (2004)	23	43
Venezuela (2004)	14	47

The VAT or GST rate corresponds to the highest rate defined in the law. Only Brazil has defined different VAT rates, between 10 percent and 15 percent. "VAT productivity" is defined as the yield of each percent point of the VAT rate, expressed as percent of GDP. The most recent available information on VAT collections is limited to 2004 and, in some cases, 2003 and 2002. The GDP used to compute VAT productivity corresponds to the same period, but the VAT rate is the one in place on 2006. Some inaccuracies can be observed for those countries where the VAT rate has changed over the past years. Sources: For general consumption tax collections in 2002–2004 (current US$ millions), Centro Interamericano de Administraciones Tributarias; for GDP in 2002–2004 (current US$ millions), World Marketing Data and Statistics; for the VAT or GST rate, PricewaterhouseCoopers' Worldwide Tax Summaries online (PricewaterhouseCoopers, 2005); and calculations by authors.
3 Of course, there are many factors other than taxes that have been shown to affect foreign direct investment. The quality of a country's governance institutions, the level of corruption, the quality and skill levels of the labor force and infrastructure, and other factors have been shown to be as important, if not more so, as determinants of foreign direct investment flows as are taxes. Even so, many of these other determinants depend heavily on the ability of a country to generate adequate revenues.

4 The regression results are:

Independent variable	Period	
	Average of 1990s	*Average of 2000–2004*
GDP per capita	9.14E-06 (0.08)	1.53E-4 (1.99)
Agriculture/GDP	−0.17 (−3.48)	−0.04 (−0.46)
Population growth rate	−0.43 (−0.48)	−0.74 (−1.01)
Constant	17.62 (7.01)	13.96 (7.37)
Observations	105	98
R^2	0.21	0.14

The dependent variable is total tax revenue divided by GDP. White corrected t-statistics are in parentheses. The equations are estimated by OLS methods. Source: calculations by authors.

5 This issue has been recently examined by Baunsgaard and Keen (2005) and Glenday (2006). These studies find, based on the analysis of central government tax collection data for a large number of developing countries and for a period of almost three decades back, that, on average, low-income countries recovered at best less than one-third of the losses from taxes on international trade through increased domestic taxes. In contrast, middle-income countries recovered around half of those tax losses, and high-income countries had no problems replacing the revenue losses.

6 See Bird *et al.* (2006) for more discussion. Also, see Martinez-Vazquez (2008) for a discussion of Mexico's tax–ratio constancy over time. Similar relative constancy can be seen in other countries (e.g., Colombia) over the decades, despite repeated tax reforms (McLure and Zodrow, 1997). Lledo *et al.* (2003) and Bird *et al.* (2006) emphasize the role of political institutions, especially those that enhance legitimacy and representation, in explaining tax effort across countries in the LAC region.

7 For example, after the Sandinista government took over in Nicaragua, the tax to GDP ratio rose very quickly in the first five years of the regime, from 18 to 32 percent of GDP, with the increase mostly coming from (regressive) indirect taxes. Nicaragua has maintained a relatively high level of tax efforts over many years and several subsequent governments since the Sandinistas left government.

8 See Alm (1999), Andreoni *et al.* (1998), Cowell (1990), and Slemrod and Yitzhaki (2002) for further discussions of the economics-of-crime approach to tax compliance. There has also been some work to expand the basic model of individual choice by introducing some aspects of behavior or motivation considered explicitly by other social sciences, such as "overweighting" of low probabilities, "reference point" effects, deviancy, personal and situational characteristics, social contexts, and attribution theory. See Smith and Kinsey (1987) for discussions and evaluations of many of these alternative theories. See also McCaffery and Slemrod (2006) for a collection of papers that discuss "behavioral economics" approaches to individual behavior, including tax compliance decisions.

9 We do not discuss here other possible relationships and distinctions among these concepts. See Feinstein (1999) and Lippert and Walker (1997) for discussions of the relationship between tax evasion and the shadow economy. Lippert and Walker (1997), for example, argue that tax evasion more often involves financial transactions with the objective of concealing income, while the shadow economy more often involves the production of goods and services with labor and other inputs.

10 Of course, we do not know precisely the relative predominance of the self-employed in developing and developed economies. Interestingly, the self-employed seem to be increasing in importance in mature economies.

11 We also estimated alternative models with additional control variables that account for the existence of particular tax handles or that represent features of the economy which may facilitate tax collections (e.g., the share of mining in GDP) or may impede tax collections (e.g., the share of agriculture in GDP). Because of the lack of data on these variables, the number of usable observations becomes quite small, so we do not report these results. Even so, the impact of variables such as GDP per capita or Shadow economy/GNP are similar to the results reported in Table 13.3.

12 To test for the potential simultaneity of the informal sector and tax structure, we ran a Hausman chi-square test with corruption as an instrument for the informal sector, and we failed to detect any presence of simultaneity.

13 For a comprehensive discussion of the WVS, see Inglehart *et al.* (2000).

14 There are other concepts that describe the same basic phenomenon as social norms and tax morale, such as "psychic cost" (Gordon, 1989), "moral sentiments" (Erard and Feinstein, 1994), "group conformity and social customs" (Myles and Naylor, 1996), and "intrinsic motivation" (Frey, 1997).

15 Some degree of tax evasion exists in every country. However, when does tax evasion become the accepted norm? Practically nothing is known about the tipping point of tax evasion, where the social norm of tax compliance switches to one of tax evasion. To our knowledge, no empirical research has been conducted on this important issue. There is, however, some experimental evidence that examines this issue. See Alm (1999) for a discussion.

16 A growing theoretical literature has formally developed this conjecture. See, for example, Gordon (1989), Myles and Naylor (1996), Bergman (2002), and Chang and Lai (2004).

17 For example, see Harris and Associates, Inc. (1988) for the United States, and De Juan *et al.* (1994) for Spain.

18 For a contrary view on the role of social norms, see Tanzi and Pellechio (1995).

19 Note that the available evidence from government budgetary information indicates that the budget cost of collecting individual income, business income, and sales taxes is generally in excess of 1 percent of the revenues from these taxes, and can sometimes be substantially higher (Sandford, 1995). However, there is little information on how these costs vary with various policy tools. It seems likely that the administrative costs change by large and discrete amounts with the scale of collections, and that they may also display economies of scale in their collections, but these aspects of the collection cost technology are not known.

20 See Martinez-Vazquez (2006).

21 See Martinez-Vazquez and Sanz (2007). Other key factors in Spain's successful experience were a widespread consensus among political parties about the need for the reform of the tax system, improved democratic governance, and highly visible enhancements in social and other public services. Martinez-Vazquez and Torgler (forthcoming) find evidence of significant changes in tax morale among Spanish taxpayers over this period.

Bibliography

Allingham, M. G. and Sandmo, A. (1972) "Income tax evasion: A theoretical analysis", *Journal of Public Economics*, 1(3–4): 323–38.

Alm, J. (1999). "Tax compliance and administration", in W. B. Hildreth and J. A. Richardson (eds.), *Handbook on Taxation*, New York, NY: Marcel Dekker, Inc.

Alm, J. and Martinez-Vazquez, J. (2003) "Institutions, paradigms, and tax evasion in developing and transition countries", in J. Alm and J. Martinez-Vazquez (eds.), *Public Finance in Developing and Transition Countries – Essays in Honor of Richard Bird*, Northampton, MA: Edward Elgar Publishing, Inc.

Alm, J., Bahl, R., and Murray, M. N. (1991) "Tax base erosion in developing countries", *Economic Development and Cultural Change*, 39(4): 849–72.

Alm, J., McClelland, G. H., and Schulze, W. D. (1992) "Why do people pay taxes?", *Journal of Public Economics*, 48(1): 21–48.

Alm, J., Bahl, R., and Murray, M. N. (1993a) "Audit selection and income tax under-reporting in the tax compliance game", *Journal of Development Economics*, 42(1): 1–33.

Alm, J., Jackson, B. R., and McKee, M. (1993b) "Fiscal exchange, collective decision institutions, and tax compliance", *Journal of Economic Behavior and Organization*, 22(4): 285–303.

Alm, J., McClelland, G. H., and Schulze, W. D. (1999) "Changing the social norm of tax compliance by voting", *Kyklos*, 52(2): 141–71.

Andreoni, J., Erard, B., and Feinstein J. (1998) "Tax compliance", *Journal of Economic Literature*, 36(2): 818–60.

Baer, K., Benon, O., and Toro Rivera, J. (2002) "Improving large taxpayer compliance: A review of country experience", International Monetary Fund Occasional Paper 215, Washington, DC: International Monetary Fund.

Bagchi, A., Bird, R. M., and Das-Gupta, A. (1995) "An economic approach to tax administration reform", Discussion Paper No. 3, International Centre for Tax Studies. Toronto, Canada: University of Toronto.

Bahl, R. W. (1971) "A regression approach to tax effort and tax ratio analysis", *IMF Staff Papers*, 18(3): 570–612.

Baunsgaard, T. and Keen, M. (2005) "Tax revenue and trade liberalization", International Monetary Fund Working Paper WP/05/112. Washington, DC.

Bergman, M. (2002) "Compliance with norms: The case of tax compliance in Latin America", CIDE, Working Paper No. 5. Mexico D.F.

Bergman, M. (2003) "Tax reforms and tax compliance: The divergent paths of Chile and Argentina", *Journal of Latin American Studies*, 35(4): 593–624.

Bird, R. M. (1976) "Assessing tax performance in developing countries: A critical review of the literature", *Finanzarchiv*, 34(2): 244–265.

Bird, R. M. and Casanegra de Jantscher, M. (eds.) (1992) *Improving Tax Administration in Developing Countries*, Washington, DC: International Monetary Fund.

Bird, R. M. and Oldman O. (2000) "Improving taxpayer service and facilitating compliance in Singapore", PREM Notes, Public Sector, No. 48, Washington, DC: World Bank.

Bird, R. M., Martinez-Vazquez, J., and Torgler, B. (2006) "Societal institutions and tax effort in developing countries", in J. Alm, J. Martinez-Vazquez, and M. Rider (eds.), *The Challenges of Tax Reform in the 21st Century*, Norwell, MA: Springer Science and Business Media.

Chang, J. J. and Lai, C. C. (2004) "Collaborative tax evasion and social norms: Why deterrence does not work", *Oxford Economic Papers*, 56: 344–68.

Cowell, F. A. (1990) *Cheating the Government*, Cambridge, MA: MIT Press.

Dabla-Norris, E., Gradstein, M., and Inchauste Comboni, M. G. (2005) "What causes firms to hide output? The determinants of informality", International Monetary Fund Working Paper No. 05/160, Washington, DC: International Monetary Fund.

Das-Gupta, A. (1994) "A theory of hard-to-tax groups", *Public Finance*, 49 (Supplement): 28–39.

De Juan, A., Lasheras, M. A., and Mayo, R. (1994) "Voluntary tax compliant behavior of Spanish taxpayers", *Public Finance/Finances Publiques* 49(Supplement): 90–105.

Dreher, A. and Schneider, F. (2006) "Corruption and the shadow economy", Johannes Kepler University of Linz Working Paper No. 0603, Linz-Auhof, Austria.

Dreher, A., Kotsogiannis, C., and McCorriston, S. (2005) "How do institutions affect corruption and the shadow economy?", University of Exeter Discussion Paper.

Elffers, H. (1991) *Income Tax Evasion: Theory and Measurement*, Deventer, The Netherlands: Kluwer.

Elster, J. (1989) "Social norms and economic theory", *Journal of Economic Perspectives*, 3(4): 99–117.

Engelschalk, M. (2003) *Creating a Favorable Tax Environment for Small Business Development in Transition Countries*, Washington, DC: World Bank.

Erard, B. and Feinstein, J. S. (1994) "The role of moral sentiments and audit perceptions in tax compliance", *Public Finance/Finance Publiques*, 49 (Supplement): 70–89.

Feige, E. L. (ed.) (1989) *The Underground Economies: Tax Evasion and Information Distortion*, Cambridge, UK: Cambridge University Press.

Feinstein, J. S. (1999) "Approaches for estimating non-compliance: Examples from federal taxation in the United States", *Economic Journal*, 109 (456): 360–9.

Frey, B. S. (1997) "A constitution for knaves crowds out civic virtues", *Economic Journal*, 107(443): 1043–53.

Frey, B. S. and Pommerehne, W. W. (1984) "The hidden economy: State and prospects for measurement", *Review of Income and Wealth*, 30(1): 1–23.

Frey, B. S. and Torgler, B. (2007) "Tax morale and conditional cooperation", *Journal of Comparative Economics*, 35(2): 136–59.

Friedman, E., Johnson, S., Kaufmann, D., and Zoido-Labton, P. (2000) "Dodging the grabbing hand: The determinants of unofficial activity in 69 countries," *Journal of Public Economics*, 76(4): 459–93.

Gallagher, M. (2004) "Assessing tax systems using a benchmarking methodology," Research Paper, Fiscal Reform in Support of Trade Liberalization, USAID, Development Alternatives, Inc.

Glenday, G. (2006) "Towards fiscally feasible and efficient trade liberalization", Duke Center for International Development, Duke University, Durham, NC.

Gomez Sabaini, J. C. (2005) "Evolución y situación tributaria actual en América Latina: Una serie de temas para la discusión", Report prepared for CEPAL (Comisión Económica para América Latina y el Caribe).

Gordon, J. P. F. (1989) "Individual morality and reputation costs as deterrents to tax evasion", *European Economic Review*, 33: 797–805.

Gorodnichenko, Y., Martinez-Vazquez, J., and Sabirianova, P. K. (2008) "Myth and reality of flat tax reform: Micro estimates of tax evasion response and welfare effects in Russia", NBER Working Papers 13719.

Gould, S. J. (1996) *Full House*, New York, NY: Harmony Books.

Graetz, M. J. and Wilde, L. L. (1985) "The economics of tax compliance: Facts and fantasy", *National Tax Journal*, 38(3): 355–63.

Harris and Associates, Inc. (1988) *1987 Taxpayer Opinion Survey Conducted for the US*, Internal Revenue Service, Internal Revenue Service Document 7292. Washington, DC.

Inglehart, R., European Values Study Group and World Values Survey Association (2000) *World Values Surveys and European Values Surveys,1981–1984, 1990–1993, and 1995–1997 [Computer file]*, ICPSR version, Ann Arbor, MI: Institute for Social Research.

International Monetary Fund (various dates) *Government Finance Statistics*, various issues. Washington, DC: International Monetary Fund.

Johnson, S., Kaufmann, D., McMillan, J., and Woodruff, C. (2000) "Why do firms hide? Bribes and unofficial activity after communism", *Journal of Public Economics*, 76: 495–520.

Kenadjian, B. (1982) "The direct approach to measuring the underground economy in the United States: IRS estimates of unreported income", in V. Tanzi (ed.), *The Underground Economy in the United States and Abroad*. Lexington, MA: Lexington Books.

Lippert, O. and Walker, M. (eds.) (1997) *The Underground Economy: Global Evidences of its Size and Impact*, Vancouver, BC: The Frazer Institute.

Lledo, V., Schneider, A., and Moore, M. (2003) "Pro-poor tax reform in Latin America: A critical survey and policy recommendations", University of Sussex, UK: IDS.

Loayza, N., Oveido, A. M., and Serven, L. (2005) "The impact of regulation on growth and informality cross-country evidence", World Bank Policy Research Working Paper No. 3623, Washington, DC: World Bank.

Mann, A. (2004) "Are semi-autonomous revenue authorities the answer to tax administration problems in developing countries?" Research Paper, Fiscal Reform in Support of Trade Liberalization, USAID. Development Alternatives, Inc.

Martinez-Vazquez, J. (2006) "An assessment of Pakistan's tax system", A report for the World Bank and the Central Board of Revenue of Pakistan. International Studies Program Working Paper No. 06-24, Atlanta, GA: Andrew Young School of Policy Studies.

Martinez-Vazquez, J. (2008) "Evaluating Mexico's tax system", in B. Moreno-Dodson and Q. Wodon (eds.), *Public Finance for Poverty Reduction*, Washington, DC: World Bank.

Martinez-Vazquez, J. and Sanz, J. F. (eds.) (2007) *Tax Reform in Spain: Accomplishments and Challenges*, Cheltenham, UK: Edward Elgar.

Martinez-Vazquez, J. and Torgler, B. (2010) "The evolution of tax morale in modern Spain", *Journal of Economic Issues*, in press.

McCaffery, E. and Slemrod, J. (eds.) (2006) *Behavioral Public Finance*, New York, NY: Russell Sage Publications.

McLure, C. E. and Zodrow, G. (1997) "Thirty years of tax reform in Colombia", in W. R. Thirsk (ed.), *Tax Reform in Developing Countries*, Washington, DC: World Bank.

Myles, G. D. and Naylor, R. A. (1996) "A new model of tax evasion with group conformity and social customs", *European Journal of Political Economy*, 12(1): 49–66.

Owens, J. (2006) "Fundamental tax reform: An international perspective", *National Tax Journal*, 69(1): 131–64.

Pommerehne, W. W., Hart, A., and Frey, B. S. (1994) "Tax morale, tax evasion, and the choice of tax policy instruments in different political systems", *Public Finance/ Finances Publiques*, 49(Supplement): 52–69.

Price Waterhouse Coopers (2005) *Individual Taxes 2004–2005, Worldwide Summaries* Hoboken, NJ: John Wiley & Sons, Inc.

Sandford, C. (ed.) (1995) *Tax Compliance Costs: Measurement and Policy*, Bath, UK: Fiscal Publications.

Schneider, F. (2002) "The value added of underground activities: Size and measurement of the shadow economies of 110 countries all over the world", mimeo.

Schneider, F. and Enste, D. H. (2000) "Shadow economies: Size, causes, and consequences", *Journal of Economic Literature*, 38(1): 77–114.

Schneider, F. and Enste, D. H. (2002) *The Shadow Economy – An International Survey*, Cambridge, MA: Cambridge University Press.

Silvani, C. (1992) "Improving tax compliance", in R. Bird and M. C. de Jantscher (eds.),

Improving Tax Administration in Developing Countries, Washington, DC: International Monetary Fund.

Slemrod, J. and Yitzhaki, S. (2002) "Tax avoidance, evasion, and administration", in A. J. Auerbach and M. Feldstein (eds.), *Handbook of Public Economics*, New York, NY: Elsevier.

Smith, J. D. (1994) "Market motives in the informal economy", in W. Gaetner and A. Wenig (eds.), *The Economics of the Shadow Economy*, Heidelberg, Germany: Springer.

Smith, K. W. and Kinsey, K. A. (1987) "Understanding taxpayer behavior: A conceptual framework with implications for research", *Law and Society Review*, 21: 639–63.

Taliercio, R. Jr (2004) "Designing performance: The semi-autonomous revenue authority model in Africa and Latin America", World Bank Policy Research Working Paper 3243, Washington, DC: World Bank.

Tanzi, V. and Casanegra de Janscher, M. (1989) "The use of presumptive income taxation in modern tax systems", in A. Chinicone and K. Messere (eds.), *Proceedings of the 42nd Congress of the International Institute of Public Finance, Athens 1986*.

Tanzi, V. and Pellechio, A. (1995) "The reform of tax administration", International Monetary Fund Working Paper 95/22, February. Washington, DC: International Monetary Fund.

Tanzi, V. and Shome, P. (1993) "Tax evasion: Causes, estimation methods, and penalties: A focus on Latin America", United Nations Economic Commission for Latin America and the Caribbean. Santiago, Chile: Serie Politica Fiscal 38.

Tanzi, V. and Zee, H. (2000) "Tax policy in emerging markets: Developing countries", *National Tax Journal*, 53(2): 299–322.

Terkper, S. (2003) "Managing small and medium-size taxpayers in developing economies", *Tax Notes International*, 13 January: 211–34.

Torgler, B. (2005) "Tax morale in Latin America", *Public Choice*, 122(2): 133–57.

Torgler, B. and Schaltegger, C. A. (2005) "Tax amnesties and political participation", *Public Finance Review*, 33(4): 403–31.

Traxler, C. (2006) "Social norms and conditional cooperative taxpayers", University of Munich Policy Discussion Paper 1201, Munich, Germany.

World Bank (2006) World Development Indicators. Washington, DC: World Bank.

Index